D1760376

Deep Rhetoric

Philosophy, Reason, Violence, Justice, Wisdom

JAMES CROSSWHITE

The University of Chicago Press   Chicago and London

JAMES CROSSWHITE is associate professor of English at the University of Oregon. He is the author of *The Rhetoric of Reason*, and has directed writing programs at the University of California, San Diego, and at the University of Oregon, where he founded the Program in Writing, Speaking, and Critical Reasoning.

The University of Chicago Press, Chicago 60637
The University of Chicago Press, Ltd., London
© 2013 by The University of Chicago
All rights reserved. Published 2013.
Printed in the United States of America
22 21 20 19 18 17 16 15 14 13   1 2 3 4 5

ISBN-13: 978-0-226-01634-4 (cloth)
ISBN-13: 978-0-226-01648-1 (paper)
ISBN-13: 978-0-226-01651-1 (e-book)

The University of Chicago Press gratefully acknowledges the generous support of the Oregon Humanities Center toward the publication of this book.

Library of Congress Cataloging-in-Publication Data

Crosswhite, James.
    Deep rhetoric : philosophy, reason, violence, justice, wisdom / James Crosswhite.
        pages.   cm.
    Includes bibliographical references and index.
        ISBN 978-0-226-01634-4 (hardcover : alk. paper)—
ISBN 978-0-226-01648-1 (pbk : alk. paper)—ISBN 978-0-226-01651-1
(e-book)   1. Rhetoric—Philosophy. 2. Plato. 3. Heidegger, Martin, 1889–1976.   I. Title.
P301.C76 2013
808' .001—dc23   2012030011

♾ This paper meets the requirements of ANSI/NISO Z39.48-1992 (Permanence of Paper).

For Marsha

Contents

Acknowledgments

One cannot even conceive of a project like this without incurring weighty debts, and one cannot complete it without accumulating many more. Thanks go, first, to my colleagues who have participated in the study and teaching of rhetoric at the University of Oregon: Suzanne Clark, David Frank, John Gage, Mark Johnson, Anne Laskaya, John Lysaker, Betsy Wheeler, Carolyn Bergquist, and Kathleen Horton. Special thanks, too, to Steve Shankman for reading and commenting on the chapter on Plato's *Gorgias*, as well as for many stirring conversations on Levinas and other related matters, and to Lisa Freinkel for reading through and discussing with me the section on the Prajnaparamita literature in chapter 8. Thanks also to James Earl and Warren Ginsberg for an unforgettable reading group on Augustine's *De Trinitate*, which ended up helping with this project in unexpected ways. I am also grateful to Michelle Bolduc for illuminating discussions about translating Perelman and Olbrechts-Tyteca's French.

Many of the ideas in this book were first tried out in oral presentations at conferences organized by the International Society for the History of Rhetoric, the Rhetoric Society of America, and the International Society for the Study of Argumentation, and I owe thanks to the organizers of those conferences for hosting vigorous intellectual exchanges and to the participants for their questions and comments, which helped me to correct and refine and develop what I have to say here. Thanks are also due to Rudong Chen for an invitation to deliver a plenary address at a meeting of the

Chinese Rhetoric Society in Beijing in 2011 (and for his wonderful hospitality there) and to deliver a series of lectures at Peking University, Beihang University, and the Communication University of China. Having the chance to discuss some of the ideas worked out in this book with students and scholars in Beijing gave entirely new inflections to some of the arguments. Finally, special thanks are also due to WooSoo Park and the Rhetoric Society of Korea for an invitation to give a keynote address at their 2010 conference and to have discussions about these ideas with students and scholars of rhetoric in Seoul. Sustained conversations about rhetoric, philosophy, and literature with WooSoo Park have also left their mark on these pages, as well as providing delightful memories.

An earlier version of chapter 3 appeared as "Deep Rhetoric in Plato's *Gorgias*" in the *Korean Journal of Rhetoric* 9 (2009): 5–57, and I owe thanks to the Rhetoric Society of Korea for allowing me to retain the rights to include that work here. Parts of chapter 2 also found print in an earlier form in "Rhetoric in the Wilderness: The Deep Rhetoric of the Late 20th Century," published in *A Companion to Rhetoric and Rhetorical Criticism* (2004), and thanks are due to John Wiley and Sons, Ltd. for giving permission to include those passages here. Thanks also to the American Forensic Association for permission to adapt and include in chapter 7 a few pages from "Awakening the Topoi," published in *Argumentation and Advocacy* 44, no. 4 (2008): 169–84. The lines from Les Murray's poem "An Absolutely Ordinary Rainbow" are gratefully included with the permission of Les Murray. Finally, thanks to Peking University and the editors of the *Journal of Peking University* for permission to include in chapter 1 parts of "Rhetoric, Equity, Freedom," an article published in the journal in 2011 (48:5).

At some point, one looks back and recognizes the good fortune one has had in one's teachers, how one's work would be impossible without them. Though I cannot name them all here, and though many would no doubt have some reservations about this project, I can and will acknowledge a few, even though some have now passed on. I am forever grateful to have been an undergraduate at the University of California at Santa Cruz, with its narrative evaluations (in place of grades) and its small undergraduate proseminars. The conscientious and wholehearted teaching of Ellen Suckiel, Albert Hofstadter, Maurice Natanson, and others has done more for me and my work than any of us could possibly have foreseen at the time. I also landed at UC San Diego at a fortunate time to pursue a philosophy PhD. Especially helpful there were Frederick Olafson,

Robert Pippin, Herbert Marcuse, Edward N. Lee, Richard Arneson, Gerald Doppelt, and Henry Allison.

Finally, I owe more than I could ever express to my children, Hilary, Elliot, and Wes, who give support and motivation for all my work, simply by coming around and being themselves; and to Marsha, wife and companion of thirty-six years, without whom this book and the person I am now could never have come about, and whose love has made the difference in my life.

Introduction

On June 12, 1806, John Quincy Adams, later to become the sixth president of the United States, was installed as the Boylston Professor of Rhetoric and Oratory at Harvard University. On that occasion, he presented an inaugural oration, which was eventually published as a preface to his *Lectures on Rhetoric and Oratory* (1810). The address begins this way:

It is the fortune of some opinions, as well as of some individual characters, to have been, during a long succession of ages, subjects of continual controversy among mankind. In forming an estimate of the moral or intellectual merits of many a person, whose name is recorded in the volumes of history, their virtues and vices are so nearly balanced, that their station in the ranks of fame has never been precisely assigned, and their reputation, even after death, vibrates upon the hinges of events, with which they have little or no perceptible connexion. Such too has been the destiny of the arts and sciences in general, and of the art of rhetoric in particular. Their advancement and decline have been alternate in the annals of the world. At one period they have been cherished, admired, and cultivated; at another neglected, despised, and oppressed. Like the favorites of princes, they have had their turns of unbounded influence and of excessive degradation. Now the enthusiasm of their votaries has raised them to the pinnacle of greatness; now a turn of the wheel has hurled them prostrate in the dust. Nor have these great and sudden revolutions always resulted from causes seemingly capable of producing such effects. (Adams 1810, 11–12)

Adams successfully, if somewhat magniloquently, articulates rhetoric's basic conundrum. Rhetoric is, on the one hand, cherished, admired, and cultivated. The field of study has a two and a half millennia history that runs from Ancient Greece through the Roman and Christian eras, through the higher Middle Ages, and then explodes with new life in the Renaissance and early modernity. It is lively and influential through the eighteenth century in Europe, where ancient rhetoric was both preserved and brought into productive contact with modern sciences. The teaching of rhetoric, too, has been a centerpiece of liberal education and often of professional training in law from the schools of antiquity, through the foundational trivium of grammar, logic, and rhetoric in medieval universities, through Renaissance humanist education, and into the eighteenth and even the nineteenth centuries. Rhetoric has, in our own time, resurged with new vitality in a number of different fields of study as well as in its importance for public life and in new media, as communication and its forms and issues become more central concerns in ever more interdependent economies, political societies, and cultures.

Rhetoric has also been despised and neglected, and its history shows cyclical declines. Rhetoric's origin is in the early democratic movements in ancient Greece, and George Kennedy (1980) has identified its phases of decline with restricted opportunities to speak to issues of public and political concern. Yet, following Adams's script, Kennedy also acknowledges the argument that in modern times rhetoric seems sometimes to decline in connection with expansions of democracy. It is difficult, as Adams says, to clarify the causes of these alternations. Another explanation sometimes given for rhetoric's modern decline places the blame on modern science and especially on the development of a science of politics. If there were found to be a scientific way of establishing the normative bases of politics (say, a substantive concept of justice), and a scientific-rational way to legislate and educate and otherwise manage human behavior to conform to these norms, then there would be a reduced need for what rhetoric offered: a capability for deliberation and judgment in conditions of uncertainty where there are conflicting conceptions of what is good. So, intellectuals and governments and universities oriented by this idea became much more focused on training for scientific-rational expertise than on cultivating the traditional rhetorical virtues of being able to discover and invent arguments on all sides of an issue, to make practical judgments about specific cases, to acquire common sense and a broad education. Most historians of rhetoric seem to note a distinct decline in rhetoric's status by the nineteenth century, and yet, following Adams's script once more, almost all have noted rhetoric's powerful resurgence, intellectually and institutionally, in the late twentieth century, and not only in Europe and North America.

I will discuss the late-twentieth-century intellectual resurgence of rhetoric in chapter 2, but here I would like to note at least briefly rhetoric's recent institutional resurgence.[1] Rhetoric's institutional decline in the last half of the nineteenth century has been broadly noted and attributed to many causes, most of which I will not consider here, but one of which was the increasing status of research in the newly emerging research universities and the decreasing value of teaching. Rhetoric, for all its vast scholarly and research interests, was always also focused on education and formation, on teaching. Education is simply an essential part of the identity of rhetoric as a field of study. This did not serve it well in the changing institutional setting in which it found itself. In the last half of the nineteenth century, it survived in fairly narrow and fragmented forms—mostly as a practice of remedial pedagogy in the teaching of writing, for example, and at best as a teaching of style as well. Class sizes were often very large. Teachers typically assigned papers that asked for personal narratives or for simple exposition of information. Teaching often consisted primarily of marking errors and focusing on correct grammar. Students were not educated to engage in inquiry or critical reasoning. They were not prepared to become informed citizens capable of participating in public debate or even of expressing themselves on important issues. The communicative capabilities students needed to take their places in work and social life were believed to be much simpler than the rhetorical tradition would lead anyone to expect. This destructive elitist attitude has not altogether disappeared, and in fact there are institutional and financial pressures that tend to maintain and reinforce it even against powerful arguments for better training in writing, speaking, and reasoning.

In the early twentieth century, in American universities, what was remembered of rhetoric was taught and to some degree studied in relation to courses on writing and speech in English departments. However, the internal tensions in English led to two important institutional divides. The first was the founding of the National Council of Teachers of English, which began as a kind of task force focused on educational policy regarding college admissions but gradually came to represent the teaching and educational concerns that were neglected by the increasingly research-identified profession of literary studies. The second occurred in 1914, when the National Association of Academic Teachers of Public Speaking split from the NCTE and became a professional organization for speech communication that promoted not only research and teaching but also the development of speech communication departments. The largest remnants of rhetoric were now divided into two separate disciplines, one having to do with writing and one with speech, though parts of what had once been rhetoric would still be studied and taught in law, in business, in philosophy, in journalism, in advertising, and in other areas. Rhetoric as a specific field of study and teaching, however, often continued in the degraded forms into which it had fallen in the late nineteenth century.

This changed drastically in the second half of the twentieth century, when the teaching of writing gained power as a research field in English departments and quickly reconnected with the rhetorical tradition. At roughly the same time, cross-disciplinary relations began to be forged among scholars in classics, philosophy, English, speech, and communication, and an interest in rhetoric grew in literary criticism, cultural studies, and other disciplines.[2] The Rhetoric Society of America was founded in 1968, and now has over 1,200 members and publishes the *Rhetoric Society Quarterly*. That same year, the journal *Philosophy and Rhetoric* published its first issue. Its editorial board included scholars from philosophy, speech, and English. That journal recently published its fortieth anniversary issue. The International Society for the History of Rhetoric was founded in 1977, holds biennial international conferences, and publishes *Rhetorica: A Journal of the History of Rhetoric*. The once seventeen-member National Association of Academic Teachers of Public Speaking has gone through many changes but has now emerged as the National Communication Association. The NCA currently has 7,700 members and publishes ten different journals, including the *Quarterly Journal of Speech*, a pillar of rhetorical studies for many years. In 2003, this explosion of work in rhetoric across disciplines led to the formation of an Alliance of Rhetoric Societies, which attempted to draw people studying and teaching rhetoric together into a loose coalition. But the resurgence has been difficult to organize, and it has not been limited to Europe and North America. In 2010, the Korean Rhetoric Society held its Second International Conference on "Cross-Cultural Conflicts and the Rhetoric of Communication" at Seoul National University. That society also publishes the *Korean Journal of Rhetoric*. The Rhetoric Society of China and the Chinese Rhetoric Society of the World also sponsor conferences. All of this is only a sampling of the recent growth in rhetorical studies.

The upshot of all this change is that organizing the resurgence of rhetoric as a field of study and teaching has become a serious challenge for contemporary American universities. The nineteenth- and early-twentieth-century decline of rhetoric has left many universities without rhetoric departments or even their fragmented remainders. In some cases, it has also left them with an institutional organization of the teaching of writing that is fraught with difficult tensions. Yet the last few decades have also seen new departments of rhetoric and writing spring up at many universities. And many English, speech, and communication departments have adapted by expanding Ph.D. study in the field. Yet Adams's conundrum seems to persist as a quandary for many American universities.

However, the conundrum of rhetoric is not simply an institutional matter. The opposite judgments concerning rhetoric that Adams noted are also related to the way rhetoric has been conceptualized.[3] Specific conceptions of rhetoric have produced specific conflicts about rhetoric and specific judgments about its value. There was from the start a conflict between the culture of rhetoric and the culture of the traditional heroic virtues of ancient Greece. There was also from the start a conflict between rhetoric and philosophy, and that conflict has continued over the course of rhetoric's history and is an essential part of that history.

The conflict between philosophy and rhetoric has taken many forms. Stanley Fish has given a famous characterization of it in his essay "Rhetoric," in which he derives a long list of dualities from Milton's description of the demon Belial. These dualities that are supposed to capture the conflict between philosophy and rhetoric include, to name just a few: inner/outer, deep/surface, essential/peripheral, unmediated/mediated, abiding/fleeting, reason/passion, things/words, realities/illusions, neutral/partisan. Underlying all of these, says Fish, are three other oppositions: a truth that is distinct from all perspectives, genuine knowledge that is independent of any system of belief, and a self that is focused outward toward truth as opposed to inward toward its own prejudices (Fish 1989, 474).

This particular way of describing the conflict between philosophy and rhetoric is endorsed most often by those who take rhetoric to land on the fallen side and take philosophy to belong to the divine contingent. These are they who, as Adams says, neglect, despise, and oppress. The rhetorical party is just as capable of demonizing the opposition, although it has not often taken that tack. It is also more than able to show itself to belong to the divine party, as it has often done. There is perhaps no reasonable expectation of a resolution to this conflict, at least not the way it has most often taken shape. There are now enough prefabricated arguments on both sides to keep debaters happy for a long time.

However, there may be some hope in not taking sides. In fact, that is what I propose to do in this book. The controversy with philosophy is internal to rhetoric; it is part of what rhetoric is. This ability to host controversy is in fact one of the most important and valuable things about rhetoric. In this, rhetoric is similar to philosophy, which carries in its own tradition questions and unresolved issues that seem continually to take on new meaning. In fact, many disciplines are partly defined by the controversies they sustain. Law, too, carries conundrums. One leads to what Steven D. Smith calls "Law's Quandary"—that law continues to appeal implicitly to natural law but that it has no clear understanding of how the idea of natural law can have survived the loss of the ontological commitments that sustained it. Another unresolved conflict we will confront later in this book is the conflict between law and justice, a conflict that appears in the works both of Plato in ancient times and of Chaim Perelman in the twentieth century, and which forms part of the continuing history of jurisprudence. Medicine, too, carries perduring conflicts about what health is, about the ways in which we should balance its costs against the costs of other goods, and about the degree to which we should sacrifice some of life's pleasures in order to preserve health and life. There are essentially contested concepts in most disciplines and professions. In the arts and sciences and in the professions, too, it is often the unfinished theories and the living questions and the gaps and the controversies that are the most interesting and important things going.

Our well-being lies not in the general theoretical solutions we manufacture for these controversies—all of those fail in some way—but rather in how well we resolve them for a specific time and in a specific place and for ourselves, through our own reasoned choices. This allows us to make necessary practical choices while keeping the larger controversy alive, which is both the honest thing to do and the useful thing to do.

We have a low view of the enterprise of knowledge and of universities and of education when we think of knowledge simply as something that can be transferred like money from one account to another, and of education as a piling up of information and accounting procedures. We in fact diseducate when we are governed by such a model.[4] Controversies are at the heart of many of the most important activities of human societies. Sustaining controversies and preserving competing perspectives is also part of what it means to preserve democratic culture, in which we continue to deliberate about the different goods we seek. Keeping some controversies open can be a way of insisting on our freedom, our freedom to change our minds or to create something new or to adapt to new conditions. Few of our achievements are unambiguously and absolutely good. Keeping the controversies in sight, and learning to live with them in a humane and intelligent way, is an essential ethical capability. It is a requirement for living with one another in a humane and intelligent way.

_____

In what follows, I will address the conflict between philosophy and rhetoric, but not in a direct attempt to resolve the controversies as they have traditionally been formulated. My aim is rather to engage in a reconceptualizing of rhetoric in a way that develops its deeper philosophical dimensions. The aim is to attempt to go behind, so to speak, the historical and conceptual dissociation of rhetoric from philosophy and to retrieve and to reconstruct and to explore a more philosophical rhetoric, a deeper rhetoric. I am emphatically not attempting to construct a new rhetorical theory. If anything, the "aim" is to prevent theory, or, at least, to stay as independent from theorizing as possible. Theorizing is appropriate inside the separate disciplines of philosophy and rhetoric, but I am attempting to stay in the philosophical moment of rhetoric, "before" the separation happens. Of course, this cannot be a goal in the sense of an end point to be reached. It is quite impossible to prevent theory or to stay independent from it in any literal sense or any absolute way. Preventing theory is rather a kind of philosophical practice, trying to keep questions and possibilities open that theorizing attempts to close down and resolve.[5] The chapters that follow will inevitably tack back and forth across deep rhetoric, a philosophical theory of rhetoric, and rhetorical theory. One movement of the work is to pursue rhetorical theory in order to discover and explore and activate its neglected philosophical background. Another movement is to pursue deep rhetoric for the purpose of preparing for more philosophically informed rhetorical theory.

One might say that, rather than attempting to construct a new rhetorical theory, I am attempting to paint a new rhetorical imaginary— a background against which we do our thinking about rhetoric and rhetorical theory. That would in some respects be accurate. I have, for example, chosen to pursue the relation of rhetoric to violence, justice, and wisdom, and these are probably not the first things that would spring to mind if one were to begin to think of the study and teaching of rhetoric. It is true that I am trying to change the context and the background against which we conceptualize rhetoric, and so I am calling up different images and associations and focusing on different primal scenes and examples. However, describing the aim this way does not capture the senses in which this is also a philosophical and scholarly labor.

The problem of method would loom large if this project were aimed at developing a theory or coming to some fundamental grounds for building a new philosophical rhetorical theory. But since the aim is to begin and to sustain a project of reconceptualizing rhetoric, something different from a conventional method is called for.

What I offer here, then, is not a systematic treatise but rather a series of closely related essays that develop the philosophical dimensions of rhetoric against the background of the history of rhetoric and especially the developments of the late twentieth century. Rather than building a theory or aiming toward a systematic development, it pursues conversations, reinterprets texts, renarrates histories, stages confrontations, offers close critical commentaries, and generally engages interlocutors, dead and living, who can contribute to conceptualizing the philosophical rhetoric that the book seeks. This approach should, at least, put the controversies about rhetoric in a new light, and give us more resources for considering the practical way we will resolve them for our time and place, and for ourselves.

———

Given the approach and the ambition of the project, it will be helpful to have a summary and roadmap as a guide. The book's first two chapters address the basic question: What is deep rhetoric? Chapter 1 begins with two apparently opposing approaches to rhetoric: Paul Ricoeur's view that the scope of rhetoric is limited by its generative seats in specific institutions and practices of ancient Greece, and Hans-Georg Gadamer's belief that rhetoric is "the universal form of human communication." Addressing this dispute requires addressing the question of the origin of rhetoric and treating the conflicting judgments on rhetoric found in Plato and Aristotle. The upshots are that there is a way of at least partially reconciling both Ricoeur with Gadamer and Plato with Aristotle, but it requires a reconceptualizating of rhetoric as deep rhetoric and a revisionist reading of Plato. Retrieving a more sympathetic Plato includes retrieving two essential Platonic notions. One is the very broad notion of logos that is at work in Plato and the sophists, according to which "logos" means speech, statement, reason, language, explanation, argument, and even the intelligibility of the world itself. Another is the notion, found in Plato's *Phaedrus*, that *logos* has its own special power, *psychagōgia*, leading the soul, and that rhetoric is an attempt to be an art or discipline of this power, or to in some sense master it, or to gain control of it, or to become the appropriate practice of this power. If logos is conceived in the broadest sense—that is, in all its senses—then rhetoric carries the very possibility of one thing's leading to another, so its scope becomes immense. The challenge for a deep rhetoric is to hold on to such a difficult pretheoretical notion without allowing it to become unformed, and to see where it leads.

The idea that rhetoric has to do with "leading the soul" by allowing things to lead to one another in specific ways immediately raises Platonic questions of where the art of rhetoric is leading. The second part of chapter 1 addresses this question by developing a coherent sense of purposeful leading even where ultimate ends may not be comprehensible. It takes on this task in challenging contexts, Plato and the Gospel of John, where logos would seem to be linked with theologies and teleologies that reify and absolutize ultimate goals. This section shows that the truth is more complicated than that. The first chapter continues in giving definition to deep rhetoric by developing a contrast between "deep rhetoric" and "big rhetoric." A controversy over "big rhetoric" has recently erupted inside the discipline of rhetoric. The controversy is over the tendency of rhetoric to expand across the disciplines and become the rhetoric of everything. I note some similarities but also explain some important differences between deep rhetoric and big rhetoric.

Another potential objection to the project is that it develops a new kind of humanism, one in which deep rhetorical capabilities define human being. The next few sections of chapter 1 address this objection by affirming that deep rhetoric is a kind of humanism, but by also arguing that it is not the kind of humanism that is obviously vulnerable to contemporary attacks. This is worked out both in specific cases, by exploring and explaining the kinds of humanism at work in the new rhetoric project in the life and writings of Chaim Perelman and the very interesting Mieczysław Maneli, and in general by elaborating the rhetorical capabilities that lie at the heart of a deep rhetorical humanism. In deep rhetorical humanism, rhetorical capabilities are the capabilities by which we go on continually defining the human, especially by saying, in each new case, what human dignity is, and what the practices are that acknowledge it, and what the laws and institutions are that protect it.

Chapter 2 continues to address challenges to the notion of a deep rhetoric as a way of further developing and clarifying the project. One challenge is discussed here under the rubric of rhetoric and ideology. Since deep rhetoric reinterprets logos and reason, can it still carry out the enlightening and liberating projects of reason as it has been understood in the modern period? The answer is yes, and the answer is arrived at through a careful analysis of some of the assumptions behind the concept of ideology and an explanation of how a deep rhetoric calls some of those assumptions into question and offers a new understanding of the way in which reason is related to freedom.

Chapter 2 concludes by returning to a more direct account of a deep rhetoric, this time by way of an exposition of how significant parts of the framework of a deep rhetoric were developed by twentieth-century philosophers. In the later twentieth century, after its near disappearance, the study of rhetoric returns as philosophy, often in the work of philosophers, and as a specifically late-twentieth-century kind of rhetoric. Burke, Perelman, McKeon, Toulmin, Gadamer, Habermas, and Walton are all treated in some way, but Gadamer is singled out for his development of a "kairotic" ontology, and the Habermas/Gadamer debate is analyzed as an exemplary instance of how rhetoric returned as philosophy.

At this point, given what many have been taught, some readers may still find it difficult to think of Plato as a friend of rhetoric and to accept the idea that Plato has a continuing relevance for the development of a twenty-first-century philosophical rhetoric. So chapter 3 shows that the *Gorgias* can be read as a defense of a deep rhetoric rather than simply as an attack on rhetoric. To carry this out, the chapter reviews the recent literature on the *Gorgias*, much of which contributes to a very interesting rehabilitation of the sophists, and shows that, in spite of its insightful interpretations of Gorgias and the sophists, much of this literature nonetheless misses subtle though profoundly important Platonic attitudes, and so fails to catch sight of vital dimensions of the dialogue. Instead of focusing on the familiar exchange between Socrates and Polus, in which rhetoric is identified as a species of flattery, the chapter centers on the exchange between Socrates and Callicles, explains Callicles' rhetorical narcissism, radically reinterprets the *nomos/physis* distinction at play in the dialogue, shows how a deep rhetorical conception of the "fitting" is developed by Socrates, identifies the way the concept of restraint places ethics prior to ontology, and highlights the very different attitudes toward *logos* that are expressed by the interlocutors. It turns out that Socrates, Gorgias, and Callicles are all assuming a very broad notion of logos, that Socrates is himself practicing the "fine" kind of rhetoric the dialogue seeks, a rhetoric that is not divorced from philosophy, and that the distinction between mythos and logos is fundamentally questionable since both can be fitting ways to lead the soul.

Chapter 4 begins to use the idea of deep rhetoric to explore and reinterpret and clarify issues that have attended the history of rhetoric but have not received the fuller attention that a deep rhetoric can provide. Here, the issue is violence. Is rhetoric, as many have claimed, a potential substitute for violence, a nonviolent way of resolving conflict? Is it the discourse of democracy, both in its historical origin and in the way it continues to inform education and public discourse? Or is rhetoric just another form of violence, a sophisticated practice of discursive power and coercion? Is violence in fact a feature of rhetoric from its origin onward?

This chapter addresses this dispute first through an extended commentary on the great myth of Protagoras, as it is offered by Plato. Protagoras claims that the rhetoric he teaches is equivalent to an education in political virtue itself and that it allows citizens to live peaceably in cities. According to the myth, the origin of rhetoric is an end to violence and the beginning of politics, as well as the birth of a new kind of human being. A deep rhetorical commentary on this myth requires drawing in the twentieth-century philosophers who wrestled with the question in a contemporary context, especially Perelman and Olbrechts-Tyteca, who believe that some notion of a freedom from force lies at the heart of claims that discourse can be free and reasonable. This commentary on the myth of Protagoras ends with a sharpening of the question and a deeper and more detailed awareness of how central the idea of a freedom from violence is for the conceptualization of rhetoric and for reason itself, and yet how subtle and persistent the occurrences of force can be.

The second part of the chapter turns to Walter Benjamin's "Critique of Violence," which argues that all rhetorical-political orders are grounded in and dependent on violence and that only a "divine" violence can end violence. This section offers a careful analytical commentary on Benjamin's essay, drawing in ancient and contemporary writers on rhetoric where they are helpful. The commentary ends with a deep rhetorical critique of the "Critique," partly on the grounds that it exaggerates its vision of violence and diminishes widespread practices of peace, which it relegates to a private sphere which is far too abstractly conceptualized as being entirely separate from the political order. Further, Benjamin's notions of violence and nonviolence are also too abstract; they are conceptualized as pure theoretical entities. His distinction between mythic and divine violence is even more abstract, to the point that he ends up reifying these violences in an ontotheological domain.

The chapter ends with an attempt to undo some of the abstractness with which the question of violence has been treated. It pursues the notion that violence is in some respects less a problem to be solved and more a form of human suffering, like pain. Pain and violence both attend human life, and neither can be completely eradicated, but all worthwhile lives and social and political orders attempt to mitigate both. Rhetoric is the mitigation of violence, not its eschatological terminus. To conclude this chapter, I explore this idea in connection with Aeschylus's *Oresteia* and a poem and a verse novel by Les Murray. The claim that rhetoric addresses the problem of violence is best understood not as a claim that rhetoric can lead to an end of violence, some condition of absolute nonviolence, but rather that rhetoric mitigates violence by making possible dynamic resolutions of conflict in discourse and in processes of justice that are practices of peace. The dynamic and incomplete justice of rhetoric that makes an active peace possible is elaborated in chapter 7.

Henry Johnstone, the founding and long-time editor of *Philosophy and Rhetoric*, once suggested that rhetoric was an attempt to be "philosophy without tears." Chapters 5 and 6 drag rhetoric through the severest kind of tear-inducing philosophy, the thought of Martin Heidegger. The first four chapters prepare the reader for this, giving a good preliminary account of deep rhetoric, but before justice and wisdom can be explained in a deep rhetorical way, the idea of a deep rhetoric must be given more philosophical definition and power, and so it is developed and elaborated in an encounter with some essential challenges of Heidegger's thought. These chapters are not about Heidegger, although there is much careful exposition here. They are rather about the way a deep rhetoric takes up certain Heideggerian challenges, the way deep rhetoric thereby achieves philosophical definition, and the way the project of a deep rhetoric exposes and corrects certain deficiencies in Heidegger's thought.

A deep rhetoric draws from Heidegger's penetrating critique of the way we ordinarily conceptualize being and beings, from his attempt to describe the specific kind of being of human beings, especially from his account of human being as a kind of transcendence, and from his continuing failed encounter with rhetoric and his usually constricted conception of logos—which a deep rhetoric aims to correct. It also aims to correct Heidegger's conception of reasoning. Heidegger also comes in for criticism for his overemphasis on the isolation of individual human existence, the idea that only silence can be authentic, and for the fact that others appear only in ghostly fashion in his writings. Deep rhetoric corrects Heidegger with a much more robust account of sociality. Chapter 6 concludes with an examination of how Heidegger's missteps and failures can nevertheless be read sympathetically as generating a challenging agenda for any conception of rhetoric that intends to endure philosophy's tears.

According to Noemi Perelman Mattis, Chaim Perelman's daughter, Perelman was reading Heidegger at the end of his life.[6] One can only wonder what Perelman's new rhetoric project would have been like if he had studied Heidegger before the project was launched. In some ways, chapter 7 imagines such a reality. It has been difficult for readers of *The New Rhetoric* to grasp Perelman's philosophical ambitions, so this chapter both clarifies those ambitions and takes them further by tuning the new rhetoric project to the philosophical keys of its time and our own, thus making its innovations more widely audible. This chapter also clarifies the senses in which Perelman and Olbrechts-Tyteca's new rhetoric project, interpreted in the light of a deep rhetoric, is a kind of cure for what went wrong in Heidegger's project.

The new rhetoric project was closely connected with Perelman's philosophical work on the concept of justice, and the reinterpretation offered here shows just how intimately intertwined those two aspects of Perelman's thinking were. The chapter opens with a clarification of the idea of justice that is based on the notions of transcendence and world that were developed in the preceding chapters. A concern for justice is not simply a concern with such matters as compensable damages and the just distribution of valued goods, but also with what it means to do justice to each other's lives and experience. This requires taking into account the way our lives are invested in each other and in the world around us. To clarify this, I consider Keith Basso's writings on the Western Apache in *Wisdom Sits in Places* and Jonathan Lear's account of the fate of the Crow people in *Radical Hope*.

This leads to a deep rhetorical reconstruction of the new rhetoric project as a philosophical-rhetorical account of how argumentation can be understood to be a way of doing justice to each other's experience and each other's lives. Because argumentation is a way of doing justice, it can also be understood to be the practice of a dynamic peace. Chapter 7 addresses the questions with which chapter 4 ended by explaining how rhetoric can mitigate violence and be a practice of peace.

Since *Deep Rhetoric* claims to accomplish a *rapprochement* of philosophy with rhetoric, it seems more than fair to ask how it stands with deep rhetoric in relation to that ancient definition of philosophy as a love of wisdom. Chapter 8 responds to this question. It begins with a review of some of the ways wisdom has been conceptualized in the rhetorical tradition, and then it clarifies the question of wisdom through a reading of the *Eumenides*, which ends with a myth of the origin of rhetoric. There, two ways of knowing and judging come into conflict in a dispute about Orestes' killing of his mother: the ways of the Furies and the old gods, on the one hand, and the ways of Orestes and Apollo, on the other. Athena hears their cases, but she delegates her authority to a human jury that is responsible for deliberating and deciding the issue. This generates the question of wisdom: how does one know how to proceed when there are two conflicting ways of knowing and judging, when there is a reasonable case to made on both sides?

Instead of simply rehearsing rhetoric's historical alliance with practical reasoning, I develop a different context for the discussion. I give (necessarily!) brief accounts of how this question of wisdom is developed in Mahayana Buddhism, in an ancient Hebrew context, and in Plato's treatment of Socratic wisdom. The question of wisdom and the development of wisdom traditions have broad cultural and historical range, and this final chapter tries, in a small but specific and significant way, to connect with these larger concerns. Having developed this background, I show how Kenneth Burke addresses this question, primarily in "Four Master Tropes," an appendix to *A Grammar of Motives*, and then how Chaim Perelman treats it, primarily in his Genoa lectures on justice. In their encounter with the question of wisdom, both Burke and Perelman become progenitors of a deep rhetoric, and the chapter concludes by explaining how this is so.

A few final caveats are perhaps in order. I must ask readers for flexibility in my use of a couple of terms. The first is "logos." Part of the aim of a deep rhetoric is to step back from basic concepts that have already been subordinated to and defined in terms of specific theories. In this respect, it strives not to ground rhetorical theory but, at times, to prevent theory, to stay with philosophy in order to expand the question and deepen the sense of what is at stake. I will use the word "logos" in a variety of contexts and for a range of purposes. Rather than give a single definition for the term, I will do my best to provide definition in the specific contexts in which the term is used. Much the same can be said for the word "transcendence." It is used to name in a very abstract manner the general way *we are always moving beyond ourselves*, whether simply in time, or in history, or in language, or in our pursuits of our goals, or even in simple perception and thought. Again, rather than attempt a general definition, I will provide definition as the term arises in specific contexts.

Both of these terms will receive increasing definition in the chapters that treat Heidegger's challenges for rhetoric, but those chapters are themselves the subject of my last caution. Chapters 5 and 6 dig into some of Heidegger's texts in a way that demands a close and technical kind of attention. I believe that the dig is worthwhile, but I admit that it may require special patience from readers who are entirely unfamiliar with Heidegger's thinking. I have done my best to make those chapters available to anyone who gives them the time and attention, but I acknowledge that it requires more than usual effort. For those who make the passage, chapter 7, on reason and justice, will appear in a brighter light.

A central task of the book is to pull the rhetorical tradition into the present time, especially by consolidating and reinterpreting the development of philosophical rhetoric that occurred in the later twentieth century. I hope that this will give us a deeper respect for the resources of rhetoric in general and so a stronger sense of its importance as a field of research and teaching in universities. I hope, too, that slowing down and exploring the philosophical dimensions of rhetoric will strengthen and inform the discipline of rhetoric itself. Rhetoric as a discipline has an important role to play in connection with how we understand many pressing matters, among them: developing democracies, new communication technologies, war and cultural and political conflict, the status of animals, environmental concerns, the task of setting free the capabilities of the disabled, public discourse that has increasingly global dimensions, and the language of market values that has come to pervade so many parts of our thought and our lives. It may also play a significant role in helping along a dialogue among the world religions. We all need all the help we can get in reasoning and communicating about these matters more wisely and clearly. And we need all the help we can get in educating the next generation to be capable of these new communicative challenges.

ONE

What Is Deep Rhetoric?

One way of approaching the question of deep rhetoric is to begin by explaining what ordinary rhetoric is and then to describe the difference between deep rhetoric and ordinary rhetoric. However, there is nothing easy or clear about that approach. The word "rhetoric" has over the last few centuries been reduced to little more than a derogatory term. Rhetoric is, in the popular understanding, a manipulative and dishonest use of language, a use of language that tries to trick or coerce people into believing something that they would not believe on the basis of the evidence alone. Or rhetoric is language that is used to lead people into doing something that, if they knew the truth, they would not do. Or rhetoric is a way of using language to manipulate emotions, to stir up anger or prejudice or fear, and so to lead people to make judgments that they would not make if they were calm and reasonable. In the popular, modern understanding, the goal is to "get beyond all the rhetoric," or to "get behind it," or to "set it aside," in order to be reasonable, in order to have a chance at finding out what is true or which course of action is best.

Because this view of rhetoric is drastically out of line with much of the history of what has been written about rhetoric, drastically out of line with a long tradition of liberal education in which rhetoric has had a central place, and drastically out of line with the idea of rhetoric that will be developed in this book, I will start with a simple statement about rhetoric that contrasts drastically with the popular conception, let it stand, and then start again.

Rhetoric is a form of human transcendence, a way we open ourselves to the influence of what is beyond ourselves and become receptive, a way we participate in a larger world and become open to the lives of others, a way we learn and change. Rhetoric is also a way the world and others become open to us, open to our giving and our participation; it is a way we teach, a way we change our common conditions, a way we form relationships and bear the lives and experiences of other people. Rhetoric is a shape taken by Hebraic wisdom, who cries out in the streets, who was present at the creation of the world.[1] Rhetoric is a shape taken by John's logos, the logos that was from the beginning and through whom all things come into being.[2] Rhetoric is also a form of the logos about which Plato pondered, saying memorably, through the agreement between Socrates and Phaedrus, that there was a special power specific to it, the power of *psychagōgia*, or leading the soul. Rhetoric, as the possibility of there being any leading or being led at all, is necessary for any finding of direction, any purpose. Yet rhetoric is also always something historically and materially specific, a specific shape taken by wisdom and word, a shape that has a special kairotic belonging to some times, some situations, some places.

We are rhetorical beings, and through rhetoric we give ways of being to each other and receive them from each other. Rhetoric is not a debased kind of communication; it is the reality of all communication, and it leads us into experiencing the world in some particular ways and not in all ways. Rhetoric is the inescapable event in all communication—the form and the direction of the influence we exert on each other. We exert such influence in every encounter because we never experience each other outside of a communicative event. Communication and the rhetoric that gives it form and direction grant us our being with each other and our being with ourselves. Ordinary rhetoric is connected with the way this influence and direction can be studied and taught, learned and used, criticized and improved. Deep rhetoric is connected with the dimensions of rhetoric that allow individuals, societies, human activities, and the world itself to take place—and so it brings the very possibility of philosophy and the sciences into its realm.

What Is Rhetoric?

Now, let us start again, differently. What is rhetoric? To begin, consider two apparently incompatible characterizations of rhetoric, both from philosophers. The first is from Paul Ricoeur (1989). He offered it in a lecture titled "Rhetoric—Poetics—Hermeneutics" that he gave in 1970 in Brussels at the Institute for Higher Studies, whose president was Chaim Perelman, one of the authors of *The New Rhetoric*. Perelman was also in the audience. Perelman's rhetorical theory develops a concept of rhetoric whose scope reaches to all nonformal communication, including inward deliberation. Ricoeur believes that this concept is too broad, that distinctions must be made among rhetoric, poetics, and hermeneutics. He argues that each has a different generative seat, a different origin, and he concludes that this limits rhetoric's scope in a specific way. Ricoeur says that rhetoric was born with the legal reforms that took place in sixth-century BCE Sicily, and he believes that rhetoric is forever conditioned, shaped, and limited by the typical discursive situations in which it arose. In this context, he mentions Aristotle's famous three: the deliberative, judicial, and epidictic contexts and genres of rhetoric. Deliberative rhetoric would be found mainly in legislative assemblies or similar contexts, forensic in the institutional settings for trials, and epidictic rhetoric would have its proper place on ceremonial occasions. Ricoeur acknowledges that there is an internal tendency of rhetoric to move beyond these contexts—specifically, he believes that rhetoric's focus on argumentation as a kind of reasoning that takes place in conditions of uncertainty, in the vast domain between arbitrary deciding and certain proof, moves rhetoric's scope outward without limit toward all discourse, even to that point of completion at which it incorporates philosophy. However, he also believes that the generative seats of rhetoric provide an unconquerable constraint on rhetoric's ambitions. Rhetoric will always have a historical and situational and quasi-institutional character.

I have two reservations about Ricoeur's account of rhetoric. First, it neglects the fact that the concept of rhetoric has a significant educational and formative dimension. The origin of rhetoric lies not simply in the new kind of speech made possible and necessary by early democratic reforms in Sicily, but also in the coincident recognition that this new artful communication could be learned and taught. This recognition spurred the development of teachers who became experts in the ways of the courts and assemblies and who offered to train young men in the arts of speech and persuasive reasoning—for a fee. But this educational dimension of rhetoric quickly grew beyond the needs of a specialized class. These arts came to be relevant to all spheres of life, from the household to the assembly. So powerful was the emergent idea of rhetoric that it spawned another transformation. The concept of an individual, free, fully developed citizen began to change to include a new kind of communicative competence, a competence that was very quickly conceptualized by rhetorical theorists as an essential competence for human beings, one without which they would be unable to develop their most human abilities. The early history of rhetoric, the history of its origin, was connected not only with specific changes in political institutions and social practices but also with new conceptions of education and of the specific nature of human beings. From the beginning, rhetoric had exceeded its institutional origins, exceeded Ricoeur's constraints.

Let me broach my second, related, reservation by moving on to some words of Hans-Georg Gadamer, originally published in 1977, words which characterize rhetoric very differently: "Rhetoric is the universal form of human communication, which even today determines our social life in an incomparably more profound fashion than does science" (1986, 17). Here is a very different definition of rhetoric, sweeping but subtle, like so much in Gadamer, apparently simple and almost hiding its central key paradox.[3] I want to develop my second reservation about Ricoeur's account of rhetoric by exploring the paradox in Gadamer's casual-looking definition of rhetoric. The paradox is this. On the one hand, "Rhetoric is the universal form of communication." What could be simpler? When and where human beings communicate, for whatever purpose, rhetoric reigns as the form of that communication. There is no qualification about its scope's being limited by its "generative seats" or by specific occasions or situations. Rhetoric is simply the universal form of human communication. Well, not simply. For Gadamer adds that "even today" rhetoric determines our social life more profoundly than science does. This suggests of course that rhetoric's power to determine social life is a historical power that can wax and wane, and it makes clear that Gadamer's claim is that even though this power can wax and wane in its historical unfolding, it has not yet waned significantly, at least not in comparison with the power of science to determine social life. But if rhetoric is the universal form of human communication, how could it increase and decrease in its power to shape social life? How could it be in a kind of competition with science to shape social life? If it is the universal form of communication, and science is not, how could rhetoric ever not shape social life more profoundly than science? In general, if it is the universal form of human communication, it cannot at the same time permit of being "more or less" the universal form of human communication. It is either universal or it isn't. This is the paradox.

Gadamer starts to clarify the paradox while still in the course of articulating it, and then we can carry out the task out from there. Rhetoric is not really even commensurate with science in this matter of shaping social life, for rhetoric conditions social life "in an incomparably more profound fashion than does science." Rhetoric may have a history of some kind, and its shaping of social life may be altered in some way by science and its history, but rhetoric's power as the universal form of human communication is somehow "incomparably" more profound. We can imagine human beings before modern science, and so we can perhaps imagine ourselves without it. However, there is something that Gadamer here calls "rhetoric" that we cannot imagine ourselves without unless we imagine ourselves as profoundly different from what we now are.

Origins of Rhetoric

To get a better idea of why Gadamer says this—even though, we must assume, he knows the stories of rhetoric's origin as well as Ricoeur does—it might help to look at some of the early testimony about the nature of rhetoric. For the very nature of rhetoric was an issue right from the start.

To take this step embroils us in a little bit of relevant controversy, though, for Edward Schiappa has set forth a strongly historicist and quite thought-provoking argument about rhetoric's beginnings that would make this step look like question-begging. Schiappa warns us not to look to pre-Aristotelian philosophy to understand rhetoric, because the concept of rhetoric was not really developed until after Plato coined the term and Aristotle refined the concept. In *The Beginnings of Rhetorical Theory in Classical Greece* (1999), Schiappa urges us to give up our anachronistic accounts of rhetoric's pre-Platonic history. Plato coined the word "rhetoric," he says, and conceptualized it in a specific relationship to philosophy, dialectics, eristics, and other specialized Platonic descriptors of what was more generally referred to in terms of *logos*. Not until "rhetoric" becomes part of a discourse that organizes it as a term in relation to other terms do we begin to understand the history of rhetoric. Only when rhetoric is differentiated from some general art of *logos*, a differentiation that begins in Plato and is almost complete in Aristotle, do we really have "rhetoric." So, if, in order to show that Gadamer's philosophical approach to rhetoric has merits that go beyond Ricoeur's more historicist approach, we appeal to what certain ancients said about the art of *logos* in general, are we not demonstrating that we have simply neglected the historicist challenge?

Well, no. And for two reasons. First, the historicist method employed here tends to be question-begging. Schiappa imagines three stages in the early development of what we now call rhetorical theory. A first stage, a fifth-century stage, represented by the older sophists, was primarily concerned with *logos*.[4] A second stage, represented by Plato, developed a new focus on an art of *logos* or speech, sometimes called by Plato "rhetoric." By the end of the fourth century, with Aristotle, a third stage had been reached, in which the split between philosophy and rhetoric was complete. Schiappa urges us not to think of the early stages in this process as essentially concerned with rhetoric. As he says, "The meanings associated with *logos* and *legein* are such that one cannot argue they mean the same thing as was later conveyed by 'rhetoric'" (1999, 34).

However, that is just the issue. If the older sophists spoke of *logos* in a general way, and Plato began to speak of *logos* and rhetoric and philosophy in such a way that there were both differences as well as identity, and then Aristotle systematized the differences so that there was not as much left to say about a general art of *logos*—well, what is the best or most helpful or truest or most desirable way to speak and write and think about these things? Schiappa seems to take the strong historicist view that we must understand the origin of rhetoric the way the people near its origin understood it, and especially the way Aristotle understood it. As he says at one point, the idea of "rhetoric derived from fifth century Greece is improbable. . . . Ahistorical definitions are misleading, unhelpful, or superfluous" (64). However, if we want to know whether a historicist or a philosophical approach to the question "What is Rhetoric?" is more helpful, we can't simply decide the issue by historicist fiat the way Schiappa does here. So, the first reason not to go Schiappa's way is that it begs the question. Our question is not simply a historical one. Our question is: What is rhetoric? And more specifically: Is rhetoric the universal form of communication or is it a particular kind of communication limited to particular times and places?

A second reason why we are not simply neglecting the historicist challenge is that there was a controversy at the origin of rhetoric about just what rhetoric is. Schiappa's neat three-part progression that resolves itself in the "completion" of the conceptualizing of rhetoric in Aristotle is a tidy way to resolve this controversy, but it is hardly a satisfying resolution for those who believe that there is something philosophical in the conflict between philosophy and rhetoric. Plato was not merely at a half-way point between the older sophists and Aristotle in some three-part problem-solving process. In the *Phaedrus* (261a-b, Fowler trans.), Socrates poses this question to his young interlocutor:

"Is not rhetoric in its entire nature an art which leads the soul by means of words (*dia logōn*), not only in law courts and the various other public assemblages, but in private companies as well? And is it not the same when concerned with small things as well as with great, and, properly speaking no more to be esteemed in important than in trifling matters? Is this what you have heard?"

That is, Socrates is asking: Isn't rhetoric an art of *logos* in general, an art whereby we have an influence on each other's souls, an art of teaching and leading one another, an art whose scope ranges from the largest public political matters to the smallest private affairs? In other words: Isn't rhetoric best understood in light of *logos* in general? Isn't rhetoric the universal form of human communication?

Phaedrus answers as a good student should, along the well-informed and knowledgeable paths that Ricoeur and Schiappa follow: "No, by Zeus, not that exactly; but the art of speaking and writing is exercised chiefly in lawsuits, and that of speaking in public assemblies; and I never heard of any further uses" (261b, Fowler trans.). Here Phaedrus gives the properly Aristotelian answer, jumping to Schiappa's stage three right in the middle of one of Plato's dialogues. He says: No, Socrates, rhetoric is not the universal form of human communication. One has judicial rhetoric, and then one has deliberative rhetoric, and so rhetoric has its institutional generative seats which limit it and so prevent it from rightly being characterized as the universal form of human communication. Rhetoric is a distinct art or discipline and not a kind of philosophy or general art of *logos*.

Socrates then carries the dialogue forward, examining the kind of speech that occurs in courts and assemblies, arguing that "the art of contention in speech [*antilogikē*] is not confined to courts and political gatherings, but apparently, if it is an art at all, it would be one and the same in all kinds of speaking" (261d-e). This is his beginning of a long argument for a conception of rhetoric as equivalent to an art of *logos*, a conception of rhetoric as something like the universal form of human communication. The long discussion eventuates in two very important claims in the *Phaedrus*. First, the attempt to conceptualize rhetoric as something that can be understood and learned independently of some more general art of *logos* is a mistaken effort, one that confuses the preliminaries or elements of an art with the art itself. Without understanding the purpose of an art of *logos*, a mastery of the techniques of *logos* is meaningless. Second, since it is the special power of *logos* to lead the soul, the art of *logos*, rhetoric itself, is the art of leading souls, and so, Socrates says, the art of rhetoric is a lot like the art of healing, and not much different from a philosophical dialectic. These are arguments for the claims that (1) rhetoric cannot be detached from deep rhetoric without losing its purpose, which organizes it as an art, and (2) rhetoric cannot be detached from deep rhetoric without obscuring the fact that rhetoric is not just an external and optional activity but is also a matter of who and what we are intrinsically.[5]

The point of all this is that Plato has an explicit argument against conceptualizing rhetoric the way Schiappa and Ricoeur and Aristotle want to. There is an advantage in valorizing the Aristotelian approach. It yields a discipline of rhetoric that is fairly well-defined and mercifully distinct from philosophy and its eternal failure to define itself. The Aristotelian approach can give an answer to the question of what rhetoric is that for most people will not cause serious problems.[6] On the contrary, for most rhetoricians, it will remove difficulties, and allow them to proceed with work in their discipline in a productive way. However, the approach does not offer a serious philosophical response to Plato, and it does not help with the project of trying to understand what a deep rhetoric would be. So it is at least an open question whether we should look at historical sources that seem to have a general, *logos*-oriented conception of rhetoric for help in answering our contemporary question: what is rhetoric?

When Aristotle subordinated and disciplined and so legitimated rhetoric, he at the same time disciplined philosophy—made it less than the whole. Plato knew that both rhetoric and philosophy were striving with a general conception of *logos* toward something like a genuine art or practice of *logos*, although the idea of an art or practice in this context is highly unstable because *logos* is not simply an optional attainment for human beings. We already participate in it in one way or another, and we could hardly be at all in its absence. Philosophy as Socrates and Plato practiced it is born in the matrix of dialogues that illuminate this *logos* that leads the soul but which is not susceptible to being mastered by a wisdom or a specific kind of knowledge. When Aristotle distinguishes between the different arts of *logos*, he converts an unmanageable truth into a problem to be solved—and he solves it in a masterful way. Rhetoric and dialectic are clearly distinguished and their separate spheres are explained. Rhetoric is subordinated, and philosophy is brilliantly elaborated and explicated, but philosophy is now a discipline to be executed and no longer a comportment—one akin to worship—toward a good that cannot be conceptualized or disciplined. The deep ethical and existential rigors of restraint and critique and intense dialogue between specific people with specific kinds of souls that need tempering and leading in specific kinds of ways in order for what is most worth pursuing to have any chance of showing itself—that kind of philosophy is forsaken for the philosophy that might plausibly make a claim to a general kind of knowledge.

One cannot deny that Aristotle's move was an advance that was productive for both rhetoric and the philosophical sub-disciplines as they are still known today. It is one of philosophy's fundamental achievements. Few people can read the *Nicomachean Ethics* now without being grateful, without wishing that those ideas were more widely understood and discussed in our own time. However, Aristotle's controversial solution is so functional that it has become identical not only with common sense but also with the structure of academic disciplines. "Ethics" is not part of the discipline of communication, but it is wise to have an "ethics of communication" course in a communication curriculum. This is rational, disciplinary compartmentalization. For Plato, ethics is not a compartment of human knowledge or a separate discipline. It is an essential dimension of all communication, in fact of all human action. Much of Socrates' critical force is aimed at the rhetoricians' attempts to separate ethics and philosophy from rhetoric, as if ethics could be something external to communication, or as if a careful discussion about what was really true and good in some case was an optional, value-added accessory to political deliberation.

Having made the case for the legitimacy of a conception of a rhetoric that preserves its deeper and admittedly difficult connections with *logos*, let us turn to the fourth century BCE, when Isocrates offered his "hymn to *logos*," an enduring account of an art of human discourse that is equivalent to reason itself. Here it is:

For in the other powers which we possess . . . we are in no respect superior to other living creatures; nay, we are inferior to many in swiftness and in strength and in other resources; [15.254] but, because there has been implanted in us the power to persuade each other and to make clear to each other whatever we desire, not only have we escaped the life of wild beasts, but we have come together and founded cities and made laws and invented arts; and, generally speaking, there is no institution devised by man which the power of speech has not helped us to establish [15.255]. For this it is which has laid down laws concerning things just and unjust, and things honorable and base; and if it were not for these ordinances we should not be able to live with one another. It is by this also that we confute the bad and extol the good. Through this we educate the ignorant and appraise the wise; for the power to speak well is taken as the surest index of a sound understanding, and discourse which is true and lawful and just is the outward image of a good and faithful soul [15.256]. With this faculty we both contend against others on matters which are open to dispute and seek light for ourselves on things which are unknown; for the same arguments which we use in persuading others when we speak in public, we employ also when we deliberate in our own thoughts;

and, while we call eloquent those who are able to speak before a crowd, we regard as sage those who most skillfully debate their problems in their own minds [15.257]. And, if there is need to speak in brief summary of this power, we shall find that none of the things which are done with intelligence take place without the help of speech, but that in all our actions as well as in all our thoughts speech is our guide, and is most employed by those who have the most wisdom.

Here in a nutshell is a concept of *logos* as equivalent to communication in its more profound senses, a concept of *logos* that does not divide the kind of reasoning we do in science and in intellectual inquiry from the kind of reason we use when we adjudicate disputes. As Isocrates says, with communicative reason, we not only deliberate about laws and invent arts and develop skills, we also educate the young and evaluate the claims of the wise. The reason with which we think when we are alone, lost in inner deliberations and arguments, is the same reason we use to speak before a crowd. As Isocrates concludes, "None of the things which are done with intelligence takes place without the help of *logos*," without communicative reason, but in both action and thought, communicative reason is most used by those who have the most wisdom.

Here, say many, is the core vision of the classical liberal arts—that there is a common activity that both pervades all the particular sciences and reaches well beyond them, into civic life and into the individual uses of reason, and that this activity can be cultivated and nourished. We can train people to be better at it. Here is where Isocrates lines up with the older sophist, Protagoras, also an educator, who attributes the same importance to *logos*. Protagoras says that the art he teaches is the art of living together in cities, and he also says (at least in Plato's dialogue) that before people discovered this art, they were unable to form societies, and were in fact less than human.

Toward a Deep Rhetoric

This takes us directly back to my first reservation about Ricoeur's account of rhetoric. Protagoras and Plato and Isocrates were all educators, and at the heart of their educational projects was a conception of *logos*. They all explored the question of whether there was some essential power of *logos*, some role it played that nothing else could play, and they all developed a concept of what it might mean to be educated in such a way that one could somehow connect with its power, be shaped by it, and learn both how to be led and how to lead the souls of others. Both Protagoras (at least Plato's Protagoras) and Isocrates accept the mythic view of rhetoric that informs the traditional account of the historical origins of rhetoric—the view that the origin of rhetoric was coincident with the advent of a specifically human kind of society, or, in more historical terms, that rhetoric originated in the democratic reforms that began in ancient Sicily.

It is at this point that we might see a slight convergence of Ricoeur's and Gadamer's views. Think of it this way. At some point in history, people begin to succeed in developing institutions and practices that are in some important respects democratic, especially in the respect that these new laws and institutions require new abilities of people, especially the ability to reason in speech with other people in order to make choices, choices about a significantly enlarged range of issues, choices once made by a tyrant or some other power or authority, but choices that must now be made by a broader range of people in a context of more open deliberation and reasoning.

We must pause here for a moment because this historical account is of course also a mythical story. Today, we would want to examine this apparent outbreak of freedom and discover what kind of unfreedom took force at the same time and supported it. We would want to focus on its effects on people who did not gain political freedoms and who were not eligible for the new education in communication. We would want to look at what communicative practices were available to them and how these were shaped by the changes going on in the assemblies and courts. We would also want to look at other societies at other times, at their own legal reforms and the communicative practices that looked similar. We would want the history to be much more complex and honest. However, we can want all this and still want to grasp why so many people of so many kinds over such a long time have used this particular historical event to wrestle with some ideas that come up again and again in many different historical contexts. For, as you know by now, it is the idea that I have set my sights on in this book—partly in order to bring it into a relation with a particular set of practices and issues in a particular time and place, our own.

When Hegel tried to think of a way to characterize the nature of these Greek legal reforms, he could say only that the Greeks seemed to come up with the idea that not one person, not a single authority, should be free, but that some larger group should be free.[7] With this notion of a larger group of free individuals, one needs of course a way for them to resolve disputes among themselves, and so the legal reforms are coincident with the recognition that more than one person should be free. However, the legal reforms are abstract and useless unless people have some real ability to use speech to resolve their disputes, to succeed in persuading one another, and so a conception of rhetoric arises both as the form of communication among free citizens and as the educational goal of the training of free citizens.

Thus, rhetoric arises in a historically specific situation, and its advent is coincident with certain laws and institutions and practices, as Ricoeur says, and yet rhetoric is also, as Gadamer says, the universal form of human communication among people who expect to be treated as free, that is, as capable and deserving of participating in deliberation and reasoning about some significant range of choices that must be made. Gadamer imagines that this expectation is still profound. If modern science has in some sense displaced rhetoric, if a culture of scientific expertise and a technology that seems to move faster than choice seem to have seized power, it is not the case that they have in any significant way weakened our expectations or our demands to participate in the choices that affect us. For, as Gadamer says in another context,[8] there is implied in every theory of science itself the idea of self-justification, which compels it to go beyond itself, both into the hermeneutic domain of argumentation and communication, where competing theories and interpretations meet, and also finally into the philosophy of science. The expectations that scientific claims must be justified and that the communicative sphere in which this justification takes place must be designed to give human individuals a role in the choices and judgments that are made are evidence that science itself is supported by the same communicative expectations as those carried to us by the rhetorical tradition.

So Gadamer, or even Plato, and certainly Protagoras and Isocrates, can admit that rhetoric has a specific origin in particular institutions and historical developments. They can even admit that rhetoric continues to be "limited" or influenced by this origin. However, if the origin is conceived as a development of concrete historical forms of education and political life that are still connected with what are now widely held notions of reason and freedom, notions whose proper legal and institutional and educational forms are still being explored, then the original institutional matrix of rhetoric does not appear to be a constraint on the range of rhetoric; it appears to be quite the opposite. The idea of a deep rhetoric is the idea of a rhetoric that takes historically specific shapes, and which divides itself into forms of discourse, but which also has generative power that is in the process of exceeding those shapes and forms. Part of this exceeding occurs in the attempt to realize the educational and humanistic ideals that rhetoric generates. Its effects are evident, too, in the universalities that it produces.[9] One could say then that rhetoric has both a horizontal, historical axis in which it assumes the specific institutional shapes by which it seems to be constrained, and also a vertical axis along which it generates ideals of freedom and reason and nonviolence, and the humane formation of human beings, ideals which reach beyond specific situations and generate motives for changing them. This vertical axis is, of course, as historical as everything else, and its specific content changes as the situations it intersects change. Every historical situation has its own verticality, its own imagination of what goes beyond the situation.

We began this chapter by asking, what is rhetoric? The question presented an immediate obstacle, because the historical meaning of rhetoric has been largely lost in our time. We have only a degraded trace of that meaning flickering in our current uses of the word. We presented an initial account of rhetoric that would contrast with the degraded notion of rhetoric and give a sense of a conception of rhetoric in terms of which we might be able to articulate the meaning of a "deep rhetoric," one that would lead to a rapprochement of rhetoric and philosophy. We considered Paul Ricoeur's claim that rhetoric would always be limited by its institutional origins in ancient Greece, and we considered Gadamer's counter-claim that rhetoric is the universal form of human communication. To gain perspective on this conflict, we considered how this same dispute arose among the Greeks during the period in which the word "rhetoric" was first used and in which the concept of rhetoric was being formed. I made a case that Plato's argument for a conception of rhetoric as belonging to a general art of logos is one that cannot be dismissed, and that it is a framework for a concept of rhetoric that would open up the dimensions of deep rhetoric. I also made a case that the apparent conflict between Ricoeur's and Gadamer's views of rhetoric could be resolved. This clears the way for a deep rhetoric, a philosophical rhetoric that will not simply be in conflict with disciplinary conceptions of rhetoric but will instead help to interpret and explain and to some extent even justify and strengthen them.

Time again for some general, provocative statements, summarizing and projecting. "Deep rhetoric" is a conceiving of all rhetoric in the context of what the ancients would call a general art of logos. It is related to the *psychagōgia* of Plato's *Phaedrus* and the art of *logos* described by Isocrates. However, it is not the name of a specific set of techniques or methods or figures or schemes, but rather it is the name of a way of transcendence, steered by logos. Rhetoric is a way of being human, a way of educating human beings, a way of nonviolence, a way of reason and freedom, a political way . . . and more. This way is in part a specific way, but it is always also just the event of forward movement itself, our constant transcendence beyond ourselves, toward something else. And so, an important question is, movement toward what? What makes change desirable or good? If rhetoric is the leading of the soul, then where is rhetoric leading the soul?

In a profound sense, this phenomenon of being led *toward* something just *is* the ethics of rhetoric. The question of whether rhetoric is ethically good or ethically bad, or what makes it which, takes for granted that rhetoric has an ethical valence, that rhetoric is readily recognized as a mode of human existence to which ethical judgments are always relevant and appropriate. Rhetoric is one of the primary ways we act ethically or unethically, in a way that accomplishes good or a way that does not. To say that rhetoric is a kind of violence or manipulation or trickery, and so a kind of wrong, is already to say that rhetoric is something that can be judged in ethical terms. From the standpoint of a deep rhetoric, rhetoric in general is always in a formal sense "ethical," meaning that it is a way human beings accomplish good or evil. How some *specific* rhetorical action is to be judged—that cannot be foretold at a philosophical or even a sound theoretical level.

However, this leaves a central, legitimate concern unaddressed. I will in this work not only attempt to develop an understanding of a deep rhetoric, but I will also be defending rhetoric as an educational and intellectual and political pursuit, and I will make this defense in the context of the notion of a deep rhetoric which I will be working out. A legitimate question is: If rhetoric is a leading of the soul by means of logos, then where is rhetoric leading? Am I not somehow smuggling in some ultimate goal or value for this rhetorical leading? This question, along with the question of *how* rhetoric leads, will be a thread in all the remaining chapters. It will receive its most focused development and discussion in chapter 7, "Rhetoric and Justice." In the remainder of this chapter, it will lead us into questions that are analogous to theological questions, and it will take us back once more to Plato, although once again interpreted in a way that goes against the usual reading. From there, it will lead us into a discussion of humanism, education, and another encounter with the disciplinary conception of rhetoric. We will also begin to work through a part of the philosophical groundbreaking that makes this work on deep rhetoric possible: Chaim Perelman and Lucie Olbrechts-Tyteca's new rhetoric project.

Some Theologies and Teleologies of Rhetoric

A legitimate concern about a rhetoric that speaks of a general art of logos is that it will universalize and absolutize the purpose it seeks to accomplish, the value of the place to which it leads. In what follows, we will consider two classical sites for thinking of logos and its ultimate purpose: Plato and the Gospel of John in the New Testament. Both Plato and John are usually taken to connect logos with an ultimate being, an ultimate value, to which logos leads. In the case of Plato, it is the ultimate Form of the Good to which logos is thought to lead us, ultimately in an act of intellectual intuition. In the Gospel of John, it is the knowledge of the highest Being, God, to which Christ the Logos leads. However, a closer look will show that even here, in texts that are saddled by tradition with the crudest kind of ontotheology, there is a conception of logos that is defined precisely by its *not* leading to a knowledge of an ultimate being. Becoming attuned to this use of "logos" will help to keep deep rhetoric from falling into some disciplinary formation of philosophy or rhetoric, or into some particular religious formation. It will instead keep deep rhetoric philosophical, in question, and not secured and limited by its knowledge of some specific, existing, ultimate being or value or goal. Yet I hope to show that deep rhetoric will in no way be left purposeless or simply abstract.

In Plato's *Phaedrus*, the art of *logos* is aligned with the special power of *logos* to "lead the soul" (261a-b, 271c, Fowler trans.). So, in the *Phaedrus*, the dialogue between Socrates and Phaedrus seeks the right kind of leading, a leading toward that which is the most genuinely attractive, toward what is best. At the beginning of the dialogue, Phaedrus is being led by a written speech of Lysias whose purpose is to persuade Phaedrus to gratify Lysias's desires. Socrates uses speech to deflate Lysias's prose and render it powerless to lead. He then uses several forms of logos, including myth and dialectic and humor and imagery, to draw Phaedrus's attention first to himself, and then toward images, and then, insofar as possible, toward philosophy, a way of life guided by a deep affection for wisdom, and thus toward a form of love or desire. As Socrates insists elsewhere, this kind of love is not a possessing or grasping of its goal or its object but precisely a not-having, a way of comporting oneself *toward* but not a way of actually knowing or grasping or achieving the goal.[10]

In the first chapter of the Gospel of John, the *logos* is said to be *pros ton theon*, "toward (the) god." However, we will see that with this logos, too, at least in some very significant receptions of it, the idea that it achieves some possession or knowledge of an ultimate being, some end of its being toward and an actual arriving at its goal—that idea is precisely what it defines itself against. If one were thinking in an ontotheological framework, where one already knew that if there is a "leading" or a "toward," then there must be an ultimate goal, an absolute endpoint, some final being or state of being toward which one was being led, then there would be grounds to suspect the idea of a rhetorical theory related to a logos that leads to this super-goal. And in the distortions of Plato and John handed down to us by those who need definite, certain, foreseeable outcomes for all their educational efforts, these endpoint-beings are the "Form of the Good" and "God," named, conceived, known, and subordinated to the reigning ontology. This relieves the anxiety of some and inspires the critical energies of others.

But let us go forward, I hope, more slowly and with less certainty. In Plato's *Republic* (506), Glaucon presses Socrates to give an account of "the Good." Socrates is reluctant, and there's quite a bit of discursive pushing and shoving between the two about whether this discussion can really be conducted. Glaucon accuses Socrates of being willing to speak of other people's beliefs but not his own. Socrates replies: "Is it your opinion that it's just to speak about what one doesn't know as if one knew?" (506c). The verb for "know" here is *oida*, which means to see or to know. Socrates is denying that he has "seen" the good in the sense of having direct knowledge or intuition of it. He is insisting still, in the *Republic*, on his ignorance. Those who claim to see when they do not, those who claim knowledge where it is not available, are not seeing the Good, but are experiencing blindness and distortions. Socrates asks Glaucon: Are those the things you want to see, "when it is possible to hear bright and fair ones from others?" (506c). The contrast between seeing and hearing is in the Greek, and it is especially noticeable because it seems to suggest that one cannot see the radiant beauty of the Good but can only hear of it—that there is something like willful seeing and then there is something like receptive listening. Nevertheless, Glaucon continues his combative striving forward and demands that Socrates not withdraw before he has reached the ultimate goal—a direct exposition of the Good itself. He demands, "in the name of Zeus," that Socrates continue. Socrates replies that he would like to be able to do what Glaucon demands, but that it is not possible, and that Glaucon's spirited desire would simply lead him to do something laughable.

Instead, he says, he can speak of what appears to resemble an offspring or child of the Good, but he warns Glaucon: "Be careful that I don't in some unwilling way deceive you . . ." (507a). This is because the discussion now is focused on something that seems to be similar to the good but the language that is to be used of it will be deceptive if it is taken in the wrong way. What follows is a discussion of the intellect as something analogous to sight—an analogy that seems to work for mathematical ideas, and is said, in the discussion, to work for other forms, but which has already been indicated to be inappropriate for comporting oneself toward the Good, and, in fact, no such claim that the Good can be "seen" is made anywhere in the discussion. When it comes to the Good, there is no direct access. The Good is not a mathematical form. There is a way toward it, but it requires a special kind of ignorance, a knowing that knowledge is not sufficient, that the good cannot be grasped in that way.

In *God Without Being*, Jean-Luc Marion attempts to explain the difference between the idol and the icon by examining the relation between seeing and knowing. His account could have been written as a gloss on Plato:

> The idol . . . by definition . . . is seen—*eidōlon*, that which is seen (*eidō, video). It even consists only in the fact that it can be seen, that one cannot but see it. And see it so visibly that the very fact of seeing it suffices to know it—*eidōlon*, that which is known by the fact that one has seen it (*oïda*). The idol presents itself to man's gaze in order that representation, and hence knowledge, can seize hold of it. . . . The idol . . . captivates the gaze precisely because everything in it must expose itself to the gaze, attract, fill, and hold it. The idol depends on the gaze that it satisfies. . . . The gaze alone makes the idol, as the ultimate function of the gazable. (1991, 9–10)

Marion is describing exactly what Socrates is trying to resist in Glaucon's spirited demands for intellectual satisfaction—a kind of idolatry. So he will offer Glaucon something *like* seeing, and move him from seeing through the thinking and intelligence that are like seeing, *toward* the good, but the good will not itself be known this way. To be carried away by one's desire to see here would be, in Socrates' language, "shameful."

To make an idol of Plato's good is to miss both the kind of being or giving appropriate to the good and also to misunderstand what human beings must achieve in order to comport themselves toward it properly. The encounter with the good is not an intellectual intuition—that is too easy. If it were an intellectual intuition, then it could be shared, insofar as we all have intellects. We could also deduce properties or implications of the good from this intellection, the way we do from mathematical truths. Intellectual intuitions are cognitive. But this is exactly *not* the case when it comes to the good in the *Republic*. One of the ironies at the end of book 6 of the *Republic* is that the book concludes with a divided line that distinguishes having opinions about things that are only imagined or at best believed from having knowledge by way of thinking and intellection about what really is—and yet this conclusion is reached by way of an untrustworthy opinion about an unreliable *resemblance* between seeing and knowing! The opinion is not knowledge and the resemblance is only apparent. These logoi are meant to be stepping stones, skipped over lightly, in just the right away. They are not meant to be foundations in the building up of a knowledge of the Good. They are not themselves a way of grasping or seeing the good. That would be a mis-leading. They are instead part of a path of logoi, a way of moving toward.

The issue comes up again in book 7 of the *Republic*, after the allegory of the cave and a long discussion of education based on the allegory and the divided line of book 6. Socrates draws the extreme conclusion of his lengthy, potentially deceptive development of the analogy between seeing things and knowing them, between the sun's relation to sight and the Good's relation to knowledge. He has already pushed the analogy to breaking at one point in book 6, where he observed that the sun not only allows for things' being seen but also for generation, growth, and nourishment. "Therefore," he reasons, "say that not only being known is present in the things, but also existence and being are in them besides as a result of it, although the good isn't being, but is still beyond being, exceeding it in dignity and power" (509b). If the good is not a being itself but is instead "beyond being," then pretty clearly it cannot be seen or known by any of the ways we see or know beings, and so the analogy has surpassed itself.

In book 7, Socrates pushes the limits yet again: "When a man tries by discussion—by means of argument [*logos*] without the use of any senses—to attain to each thing itself that is and doesn't give up before he grasps by intellection itself that which is good itself, he comes to the very end of the intelligible realm just as that other man was at the end of the visible. . . . Don't you call this journey dialectic?" (532a-b). Glaucon is agreeable, but again he wants Socrates to go further, to complete the task. He wants to know exactly what this dialectic is, this movement through logoi, and he wants a description of how it conducts us to the Good. "For these, as it seems, would lead at last toward that place which is for the one who reaches it a haven from the road, as it were, and an end of his journey."

And this is exactly where the analogy breaks down for the final time: "You will no longer be able to follow, my dear Glaucon . . . [because] . . . you would no longer be seeing an image of what we are saying, but rather the truth itself, at least as it looks to me. Whether it is really so or not can no longer be properly insisted on" (533a). The point is that the Good is not a being that can be seen and then described accurately. *Logos* leads one toward it, but does not arrive at it as at a destination, as if it were traveling in a kind of spiritual-intellectual space through the lower forms, up through beauty and justice until finally it reached that highest being, the Good. All of that is simply an image, an image that one can indeed "see" in an "idolatrous" way. The Platonic *logos* is a leading, not a seeing or grasping or knowing. It is more a reverent way of inquiry than a method for reaching final conclusions or arriving at a knowledge of the final being. The latter can simply not be a realizable goal for a Socrates whose essential intellectual virtues include ignorance.

In fact, there are plenty of suggestions in Plato that ignorance and love are dimensions of philosophical rhetoric that keep one open and attuned to the good in a way that knowledge cannot. "Attuned" is of course a metaphor that tries to capture the comportment toward the good in light of the *Republic*'s insistence that everything that is comes to be only by way of the good, which is then not a being but a kind of giving of being, something to which one must become attuned without actually seeing/knowing it as an object. And "at*tuned*" seems to be appropriate, too, in relation to Socrates' dictum that the dialectic is itself a kind of song. The good does allow the dialectic, and life itself, to be experienced as a journey. And *some* kind of encounter of the good is clearly possible. However, it is not an intellectual intuition, and it is not simply cognitive. Whether it really is as it shows itself in the encounter or not "cannot properly be insisted." And yet moving toward "it" is the whole point.

Similarly, in the Gospel of John, in which the *logos* is said to be *pros ton theon*, toward God, there is a sense in which the *logos* never makes a final, journey-ending arrival at the god, or God. Instead, the *logos* is the dynamic movement toward and into G-d.[11] If it arrived at G-d as at a goal, as at the being named "God," it would no longer be in movement toward G-d. It would be one independent entity that had moved through some kind of space to arrive at another independent entity. Or it would be language or thought or reasoning that finally made God comprehensible, and so was responsible for God's being known. Then the *logos* would be the fulfillment of gnostic or rationalist philosophical-religious projects. Neither Plato nor John develop that kind of project. Both preserve the dynamic character of *logos* and the idea that that toward which *logos* leads will always exceed the forms of comprehension that lead toward it.

Many of the more neglected parts of the traditions of Christian theology focus carefully on this incomprehensibility of G-d, especially the

Orthodox traditions. However, even in the Western Latin tradition, this incomprehensibility is a persistent theme. For Augustine, in *De Trinitate*, faith in a comprehensible God is "feigned faith." Throughout the book he wonders, just as he does in *Confessions*, whether the God he loves is the "true God," something he could never know because he did not have sufficient knowledge of the true G-d. His "solution" in *De Trinitate* is to love the love with which he loves, for that love is G-d, for G-d is love, and the truest love is the love of G-d, which is just as present in love of neighbor (8.5.12; 253ff.). The sense in which love can be said to be true is a much more important one for Augustine than the epistemological sense of "truth."

In *Confessions*, this movement away from a being that can be comprehended, grasped, known, is an indirect movement toward Augustine's own intense, restless, passionate questioning, his seeking of God, as that wherein G-d is acting. In book 7, chapter 10, where Augustine recounts his search for God, his search outward through every means and his search also down through the labyrinth and deceptiveness of his own inwardness, his grand survey of everything that exists, he concludes that nothing of it was G-d. And yet, he says, in the long prayer that is the *Confessions*, that he was near G-d in this very searching: "You were what I heard teaching and guiding . . ."(7.10.65; 251). (Here is the metaphor of hearing again.) This hearkens back to the opening of *Confessions*, where, after puzzling over the paradox of seeking something that one does not comprehend, Augustine asks: "Or is calling for you itself the way to recognize you?" (1.1.1; 3).

The *Confessions* is a long *via negativa*, question answering question, with every concept of God found wanting, every appearance of God in creation found to be an illusion. Augustine is nothing if not consistent about this. The *Confessions* ends with a discussion of G-d's goodness and rest. However, at this end, one achieves no knowledge and reaches no final goal. Instead Augustine asks yet more questions: "What man can explain this to another man? What angel to an angel, or what angel to a man?" As always, Augustine gives his ultimate answers in the guise of penultimate questions, for the "answer" is: "Only to you can we pray, only from you can we hope, only at your door can we knock. Be it granted, be it filled, be it opened." Here, the book ends. It ends with questions, and it ends with praying, hoping, knocking—all forms of seeking and moving toward, not forms of arrival or fulfillment. There is no ultimate comprehension or experience of direct contact with a Superbeing for whom one is searching. There is prayer, towardness. This is, for Augustine, what we are:

a being-tilted-toward an ontologically fugitive and incomprehensible G-d who is not in any ordinary sense a goal or a being or a purpose from whom we can deduce the appropriate uses of logos.

In trinitarian philosophical theology, the being of G-d was sometimes described in terms of *perichoresis*, a word that names the way the members of the Trinity do not have their being simply in themselves but rather give being to one another, dynamically. In John's gospel, the *logos* is, like the Good in Plato, that by virtue of which anything has its being. It is that which gives intelligibility, the Johannine "light of the world." And what is perhaps most interesting here is that "in the beginning," the word (*logos*) was not only moving dynamically toward God, but that the word *was* God. That is, the "way" or "path" is also that toward which the way leads. This cannot be taken to be sheer, undifferentiated identity—that would be an ontotheological reification. It is beyond our purpose here to delve into the theological treatments of this issue, which are innumerable, but the concepts of participation and *perichoresis*, with their many inflections and forking trails of thought, would be the field into which such thinking would head. However, the issue is familiar enough. It is sometimes said of the Islamic hajj that each step of the journey must also hold its destination. Or, as Gary Snyder's Zen teacher told him, "The perfect way is without difficulty. Strive hard!" (1990, 149). That is, you are already in some sense at the end of the way, but responding to that fact is not easy. Understanding the nature of the participation, the way in which the being of the way and its end are given and received to and from each other—that is not an easy matter either for thinking or for practical reasoning. The issue appears repeatedly in theological thinking, and insofar as we press this question of an ultimate goal on the project of a deep rhetoric, such formal issues will arise here.

And so, a deep rhetoric will regularly encounter the phenomena of directionality and "leading," the question of purposefulness and goals—a kind of theological and teleological challenge. However, this encounter in no way requires its absorption into the ontotheological tradition. In fact, rhetoric's going deep requires just the opposite. It requires the struggle for thinking in which Plato and Augustine and Jean-Luc Marion and Emmanuel Levinas have all engaged, though each in a different way: a questioning of the priority of ontology on the ground that ontology is itself a communicative phenomenon, an effect of logos. The logos of rhetoric is always on the way somewhere, never arriving at a final end, traveling through time and human inwardness and making direction and purposefulness possible—and yet always taking place and taking shape at some particular place at some particular time in some particular circumstance. The project of a deep rhetoric is not grounded in the assumption of a super-goal, but instead explores the way in which rhetoric makes possible the experience of human purposefulness itself.

Suspecting Universality

If there is a basic ground for suspicion of a deep rhetoric, it is not in some super-value that deep rhetoric has smuggled in under its coat. This does not mean that there is no ground for suspicion at all. Deep rhetoric does generate certain universal expressions, and this would be a good place to address, in a brief and general way, some questions that are sure to arise as we move forward. Since we are speaking of human actions and human societies, the basic suspicion of universality is an ethical and political suspicion: that any conceivable universality is not really universal but is a partial interest masquerading, so to speak, as a universal interest. This means that the interests of some are being obscured, even denied. This fear is related to a deep rhetoric in several ways, but one way relates to rhetoric's conception of reason as a process. Rhetoric's powerful attempt to offer a theory of reason, a theory of argumentation that explains how arguments can be reasonable without being compelling, generates universals of process—conditions and procedures whose aims are to ensure that argumentation will be nonviolent (so, for example, threats of violence are not features of reasonable argumentation) and procedures that assure that the process will be just (and the rule of justice governs argumentation almost everywhere). These procedures of just reasoning are an attempt to realize a kind of equity among interlocutors, equity among those in conflict. I will focus on these generative ideas of nonviolence and justice in chapters 4 and 7, but it is important to note here that they will emerge in claims of fairly universal scope, and they will deserve the critical scrutiny that all such claims deserve.

One way to temper the suspicion of these universals is to acknowledge that they are internally dynamic, that they are critically and creatively unstable. They each have an abstract, fairly indeterminate meaning, and this is in an unceasing interaction with a more specific and concrete meaning. Consider that it is not difficult to draw even skeptical critics into an agreement that justice should be pursued. However, it is very difficult to draw conflicting parties into an agreement about the content of justice, in concrete and particular terms, in a specific case. This is a well-known feature of the concept of justice, one that was pivotal in Chaim Perelman's development of the new rhetoric project. John Rawls

(1971) imagines that what we seek in the case of justice is a "reflective equilibrium," in which we keep trying to find a balance between our general concept and principles of justice and our particular judgments about justice in specific cases, modifying things on each side as we go along. So, universals are not simply absolute concepts that hide partisan interests; they are concepts in motion, interacting with judgments that conflict with them, changing, having a direction, or path. They are, in Emerson's words, vehicular and transitive, like all logoi.[12]

This sheds light on another feature of these universals: they are criticizable in a way that particular judgments are not. If one were to say that a particular action was unjust, or violent, or unwise, without offering any justification based on some larger conception of why the action was unjust or violent or unwise, then one's judgment would not be criticizable in the usual sense. Without an "It was unjust *because* . . . ," the statement could be rejected or ridiculed, or one could have a fight about it, but there could be no criticism that involved reasoning. Arguments that make use of concepts like justice invite criticism; they are open to challenge and change in ways that specific judgments are not. When we want to open specific judgments up to scrutiny, we often do so by asking people to give their reasons for their judgments, to reveal the more general ideas and beliefs at work in their reasoning. The attempt to express these general principles in the most universal form has valuable critical potential. It opens up conversations that allow us to take direction and to change direction. Once again, this becomes possible only when such universals are themselves experienced as transitive, as stepping stones, as leading somewhere.

Deep Rhetoric and Big Rhetoric

Over the last few decades or so, within the discipline of rhetoric as it is practiced in the U.S., a controversy has broken out about the scope of rhetoric as a discipline. In fact, such a controversy permanently attends the discipline, although it is not always noticed. Certainly Kenneth Burke, Richard Weaver, Chaim Perelman, and many other rhetorical theorists of the twentieth century held to an expansive conception of rhetoric, one that went well beyond the range of most disciplinary conceptions. However, the controversy reached a new pitch in the 1990s with a flurry of publications, many of them sparked by Dilip Gaonkar's work.[13]

The idea of an expansive rhetoric developed in some specific ways during this period, and it will prove helpful to distinguish the development of this expansive rhetoric from the deep rhetoric I am trying to develop here. Edward Schiappa uses the term "big rhetoric" for "the theoretical position that everything, or virtually everything, can be described as 'rhetorical'" (2001, 260), and he connects big rhetoric with the popularization of rhetoric, the spreading out of rhetorical studies to many different kinds of subject matter, across many disciplines.

Schiappa suggests that there are two rationales for big rhetoric: symbolic interactionism and an epistemological rationale. He condenses symbolic interactionism into the argument that since all persuasive actions are rhetorical, and all symbol/language-use is persuasive, then all symbol-language use is rhetorical, and he links this argument to the views of Kenneth Burke and Richard Weaver. This account of symbolic interactionism is a little surprising, since symbolic interactionism is often understood as a sociological theory, developed over against behaviorism, that insisted that actions were never pure behaviors that triggered other actions, but that actions always had to be interpreted, that they had social meaning, and were never simply brute facts. However, one can still see the lineage of the rationale: if actions are not simply brute facts, but symbolic, then they carry meaning whose truth is not just an observed fact but rather depends on an interpretation. An interpretation is only one way of understanding something, and one accepts it only if one is in some way persuaded to accept it. So all actions, insofar as they are understood, carry persuasion. Since persuasion is the subject matter of rhetoric, all action is the subject matter of rhetoric. If one extends this idea to artifacts or anything that has cultural meaning, then just about everything is rhetorical.

Since the deep rhetoric I have been pursuing here is guided by the philosophical hermeneutics of Gadamer, it is consistent at many points with the hermeneutical orientation of symbolic interactionism. However, there are also some potential differences, depending on exactly how one interprets symbolic interactionism. First, a deep rhetoric seeks after the senses in which we *are* rhetorical even before and behind and in addition to whatever symbolic actions we *take*. And this rhetorical ontology is not primarily concerned with a "self" that is constructed as an object to be understood, or even with the various theories of a "self," but rather with *the ability to be a self* and the different ways of being that involves. We *are* a capacity for receiving and giving our being to each other. This is not exactly the same as persuasive action.

Further differences become apparent in relation to Schiappa's second, "epistemological" rationale. Here the general idea is that "the philosophical criteria used traditionally to separate 'higher' ways of knowing,

such as 'science' (as *epistēmē*) from 'rhetoric' (as *doxa*), have been cri-
tiqued persuasively" (2001, 262). Here Schiappa refers us to Perelman,
Toulmin, Kuhn, and Robert L. Scott; however, the list could be much
longer. Again, the deep rhetoric project is consistent with this strand of
big rhetoric. A deep rhetorical approach looks for the ways in which all
knowledge is communicative—even and especially in that the criteria for
adjudicating knowledge claims are communicative and not purely logical
and empirical. Beyond this, logic and empirical science themselves have
a communicative substrate.

However, this level of epistemological discourse, as important as it is,
is not the sole focus of a deep rhetoric. The communicative provenance
and life of epistemological discourse have ontological and ethical dimensions that shape the way we conceptualize and reason about reality. Deep
rhetoric is not an epistemological project because epistemology makes
too many assumptions about matters that a deep rhetoric wants to explore through a less presumptuous kind of questioning. Knowing cannot be isolated from the other dimensions of transcendence on which it
depends—at least not without obscuring its own lack of independence
and begging some important epistemological, ontological, and ethical
questions.

A further difference between big rhetoric and deep rhetoric is that a
deep rhetoric tries to pay attention to communication independently of
the splitting of rhetoric and philosophy into distinct disciplines. Deep
rhetoric explores and questions that disciplinary formation and the theoretical frameworks it establishes, and it attempts to forge a new approach
that depends on preventing those theoretical frameworks from establishing themselves. One way to begin to weaken these disciplinary powers is
to let them confront each other and cross one another's boundaries. This
is, in a way, inevitable. For if rhetoric has now become big rhetoric, then
on the path of its expansion it must meet its eternal nemesis, philosophy.
It meets it not only because the rhetoric of philosophy is one part of the
expansion process, the part in which rhetoric takes philosophy as its subject matter, but also because philosophy is in competition with rhetoric
in regard to the claim to be a special kind of knowledge of knowledge.
Philosophy can easily accept the sociology of knowledge as a branch of
sociology because the sociology of knowledge need not compete with
philosophy in a direct way. For example, it doesn't in Berger and Luckmann's classic *The Social Construction of Reality*. However, the rhetoric of
philosophy does compete with philosophy—at least, it does when it pursues the process of expansion. For example, when Alan Gross writes that

he wants to reduce science to "rhetoric without remainder" (1990, 33), and to reconceive dialectic and logic as special rhetorics defined in terms of and subordinated to a more general rhetoric, he is placing rhetoric not in competition with science but in competition with the philosophy of science—which, if Gross's project proved successful, would have no subject matter left for itself that was not even more deeply and properly the subject matter of rhetoric. This is intolerable for philosophy because the only metaphilosophy that philosophy can admit is philosophy itself. But what is philosophy? What is philosophical knowledge? How is it justified? These, too, are questions that are supposed to belong only to philosophy itself. However, if rhetoric is to pursue the path of globalization and take on the burden of metaphilosophy, it must directly challenge philosophy's self-understanding.

This provides one motivation for the term "deep rhetoric." Rather than describe this project of rhetorical metaphilosophy as simply one part of an expansion process, I want to acknowledge its special character by integrating it into the concept of a "deep rhetoric." In its unique interaction with philosophy, a deep rhetoric would face six central challenges that would distinguish it from other aspects of big rhetoric's more horizontal expansion.

First, the challenge of developing a nonreductive rhetoric of philosophy. When we speak of reduction, we usually have at least two things in mind. First, the translation of one set of terms into another set of terms, and second, the sweeping away of a set of understandings which were mistaken, understandings that were associated with the first set of terms. That is, reductionist accounts usually get rid of something beside just terms. Such a project would simply amount to a reduction of the discipline of philosophy to the discipline of rhetoric. The project of a deep rhetoric is not the reduction of philosophy to rhetoric, but the discovery of the inseparable philosophical-rhetorical dimensions they share. Deep rhetoric can and should for the most part leave philosophical terms and philosophical reasoning alone. However, it will offer a different account of what is actually happening when these terms are used and when this reasoning takes place, a different metaphilosophy, one that clarifies the communicative dimensions of philosophy that philosophy has, at times, left unacknowledged.

This can be explained further in relation to the second challenge a deep rhetoric faces: the development of a rhetoric of reason. Chaim Perelman and Stephen Toulmin and Michel Meyer have all contributed to this kind of rhetoric, and I hope that I have made a small contribution in my book of this title. Once again, a deep rhetoric does not simply discover that a whole set of arguments is suddenly invalid, or that a whole set of philosophical interests is foolish. Much of its work is done at the level of metaphilosophy. Deep rhetoric gives a different account of what is happening when we give philosophical accounts and justifications of reasoning and argument—however, also, in the case of a rhetoric of reason, it gives a different substantive account of what happens when people reason, when they argue. It acknowledges the communicative dimension of all argumentation, the fact that, as *The New Rhetoric* puts it, "it is in terms of an audience that an argumentation develops" (5). A deep rhetoric also offers a different justification of the activities of reason. These justifications go to the ethical and ontological and sometimes the political dimensions of human transcendence. A deep rhetoric illuminates the senses in which reason is a kind of justice, the subject of chapter 7. In this, it keeps to its characteristic recognition that ethics precedes ontology.[14]

Third, although a deep rhetoric does not pursue a program of reductionist "translation," it does seek to reinterpret the *meaning* of major philosophical terms—in fact, it must, because part of traditional metaphilosophy is a general account of the meanings of these terms. Terms such as "truth," freedom," "essence," "violence," "peace," and "wisdom" do not suddenly become obsolete or passé—the way, say, in some new historicist work, the word "freedom" is never used but is instead replaced by the word "mobility," an obvious reduction. However, the meanings of the words do change. For example, metaphysical and epistemological terms tend to receive practical, ethical, and political interpretations. Again, I believe that Chaim Perelman and Lucie Olbrechts-Tyteca have advanced this project several large steps already.

A fourth challenge faced by a deep rhetoric is to develop a rhetorical "anthropology" without reifying what it is trying to bring to light. I am reluctant to use the word "anthropology" because it suggests a disciplinary conception of "anthropos," perhaps a reification, and not the dynamic kind of humanism which is a dimension of a deep rhetoric. However, philosophy has traditionally constructed philosophical anthropologies of all sorts, from conceptualizing human beings as "political animals" and "rational animals" to viewing them as an understanding of being or as the entity whose essence is its existence. A deep rhetoric not only accounts for the use of these concepts in argumentation and the persuasiveness of the arguments that support them, but also inevitably supplements them with its own conception of human being as communicative transcendence.

In a way, this breaks with the old conception of philosophical anthropology, but in other ways, the right ways, it also continues that tradition. I broached this issue once before in a polemic against van Eemeren and Grootendorst's theory of fallacies when I described what I called the "strong interpretation" of the priority of rhetoric to the other human sciences (Crosswhite 1995). According to this view, what human beings are, what the "socio" of sociology is, is already dependent on rhetoric—on the coming to be of rhetorical communities. This is the point of Protagoras's great myth and of Isocrates' famous description of rhetoric—and of the tradition of rhetoric that follows along Protagorean-Isocratean lines. The origin of the Western tradition is conceived by way of myths and stories about how rhetoric draws human beings out of a "pre-human" state. In this tradition, what is at stake is whether we will *accomplish* our humanity or not (and this is by no means a settled question), and our fate in this respect is bound up with our relation to rhetoric.

There are good reasons for stressing the continuity of this effort with a certain kind of humanism rather than trying to cast it as a post-humanist effort, even though there will also be some important divergences from traditional humanisms. Deep rhetoric's humanism lies not in the crude essentialism of a reified humanity but in the project of accomplishing our humanity, of achieving freedom and reason as ways of being human, freedom and reason now conceived as ethical and rhetorical projects motivated by hope rather than as metaphysical and logical realities. In this light, not only are "anthropology" and "sociology" dependent on rhetoric for a justification of their reasonableness, but even the entities with which they concern themselves—human beings and societies—are dependent on the occurrence of rhetoric in order to come into being at all. Giving an example of what a rhetorical humanism might look like will be the focus of the next section.

All these parts of a deep rhetorical project go on at the level of philosophical rhetoric and, at times, perhaps, rhetorical theory. However, deep rhetoric also has a special kind of practice. The practice of deep rhetoric is the practice of philosophical reasoning and leading that no longer has a traditional epistemological foundation. The fifth challenge for a deep rhetoric, then, is to attempt a communicative practice that acknowledges and best clarifies the transcendence that it is attempting to describe. This will happen in many ways, and in conversation with many other perspectives. However, it will not happen as a systematic theoretical attempt, and will not eventuate in some specific new rhetorical theory. The kind of philosophy with which it identifies is the philosophy of Plato and

Gadamer—that is, a persevering questioning, and so, in important respects, a *prevention* of theory, although this prevention is a necessary prologue and accompaniment to any genuine and conscientious theory-building. The form that this elaboration and exploration of deep rhetoric takes will thus be necessarily essayistic when compared to a systematic theoretical account of rhetoric. The form will also be dialogical and hermeneutic, engaging in critical conversation with other perspectives on rhetoric in an effort to deepen the interpretation of rhetoric (and violence and justice and wisdom) that they have provided.

Sixth, a deep rhetoric faces the challenge of a new dialogue with critiques of reason and with the philosophical term "ideology"—a part of the project I want to take up in the next chapter in a little more detail, because many people doubt that rhetorical theory can defend reason in the vigorous way that philosophy sometimes has.

Rhetoric and Humanism

In elaborating the notion of a deep rhetoric, and in defending it against theological and teleological misunderstandings, we have uncovered, for some, another ground for suspicion: deep rhetoric appears to be a kind of humanism. After all, the passage from Isocrates says explicitly that there are capabilities that are essentially human, capabilities that distinguish human beings from animals, and in which human beings find their fulfillment. The suspicion here is that any humanism of this kind is an essentialism, a depriving of human beings of their abilities to change and to differ from one another. It is a marking off as somehow less than human those who lack these capabilities, or have fewer of them, or have them less powerfully. Humanism may also take shape as a denial of our religious capabilities, as a valorization of abstract rationality over against all other virtues, or as a denial of our interdependence and commonality with what is not human—or, in the words of David Abram (1996), with the more-than-human.

The reasons for this concern are not only legitimate but ethically and politically essential. However, the question is whether our critical efforts are best realized by a broad, abstract, unceasing attack on any appearance of an effort to say what is "human," or whether they are better focused on the specific humanisms that deprive us of freedom, distort our capabilities, prevent social change, and oppress and persecute those who somehow do not align with the standard. And the answer is that they are better focused on the latter. First, our efforts may actually do some practical good there. Second, humanism is not only unavoidable, it is also an invaluable creative and critical idea. It is unavoidable because even to say that "there is nothing human beings are like . . . nothing it is to be human" is to say something very interesting about what it is to be human. If we can reasonably explain what continental drift is, and what lowland gorillas are like, but cannot say anything of the sort about human beings, then that is to say something profound about what it is to be human. But beyond this, humanism is an idea into which we have poured our ethical and political creativity and a great deal of our decency. It would be destructive, concretely and historically destructive, to surrender it. Are there things no human should suffer? Is human dignity something to strive for? Are there human capabilities to be nourished and human rights to be protected? Can one make sense of these without some kind of humanism?

Rhetoric as Humanism: Mieczysław Maneli

Some kind of humanism is central to a deep rhetoric project. Rhetoric is an event of human being, a way we are human. It is a way we are with ourselves and become ourselves. It is a relation we have to the power of logos that activates and develops our human abilities. Rhetoric was closely related to humanism for over two millennia in the West. In the deeper rhetoric of the twentieth century, that close connection is reasserted. In this section, I would like to explore one way of making the connection between rhetoric and humanism—that of Mieczysław Maneli, considered especially in light of his encounter with Chaim Perelman's new rhetoric project. This discussion will also move us directly to the twentieth century, when a larger, more philosophical conception of rhetoric, one closer in some ways to Plato's conception, began to be developed by a number of different thinkers.

In *Perelman's New Rhetoric as Philosophy and Methodology for the Next Century* (1994), Mieczysław Maneli goes so far as to identify Chaim Perelman's new rhetoric project with the project of humanism itself: "The new rhetoric is modern humanism," he proclaims, and then elaborates:

The struggle for humanism never ends. . . . The most essential features to a humanistic approach to life are: individuals should be given the chance to develop their personal talents and energies; they should be able to be creative and to become happy. . . . [Their} essence and value is creativity and self-determination. . . . Once the New Rhetoric took as its basic proposition that nothing is absolutely good or sacred except human dignity, one must constantly search for higher values, for better forms and ways of

45

life. There are three specific areas that are especially important for modern humanism: social and individual justice, freedom from oppression with a genuine opportunity for a decent life, and tolerance and privacy. (124–25)

Notable here is that humanism is not realizing a specifically human essence—say rationality—but struggling for human dignity, and dignity is itself conceived as a freedom to develop one's capabilities and to search for better ways of life. This requires justice, freedom from oppression, a decent life, privacy, and tolerance. Maneli identifies this humanistic project with Perelman's new rhetoric project. This is worth looking into in some detail.

Mieczysław Maneli's book on Chaim Perelman and the new rhetoric labors in an obscure and complex genre—at times a kind of memoir, at others a eulogy, at still others a commentary, at yet others a detailed attempt to work out issues in legal theory and political philosophy, with the help of concrete historical examples which generate some independent Manelian commentary. Existential and historical concerns pervade its approach to conceptualizing humanism and the new rhetoric. The book also makes enormous claims:

The philosophy and methodology of Perelman are instruments which can help to elaborate new ways of thinking and acting, new critical approaches to every social, political, and juridical institution, be they in the east or in the west. The traditional divisions of left and right, of progress and justice, of human rights and privacy, of state sovereignty and internal autonomy, must be revised extensively. Today the New Rhetoric is the most consistent method of searching for new approaches. (1)

Maneli's humanism amounts to a practical struggle for human dignity informed by a social philosophy that is an expression of rhetorical theory.

The question at issue in Maneli's interpretation of Perelman is: How does one get from a rhetorical theory of argumentation that, if it is completely successful, establishes at best the mere "possibility of a human community in the sphere of action when this justification cannot be based on a reality or objective truth" (NR 514) to a social philosophy that has critical and constructive evaluative power, and is the appropriate philosophy and methodology for the post-communist world, for the post-colonial world, and even for the liberal-skeptical West?

Part of the answer will be a change in expectations, a willingness to dim the bright lights of dogmatism, naturalism, absolutism, and skepticism and learn to see in the softer light of rhetorical mindfulness. Maneli's humanism is a broad, synthesizing idea, and it is sometimes difficult to grasp as a whole. But one can get a glimpse of his direction if one stresses the word "human" in the quote above. Perelman's rhetorical theory is aimed at establishing "the possibility of a *human* community in the sphere of action." But before I develop this question and reconstruct Maneli's answer to it, I want to sketch the broader human and practical background to this issue—mostly relying on Maneli himself, since it is his views I am concerned with here—and say a little about the lives of Chaim Perelman and Mieczysław Maneli. This will make the idea of humanism less conceptually neat but more meaningful. For there is without a doubt an existential dimension to Maneli's conception of humanism.

Maneli's Perelman

"Chaim Perelman was a product of European humanism" (116). We might stop for just a moment here. I believe that Maneli wants this word "humanism" to ring with most of its historical meaning, but he also wants it to stress his own conception of humanism according to which the essential principle is: "Individuals should be given the chance to develop their personal talents and energies; they should be able to be creative and to become happy" (124). Going on with Maneli:

[Perelman] read all the chief scholarly and literary works in their original languages. . . . Perelman was a Belgian, a Jew, a Pole and an authentic cosmopolitan. (116). . . If one prefers to call Perelman a Polish Jew, then only in the sense suggested by Czeslaw Milosz . . . [a] special original category of Jewish-European intellectual, different from all other Jewish and non-Jewish categories of intellectual. . . . Indeed he was a Belgian patriot always stressing his Belgian spiritual association, especially in the presence of foreigners. He consciously sought to overcome all narrow nationalistic and caste barriers. (2) . . . Although born in Poland, Perelman moved to Belgium as a young man. . . . In the 1930s he returned to Poland in order to learn firsthand about the achievements of the then famous Polish school of logic, mathematics, and positivist philosophy. . . . During the Nazi occupation, Perelman was active in the Belgian resistance, and, while in hiding, lacking any access to libraries, wrote his great essay *On Justice*. . . . His ability to concentrate on and produce a study of such an abstract and lofty ideal during the darkest days of European and his own life, filled with horror, throws a meaningful light on the author. . . . After WWII, Perelman assumed the first name, Chaim, as an outward sign of his solidarity with the nation the Nazis tried to extinguish. . . . Perelman was uniquely able to combine his nationality and his humanity in his writings. He was an ardent Belgian patriot, [and] he preserved close ties with Polish scholars and Polish culture at the same time. (116–18)

Maneli emphasizes the specific influence of being a Pole and a Jew on Perelman's thinking. He says that Perelman was aware of two distinct currents in Polish history—the one that in the Middle Ages promoted, "while the Jews were being massacred all over Europe . . . a haven of peace and hospitality under the dynasties of the Piasts, the Jagiellons, and their successors," and the other the current of anti-Semitism that grew especially powerful in the twentieth century with reinforcement from German and Russian anti-Semitism. Between 1918 and 1939, Perelman witnessed the development of something else—"a backward and undemocratic state [that was also] a country where many nationalities lived together and where creative liberal thought and art thrived." Maneli draws an interesting conclusion from this: "The strange and unbalanced conditions there, nevertheless, were a source and inspiration for the Poles and for the Jews. Their love-hate affair was at once stimulating and numbing. This gifted Belgian, influenced by this atmosphere, was destined to create something innovative" (118).

There is much in this portrait to unpack—the hybridity and multiplicity and inner conflict of identities producing a greater integrity instead of a loss of integrity, and the implicit suggestion that moving through these identities without ever leaving any of them behind was partly responsible for the step to rhetorical reflection. But what is most significant here is irrepressible hope—both in Perelman and in Maneli's writing about him. Out of Perelman's being forced into hiding comes an essential work, *De la justice*. As Maneli says at the conclusion of this section of his book, "[Perelman] was able to transform all the disadvantages of his origin and background to powerful advantage and to a source of inspiration" (118). This is using the vale of tears for a well. This hopeful hermeneutic of history is part of what makes Perelman's new rhetorical turn possible, and, as we shall see, part of what makes possible Maneli's interpretation of legal positivism as legal realism.

However, there is also here a matrix for the emergence of humanism. In this transnational and transcultural movement and hybridity, and in the experiences of anti-Semitism and Nazi outrages against humanity, one finds Perelman pondering justice, one of Maneli's three pillars of humanism, and, in the new rhetoric project, an idea that aims at the kind of universality that will allow for "*human* community." This justice-thought-out-of-suffering will turn out to be not only the motive for but also the substance of Perelman's rhetorical theory of argumentation.

Maneli's Maneli

Maneli began his studies immediately after the war and took degrees in law and economics. He worked as an assistant to a philosophy professor, Czesław Nowinski. In 1954 he received his doctorate in law and become a Dozent at Warsaw University. In the 1960s, he became founder and chair of the History of Political and Juridical Doctrines. In 1962 he was appointed head of the Polish delegation to the International Commission in Vietnam. His book *War of the Vanquished* reflects on his Vietnam service. Years before the end of that war, Maneli saw clearly that all sides would be diminished by the conflict. The book contains achingly depressing accounts of Maneli's futile diplomatic attempts to locate an interlocutor with any common sense, any doubt about the current party line, any nascent leanings toward tolerance, freedom, or peace. Maneli's later work would focus on law, on freedom, and on tolerance.

Over fourteen years, from 1954 to 1968, he wrote six volumes of *The History of Political and Juridical Doctrines*. Two volumes of this work won Maneli an award from the Minister of Higher Education in Poland—the same man who, one year later, in 1968, signed a letter dismissing him from the university for anti-socialist ideas and lectures.

Maneli's later *Freedom and Tolerance* is a systematic historical exploration of the ideas of the title. However, Maneli is not simply a traditional liberal. His liberalism is of a specifically postcommunist sort, formulated out of a Polish context, and complicated by his exile in New York City. (Maneli had concluded that since he could pursue his work on freedom and tolerance only outside of Poland, he had a *duty* to leave.)

Maneli's earlier life is captured in an undated letter he wrote to a correspondent addressed only as "Zvi." My colleague at Oregon, David Frank, interviewed Maneli not long before his death in New York and has provided me with a copy of the letter. Maneli reports that his social and political activity began in the fall of 1942 in the Warsaw ghetto, after the first phase of the extermination of its inhabitants. The victims included his parents and nearly all other members of his family. During the April 1943 uprising, he was arrested by the SS, taken to the *Umschlagplatz*, and put on a train to Treblinka. He jumped through a small window of the freight car and escaped. In May he was arrested, and again escaped. After a futile attempt to join the Armia Krajowa (he was refused on the grounds that the army already had too many Jews), Maneli was soon arrested again, again taken to the *Umschlagplatz*, and eventually transported to

Auschwitz Buna-Werke. With the help of German and Polish political prisoners, he escaped from there in 1945.

I relate this story to show that Maneli's account of Perelman's innovation and creativity and his ability to draw inspiration from dark days is an account that has many parallels in his own life. These parallels help to explain, in part, Maneli's transformation of *The New Rhetoric* into a social philosophy. There are several dimensions to Maneli's rewrite of Perelman. All are revealing of the breadth of his notion of humanism. Here, I will focus on only one: Maneli's attempt to combine his "legal realism" with *The New Rhetoric*, since questions of law and justice are at the heart of the relation between humanism and rhetoric.

Perelman and Maneli both use a hermeneutic of hope to advance their projects. Perelman's original question in *De la justice* was: can assertions of value be given reasonable justifications? Laboring in the 1940s, within a logical positivist framework, the answer was: no. However, years later, working with Lucie Olbrechts-Tyteca and the vast collection of examples collected in *The New Rhetoric*, the answer became: yes. The argument in its most general form is that a concrete tradition of successful reasoning about difficult practical issues surrounds us—in fact, pervades our history and our lives—and we can use the successes of this tradition as precedents to reason about value for ourselves.

Maneli makes a surprisingly similar move regarding the authority of law in his reworking of legal positivism into legal realism.[15] What, he asks, is the justification of the authority of law? Maneli answers that the *process* by which law is made justifies and gives authority to law. In this process, people may reason from all sorts of principles—natural law, the will of the people, theological principles—but none of these can directly justify law; only the process can. And this process has been secured historically in positive law, which justifies the substantive outcomes of that process. However, this legal positivism needs historicizing; it has not been in all times and places "true." Maneli argues that legal positivism developed historically in resistance to dogmatic concepts of law and in connection with the development and elaboration of democratic theory, the rule of law, and individual rights (84). In this era, which is still our own, law has made progress. Maneli's primary examples are: the Charter of the United Nations, the Universal Declaration of Human Rights, democratic constitutions, and laws against racism and colonialism.

Maneli's humanism and his legal principles are matters of historical struggle and change. For Maneli, there are no self-evident principles of substantive law that are exempt from the demand that they be justified through process. A just process—a process that allows people to determine for themselves what laws should be—is the source of all justification and all law. This is Maneli's humanism. This just process will itself change and develop historically as our environments and our hopes put new pressures on our conception of human dignity. But rhetoric—specifically Perelman's new rhetoric—describes this process for our time. It is, as the title of Maneli's book puts it, "philosophy and methodology for the next century."

This means that, for Maneli, rhetoric is not simply a consciously applied art of communication. Rather, it is the form of our being human, the form of our social *dignity* as human beings, and the form of the occurrence of justice and law.

Maneli's positivism is also, he says, a kind of legal realism. Law is the accumulation and expression of real historical achievements in the promotion of human dignity. This dimension of law is not recognized by conventionalism or nominalism. Maneli emphasizes that realism does not capture some universal, timeless essence of law. Rather it holds for a period when "law 'pervades' the life of nations to an incomparably greater degree than [in the past], when the norms of international law and morality are . . . permeating deeper and deeper into everyday life, when states of various political and social structures coexist on this globe and cooperate with one another despite their basic differences and antagonisms." These laws, he says, "are being expounded as something living and can be enriched or impoverished by new requirements of life." In such a period, legal realism provides "a fruitful promise for the future" and supplies "instruments of cooperation" (111).

To put it in other words, the law is *about something*, and that *something* unfolds itself, or doesn't, in the history of law. For Maneli, the law is *about* human dignity and happiness, which come to historical presence in relation to whatever freedom, tolerance, and justice the law realizes. The process of rhetoric as Perelman describes it in *The New Rhetoric* is the giving of the freedom and tolerance and justice that provide the social space for human dignity to make its advents.

What is the same in Perelman's rhetorical theory and Maneli's legal theory is that each attempts to ground itself in historical realities. In so doing, each is offering an interpretation of historical facts guided by a hermeneutic of hope—and here I am thinking of Gadamer and his observation that hope is not an empirical hypothesis; it depends on granting some facts a privilege over others and joining one's anticipations to those. Hope is *not* an attempt to *predict or generalize or draw a logical conclusion*. One could counter Perelman's case with a treatise that showed how innumerable examples establish that the most significant historical conflicts fall immovably outside the framework and starting points he delineates as the conditions for argumentation. One could add countless cases where conflicts fall within the framework but where the arguments themselves are still unconvincing or balance each other out. One could conclude that Perelman's "possibility" remains entirely abstract. One could argue against Maneli similarly that the period in which legal positivism became true law also saw terrible regressions and failures, and looking over the record as a whole one could produce not only laws that worked in the opposite direction but also laws that were formally in accord with his principles and yet functioned in such a way as to disguise the real means by which conflicts were settled.

Maneli knows that these cases can be made. To understand history, he says, "one must impose an interpretation . . . [but] what measure do we use to determine what is more or what is less important" (79)? He rejects the simple idea that history is merely our own political interests projected onto past events, though he is completely open about the practical justification of his own account: it provides, he says, "a fruitful promise for the future." And fruitful, for Maneli, means productive of dignity, creativity, freedom, tolerance, justice, and happiness. However, he attempts to restrain the effects of narrow, presentist interests by promoting the testing of this historical interpretation against open and in principle interminable argumentation with those who object to such a project.

These arguments succeed, insofar as they do, largely through an appeal to precedent, and with a little new rhetorical analysis we can see how this works. Precedence and justice are closely connected for Perelman, and they rest finally on the quasi-naturalistic force that he calls inertia and which he compares directly with physical inertia.[16] Preserving matters as they are does not require argumentation; changing them does. The critical difference between rhetorical inertia and physical inertia is that physical inertia knows no temporal gaps; rhetorical inertia does. *We* must contribute to the quasi-natural power of inertia by connecting precedents to existing situations; we must fuse the temporal horizons.

And this is what both Perelman and Maneli do. Perelman faces the failures of logical positivism and the collapse of Europe into holocaustal violence, and then connects the postwar possibilities presented by the UN and other international efforts to a recovery of the lost potential of a tradition of rhetorical reasoning. Maneli comes out of the same situation and responds to it similarly, but also judges that Perelman's work needs to be made more historically concrete so that it can provide "fruitful promise for the future." The specific future Maneli has in mind is threefold: (1) the transition of post-communist nations to new, democratic political lives; (2) the transition of postcolonial nations to fully participatory democratic futures; and (3) the West's need to move beyond its denial of the meaningfulness of ideological conflict and beyond its authoritarian consumerism. Maneli wants precedents with deliberative teeth, and so elaborates his legal positivism as legal realism and fills the inertial gaps between precedents with a thesis of historical progress—and he wants the new rhetoric project to help to consolidate this progress. In this way, *The New Rhetoric* gains something like the content of a social philosophy.

Maneli acknowledges that the new rhetoric seems not to be a social philosophy because it provides only a theory and means of reaching reasonable solutions to conflicts while a social philosophy has something like its own values and goals. Here I quote directly from Maneli: "However, in our time, once such values as human rights, respect for legality, freedom from hunger and religious oppression, are *uncontestable human values* acknowledged even by international and municipal law, then we must agree that the situation has changed dramatically. Today the problem is how to preserve, secure, and enhance these values" in the face of a world in which they continue to be endangered (115).

Maneli's Legal Realism

I want to secure this grasp on Maneli's realism before moving on. Chaim Perelman had already recognized that some values are for all practical purposes universal—no one is against freedom or justice when they are expressed as what Perelman calls "abstract values." Maneli's transformation of the new rhetoric is to claim that these abstract values have been realized more concretely in our time as law—and especially international law. Maneli knows the interpretive nature of this claim, but he still believes that it is appropriate to call his perspective legal *realism*. Maneli's legal realism is a unique blend of legal realism with a subtle form of philosophical realism. It is a kind of legal realism in that it rejects the idea that law is an autonomous system, separate from social change and politics, that works out its principles and actions in a strictly logical fashion. And yet Maneli also holds that law is more than just the uses we make of law in our time and place. Law is about something. Philosophical realism of any kind may sound anachronistic to contemporary American ears. The intellectual history of much of the most recent past, at least in the U.S., has been to emphasize the "social construction" of everything that plays a role in a social controversy in order to take it out of the realm of an unchanging nature or mind and bring it into the realm of the "constructed" so that it can be subject to being changed by human beings. This is a form of contemporary humanism. However, for Maneli, dividing the world between the natural and the constructed is not sufficient; it is simply not subtle enough to conceptualize significant social change.

While surveying the ruins of postwar Germany, Perelman is said to have remarked, simply and sovereignly, "This is not Europe." I am tempted to say that for Maneli, as a Jew and as a Varsovian, something like all natural truths about human beings came to an end between 1939 and 1945. There is no more "real" in the naïve sense. So there can be no realism that is somehow linked to the unchanging verities about human life and history. In fact, Maneli says explicitly that his realism is to be contrasted with any attempt to formulate a natural law or natural justice. His real is in part epiphenomenal on history, dependent on it but not directly identical with it, requiring interpretive imagination and hope, but not for that reason less real. The real comes to presence kairotically. And it does so in human history, in processes that promote human dignity— or do not. So Maneli's real is in that respect not purely epiphenomenal. It has the power to react on the history that generated it.

For Maneli realism is ultimately new rhetorical realism. The *result* that a new rhetorical social philosophy achieves is itself part of a continuing process of argumentation. This is necessarily so because, as Maneli says, argumentation is an "infinitely progressive process." It has phases but no natural limit or end point. Because of this, the social philosophy it does produce is, so to speak, *weak* in contrast to the *strong* social philosophies of the past. Of course, Maneli takes this to be a strength. The limitation of being able to offer only partial, for-a-time solutions to conflicts is a protection against totalizing ideologies. In some of the loveliest lines of his book, Maneli even offers a portrait of ideal orators who embody these principles: "The new rhetoric may be the only philosophy that praises those who ruminate, hesitate, are reluctant, doubtful, but ultimately able to act prudently" (13). Later he characterizes these new rhetorical heroes as "people who are more critical than ever before and at the same time more tolerant in their beliefs and cooperation" (139). These are the humans of rhetorical humanism.

Maneli knows that his new rhetorical realism is a tentative and uncertain achievement, yet he is wholeheartedly committed to the project. Humanism is a struggle. Maneli holds that the new rhetoric maintains that social contradictions are real, that there can be no legitimate political order that does not recognize the fact of moral pluralism and the necessity for compromise and a balance among goods. Maneli also tolerates another kind of contradiction (the emphasis is added): "We are *sure* that the development of democracy and the culture of society and its involvement in the process of argumentation and counter-argumentation *can* create a climate which will make the return of despotism *impossible*. Nevertheless, there are no guarantees" (132). The certainty of this possibility of an impossibility is a kind of hope—a guide and support for hopeful struggle that has also become reasonably prudent. It goes forward with the recognition that there is no guarantee that the impossible will not return.

It is not really a very impressive trick to transform rhetorical theory into social theory; rhetoric has been social theory since its own mythical origins in the sense that it is a theory of how to conduct certain kinds of public deliberations effectively—how to authorize courses of action, policies, laws, and legal judgments through speech in the framework of institutions that are to some degree democratic. And conceptualizing rhetorical practice in a way that locates it at the ground of social value is not new either. Protagoras's great myth (in Plato's *Protagoras*) and Isocrates's hymn to logos both do this. And Perelman's rhetorical theory is already explicitly a social theory, and not only contrasts its own approach to social conflict with dogmatism, skepticism, and especially violence, but culminates in a manifesto that locates social authority in (1) shared historical linguistic practices that are already acknowledged; in (2) a formulation of its overall aim as giving meaning to human freedom, a state in which a reasonable choice can be exercised; and in (3) the "justification of the possibility of human community in the sphere of action when this justification cannot be based on a reality or objective truth" (514).

What is specific to Maneli's work is that he develops these social-philosophical dimensions of Perelman's thought not simply as a way to justify teaching rhetoric, as in Protagoras and Isocrates, or as a method of interpretation, or as giving meaning or providing a philosophical understanding of freedom and communal action as in Perelman, although what he does do is closely linked to Perelman's accomplishment. Rather, Maneli's contribution is to extend Perelman's philosophical account of reasoning into something like a nascent philosophy of history and especially of legal history, as well as a nascent account of a political practice that would be not so much an application as an enactment of the rhetorical theory—for, after all, argumentation is a process in which one participates and undergoes unforeseen change. It is not a theory of where one should end up in history and how one should get there, but neither is it skeptical about there being social goods that we can achieve in practices and institutions governed and animated from within by argumentation.

In the end, in the tradition that Maneli is renewing, rhetoric is not only humanism in this very complex sense, it is also philosophical anthropology—the philosophical elaboration of the human—joined to the philosophy of law and history, and in fact to social struggles themselves. It is a dynamic humanism, in which human dignity is always at stake, always in question, always generating new historical and political and ethical demands. It is this kind of humanism, this rhetorical humanism one can see taking shape in Perelman and in Maneli, that motivates and guides a deep rhetoric, which itself takes shape in the matrix of the new rhetoric project.

A deep rhetoric goes back behind and beneath the origins of disciplinary rhetoric to recover a rhetoric that is equivalent to our being-in-logos, that part of being human that lies in our being capable of transcendence toward others and toward ourselves. For transcendence is communicative; it bears meaning and influence. We *are* meaningful communicative activity with ourselves and others. It is part of the form of our existence, without which there would be nothing. Since transcendence always moves toward something, and influence is always influence in some direction, the question of whether there is some overall purpose to rhetorical transcendence, some overall goal, will always arise, and so deep rhetoric will always generate formally "theological" and teleological and ethical questions.

And since rhetoric is about developing and directing human transcendence, it will also always be connected with some kind of humanism—some set of notions about what human beings are and where they stand in relation to other entities and to the fact of there being other entities at all. However, a deep rhetoric will go behind and beneath ontotheology because that is only one particular possibility of transcendence, one that in fact blocks our awareness and diverts our practices of transcendence. In this effort, a deep rhetoric will also have to prevent its own humanism from congealing into something reified and dogmatic.

One irony in this project is that theology and humanism are often taken to be projects that are polar opposites to each other. Here, they resemble one another in that they are each generated—the first, in a formal way—from the project of a deep rhetoric, and they each have absolutizing tendencies that will derail the project of a deep rhetoric if they are allowed to take hold. The central distinction here, then, is not between "religious" thinking and "humanism," but between, on the one hand, (1) thinking that forces gods or human beings into the ontotheological frame in which they are static beings-with-properties that can be "seen" and known and grasped in grammar by human beings, who can then deploy that knowledge and language for whatever the currently reigning purposes and forms of desire are, and, on the other, (2) thinking that is more restrained and that can stay with moving-toward without arrogating to itself an ability to grasp or comprehend the ultimate goal that sets all beings in their places. In this light, rhetorical humanism would not be an "exclusive humanism," as Charles Taylor (2007) uses the term, because it does not deny that human flourishing might require directing ourselves toward the more than human—nor does it affirm that it does. Deep rhetoric is a kind of humanism, though neither an exclusive humanism nor a religious humanism. It is "agnostic" in that respect. However, although deep rhetoric does not include a conception of some ultimate fulfillment for human capabilities, it does have an approach to rhetorical capabilities themselves, the subject of the next section.

Rhetorical Capabilities

We began this chapter by posing the question, What is rhetoric? The aim was to give definition to deep rhetoric on the basis of this initial clarification of what rhetoric is. The question led us into a discussion of the origins of rhetoric and into some controversies about the way rhetoric was conceptualized in the beginning and the proper way to conceive of it now. We discovered a basic division between those who have thought of rhetoric as a limited discipline and those who have thought of rhetoric as being more closely connected with philosophical concerns and linked with far-reaching questions about humanism and human purpose, and linked, too, with questions that are formally similar to theological questions. The discussion discovered ways in which a deep rhetoric could avoid the negative and dogmatic drag of ontotheology and humanism, and it led to a first sketch of a philosophical rhetoric that could be deep and humanistic without being ontotheological or dogmatic. This discussion produced a slowly evolving sketch of the difference between rhetoric as a discipline and deep rhetoric, a difference internal to any completely conceived rhetoric, and so a difference that both distinguishes and reconciles.

Before we move beyond this preliminary account of a deep rhetoric project, it will prove helpful to go ahead and fill out this effort with an exploration of the idea of rhetorical capabilities, for they allow a further contrast between deep rhetoric and a disciplinary rhetoric. For disciplinary rhetoric, rhetoric is a conscious art (or an informed practice) that is based on ways that people communicate naturally but which improves those ways through research, study, and practice. This art can be learned and taught to others. This project has immense educational value, and must be supported in every way possible. A decline in the status of rhetoric as a discipline threatens to undermine the informed and skilled communicative practice that is essential to truly democratic societies. This cannot be said strongly enough.

However, disciplinary rhetoric can also produce distortions if it is completely severed from a deep rhetoric and its philosophical concerns. The communicative actions and formations that the discipline of rhetoric studies are, from a deep rhetorical view, only the most visible aspects of a way that we are and a way by which we continually come to be. They have ethical-ontological dimensions that are not accessible to ordinary social-scientific methodologies. From this perspective, rhetoric as a discipline is also a partial and limited approach to human actions that require being both philosophically interpreted and also situated in social, cultural, political, educational, and even psychological contexts before they can be genuinely understood. It is only in certain developments of these contexts that rhetorical capabilities can be cultivated at all. This approach requires broad transdisciplinary and metadisciplinary considerations that are not, perhaps, as productive of theory and research as disciplinary work, but which do make clearer the significance, value, and limitations of rhetoric as a discipline. Rhetoric gains its disciplinary strengths by setting limits for itself and by not becoming entangled in endless philosophical disputes. This is absolutely necessary from the standpoint of organizing research and teaching in an institutional framework. However, this also means that the discipline cannot follow arguments wherever they lead. And it means that its understanding of itself is not complete. An exploration of the idea of rhetorical capabilities will help to demonstrate what a more complete approach would look like.

The deep rhetorical approach to rhetorical capabilities is informed in part by the way the concept of capabilities has developed in political theory. If one thinks of what is required to participate in a political community, one probably thinks of legal rights and freedoms—the kind described, for example, in the U.S. Bill of Rights, especially freedom of speech and assembly. Without these legally protected freedoms, it would be difficult to participate in democratic government in an equitable way either directly in political deliberation or indirectly in opinion-shaping communicative actions in the public sphere. However, critics of various kinds have pointed out that mere liberal rights, merely abstract freedom, are not sufficient for giving people even the roughest equity in these respects. To put it crudely, it does not do much good to have freedom of speech if one is dying of a curable disease because one cannot afford health care or if one is uninformed about the issues that are affecting one's conditions of life. Further, rights and liberties are usually conceived along lines of noninterference. They ensure that others cannot legally stop us from engaging in certain kinds of actions, and so they separate us; however, they do not themselves conduct us into any kind of cooperation or common enterprise. This fact is related to a third criticism of liberal rights. They operate with a merely "negative" notion of liberty, securing rights and developing procedures, but without providing any positive conception of human flourishing in community and solidarity. One could in principle have a perfectly healthy "liberal" society that was also a society that was full of misery and suffering and in which very few achieved happiness. The same general criticism would hold even if one adds considerations of income and wealth. Liberal rights plus wealth will not make people who are diseased or ignorant or unable to reason capable of pursuing their own well-being or their conception of what is good.

One way to sum up these kinds of concerns is that a liberal rights based approach is focused on the abstract means by which people seek something else, say, happiness, or well-being, or the good, and yet one may have these abstract means without actually being able to accomplish one's goals at all. A capabilities approach is an attempt to bring these means closer to the ends by focusing not only on someone's right to do what he or she values but also on his or her "capability actually to do things he or she has reason to value."[17] No rights are lost in this shift of focus; rights and freedoms are as important as ever. However, the focus becomes the real opportunity to choose and to do what one has reason to value, or what is sometimes called *substantial* freedom. Martha Nussbaum has attempted to make a list of capabilities, and includes such things as being able to live a reasonably long life, to be able to be healthy, move from place to place, be secure from violence, to think and reason, and so on. She also includes a capability for justice and friendship and for practical reasoning. Amartya Sen has expressed reservations about the possibility of such a list on the grounds that any such list is revisable through continued public deliberation in continually changing conditions, but there are good reasons to believe that he thinks of actual capabilities along the same lines as Nussbaum.

I do not propose to add in any technical way to the capabilities approach of Nussbaum and Sen, which is far more elaborate than I have begun to indicate here. Many of what I will call "capabilities" will be "functions" in their parlance—that is, smaller parts of more general capabilities. However, rhetorical capabilities do play a role similar to the capabilities that they have made the heart of a theory of justice. Rhetorical capabilities are connected with an idea of what it means to be human and what is required to participate in a democratic society. They require and are associated with the development of legal rights and liberties connected with a specific kind of humanism; however, they go beyond such abstract rights to conceptions of real abilities that are the goals of a liberal education and the substance of actual democratic practices. Not incidentally, a capabilities approach also gives us a way of taking incapabilities and disabilities seriously, something we will not explore in detail here but which has great importance in rhetoric's concrete projects of education and formation. Capabilities also play an important role in understanding the relation between rhetoric and justice that will be explored in chapter 7.

To explore the idea of rhetorical capabilities, I will focus on the opening chapters of *The New Rhetoric* in which Chaim Perelman and Lucie Olbrechts-Tyteca describe the rhetorical framework (*les cadres*) within which argumentation takes place, a section of the work that I will return to several more times in this book, in different contexts and for different purposes. In part 1 of their treatise, Perelman and Olbrechts-Tyteca mark off a delimited space within which rhetorical capabilities can arise and take shape. They begin by distinguishing between demonstration and argumentation. Demonstration is not within the bounds, the framework, of rhetoric. They think of demonstration as purely formal and symbolic and not occurring in natural language. Mathematical proofs are exemplars of demonstration. One sees the proof or one does not. One understands the axioms and the rules of inference, and one uses them correctly or consistently or not. However, demonstration alone, without the support of argumentation, does not result in one's making a different choice about a belief, or a course of action, or a purpose to pursue. It does not aim at leading someone in a direction by means of language. For that, we must move into the realm of rhetoric and argumentation.

Argumentation takes place only within certain bounds. This is one of the meanings of "framework" (*cadres*), the bounds within which something can take place, a milieu in which something comes to be and can be what it is. In this case, the framework marks off the field in which the rhetorical action of argumentation can take place. We can think of this requirement as a first attempt at describing deep rhetorical capability— out of which and in terms of which any conscious or trained capability will have to develop.

The first requirement is what *The New Rhetoric* calls "le contact des esprits." It is an interesting phrase because contact is one physical body touching another physical body. Contact between "esprits" must be a different kind of "contact." This most general capability I will here call "transcendence," an ability to go out of ourselves and meet each other in language of some kind—a natural language, primarily, but in any symbolic action or medium that is capable of sustaining communicative meeting. On the one hand, this transcendence is an ontological "capability," something we are rather than something we achieve, and so not an ordinary capability at all. On the other hand, however, ontological transcendence becomes concrete in specific acts, and we can succeed and fail to varying degrees in actually meeting one another in this transcendence. It is in this sense of its becoming concrete that transcendence can be understood as a capability for "contact."

"Esprit" is best understood as our ability to lead our *lives*, in which everything depends on the way we lead ourselves and each other. This general ability is always shaped by the particular lives we have already led. This French word is in other contexts the "breath" of life, the breath God breathes into the living, the Holy Spirit. "Esprit" has been used for the incorporeal, the immortal, the dynamic part of the mind, thinking substance. The word is employed in many, many ways. However, "esprits" is best not understood, primarily, as "minds" or "spirits." That would be to make too many ontological assumptions. If we think of the contact of *esprits* here as the meeting of lives, in their capacity to lead and be led, we will avoid reifying it, or objectifying it, or spiritualizing it—and so dragging in a legion of assumptions that could very well prevent us from understanding it. If we think of lives coming into contact, we will stay closer to the event.

"Esprits" is often translated as "minds" in the English edition of *The New Rhetoric*, and although this is not altogether wrong, it can be misleading. When the translators give us the phrase "the mind's adherence" for "l'adhésion des esprits," they don't give us what we need to experience what Perelman and Olbrechts-Tyteca are struggling to say. The language of "mind" leads us to wonder how it is that theses can "stick to" a mind, what makes some mental event sticky or not, and what the mental act of "adhesion" is. However, if we think of the way someone's life can, in time, stay with, keep faith with, adhere to a conclusion it has reached about how to act, or how not to act, or what purposes are the most important, or what communities it will cast its lot with, then we are much closer to the issues with which *The New Rhetoric* actually grapples. The "adhesion of spirits" describes our capability for transcendence insofar as we can keep faith with or be loyal to what has come to us from each other's influence. Rhetorical capability in general is an openness to influencing each other in the way we lead our lives.

When it comes to what *The New Rhetoric* calls argumentation, the specific kind of openness that is needed requires itself another, specific, developed capability—the ability to form *communities* capable of contact: "For there to be argumentation, it is necessary that, at a given moment, an effective community of *esprits* be realized" (*Traité*, 18). This requires an accord, "in principle," on the formation of this community. This is no small matter. *The New Rhetoric* says "in principle" because in most cases we have never decided, actually, that and how the communities to which we belong should have been formed. However, to the degree that we do not consent to their formation, or the way they are formed, then argumentation will not be taking place for us. In any case, this is another capability, the capability to form communities with each other. A further capability is to be able to decide to debate together a specific question. Clearly, not all actual groups have the capability to form even this degree of community.

The New Rhetoric points out that this capability for community is also internal to individuals who deliberate inwardly. They must be capable of forming communities with themselves, of coming to accords with themselves, and obviously this is not just naturally the case with many people. We are not always in a condition where we are ready to discuss some issues with ourselves.

This capacity for open transcendence toward others and ourselves, in a community of *esprits*, is what we are, as rhetorical beings. However, this capacity is developed weakly or strongly, and it is realized in involuntary and compulsive ways as well as in ways that keep openness itself an issue for us. Our own rhetorical capability can in fact also be something about which we reflect and deliberate and make choices and something toward which we comport ourselves in complicated ways.

When it comes to realizing this capacity for forming rhetorical communities, *The New Rhetoric* lists several more specific requirements, by no means a complete list: a common language, a reason to have a discussion, shared rules or understanding for how the discussion will be held, common techniques of communication, agreement on an audience (who will have the authority to judge the argument), attaching some importance and value to the views of one's interlocutor/audience, having the attention of others, and a willingness to change one's mind.

We can, with some effort, translate these into capabilities: the capability to learn and share a language. The capability to recognize or imagine reasons to have a discussion. The capability to develop and share an understanding of how a discussion will proceed. A capability to speak or write or sign or design or employ some shared technique that will achieve the openness necessary for argumentation. The capability to share an audience, to recognize a common judge—an ability to grant jurisdiction. A capability for experiencing and acknowledging the significance and value of the views of others. A capability to gain the attention of other people. The capability to change one's mind—and one's life—when the experience of argumentative transcendence calls for it.

These capabilities can be understood in different dimensions of their activity. First, they are elements of a philosophical-rhetorical anthropology. It is interesting, however, that *The New Rhetoric* does not equate *esprits* directly with human individuals. It is possible for this contact of *esprits* to take place within an individual. Nevertheless, this capability for contact determines what human beings are as rhetorical beings, and so the general capability for these conditions—the capability for realizing the more concrete and specific linguistic, psychological, social, and political conditions for argumentation—makes up the ontological potentiality-for-rhetoric of human beings. Second, these capabilities, in their concrete development, can be cultivated and trained to make them more effective. Third, these capabilities and their development are something like primary goods. Having these capabilities in a developed form is always good in itself because it is a realized power of freedom, as well as being one of the primary ways we achieve other goods. Therefore, fourth, in any political order in which the capacity for self-determination and the formation of voluntary communities are fundamental, these capabilities will be protected and undergirded by formal rights and liberties that allow their development and expression. Fifth, any society in which these capabilities are basic will organize itself to give people the power to develop and use them—the health and personal formation and education and access to technologies and forums and the experience and practice necessary to develop them to an optimal level.

To conceive of rhetoric in light of capabilities is a complex project, and disciplinary rhetoric accomplishes parts of this program very well. However, a deep rhetoric pushes rhetorical understanding across the boundaries of disciplinary rhetoric, toward a philosophical approach to understanding rhetorical capabilities ontologically, as part of the structure of transcendence, as well as toward a concrete critical consideration of what psychological, educational, social, technological, and political conditions will allow these capabilities to flourish.

TWO

What Is Deep Rhetoric? II

In chapter 1, the question of deep rhetoric was approached by first asking about rhetoric itself. This led to an exploration of the origins of rhetoric and to a distinction between two kinds of rhetoric: (1) rhetoric as a specific art or discipline that treats communication in specific, limited contexts, and (2) rhetoric as a more philosophical endeavor that is concerned with logos itself in all of its dimensions and uses. This second kind of rhetoric is more like the deep rhetoric with which we are concerned. The first chapter considered a number of challenges to this project—that the word "rhetoric" should be limited to the discipline of rhetoric because the word and the more specific art of rhetoric took shape at the same time; that the discipline of rhetoric could study the methods and purposes of communication because those purposes were connected with specific institutional contexts, whereas a deep rhetoric would be left trying to consider the purpose of communication itself, which would involve it in a teleological and formally theological labyrinth from which it would be unable to escape; that a deep rhetoric would inevitably have to ground itself in a questionable, essentialist humanism; and that a deep rhetoric was nothing more than a big rhetoric, an expansionist project of the discipline of rhetoric.

In light of these challenges, chapter 1 went on to give definition to a more seasoned conception of deep rhetoric, and of its humanism, and included an elaboration of some of the internal tasks it generates for itself: a nonreductive rhetoric of philosophy; a rhetoric of reason; a reinterpretation of philosophical terms and concepts; a further development of its philosophical anthropology, or its humanism; the development of an appropriate communicative practice for its own elaboration, one that will be more essayistic and dialogical than systematic and theoretical; and a confrontation with the critical term, "ideology."

In the chapters to come, "violence" and "reason" and "justice" and "wisdom" will receive deep rhetorical reinterpretations. Dialogues with other thinkers and with the rhetorical tradition will be carried on in these reinterpretations. In chapter 3, an explicit dialogue will be carried on with Plato's *Gorgias* and with some of the commentators on that dialogue because a re-reading of Plato on rhetoric is one of the best ways to clear the obstructions from the historical path that once could have led to a deep rhetoric, and thus to rethink the rhetorical tradition. Chapters 5 and 6, on Heidegger and rhetoric, will set up a dialogue that both uses and also criticizes Heidegger to open up a clearer philosophical approach to a deep rhetoric, one that does not make assumptions that undermine the project from the start.

In this chapter, I would like to begin by addressing the question of ideology directly. After that, I would like to connect the project of a deep rhetoric with the history of philosophical rhetoric in the twentieth century, for what I am calling deep rhetoric began to take shape in a number of thinkers then, especially after the Second World War. This tracing of the historical development of deep rhetoric will help to give further definition to the idea, and it will help to explain the practical significance of deep rhetoric and to clarify the nature and the value of rhetoric as a discipline, as a field of teaching and research.

Rhetoric and Ideology

In this section, I would like to bring the concept of a deep rhetoric to the complicated whorl of competing views that carry out their struggle under the umbrella term of "ideology." Part of the project of a deep rhetoric is to reinterpret traditional philosophical terms that have had a philosophical grounding. Here, I will carry out this reinterpretation of ideology specifically in relation to argumentation, for argumentation, as a form of reason, typically makes special claims to be closely connected with counter-ideological forces of thought. The central question is: can a deep rhetoric preserve the enlightening and liberating energies of reason as it carries out its reinterpretations of reason and ideology?

"Ideology" is a term that moves across philosophy both in its epistemological and political dimensions. Grounded there, it also operates in political theory and throughout the social sciences. Historically, the word has several unrelated and conflicting definitions and uses, but some of the conflicts are almost a part of the meaning of the term. Let me begin by approaching this in a historical way.

In the broadest sense, and in the tradition that includes both Marxist and non-Marxist conceptions of ideology, the question of ideology might be formulated the way Hans Barth formulated it over fifty years ago in *Truth and Ideology*: What are the obstacles to gaining knowledge? What are the obstructions that prevent our ordering our lives according to reason and nature? Barth develops this formulation of the ideological question from an examination of Bacon's theory of idols and from the writings of late-eighteenth- and early-nineteenth-century French theorists of ideology. Few people writing about ideology in the last twenty-five years would accept this formulation because its terms seem now to be quintessentially, shall we say, "ideological." That is, "reason" and "nature" and "knowledge" are all contested terms, all objects of something like "ideological" critique. They all seem to protect factional interests or particular interests behind the guise of a universal term.[1]

This brings us directly to two of the central defining conflicts of the theory of ideology. First, the problem of ideology and science, or ideology and reason, or ideology and knowledge: does the concept of ideology assume a non-distorted kind of thought, a mode of knowledge or science that is not affected by ideology? It's hard to imagine how it could not. The Marxian tradition has usually insisted on this kind of distinction. At several points, Marx both identified the process of how ideology was produced (apparently in a non-ideological description of the process), and he made clear that there really was a science of society that could identity the laws by which history operated. This requires a strong distinction between science and ideology, one that many Marxists have upheld. Lenin made this distinction not only at a theoretical level but also at the practical level of identifying which social groups in a society had real scientific knowledge of the functioning of history and which did not. Despite his more subtle conception of how deeply we are held in ideology, even to the point where, as subjects, we are constituted by it, Althusser, too, insisted on a strong science/ideology distinction, at least for the purposes of understanding how we are ideologically "inscribed."

Something of the same distinction was at stake in the dispute about ideology and science that was played out in the late 1990s among left intellectuals in the U.S. when the journal *Social Text* published Alan Sokal's faked 1996 article, "Transgressing the Boundaries: Towards a Transformative Hermeneutics of Quantum Gravity." The article claimed that physical reality was a linguistic construct and that quantum gravity was a politically progressive idea. Sokal's aim was to expose the ignorance of the poststructuralist left and its view of science as ideology. He believed that the editors of the journal would not recognize a parody if it bit them in the leg, which it did. However, behind the scandal-mongering was a serious conflict among the disputants about just where the science/ideology line should be drawn. Behind the scenes, the poststructuralists, who were skeptical about the coherence of the distinction, were lined up against the more traditional Marxian-oriented critics, who held to a very strong version of it. However, one need not be a Marxian to have this problem. To use the concept of ideology in a critical way is, at least implicitly, to claim that there is some non-ideologically distorted way to reason, judge, and communicate.

A second defining question is to ask whether ideology is a critical or a descriptive term. As a critical term, ideology describes a distortion of thought, one that can be identified as such by what must be in principle an undistorted kind of thinking. That is, again, the critical concept of ideology seems to require something like a concept of knowledge or science or reason that is undistorted. However, as a descriptive term, the requirement is not so steep. As a descriptive term, the concept of ideology might be thoroughly historicized, or ideology might be taken to be a natural part of the formation of particular groups—cultures operating in specific material or social or economic (or race or class or gender) contexts that limit or condition thought in specific ways. In this descriptive perspective, all intellectual formation is ideological because all intellectual formation is limited and shaped by its context—and this context is finally the context of the historical projects of specific groups.

However, the descriptive account does not easily escape the problems of the critical view. For we can always ask: What about the descriptions of intellectual formation? Are they also limited—shaped by their specific context? If so, what is their reliability? What is their authority? Their claim on anyone not operating in that context? Or further: If accounts of intellectual formation are just "descriptive," how do we *judge* competing intellectual formations, competing ideological powers?

This is enough to get us started. The question of ideology is, in this basic formulation, a clearly philosophical problem. Is there a kind of knowledge, a kind of reasoning, that is *not* ideological? Is there something like philosophy or science that is not shaped and conditioned by ideological powers? And what is it that is distorted by ideology? What goes wrong in ideological distortions? A deep rhetoric, in trying to accomplish its goal of serving as a metaphilosophy, must give some account of this science/ideology or philosophy/ideology distinction. In its anthropological dimension, there is also a role for it to play. The most general form of the question about ideology is a question about human finitude and human error. What is it about human beings that prevents their gaining satisfactory knowledge, prevents them from reasoning in satisfactory ways? What goes wrong with human thinking in general? Clearly, a rhetoric of reason and a rhetorical account of the critique of reason are just as immediately involved.

One more feature of the deep rhetorical project comes to the fore here, and that is the non-self-grounding character of rhetoric. It comes to the fore in a very specific way. One of the claims of reason, science, and philosophy in their traditional forms is to be self-grounding—to be founded on no authority other than reason itself, or reason and sense-experience, observation. No powerful economic base, no ruling class or dominant group, is supposed to be able to affect the nature of reason. Reason's nature arises from itself. It is, in the words of Kant, a spontaneous activity, beholden to no cause, shaped by no interest.

Rhetoric makes no such claim for itself. In fact, rhetoricians have always paid close attention to the conditions and causes of reasoning and deliberation. The rhetorical tradition has focused on the way arguments depend on audiences and their passions, on common cultural understandings, on how arguments arise from particular exigencies, how speakers and audiences adapt to one another, how the convincing character of a speech depends on the projected character of the speaker, and so on. This is one reason that rhetoric has been traditionally subordinated by philosophy as a discourse suited to getting one's way, and to achieving particular purposes. It is not a discourse of freedom in the sense that philosophy is. It is not characterized by spontaneity.

However, for this very reason, rhetoric has a supersensitivity to what, from a philosophical point of view, might look like ideological formation. A rhetorical account of reason knows that reasoning is dependent not only on a shared language and agreed upon facts but also on what we call values and on membership in a particular community of reasoning, a community that shares certain understandings and goals.

If we look back at the rhetorical tradition, the situated, background-shaped character of rhetorical discourse is something that has not only been acknowledged but has also been an essential part of what students of rhetoric have studied and made use of. Sharon Crowley has tried to capitalize on this fact in her textbook *Ancient Rhetorics for Contemporary Students*, in which she describes the interpretive network against which facts gain meaning as "ideology" (1994, 6).[2] At another place, it is the *sensus communis* that is called "ideology." Often, she says, this *sensus communis* resides in the language itself, and is "hidden from conscious awareness" (53). She devotes lengthy discussion to how the use of topics is influenced by ideology, and she refers to the ideological forces at work in authority and in extrinsic proofs as well (50ff.). And she is right to make this connection. Rhetoric works in a world that is already shaped by power and interest. Its reasoning is not spontaneous and free—at least not absolutely so. It depends on the possibilities of communication and reasoning that have been determined by the situation in which it finds itself. And this situation has many features that are—to someone like Crowley, and to me as well—reasonably called "ideological."

One way to begin to sort through these features in a systematic way is to start with rhetorical-theoretical accounts of what must already be in place for reasoning to occur. In what follows, I draw heavily, at least at first, from Perelman and Olbrechts-Tyteca's *The New Rhetoric*. For this book is, of all the rhetorical treatises I know, the most keenly aware of the tradition of thinking about ideology and the way that a rhetoric of reason is a kind of response to that tradition.

In *The New Rhetoric*, the enabling background for argumentation is analyzed into framework (*les cadres*) and starting point. In regard to framework, the most general requirement for argumentation is, as we have seen, the contact of *esprits*, even a community of *esprits* (NR 14–17). This is not a requirement in logic or in modern philosophy. However, rhetoric's view of reason is that it is grounded in particular, already existing human communities and what their members have in common. This includes, first, a common language—not just the general possibility of language and not simply a formal language or logic but an actual natural language. Natural languages are rich with specific attitudes toward the world and social life, what is appropriate and what is not. For example, the grammar of formal and informal address; the style of speaking to superiors and inferiors; and the semantics of insult, which relies on specific conceptions and valuations of race and sex/gender.[3] Natural language both reflects and organizes social life in an ideological way.

Second, there must be rules, practices, perhaps institutions for starting, conducting, and ending a conversation, even for merely getting the attention of an audience. These rules will ordinarily express a particular conception of fairness, of common interest, and of appropriateness. They will give hope to potential interlocutors that they have a fair chance to accomplish their goals. Without reasonable fairness, the discourse will not be true argumentation, at least not as we have come to understand it. Over the long run, these rules become sophisticated procedures of justice, shaped by the common situations in which conflicts arise. However, these rules may not capture everyone's intuitions about fairness; they may be acceptable, for example, only for those who succeed in gaining access to argumentative forums. Thus, they may well be ideological in the classical, critical sense. And as new groups are enfranchised, the rules may lag behind the intuitions about equality.

Third, there must be a motive, a reason to argue. From a rationalist point of view, such a motive might seem adventitious. However, argumentation is not disinterested, not pure and self-grounding. One expects that there may be benefits from entering into an argument, and one enters into argumentation with an eye toward those benefits. This influences one's argumentative behavior. However, the rules of equity that define an argumentative situation introduce an unpredictability into argumentation; they aim toward a common good, and toward something different from the simple goals of an interested party. One may enter an argument and find that one has committed oneself to much more than one had realized, something much broader than a private interest. The fact that this supervenient commitment arises within argumentation from what might at first have seemed to be an adventitious motive helps to reveal the thought-provoking way in which argumentation, rhetorically conceived, could generate counter-ideological events from within ideologically constrained situations.

Fourth, there must be someone whom one wishes to convince with the argumentation, an audience. Since audiences are the judges of the quality of argumentation, the ideology that shapes the audience's judgments will have a strong influence on the kind of reasoning that will take place. A speaker or writer must at least partly confirm this ideology in order to argue with someone at all. Beyond this, one also excludes some people from one's audience, and this exclusion too shapes one's reasoning, gives it an ideological or interested cast. The reasoning seems to be reasoning, and yet it counts as good reasoning only for a particular group.

The situation in which all these different factors come together, the rhetorical situation, is ideologically structured and is ideologically productive. The ideological background of different speaking situations—the audiences and rules for proceeding, and the motives and terminologies that bend argumentation in one way or another—tends to generate different discourses, the classical epidictic, legal, and deliberative contexts, or our own discourses of professions and disciplines. Even judging one discourse to be more appropriate in a situation than another is a highly ideological, profoundly interested judgment—even though entire societies can reach extensive agreement on these matters. These discursive formations and their effect on reason are a focus of a great deal of contemporary attention. The rhetoric of inquiry has investigated these discursive formations in the disciplines, and Michel Foucault has written compellingly interesting archaeologies and genealogies of professional and institutional discourses.

Ideology in the sense developed here, then, is the necessary background to the deliberate communication in which we engage. With argumentation, it is that about which we do not argue but which instead makes argument possible, both the form of argumentation as a kind of discourse and the content of argumentation in its reliance on unquestioned facts and truths and values and presumptions about good argumentative strategies and techniques.

In *The New Rhetoric*, epidictic discourse maintains this ideological background—the conditions for the possibility of argumentation.[4] This background is not a matter of choice but rather that which makes reason and choice possible, practicable. And even the maintenance of ideology is ideological. As Perelman and Olbrechts-Tyteca write, epidictic tends to defend traditional values, and is a procession rather than a struggle. In fact, epidictic tends to make the ideological move par excellence: "Being in no fear of contradiction, the speaker readily converts into universal values, if not eternal truths, that which has acquired a certain standing through social unanimity. Epidictic speeches are most prone to appeal to a universal order, to a nature, or a god that would vouch for the unquestioned, and supposedly unquestionable, values" (*NR* 51).

Here we come very close to themes in the Marxian tradition of thinking about ideology. The Marxian approach to ideology is probably best known for two of its features. First, the base-superstructure approach, in which the economic base, or the relations of production, express themselves in, or condition, or cause, the superstructure, the ideological formations of law, religion, and, in some versions, culture in general. Here are Marx's famous lines from the preface to *A Contribution to the Critique of Political Economy*:

In the social production of their livelihood, men enter into definite, necessary relations that are independent of their will, productive relationships that correspond to a definite stage of development of their material productive forces. The sum total of these productive relationships constitutes the economic structure of society, the real basis on which a juridical and political superstructure arises, and to which definite forms of social consciousness correspond. The mode of production of the material means of existence conditions the entire process of social, political and intellectual life. It is not the consciousness of men that determines their existence; on the contrary, their social existence determines their consciousness. (Marx 1904, 11–12)

Part of what is essential in this picture is the unilinear direction of ideological development, from base to superstructure, and the consequent implication of a dominant ideology, one governed by the economic base. This is part of the picture that Perelman and Olbrechts-Tyteca reject. Importantly, it is a part of the picture that most Marxian and post-Marxian thinkers also came to reject, and even in Marx it is not always consistently maintained.

Perelman and Olbrechts-Tyteca come closest to entertaining the notion in their analysis of classical and romantic uses of *topoi*, the way different *topoi* tend to become dominant in different periods, to become ideologies that govern whole societies. However, in the end, they believe that particular situations determine the ideological background at play in reasoning even more than social-ideological wholes do. After broaching the idea of a dominant topical ideology, or topics that might govern whole social movements, they back off and say, "It should be observed, however, that the use of certain loci or of certain lines of argument does not necessarily characterize a well-determined cultural milieu but may be, and frequently is, due to the particular argumentative situation" (*NR* 96). They follow this with an argument opposing Ruth Benedict's claim about there being a specific Japanese mind, a Japanese ideology, explaining the use of the *topoi* in question in terms of Japan's particular place in the war and at the negotiating table—situations from which Benedict drew. Rhetorical theory of this sort provides a general account that allows one to describe both large social-ideological formations and particular ones that operate counter to the larger ones.

In general, rhetorical theory has always kept alive an interest in particular situations and on all the available means of persuasion, and here it stands aligned with most of the recent work on ideology. The poststructuralist approach of Ernesto Laclau and Chantal Mouffe (1985) rejects the notion of a base or center, and even rejects the concept of "society." The thesis of the impossibility of society is that society is not a totality. No "hegemony" can suture social difference into a whole. No single social power is the underlying cause of the others. Foucault, too, believed that the concept of ideology was inevitably contaminated by the unilinear determinism of Marxism, and this was one of his reasons for rejecting the concept in favor of the concept of a discourse and of the body as a site of power struggles. He believed that power was distributed throughout micro-operations, strategies, and technologies—not in a unilinear way but in a whole system of polymorphous dependencies. This, too, is the general tendency of a deep rhetoric that would follow from Perelman and Olbrechts-Tyteca's work.

However, there is a second strand in the Marxian tradition that the new rhetorical concept of epidictic lines up with very neatly, and it is, I think, the part of the tradition that is more useful. This Marxian approach traces the way a particular mode of economic development and a particular set of economic relations get translated into a set of expressions and relations that claim universal validity and verity. The core of the Marxian notion of ideology is this mistranslation of something particular, something factional, something that benefits a particular class of people, into theories, values, presumptions, *topoi*, laws, institutions, practices that claim to have a universal range or scope. This is the main function of epidictic, this converting of a temporary and limited agreement into something that appears to be universal and necessary, something powerful enough to stand uncontested in argumentative situations. This is also a generalizing move that can take place as a result of particular arguments, but I want to highlight the epidictic dimension of ideological formation just now.

For it is here, too, that rhetoric offers something more than just a descriptive concept of ideology. Virtually all aspects of the framework and the starting points of argumentation are descriptive; these are necessary features of any argumentative situation. In describing this situation, rhetorical theory is descriptive. However, there is something inescapably critical about identifying this universalizing moment of epidictic, this exaggeration of agreement. We know from the very description that there is something amiss about this universalization, that what is being universalized is really not universal at all, and we suspect immediately that this universalization is interested, that it benefits not everyone but some people more than others.

Perelman and Olbrechts-Tyteca even highlight part of this operation when they describe how a "reference group" is necessary to identify what presumptions can be taken for granted in argumentative situations. That is, we have in mind a group of normal, competent, nondeviant individuals, who have a certain kind of knowledge and memory and intelligence and range of experience, and this group—an ideological formation that embodies the norm—determines what presumptions we can reasonably make. It cannot be determined simply by empirically working up what a group of average people would know, remember, believe, and so on; it is an ideal, with some normative force. This reference group is also unstable, adding and dropping members as argumentative situations change, and conforming sometimes more and sometimes less to what a largely representative group would be like. Appeals to what a "reasonable person" would believe or how he or she would act in a given situation are appeals to such a reference group. Perelman and Olbrechts-Tyteca also note that in any argumentative situation there are usually multiple reference groups in conflict with each other, and so multiple conflicting ideologies at work.[5]

The universalization of factional interests is also what Kenneth Burke identified as most distinctive in the theory of ideology. In *Counterstatement*, he used a notion of ideology according to which ideology was roughly equivalent to the cultural background of symbolic action, or sometimes simply to "culture" itself. However, even in *Counter-statement*, he insisted that it could vary from individual to individual and that its cultural regularities were interrupted by subcultures with different ideologies. At one point he even said: "An ideology is an aggregate of beliefs sufficiently at odds with one another to justify opposite kinds of conduct" (1968, 163)—perhaps the best definition of the term ever.

However, it is in *A Rhetoric of Motives* that he discusses the concept explicitly and at length, finding between Bentham and Marx a general agreement on the critical dimension of the concept:

It might be said that the Marxist analysis of rhetoric is primarily designed to throw new light on Bentham's 'Fallacy of Vague Generalities.' Otherwise put: As a critique of capitalist rhetoric, it is designed to disclose (unmask) sinister *factional* interests concealed in the bourgeois for benign *universal* interests. . . . All told, Marx thus forged a formidable machine; and he could apply it to shatter as deceptive 'ideology,' traditions which had been the pride of mankind, but which in being upheld by economic and social classes that got special advantage from them, and in being put forward as universally valid, thus protected factional interests in the wider, more general name of universal interests. (1969b, 102–3)

One could predict the course of ideological-critical reasoning in post-Marxist thought from just this simple description of the way ideology works. At the core of feminist criticism, of post-colonial thinking, at the core of all the concerns about race, class, gender, sexual orientation, ability, is the key critical approach of unmasking universals—universal conceptions of human bodies and human nature—as particular, interested, factional representations that work against certain groups. The formation of these particulars into universal notions that operate in the background of argumentation and reasoning is the heart of ideological-discursive formation.

This feature of the analysis of ideology aligns with the view that ideology has a kind of psychological and social validity for the people who live in terms of it. Ideology manifests itself as a necessary feature of their reasoning and action, or at least they regarded it that way. This brings us close to seeing ideology as "hegemony"—as an organization of consent without recourse to violence or coercion. Powerful "factional interests" may desire and *seek* this consent, but simply in the course of reasoning within a certain context, popular knowledge and culture *self-organize* into a process of *producing* this assent. The question for the theory of ideology is whether there is coercion in this or not.

Certainly, the background of argumentation along with its epidictic maintenance provides a good example of this kind of hegemony. It is functional. Since it allows people to reason efficiently, it carries a natural psychological validity. However, the question about coercion is also relevant to questions about the epidictic strengthening of consent. For Perelman and Olbrechts-Tyteca, epidictic is an essential part of education, the education of individuals into a community of reasoning, a rhetorical community. Epidictic is educational because it concerns the strengthening and transmitting of facts and values and truths and presumptions and hierarchies about which there is more or less social unanimity. Epidictic becomes propaganda only when it strengthens ideas that run counter to the taken-for-granted agreements of a community.

This easy distinction is troubling for anyone who sees some degree of truth in Althusser's identification of educational institutions as an essential kind of ideological state apparatus. And it is very difficult, from a deep rhetorical point of view, not to see coercion at work in the establishment of the framework and starting points of argumentation. Rhetorical theory—rightly, I think—has a tendency to emphasize the flexibility and complexity and even internal contradictoriness of the background. Ideology enables a great deal in all directions. The dominant ideology thesis and the old Marxist unilinear base-superstructure view are oversimplifications. Yet it is difficult not to see that those features of our lives which are most resistant to change and that continue to work against groups who are treated inequitably are reinforced and maintained by the ideological-discursive "education" of human beings. Beyond this, however, from a rhetorical point of view which takes argumentation to be a sphere of human freedom, a sphere of reason and choice—and Perelman and Olbrechts-Tyteca say that the whole purpose of *The New Rhetoric* is to establish the possibility of a community of freedom in relation to action—from this point of view, it is hard not to see the background and the working of epidictic and the reaffirmation of the background and the work of epidictic in particular argumentative situations as terrific examples of coercion. After all, we don't argue directly about what is taken for granted. The starting points have been defined in part by their having been withdrawn from argumentation. If we don't choose them, if they have been somehow infused into us from outside, isn't that coercion? Isn't there violence, as some would put it, in the very advent of subjects?

It's a difficult question, for thinking about hegemony and for rhetorical theory. From the standpoint of a deep rhetoric, with a profound interest in the rhetorical formation of human beings, there is nevertheless a sense in which "coercion" and "violence" are not the right words. In *The Rhetoric of Reason*, I called this coercion being claimed before one can even make a claim. A rhetorical community has claimed us and made us members independently of our choice and reason. This is the way we are formed. Coercion seems to arise only when we are forced to do something against our will; however, this does not accurately describe our formation as people who become capable of making choices. On the other hand, we were forced to be something about which we had no choice, and this does seem to be a "violation" of some strange kind, the kind that Levinas explores in his work.

One key to the question seems to be the extent to which we have been formed in such a way that our reason works against us, whether we are deeply complicit, when we reason, in projects that we to some degree and in some way oppose. From a deep rhetorical perspective, such a situation is likely, although the matter of degree is important here. Our lives are grounded in complicated backgrounds that are sedimented with interests of which we often have little awareness. A great deal of what makes a life a progress toward something is our discovery of the way our reasoning is complicit in these projects we do not support. This is what much of the critical study of discourse is about—the ways we rely on a background that works against people with whom we are trying to communicate, people who are sometimes ourselves.

In such a context, a different question seems to be the decisive one. How does argumentation, conceived rhetorically, increase our freedom with respect to the ideological background, make it a matter of choice rather than a matter of hegemonic coercive noncoercion? How does reason increase freedom and exert a counterforce to the force of ideology? To answer this question rightly—that is, to amplify and adumbrate the

answer rightly—requires the notion of a deep rhetoric, and requires returning to the background of argumentation from a slightly different
angle.

There is in the framework of argumentation, in the conditions for the
contact of minds, the definition of a direction that moves against ideological power. We ran across it first in the condition of needing a motive
or reason for arguing when I mentioned that this motive is a starting
condition and not a continually constraining one. Rules and protocols
for argumentation usually prevent one from breaking off argumentation
without a good reason. It often happens that we begin to argue out of
a particular motivation and then find out that committing ourselves to
argumentation was a commitment to more than we knew. We might be
asked to reflect on and argue for some of our presumptions. Our arguments might not convince the way we had expected. We may be forced
into reflection on our techniques and on our topics, our general premises.
We may encounter someone very unlike ourselves, and argumentative
contact with that person might have surprising results.

All of this follows from another condition of argumentation, a condition for what Perelman and Olbrechts-Tyteca mean by the contact of
esprits, that goes beyond just getting information about another mind or
trying to influence it. In order for argumentation to take place, one must
be willing, in principle, to be convinced of the other person's point of
view. If one were not willing to do so, and this fact were discovered, there
would be sufficient grounds for saying that one was not really engaged
in argumentation at all but just appearing to. One's own view was never
really up for argumentative exploration or testing. It is certainly possible
to think up and produce arguments about issues about which one was
unwilling to change one's mind. However, it is not possible to address
each other as the audience for the argumentation without this condition.
The arguers must agree on the audience, the judge of the argumentation,
and this means that the arguers must have conceded to the audience the
authority for judging the argumentation. They must agree to accept the
judgment. In actual circumstances, this acceptance may be a matter of
degree, or a judgment may be accepted provisionally, or legally, without
winning full acceptance, but the principle still holds.

This willingness to accept another person's point of view, to give up
one's own in favor of someone else's, is part of the risk and adventure of
argumentation. It is also what opens up the possibility of the new. And
it is also an essentially ethical dimension of reasoning. It is an expression
of the inherent equity-seeking force of argumentation, a force that takes
more specific shape in the way a conception of justice is always at work in

argumentation and reasoning. It is no accident that Perelman found such deep links between the notions of justice and equity on the one hand and argumentation and reason on the other. It is no accident that Perelman and Olbrechts-Tyteca found the rule of justice to be at the heart of what made some arguments stronger than others. Argumentation is the arena in which we seek justice in relation to claims, an adjudication of points of view, some way of opening ourselves to each other's experience, each other's perspectives, that will do justice to the differences and also make these differences available to each other. The contact of *esprits* is all about creating the possibility of opening ourselves to each other's experience and ultimately each other's lives.

This condition of having to be willing to change one's mind is the reason that rhetoricians, who have always thought of reasoning in a social context, have also always been keenly attuned to the fact that one's interlocutor or audience is not a matter of indifference. Aristotle pointed out that one doesn't reason with just anyone about anything. When one enters an argument willing to take the other person's point of view, one sometimes risks a kind of degradation. However, whom to argue with is not an easy matter to determine. The person we may most need to reason with might be an enemy of our present point of view, our present attainments, but also a profound friend of our next self, the one we are hoping to become, without yet knowing it very clearly.

It is this force of respect and equity and openness, which arises within highly ideological contexts, that also gives life to a countercurrent to that context—counter, at times, not only to one's supposed interests but also counter to the presumed starting points of argumentation itself, counter to the operative ideology. However, the deeper point here is that this dimension of argumentation, in its very concept—that is, in principle—is counter to all ideologies. It harbors within it the serious entertaining of the idea that one may be wrong, deeply wrong, that in fact most people may be wrong—that there might be an interlocutor who will make such deep challenges, who will question the presumed ideologies. This counter-ideological opening that grounds argumentation is the price to pay for cooperation, learning, newness, reason. We enter a situation supposing that we can use other people (or even ourselves) better to accomplish our purposes, but we end up learning from them that we can accomplish better purposes.

This is a vector, a direction, a logos that a deep rhetoric of argumentation uncovers. It is a *toward* of reason itself. In order to discover it, we need partial, interested motives, and limiting conditions. However, these partial or interested conditions give rise to or reveal something else very different. In Johannine terms, we begin to speak the language of signs, the interested language of the *sēmeion*, in search of certainties, proofs, much like the crowds of those early scenes in John's gospel. However, along those semiotic routes, we come into contact with something else, with the logos. In the prologue, the logos is said not to be a thing but a direction, a *pros ton theon*. This logos moves in and against the semiotic languages of human beings; it makes them possible, but it works strongly against their certainties and ideologies. It undoes ideological expectations about ethnicity (say, being a Samaritan) or about gender (say, being an adulterous woman) and certainly about class.

This conception of logos is also at play in Plato's idea of the *dynamis* of logos, its specific power to lead the soul—that is, to lead it in a direction, sometimes, in Plato, called an ascent. This leading is finally, not just the *dynamis* of logos, but for the Socrates of the *Phaedrus*, the completion of rhetoric, a true rhetoric—not the incomplete rhetoric of a Lysias, whose central flaw is, surprise, surprise, to hide a private interest under the cloak of a universalist discourse.

To return, then, to the idea of a deep rhetoric, this direction of argumentation is, again, something that contemporary rhetorical theory must work to retrieve from millennia of philosophical and theological reifications. Doing so will help rhetoric discover again the communicative truths in which philosophy is grounded but which philosophy keeps misrepresenting as truths about things, about beings or being, as metaphysical and epistemologically oriented truths. This retrieval and rediscovery will enable rhetoric to translate philosophical terms into communicative ones, back into rhetoric, without losing the passion of philosophy for something more, something that is not one more expression of an ideology, and without losing a sense that reason is closely related to freedom.

This capacity for logos, and for equity and acknowledgment that might call one's own positions into question, is also a deep rhetoric's contribution to philosophical anthropology and its response to the recent demise of a humanism whose conceptions of human being seemed all to be ideological reifications. The logos of rhetoric cannot be arrested at a particular destination. Its essence is its onwardness, which is a word of Emerson's. This is, by the way, the Emerson who wrote: "I do not often speak on public questions;—they are odious and hurtful, and it seems like meddling or leaving your work. I have my own spirits in prison;—spirits in deeper prisons, whom no man visits if I do not" (1911, 217). Which I take to mean: I cannot confine myself to speaking within the acknowledged semiotic codes of my time, within the accepted ideologies, or discourses. There is not only a prison or slavery acknowledged within these ideologies, including the ideology of abolitionism, but there is a deeper slavery and imprisonment, in the ideologies that keep us in the business of slavery and imprisonment regardless of who is enslaved or in jail at the time.

Although it is not actually true, as Emerson says here, that he seldom wrote or spoke or acted on public issues, I believe that the sentiment he is expressing is genuine. Onwardness is a being directed, an experiencing of *psychagōgia*, of the specific power of logos in the deepest sense as a power which first allows anything to lead to anything at all. In this instance, it is a case of what leads from "deeper prisons" to freedom, freedom from the "ideologies" that keep us enslaved even when we are busy with the projects that we believe are leading to freedom for those who are enslaved.

Emerson speaks most consistently of this onwardness in his essay "Circles" (1987), and it would be interesting to think of ideology critique in relation to that essay. In "Circles," this onwardness-without-a-final-goal is portrayed both as liberating and as threatening to one's sanity. The challenge is to maintain a sense of direction and of freedom in the absence of a clear grasp of an ultimate goal. The question is to know how to move *onward* and not simply *away from* or *beyond*. To explore the seriousness with which Emerson ultimately takes this to be a rhetorical issue would require a chapter of its own.

However, before moving ahead, I would like simply to note one more Emersonian text, a text more directly relevant to rhetoric and to our concerns with ideology. Here is a crucial journal passage of June 1846, also worked into the second "Eloquence" essay: "The orator must ever stand with forward foot, in the attitude of advancing. His speech must be just ahead of the assembly, ahead of the whole human race, or it is superfluous. His speech is not to be distinguished from action. . . . I must feel that the speaker compromises himself to his auditory, comes for something—it is a cry on the perilous edge of the fight,—or let him be silent" (1904, 115–16). "Eloquence" is one nineteenth-century word for rhetoric, and Emerson is here very clearly concerned with its power to lead, to be "ahead." Logos is also very clearly conceived here as action, movement in a direction, and this action can be a justly ordered interaction with others who are also in movement, and *who help us to determine what counts as a foot forward and what does not.*[6]

This critical recognition rescues Emerson from the threat that attended the solitary thinker in "Circles." This deep rhetoric, which assumes profound responsibility for those it addresses, also takes direction from those specific others it addresses. This is not a scene in which the speaker knows the goal and leads others to it. On the contrary, the speech is, at the deepest level, "a cry on the perilous edge of the fight," and the fight here is for direction, for logos, for the simple ability to put one foot in front of the other. The advance would not be possible if the speaker did not "compromise himself to his auditory."

There is a great deal happening in this phrase. First, Emerson uses "auditory" instead of "audience," and this suggests then not only the audience, the specific others, but also the place, the auditorium or room in which the speech takes place, and so the receptivity possible on that occasion and in that setting. One must compromise to one's place and time as well as to those specific others. The "solution" here is not a general solution but a specific one, rooted in the possibilities of the occasion, even though the stakes are, for this speaker and audience, very high. Second, the speaker must "compromise" not only in the sense of working through differences and reaching an agreement, but also in that more archaic and etymological sense—and Emerson was always attuned to etymology—of "promising together." That is, the compromise is also a promise that joins the parties together in advance toward the future, in a step forward. This is *le contact des esprits* reaching into the deep rhetorical level of the very formation of a community that hopes to share a future.

Emerson, who once wondered why he had never been offered a chair in rhetoric, often pushed to the edge of a deep rhetoric, and is a presage of what was to come in the next century. However, I want to turn now to the late-twentieth-century movement toward a deep rhetoric, in which the wall between philosophy and rhetoric was pretty much torn down.

The current chapter continues the preliminary development of the idea of deep rhetoric begun in chapter 1. We began this chapter by raising the question of how a deep rhetoric would meet the challenges of ideology critique. Because rhetoric is not self-grounding, and because rhetorical argumentation relies on existing situations for the framework and starting points of argumentation, it seems to be especially vulnerable to ideology critique. However, a deep rhetoric conceives this dependence as a strength because it emphasizes the "occasional" character of argumentation, and so undoes the science/ideology distinction on which most ideology critique relies. Rhetoric does not attempt to locate itself outside the world within which it operates. Instead, it tries to be fitting to its time, to make the most of its time, to fulfill the potential of its time. This is to be "occasional" in the deep rhetorical sense. It shares Hegel's view, expressed in the preface to the *Philosophy of Right*, that philosophy "is its own time apprehended in thoughts" (11), but it would reformulate this adage as: philosophy is its own time, thought out of its own time, in terms of its own time, reaching toward an audience beyond its time.

Rhetorical argumentation also grounds itself in an openness to others that is brought about in the conditions for a contact of *esprits* that seeks a very different way of finding freedom from the constraints of ideology. Ideology critique's conception of itself or of some other science or way of knowing that can be contrasted to ideology is different from rhetorical argumentation's openness to the other, which is essentially an openness to something that cannot be perfectly known or controlled. If with hegemony ideology reproduces itself effortlessly within the realm of the known and the rationally calculable, with rhetorical reason and its contact of *esprits*—which includes the willingness to change one's mind because of another person's reasons—the authority of what is said to be known and calculable is, in principle, suspended. This openness to the other that is also an openness to the new is a potential counter to whatever ideology has achieved a measure of force in one's reasoning, and the potential beginning, too, of a newly conceived social future.

There is much more to say about the form of this openness. For example, the question of how it can achieve the reasonableness associated with good argumentation will have to be addressed. The question of how far the reasoning and conclusions can extend beyond the immediate occasion will also have to be faced. These questions, and more, will be addressed in chapter 7, on reason and justice. There is more to be said, too, about the way in which deep rhetoric addresses the challenges presented by a very generalized notion of ideology that goes to the brink, if not over the brink, of a relativism that despairs of reason, and this will be addressed, in part, in chapter 7, too, and also in chapter 8, on rhetoric and wisdom. However, there is more that needs be accomplished in this preliminary sketch of deep rhetoric before we can speak to those questions with the seriousness they deserve. Since a deep rhetoric began to take shape in the twentieth century and especially in the late twentieth century, I want to turn to that development as a way of filling out the preliminary conception of a deep rhetoric.

The Deep Rhetoric of the Late Twentieth Century

Although deep rhetoric lies at rhetoric's origins and never entirely disappears in the history of philosophy and rhetoric, it does tend to lie dormant during much of the modern period. The philosophical and scientific revolutions of early modernity caused a reordering of intellectual activity that has still not settled or resolved itself. The decline of confidence in rhetoric's ability to describe or improve the power to reason in language and the consequent disqualification of rhetoric as a means for settling intellectual controversies played themselves out in the sixteenth and seventeenth centuries.

By the eighteenth century a man like Giambattista Vico could express the sense of what had been lost in a poignant and powerful way. In *De nostri temporis studiorum ratione* (1709), Vico exposes the narrowness of contemporary education, its myopic focus on the teaching of analytical-critical attack with no corresponding or counterbalancing education in the imagination or invention of arguments. Vico is unstinting in his praise of the achievements of modern thought, but he is also relentless in his exposé of the limitations and destructiveness of its educational project. Vico makes a deeply felt case for the recovery of the topical tradition, in which the forms by which arguments could be imagined and elaborated were near the heart of the liberal educational project. A central part of his argument can be put quite succinctly:

In our days . . . philosophical criticism alone is honored. The art of 'topics' . . . is utterly disregarded. . . . This is harmful, since the invention of arguments is by nature prior to the judgment of their validity . . . so in teaching, invention should be given priority over philosophical criticism. (Vico [1709] 1990, 14)

Vico is especially interesting for us today because his words failed to have their desired effect, at least in his time. By the nineteenth century, what marked rhetoric above all was, in the words of one historian, "the curiously irrelevant character of rhetorical education," with its elocutionary and belletristic preoccupations (Conley 1990, 236).

In the twentieth century, a more final end was reached as the vestiges of the rhetorical tradition began to disappear altogether. Chaim Perelman's story about his own rhetorical education stands for this process as a whole: "While still enrolled in high school, I had the privilege of taking the last course in rhetoric offered in Belgium. In 1929, rhetoric was removed from the curriculum both in high schools and in the universities. . . . Not surprisingly, therefore, rhetoric, in my opinion, was dead" (1984, 188–96.) This does not mean that rhetoric was in fact dead. The elocutionary movement, for example, relied on classical sources and produced scholarship and theory. It was taught in the schools and at the higher level, and it had a significant popular impact. However, the tradition of rhetoric as a deliberative, inventional art that might orient a liberal education was, if not dead, scattered in pieces across the intellectual and educational landscape.

The impact of rhetoric's dissolution and scientific philosophy's consolidation of power eventually helped to contribute to the intellectual crises of the early twentieth century. This fact is most clearly seen from the standpoint of philosophy's disastrous success in destroying rhetoric's claim to have a significant role in the enterprise of reason. The early modern attempts to develop a science of society that would produce the same mastery and control of social life that scientific method was promising with respect to nature were central defining projects of the philosophy that had dismissed rhetoric's powers as a deliberative and inventive art. By the early twentieth century, new developments in formal logic and the triumph of scientific method had produced one of the leanest, most rhetoric-free conceptions of philosophical method ever: logical positivism. This method allowed only "sense-data" and logical operations (including scientific method but with reservations about induction) to count in the production of knowledge. "Reason" was pretty much limited to formal operations (mathematics and logical proofs) and scientific method. This led to a reinterpretation of ethical discourse as having merely "prescriptive" or "emotive" meaning and in all cases having no "truth value."

This left most significant human controversies outside the province of reason, subject to whatever irrational powers managed to hold sway. Against these failures, and against the practical failures that issued in the violence of the early twentieth century— violence generated in part by those who, from one side, believed that a "science" of history that revealed its laws was possible, or, from another side, that reason was in fact useless in connection with significant social and political conflict, or yet from a third, that reason was an ethnic or racial property that varied from people to people—one could well ask the question of what promise reason still held for resolving human conflict about significant matters. In fact, this question was asked in a serious way in a movement of thought that can only be understood as the resurrection or re-creation of rhetoric in the late twentieth century. However, this resurrection of rhetoric is not simply a revivification of traditional disciplinary rhetoric; it is much more. It has the markings of what I have here been calling a deep rhetoric.

To understand this re-creation of rhetoric, one must adjust one's focus in some specific ways. Rhetoric does not come again primarily as a reformation of education or out of academic departments and schools which have custody of rhetoric's tradition. Instead, it returns out of the crisis of philosophy and in the wake of the holocaustal destructiveness of the European wars. Rhetoric returns in part as a recovery of the tradition but in greater part as the addressing of an urgent contemporary need, an original rethinking of reason against its narrowing during the modern period. If modernity can be thought of as the process of the intensifying divorce of rhetoric and philosophy, the late twentieth century can be thought of as their rapprochement and remarriage. This is not to dismiss the efforts of early-twentieth-century rhetorical theorists. Kenneth Burke's autochthonic, nearly magical, single-handed recreation of rhetoric is still hardly absorbed by rhetorical theory, and I will have more to say about in chapter 8. However, in the period from about ten to fifteen years after the Second World War until late in the twentieth century, rhetoric was re-created, from several sites, out of the ashes of modern philosophy, and with several specific characteristics.

First, rhetoric returns as philosophy. This is well known and broadly acknowledged, even if the claim may at first seen controversial. In Bizzell and Hertzberg's widely used anthology, *The Rhetorical Tradition* (2000), the final section, on "Modern and Postmodern Rhetoric," includes selections from, among others, Chaim Perelman, Stephen Toulmin, Michel Foucault, and Jacques Derrida. In Thomas M. Conley's *Rhetoric in the European Tradition* (1990), the final chapter is titled "Philosophers Turn to Rhetoric" and includes sections on Richard McKeon, Stephen Toulmin, Chaim Perelman, and Jürgen Habermas. What I will show here is that when philosophers turn to rhetoric, they are turning to a rhetoric of a specifically late-twentieth-century sort, a rhetoric made of late-twentieth-century philosophical thinking. So while it is true that in the late twentieth century "philosophers turn to rhetoric," it is even more true that rhetoric returns as philosophy. It is not simply that philosophers are developing theories of rhetoric—they have always done this—but rather that they are developing rhetorical frameworks as ways of addressing philosophical questions that have become unaddressable in purely philosophical terms. Rhetoric returns as an enlargement of philosophy.

However, second, rhetoric does not return in a perfectly unified or systematic way, but it arises in very different ways in the work of a number of different philosophers working completely separately at about the same time. And the philosophers by way of whom rhetoric returns are in some significant respects speaking from outside of the strongholds of institutional philosophy, whose own center is not holding. Chaim Perelman was trained in law and in philosophy, born in Poland, and wrote in French, from Belgium. Richard McKeon was an American philosopher who worked with the interdisciplinary "Ideas and Methods" committee at the University of Chicago and with UNESCO in the postwar years.

Stephen Toulmin's famous *The Uses of Argument* (1958) was referred to by his colleagues as an anti-logic book and was met with barely restrained hostility. Jürgen Habermas worked at the Frankfurt Institute for Social Research under Theodor Adorno, and has become the most famous second generation Frankfurt School critical theorist. I will add to this group of philosophers-out-of-the-mainstream one other figure, through whom rhetoric also returned, but who was also the quintessential German academic philosopher, Hans-Georg Gadamer. Gadamer's philosophical hermeneutics is itself a major part of the return of rhetoric. Finally, the entire North American "informal logic" movement is in some essential respects a return to rhetoric, and nowhere more than in its most productive spokesperson, the Canadian philosopher Douglas Walton. Perhaps this simple list can show more clearly than anything else the ways in which philosophers working in very different contexts found themselves forced to re-create rhetoric as a way to address the philosophical challenges of the late twentieth century.

Third, the overriding context of this development is the violence and destructiveness of the early twentieth century and the failure of philosophy to articulate a conception of reason that might address this violence and redeem reason's promise. The core motive for the recreation of rhetoric arises from this context. Gadamer's *Truth and Method* appeared in German in 1960. Toulmin's *The Uses of Argument* appeared in 1958. Perelman and Olbrechts-Tyteca's *The New Rhetoric: A Treatise on Argumentation*, also appeared, in French, in 1958. These are all postwar works in a profound sense, written out of the milieu of the destruction of Europe, and it is worth asking whether any other three years in history have produced works with such deep significance for a philosophical rhetoric. Habermas, who belonged to the Hitler Youth as a very young man, begins to publish shortly after this, pursuing with great passion and energy his liberal-democratic but Marxian-influenced program of a theory of communicative reason. McKeon's postwar work with UNESCO situates him precisely in this same intellectual milieu. The informal logicians may seem like an exception to this; however, informal logic's beginnings are, in a second wave of the same concern, a response not to the World Wars of the early part of the twentieth century but instead to the continuing violence of the late twentieth century, in particular the Vietnam War, and to the irrelevance of formal logic to the significant demands placed on reasoning by the social conflict and violence in the U.S. that attended that war. As it has developed, it has found itself face to face with the task of recreating a rhetorical approach to the theory of argumentation.

Fourth, this resurgence of rhetoric is characterized by a special concern with reasoning and argumentation. The philosophical return of rhetoric is a belated response to Vico's plea, a turn toward argumentation that will take a topical rather than a logical approach and will show promise of creative and not strictly critical-evaluative power. All the philosophers I have mentioned are centrally concerned with reason and argumentation in natural languages that will proceed without formal rules or method, with arguments that will succeed in resolving conflict and generating understanding even in conditions of continuing uncertainty. The standards for rationality and the criteria for successful argumentation are in each case social and communicative, and this is the essence of the rhetorical return at work in all these philosophers—the move from a strictly logical standard of rationality to a communicative one.

Fifth, this reclaiming of reason by rhetoric forces rhetoric out of its limited roles as a practical oral or verbal art limited to a specific range of occasions into an expansive architectonic rhetoric and into the deep rhetorical role of metaphilosophy. The topics, or conceptual matrices, that rhetoric describes are the generative seats of reason, of social formations based on the achievements of reasoning, and of fundamental philosophical activities and frameworks. Rhetoric both describes these formations and activities and is itself the process by which they come to be. Rhetoric is the discipline of disciplines, the philosophy of philosophy, and is the creation and self-knowledge of social forms. When Richard McKeon writes that "invention extends from the construction of formal arguments to all modes of enlarging experience by reason as manifested in awareness, emotion, interest, and appreciation" (1987, 59); when Henry Johnstone writes that "rhetoric is the means, the only means I know of, for generating and maintaining consciousness" (1970, 333); when Perelman and Olbrechts-Tyteca say that a universal audience attends all philosophical argumentation and that an undefined universal audience attends even that attending (*NR* 35); when Gadamer writes that rhetoric is the "universal form of human communication" (1986, 17)—they are all catching a view of this architectonic power and responsibility of rhetoric.

In what follows, I will explore in more detail the ways these twentieth-century thinkers recast the idea of rhetoric—in their treatment of kairotic being, in their recognition of the architectonic power of rhetoric, in their turning to law as a prototype of reason, in their return to the human voice, and in their merging of philosophy and rhetoric, specifically in the Gadamer-Habermas controversy.

Gadamer and Kairotic Being

One of the traditional ways of distinguishing philosophy and rhetoric has been to say that rhetoric is concerned with the essentially occasional, with practical matters, ceremonial matters, conflicts and choices that are specific and must be addressed one at a time and not in general. Philosophy, on the other hand, is concerned with what is not simply occasional, but rather with what transcends occasions, with being itself and not its temporal and accidental manifestations, with theory and not with practical exigencies and particular situations. Gadamer's account of the temporality of works of art and of understanding itself abolishes this distinction. Works of art are historical but not in the sense that historicism would give to the word. For historicism, works of art are intelligible only in light of the historical background out of which they are produced or out of the historical context in which they are interpreted. For Gadamer, works of art do not belong to time as objects that exist at one time and not another, but unfold their intelligibility in and over time, in a back and forth between the contexts of their production and the contexts of their reproduction and reception. Further, part of what they *are* is what they are *about*, and this too unfolds over time. Their manifesting and clarifying what they are about depends on time in the sense of *the right time*; it depends on the conditions of reception being appropriate to what the works have to give.[7]

In the lecture titled "Rhetoric—Poetics—Hermeneutics," which was discussed in chapter 1, Paul Ricoeur insists on a distinction between philosophy and rhetoric based on rhetoric's adaptation to and dependence on particular occasions. And, as we have seen, Gadamer denies it: "Rhetoric is the universal form of human communication, which even today determines our social life in an incomparably more profound fashion than does science" (1986, 17). Gadamer does not say this casually or accidentally. The statement belongs in a systematic way to his philosophical hermeneutics, so it is important to clarify the single most significant philosophical change that allows Gadamer to make this statement, that in fact allows a rapprochement of philosophy and rhetoric. We must consider briefly the kind of being that Heidegger and especially Gadamer have helped to clarify. For Gadamer, being is always timely or "kairotic," and is dynamic in the sense of being-at-play in any event of understanding. Let me try to clarify very briefly just this feature of the timely and historical coming to presence of things.

Gadamer explains timeliness first in relation to works of art, but he then generalizes this idea to understanding in general. Works of art do not have their being at simply one point in time. This is counterintuitive in some respects. Surely Verdi's *Requiem* was ontologically finished once and for all in 1874, Sophocles' *Antigone* in about 440 BCE, Shakespeare's *King Lear* by about 1606. And yet this is what Gadamer wants to deny. The claim that these works make, their capacity for provoking an experience of truth in very different historical periods and situations, is a kind of being they have over time. And their being just *is* their making a claim and participating in an experience of truth. That is what an artwork *is*. It *is* not a manuscript or a canvas or a musical score and libretto. When the "Libera Me" from Verdi's *Requiem* was played at Princess Diana's funeral in 1997, its being was revealed in a new way. New claims were made on its auditors, and new experiences of what the *Requiem* was *about*, new experiences of truth, took place. In the long history of performances of and commentaries on and rewrites of *Antigone*, it is the *Antigone* whose being and meaning are unfolded.[8] It is the claim of the play itself that we experience in each case. When *King Lear* shows up one more time on film or video, through whatever medium or device, it is *King Lear* itself that shows up, and if the moment is right and the performance succeeds in making the play contemporary once more, then it puts the play into play with us in such a way that we experience the play's truth once more. Again, this is an event of *King Lear* itself. The work *is* its making a claim; it *is* its being an event of truth—and what Gadamer means by an event of truth is: an event in which something is clarified, an event in which we learn something.

Now, clearly, not every wild interpretation or rewrite of *Lear* is experienced as an interpretation or event of the work. Is Jane *Smiley's A Thousand Acres* an event of Lear? Is Jean Anouilh's *Antigone* an event of Sophocles' play? The fact that we can argue about such questions in a sustained and meaningful way is evidence that we do assume that it is possible for these works to reappear in new ways. They can make a claim on us in our own time; their ability to be a making of a claim and an event of truth has a history. However, it must also be granted that works seem to wax and wane in this respect. That is, their being as a work is not only historical but also kairotic. Their being able to make a claim on us depends on the situation in which they are received. The interests and assumptions and historical knowledge and methods of a time must be such as to make a work accessible. Historical events and works of art and, really, everything that we understand are not uniformly available to us. Rather, the skills and instruments and interests and questions and all of the pre-understandings that are definitive of our time help to decide whether *Antigone* will go on unfolding *in our time*, whether, say, Hildegard of Bingen's music and art will come alive for us, whether Verdi's *Requiem* will have a chance to come to us in a new and powerful way, whether *Lear* will continue to be a tragedy that should always be remembered or will become more like a pitiful story that has to be overcome.

Although I've developed a few examples of works of art, it is not difficult to imagine extending this analysis, with revisions, to the different kairotic coming to presence of theoretical physical particles or concepts of justice or species concepts or anything else that must be understood. This being-at-a-time is kairotic being, and when it becomes our way of understanding being, then some of the underpinnings of the rhetoric and philosophy distinction start to give way—especially the distinction between what is abiding and what is fleeting, what has constant presence and what has kairotic fullness. Rhetoric has always lined up with *kairos*. In speaking for a communicative purpose, one knows that one cannot say just anything at anytime to anyone. Communicative situations simply do not allow all things to be said and to be understood indifferently. The rhetorical tradition is a long tradition of trying to identify how situations shape and lead and both make possible and limit the possibilities of communication and productive understanding. Comprehending this kairotic understanding of being that Gadamer has developed helps one to understand how Gadamer can claim that rhetoric is the universal form of human communication, for it is the universal form of the disclosure of anything that can be said to be. However, this by no means puts it into a necessary conflict with philosophy. Something comes to presence in the experience of the work of art, in an experience of truth, in learning anything at all. Part of getting the relation of philosophy and rhetoric right involves bringing to presence this coming to presence itself and recognizing the historicity of it without reifying history or the being of beings or what works of art are about.

The Architectonic Power of Rhetoric

As the universal form of human communication, rhetoric is also the generation and description and use of all the subforms it contains. That is, rhetoric is the power both to invent and to organize and comprehend the different forms that communication takes, the discourses of the different disciplines and professional fields, the discourses of different historical periods, of different social groups. For Richard McKeon, rhetoric's architectonic power goes beyond even what is traditionally thought of as the range of the "verbal":

There is every reason to think that the [architectonic productive] art we seek is rhetoric with a theoretic orientation. . . . The problem of constituting such an art and applying it once constituted is one of rejoining eloquence and wisdom, rhetoric and philosophy. . . . The new architectonic productive art should become a universal art, an art of producing things and arts, and not merely one of producing words and arguments; but the first step in constituting and using an enlarged objective rhetoric should be the reformulation of the structure and program of verbal rhetoric and its subject-matter. . . . We seek to produce it in concrete experience and existence by rejoining reason and sense, cognition and emotion, universal law and concrete occurrence. (1987, 12–13)

Such a rhetoric is still barely realized, yet this same vision of rhetoric's architectonic power has been forwarded and developed by other late-twentieth-century philosopher-rhetoricians. In *Human Understanding* (1972), in a development of the ideas he had put forward thirteen years before in *The Uses of Argument*, Stephen Toulmin describes the way that reason is constituted by a variety of different rational enterprises, each with distinct purposes, each adapting to the exigencies it faces, and each producing conceptual change as it adapts. In fact, Toulmin locates the rationality of these enterprises in the procedures they have for generating conceptual change. Rationality is, so to say, a feature of change and not a feature of a changeless system of thought. The structure and division of these enterprises are not a result of formal or logical considerations of reason's applications, or the way reason "naturally" or logically breaks into fields, but rather are a result of the changing historical purposes of human societies.

These procedures, which frequently take the form of argumentation, are not simply formal procedures. Describing the nonformal rationality of argumentation has been a thread in all of Toulmin's work, and it has brought him into closer affiliation with the rhetorical tradition of topics and argument than with earlier twentieth-century logical models of argumentation. Near the conclusion of *Human Understanding*, where he is trying once again to describe the procedures that produce reasonable conceptual change but also conceptual change specific to different rational enterprises, he describes something like the topical-architectonic function of rhetoric envisioned by McKeon.

The question at issue in Toulmin's discussion is how conceptual change is possible—that is, how a new set of concepts overtakes an old one. If one tried to explain this process of change simply in terms of formal relations, one would fail because articulating formal relations depends on having a single set of concepts, not two conflicting ones. At this point, Toulmin brings in an analogy invented by Gilbert Ryle in which making a formal inference is compared with taking a journey along an existing road. However, justifying that inference is compared with laying out the road in the first place.

Toulmin's gloss is important:

Once we have an established network of roads in any area [i.e., a constitutive way of making inferences and producing knowledge in any enterprise/discipline/profession], the question 'Which is the right way from A to B' acquires a determinate sense. At the earlier stage of surveying for the road network, by contrast [i.e., during the development of an enterprise or during a time of controversy and conceptual change], no such single-valued questions arise, and all of the operative questions are comparative ones—e.g., 'Which of the alternative lines for a road would give us a cheaper, faster, more direct, and/or environmentally less damaging way of linking A to B?' The tasks of constructing novel sets of concepts in any field of enquiry and refashioning existing concepts so as to go beyond the scope of currently established procedures likewise raise comparative questions, about what changes would be 'better' or 'worse,' rather than single-valued ones, about what step is 'correct' or 'incorrect.' (1972, 487)

Anyone familiar with the rhetorical tradition will hear the reinvention of topics here at the exact point at which rational enterprises are born and acquire their rationality. These underlying comparisons that Toulmin is after, and which begin to look more like ethically inflected concerns than pure theoretical interests—even though they are at the *archai* of rationality itself—are what the topical tradition collected and saved and passed on to human beings who wanted to acquire a greater ability to reason and resolve controversies and discover new things: comparisons by similarity—by induction, for example, or by analogy, like Ryle's own analogy here. Or by differences. Or by degree—the greater/lesser, the end/means, the scarce/abundant, the more desired/the less desired, the desired by the wise/desired by the ignorant, and so on. All these were not merely general descriptions of how people do in fact reason but were much more importantly tools and sources from which people learned to draw, invent, and create new arguments in times of controversy and change, to produce not simply single-value solutions but a *copia* of possible solutions.

Lucie Olbrechts-Tyteca and Chaim Perelman have also developed this vision of the architectonic dimensions of rhetoric, and again, although I can only gesture at this, it is worth pointing out. In their discussion of topics in *The New Rhetoric*, where they speak explicitly of the "systematization of loci," they sketch an approach to the periodization of intellectual history founded on topics. They amplify the senses in which the classical outlook was illuminated primarily by the topic of quantity while the Romantic outlook was guided primarily by the topic of quality (*NR* 95–94). They carry this approach further in the following sections on the agreements and procedures of reasoning of special audiences, the audiences that constitute the various disciplines and professions and their fields of knowledge. *The New Rhetoric* in fact pushes this architectonic program through to its completion, describing the workings of the universal audience that are constitutive for philosophical reasoning, and so the new rhetoric project incorporates dialectic into this philosophical rhetoric—again, part of what McKeon envisioned.

Rhetoric and Law

The return of rhetoric in philosophy is also a return to law as the prototype of human reasoning, and so a return, really, to the original interests of rhetoric in the legal reforms of sixth-century Sicily and the *controversia* of Cicero. This move is definitive for Toulmin's theory of argumentation. As he says explicitly in *The Uses of Argument*, "Logic (we may say) is generalized jurisprudence" (1958, 7). He says this because the parallels between argumentation and legal process go too far to be conceptualized only as parts of an analogy. Nevertheless, he also knows that he must establish the case. In his own theory of argumentation, says Toulmin, "The nature of the rational process will be discussed with the 'jurisprudential analogy' in mind: our subject will be the *prudentia*, not simply of *jus*, but more generally of *ratio*" (8).[9]

Gadamer's hermeneutics is also a turn to law as a paradigm of interpretive reasoning. In a central section of *Truth and Method*, "The Exemplary Significance of Legal Hermeneutics" (324–41), Gadamer explains this paradigmatic function of law. "Legal hermeneutics," he says, "serves to remind us what the real procedure of the human sciences is. . . . Legal hermeneutics is no special case but is, on the contrary, capable of restoring the hermeneutical problem to its full breadth and so restoring the former unity of hermeneutics, in which jurist and theologian meet the philologist" [the philologist, we might add, as architectonic rhetorician] (2003, 327–28). The specific idea Gadamer develops in this section is the idea of application. In the application of an existing law or precedent to a new case, something creative or inventional happens. One discovers something new *about the law or precedent*: "Application does not mean first understanding a given universal in itself and then afterward applying it to a concrete case. It is the very understanding of the universal—the text—itself" (341). Gadamer applies this legal idea of application to human understanding and reasoning broadly and in fact takes it as a key to unlocking the relation of past and present.

Perelman, too, participates in this return. He was trained in law; his first publications had to do with legal concepts, specifically justice; and *The New Rhetoric* as a whole rests very heavily on the ideas of precedent and justice—to the degree that the very idea of the strength of arguments, which according to the theory the book lays out should rest entirely on some kind of audience, ultimately rests instead on the rule of justice (*NR* 464–65).[10]

This convergence on using law as the prototype of reasoning instead of geometry or mathematical logic is another central event in the return of rhetoric in the late twentieth century. This brings reasoning back to a concern with difference and conflict and controversy—and not only with how the violence and suffering they produce might be mitigated, but also with how they might be transformed and used for purposes of discovery and increased understanding.

The Human Voice

Finally, the return of rhetoric is its return to human speech, or dialogue. The constriction of reason into sense data and logical operations was the constriction of the human voice. Sense-data are silent, and logical operations require only a single mind or computational agent. In fact, any conception of reason as only a formal system does away, in principle, with the need for dialogue. On the other hand, the return of rhetoric occurs in the development of explicitly communicative theories of reason.

Stephen Toulmin's *The Uses of Argument* begins in a way that sets it apart from all other English-language argumentation theory of its time. In the reigning logical models of argumentation, arguments consisted of propositions and their formal relations to each other. Toulmin's first chapter begins this way: "A man who makes an assertion puts forward a claim—a claim on our attention and to our belief" (1958, 11). This bold stroke completely resituates argument, radically alters its scene. Here it is a matter not of propositions but of claims. Claims are not propositions but speech acts, and they are made on someone and to someone; they are essentially social and implicitly dialogical actions. In his exposition of his famous ordinary argumentation model, the dialogue becomes explicit in that the argument goes forward only in response to an interlocutor who plays the role of questioner or challenger to the claim. This produces the need for a reason. If the reason's support for the claim is not immediately compelling, another question may produce a warrant, and if that warrant is also questioned, then backing for it is put forth. At this point, however, the dialogue has reached its altitudinal limit. The backing is a constitutive feature of a rational enterprise. Without some agreement at this level, the argumentation cannot go forward because what Toulmin calls the procedures of reason are not in place.

Toulmin's model is thus dialogical through and through. The parts of his model are conceptualized in terms of speech acts that are in principle communicative and dialogical. The need for reasons, warrants, and backing are all a function of a challenger or questioner. And the procedures of the enterprise in which an argument takes place are there to make a dialogue possible, to allow answers to questions to *count as* answers to questions for partners in the enterprise. This dialogue of voices speaking a natural language is worlds away from the voiceless model of propositions and their formal relations.

In *The New Rhetoric*, Perelman and Olbrechts-Tyteca also make communication between speaker and audience something internal to their very conceptions of reason and argumentation. In explaining why they have chosen to name their work "The New Rhetoric" and not "The New Dialectic," they emphasize that the idea of dialectic has not always stayed faithful to the communicative character of argumentation but has often drifted toward formal analysis that makes no reference to the communicative agents that are supposed to be offering and considering the arguments. And so, they forge their alliance with rhetoric and its tradition, for the theory's fundament is its commitment to the idea that "it is in terms of an audience that an argumentation develops" (*NR* 5), and everything from the available means of persuasion to the standards by which arguments are measured is relative to audience. Their departure from the rhetorical tradition, they say, is simply their radical insistence on this principle, their expanding the idea of audience to include all audiences for argumentation, including philosophical ones, and so they announce their participation in the return of rhetoric as philosophy, even metaphilosophy.

Douglas Walton's productivity as an argumentation theorist over the last four decades is unmatched. Many of his works explore and retheorize single "fallacies" or argumentative forms. However, in his 1998 *The New Dialectic*, he draws on his work with Erik Krabbe to build a general framework for the theory of argumentation he has been working toward. He has never been tempted to use formal standards to distinguish between forms of argumentation that are legitimate or reasonable and those that are not. A central idea of his work on fallacies is that there is a "basic problem" that the fallacy theorist must face: the fact that arguments that have what has been traditionally identified as a fallacious form are nevertheless sometimes reasonable in a particular circumstance. In *The New Dialectic*, he elaborates a theory of the kinds of circumstances there are in terms of a theory of the kinds of argumentative dialogues there are. The general idea is that each kind of rational dialogue is constituted by its own goals and rules of procedure. One is arguing reasonably as long as one keeps the rules. One runs into difficulties when dialectical shifts occur and an interlocutor suddenly changes the kind of rational dialogue being conducted.

Those familiar with the ancient tradition of distinguishing rhetoric and dialectic will wonder whether Walton's work is better understood as belonging to the new philosophical rhetoric or to the tradition of dialectic whose flag Walton adopts. The question is whether Walton's dialectic is a subfield of the new rhetoric or not, whether it is itself more reliant on something like topics than on formal procedures, whether it is generative of the network of roads produced by rhetoric's architectonic power, and whether its reliance on communication is deep—whether the voices of this dialectic create and judge the forms it takes, the governing procedures of the dialogues, or whether these forms and procedures are in some sense a priori and have their authority independently of voice. I believe that the answer in connection with Walton's new dialectic can only be discovered when the still unasked question of the rationality of dialectical shifts is more fully developed. The rules that are constitutive for Walton's different dialogues are like Gilbert Ryle's existing networks of roads. However, there is no dialogue on dialogues that has the same kind of rules. Dialectical shifts are attempts to create new roads among the different rational enterprises represented by the different kinds of rational dialogues Walton describes. From the standpoint of the individual dialogues, such moves are "fallacies," impermissible, traffic violations of sorts. However, such moves are clearly sometimes necessary. Our different rational activities draw from all the kinds of dialogues, and the important thing is to know when to shift dialogues, and why, and with whom. These dialectical shifts, then, will rest on the same invention and discovery of deep comparisons that Toulmin described in *Human Understanding*, and whether they will be acceptable or not will depend not on some specific rule applicable to the roads already laid out, but on the acknowledgement by the participants in a controversy that such shifts are in some sense more productive or valuable or appropriate than simply continuing to drive the known network of roads.

Walton recognizes this, of course. When investigating how to judge whether a dialectical shift from one dialogue form to another is licit or illicit in a particular case of argumentation, Walton proposes two complementary questions. First: "Is the new dialogue supporting those old goals, or at least allowing forward movement on their fulfillment, or is it blocking them?" (1998, 201). This first question is the general pragmatic question that guides Walton's theory of evaluation. If the answer is that the shift is continuous with the goals of the dialogue, then there is no issue, no occasion to ask further critical questions. However, if there is a question whether the shift is continuous with those goals, then a further question must be asked. The first question establishes whether or not there was a shift. However, merely noting that there has been a shift carries no normative force. The second question is: "Was the shift agreed to by the original speech partners, or was the shift unilateral, or even forced by one party?" (201). This second question is the rhetorical question that actually addresses the issue of normativity. If there is no agreement, if there is force, then the shift was illicit, and a negative evaluation is possible. There is bad reasoning going on.

I take this to be a strength of Walton's approach. Dialogue genres are highly conventionalized forms of speech and argument; they embody what most of us agree on most of the time when it comes to the discursive means for achieving a goal. However, there is no logical necessity in the relation between the means and end. Unusual situations with unusual challenges may well allow or even require unusual means. Who is to judge these cases?

Who else but the judges, the audience, the participants in the dialogue? A guiding thread of the new theory is that the logic has changed from a logic grounded in the nearly self-evident force of a prohibition against asserting contradictory propositions to a dialogue logic grounded in a prohibition against breaking one's commitments to one's dialogue partner, one's audience. One's partner, one's audience, becomes the judge of when this commitment is violated both because the genre constraints do not have sufficient normativity and because what is required for good reasoning is agreement among the dialogue partners that an acceptable goal is still being pursued. So, when it comes to establishing what is normative, the theory becomes a rhetorical theory, essentially a reception theory of rationality.

The Habermas/Gadamer Debate

These moves toward dialogue on the part of Toulmin, Perelman, and Douglas Walton are events in the general return of rhetoric. However, this return of rhetoric is especially notable and compelling in the Habermas/Gadamer *Auseinandersetzung*. In their famous debate of the 1960s and 1970s, the question at issue was exactly how deeply the dialogical character of reason goes, whether there is some rational perspective outside of intellectual controversies from which they can be judged, irrespective of the conclusions of the participants. Both Gadamer and Habermas developed powerfully dialogical conceptions of reason. In a brilliant and definitive section of *Truth and Method* titled "The Hermeneutic Priority of the Question" (362–79), Gadamer argues not only that the dialogue of question and answer is definitive for reason and knowledge but that "the structure of the question is implicit in all experience. We cannot have experiences without asking questions" (362).[11] This principle of the "primacy of conversation" (369) helps Gadamer to explain why "knowledge always means precisely considering opposites" (365). Only in the dialogue of question and answer is the subject matter itself opened up: "To conduct a conversation means to allow oneself to be conducted by the subject matter to which the partners in the dialogue are oriented" (367). Only when the different possibilities are explored in dialogue can the best judgment be reached. Actual dialogue is the dialectical path to knowledge itself.

The critical question I would like to raise here is whether this Gadamerian dialogue can be formalized into a dialectic that is not dependent on the actual people in the actual circumstance discussing the actual subject matter—whether there are rules or standards that do not ultimately depend on the consent of these interlocutors. I would like to claim that if there are, then we have a dialogue that is better understood in a formal and strictly dialectical way, and not as a return of rhetoric. If however, the interlocutors and/or audiences are the ultimate judge, if there is no formal method to which dialogue must conform, then we have here the return of rhetoric as speech and dialogue, as deliberative and inventional, and as a process of reason.

Gadamer makes his answer unequivocally clear: "There is no such thing as a method of learning to ask questions, of learning to see what is questionable" (365). Rather, he insists, questioning depends on a knowledge of one's ignorance, on a Socratic intellectual virtue, an ability to resist the pressure to be held by an opinion. The "art" of questioning, of participating in the question and answer dialogue that leads to knowledge, is no real *techne* at all. It cannot be formalized: "The 'art' of questioning is the art of questioning ever further—i.e. the art of thinking. It is called dialectic because it is the art of conducting a real dialogue" (367). In the end, this view is realized by Gadamer's deeply anti-Platonist Plato: "The literary form of the dialogue places language and concept back within the original movement of the conversation. This protects words from all dogmatic abuse" (369). Gadamer does not make the explicit distinction between formal dialectics and rhetoric that I am insisting on here, but in the context of the question of the advent of a third age of rhetoric, his move is a significant one.

The critical issue can be highlighted even more sharply in the conflict between Gadamer and Habermas. Habermas is himself one of those late-twentieth-century philosophers through whom rhetoric returns. He has developed an elaborate pragmatic theory of communication that is supposed to realize some of the aims of traditional critical theory. He constructs a consensus theory of truth, holding fast to the attempt to reinterpret traditional philosophical principles along communicative lines. In order to distinguish between rational consensus and de facto consensus, he creates his "counterfactual" idea of an "Ideal Speech Situation," in which all the distortions of communication produced by inner and outer constraints, by differences in power, by covert strategic actions, and so on, are eliminated. The only motive in play, consciously or unconsciously, is the search for truth. In these respects, and in many others, Habermas's turn to communicative standards of rationality is part of the general return of rhetoric as philosophy.

However, in his exchange with Gadamer, Habermas's critical-theoretical standpoint will not allow him to go all the way to a kind of rationality that is finite, situated, and adapted to and dependent on historical circumstance and the judgments of real interlocutors who reason from within such a situation. In his review of *Truth and Method*, he argues that deliberation in such a context cannot be rational unless it achieves a reflective knowledge of the historical processes that have conditioned it. Such reflection enables us not simply to act from out of a context handed down to us by a tradition, but "to designate the conditions outside of tradition under which transcendental rules of world-comprehension and of action empirically change" (Habermas 1990a, 241). That is, Habermas wants a scientific-philosophical understanding of something like the laws of history that can themselves somehow be known by reflection that takes one outside of the influence of the history that has been produced by such laws. This would allow the reflective critical theorist who has achieved such knowledge to be able to judge the communication of people who claim to have reached a rational agreement with one another. The critical theorist, because of his or her knowledge of how history conditions the communication in question, might reasonably overrule the interlocutors, who might lack such knowledge. Gadamer's apparent dialogue is exposed as a context of force and domination. By contrast,

Truth is that characteristic compulsion toward unforced universal recognition; the latter is itself tied to an ideal speech situation, i.e. a form of life, which makes possible unforced universal agreement. . . . It is only the *formal anticipation* [emphasis added] of an idealized dialogue, as the form of life to be realized in the future, which guarantees the ultimate supporting and contra-factual agreement that already unites us; in relation to it we can criticize every factual agreement, should it be a false one, as false consciousness. (Habermas 1990b, 267–68)

Here we have returned to another version of the ideology question, with Habermas taking the position that the critical theorist has secured a perspective on the more ideologically constrained perspectives that are not accompanied by critical theoretical awareness.

To amplify his contention, Habermas develops an analogy with psychoanalysis. Just as the psychoanalyst can decode the systematically distorted communication of neurotics, so the critical theorist can decode the systematically distorted elements of the communication that produces de facto but ultimately false consensus.

The issue is utterly compelling for anyone familiar with the history of philosophy and rhetoric. Both Habermas and Gadamer are philosophers for whom communication and dialogue are central concerns, who have in large part given up on the notion of a priori knowledge and strictly logical-analytical standards of reason. Both are essentially concerned with how to find the measure and standard of rationality within communication itself. In this sense, they have both tilted far toward the rhetorical side of the rhetoric-philosophy continuum. However, when pushed far enough by Gadamer's philosophical hermeneutics, Habermas returns to something like a scientific or methodological or traditionally philosophical standard—a "formal anticipation of an idealized dialogue," a social-philosophical critical science analogous to psychoanalysis, even a reflective knowledge of the laws of history—something, anything, that will free us from the communicative distortion by the very forces that make a particular situation a particular situation, but without actually removing us from the realities of communication.

Gadamer's reply is equally compelling, and it includes a culminating manifesto of the return of rhetoric in a unification of the projects of rhetoric and hermeneutics. First, he agrees with Habermas that there is specialized scientific knowledge that operates according to method and that critical sociology may well use this kind of knowledge. However, he insists, such knowledge makes its claim and achieves what authority it has from within the dialogue of knowledge and not from outside it (Gadamer 1990, 297). Scientific-critical expertise is itself in need of the same kind of critical reflection on itself that the other interlocutors in the dialogue are. In fact, the different arguments and perspectives that are achieved in the challenges among the interlocutors provide the opportunity, even the possibility, for scientific and methodological understandings to achieve this kind of reflection.

Second, Habermas's critical theory of communication is in search of a criterion for truth. Habermas finds hermeneutics wanting because it does not produce such a criterion. However, philosophical hermeneutics is not trying to come up with a formal criterion for truth. A central idea of *Truth and Method* is that truth and method are in tension with one another, that truth is an event that cannot be completely constrained by methods and their truth-criteria. In fact, as Gadamer delights in pointing out, Habermas's own "Ideal Speech Situation" was not created in or justified in an ideal speech situation itself, so how can it account for its own truth? The universality of hermeneutics subsumes even Habermas and his ideals. The real purpose of hermeneutics is different, and here the sense in which rhetoric and hermeneutics are part of the same intellectual project begins to come into focus: "Hermeneutic reflection is limited to opening up opportunities for knowledge which would otherwise remain unperceived. Hermeneutic reflection is not itself a criterion of truth" (1990, 284). Can you hear the ring of this? Hermeneutic reflection produces copious discovery/invention of arguments—hitherto undiscovered *opportunities* for knowledge.

The convergence of rhetoric and hermeneutics intensifies, and this is third, when Gadamer charges Habermas with not really understanding dialogue, which is defined by its faithfulness to *controversia*, to genuinely seeing from different perspectives, to acknowledging genuine difference. The ideal speech situation, he says, is modeled on the old idea of pure intelligence and the truth that would be produced by such a pure intelligence. He adds that he himself does not think of hermeneutic dialogue going on only in ideal conditions, and he charges Habermas with a dogmatic prejudice when he denounces as "coercive" and "unreasonable" all those real situations in which real people believe that they have reached real agreement about matters in which they themselves have a stake and around which they are willing to orient their lives—matters such as love and friendship and work. That is, Habermas's critic is able to judge, on the basis of an ideal of communication, the actions of people with which he or she has never communicated, whose perspectives have never been mutually acknowledged in argumentation: "A critique which in general opposes the prejudices of another individual or the dominant social prejudices because of their coercive character and, on the other hand, claims to dissolve such a delusory relation by communication finds itself . . . in very bad circumstances. It must ignore fundamental differences" (Gadamer 1990, 288). Habermas's critical theory of communication lacks what a rhetorical theory of controversial reasoning insists on: "It belongs to the concept of reason, that one must always reckon with the possibility that the opposite conviction, whether of the individual or in the social realm, could be correct" (294).

Fourth, Habermas's critical theory cannot answer a very important practical question. In psychoanalysis, the patient has already acknowledged needing help and has acknowledged the expertise of the analyst. This permits the analyst to assume power over the patient and communicate strategically in relation to the patient. In the analogous situation, asks Gadamer (289), in which the analyst is the critical theorist and activist, under what conditions, given what understanding of social reality, is it out of place to assume such power and strategic control over others, and in what conditions is it not out of place? The point is that the original agreement between the analyst and the patient has no analogue in the case of the critical theorist and social groups. One can easily detect the implicit call for hermeneutic dialogue and reflection here.

Finally, Gadamer works an intriguing unification of hermeneutics and rhetoric into this discussion, and expresses in a powerful way the practical, situated, kairotic character of the human experience of the good. At this point, I will let Gadamer conclude for himself. First, with this deep identification of philosophical hermeneutics and rhetoric:

Hermeneutics and rhetoric share this area . . . of convincing arguments. In modern scientific culture, the defense of rhetoric is difficult. . . . Vico rightly presses home a unique value found here: *copia*, the abundance of viewpoints. [Habermas' assertion] to the effect that rhetoric contains a coercive character and must be circumvented in the interest of coercion-free rational dialogue seems to me to be shockingly unrealistic. If it is the case that rhetoric contains a coercive moment, then it is nonetheless certain that social praxis . . . would not even be conceivable without this coercive moment. . . . The concept of manipulation is in this context genuinely ambiguous. Every emotional influence occurring through speech is in a certain sense such a manipulation. But this is not just an empty social technique. . . . Aristotle had already characterized rhetoric not as a *techné*, but rather a *dynamis*, so strongly did it belong to the *zoon logon echon*. (1990, 292)

Gadamer presses the point home not only in his rejection of the idea of a theoretical elite who know the social good but also in his insistence on the kairotic experience of the good in the particular hermeneutical-rhetorical situation:

> The human good is something to be encountered in human praxis, and it is indeterminable without the concrete situation in which one thing is preferred to another. This alone, and not a counterfactual agreement, is the critical experience of the good. It must be worked through in the concrete circumstances of the situation. An idea of the correct life as a universal idea is 'empty.' Herein lies the portentous fact that the knowledge of practical wisdom is not a knowledge that is conscious of its ascendancy over the ignorant. (293–94)

Here, too, is a profound conception of democratic rhetorical humanism—that the good lies in human choice and action and not in abstract ideals, and that there is no "knowledge of practical wisdom" that would justify the status or actions of a critical-theoretical or noble elite.

The Gadamer-Habermas Controversy is probably the most significant philosophical exchange of late-twentieth-century philosophy. Gadamer draws on the classical and rhetorical traditions, on his vast knowledge of the European humanistic tradition, and on his immersion in German philosophy as passed down to him, in part, from his teacher Martin Heidegger. Habermas places himself squarely in the modern tradition of enlightenment and tries his best to unite traditionally Marxian social and political concerns with the progressive dimensions of liberal-democratic theory. He joins the depth of the German philosophical tradition and the critical perspectives of Marxism to the liberal and progressive and democratic and natural-scientific interests of the rest of European philosophy and social thought. And yet both are ultimately committed to carrying forward their philosophical projects within a communicative framework, and the issue that draws forth their energies is an issue that one might say is internal to the self-understanding and history of rhetoric: the extent to which successful communication can be described formally and understood and judged by formal standards. In this discussion, there is no question of *logical* standards or forms, or standards or forms that might be found somewhere outside of actual communication. Instead, the question is the form or nature or the standards that are internal to communication, found in rhetorical activity itself. Rhetoric returns as philosophy here not simply as one side of a controversy but as the very framework in which the controversy takes place. The question is whether we are to go all the way to Gadamer's deep rhetoric in which theoretical and practical reason are both held within the hermeneutical-rhetorical situation, or whether with Habermas we hold on to a distinction between theoretical and practical reasoning, and search for ways to release theoretical reason from its dependence on this situation.

The relation between philosophy and rhetoric has always been a dynamically unstable one. However, the late twentieth century shows a remarkable development when thought against the conventional history. Late-twentieth-century philosophy becomes the matrix from which rhetoric is, once more, born again. This return is all the more remarkable because it is especially evident in two German philosophers, two unparalleled inheritors of the tradition of German Idealism, inheritors of Kant's famous devaluations of rhetoric in the Third Critique and Hegel's consistent denunciation of Ciceronian rhetoric as nothing more than popular philosophy—that is, not philosophy at all. And the story of how, in philosophy, we get from "not philosophy at all" in the 1820s to "the universal form of human communication" in the 1960s is part of the story of what has happened with rhetoric inside the history of philosophy.

————

The aim of the first two chapters has been to give some preliminary definition to the idea of deep rhetoric by showing how a larger conception of rhetoric as a philosophical endeavor has accompanied rhetoric ever since it was first conceived as a specific art or discipline. This larger conception of rhetoric is clearly evident in Plato, and while Aristotle conceptualizes rhetoric as an art, and so provides it with disciplinary limitations, he also understands that rhetoric is a special human capability and not simply a developed art. This larger conception of rhetoric comes to the fore again when rhetoric returns as philosophy in the late twentieth century. However, to develop and clarify this more philosophical kind of rhetoric requires addressing a number of questions and challenges. We have begun to address some of these—the question of whether and in what sense logos has a purpose; the question of whether this larger conception of rhetoric has enough definition to guide research and teaching, and what its implications are for disciplinary rhetoric; the question of rhetorical humanism; the challenge of addressing the issues that would arise from a rapprochement of philosophy and rhetoric, including a rhetoric of reason; and the challenge of explaining how a philosophical rhetoric would stand up against ideology critique.

In the next chapter, I will address another challenge. I have several times referred to deep rhetoric as a return to conceptions of rhetoric and of logos found in Plato's dialogues. Yet, Plato is commonly taken to be rhetoric's greatest critic, who distinguishes absolutely between philosophy and rhetoric, so this way of giving definition to a deep rhetoric seems mistaken from the start. Many people have recognized that Plato develops a favorable view of rhetoric in the *Phaedrus*, where rhetoric and philosophy do undergo a rapprochement. However, this is also usually taken to be a minor and undeveloped digression from Plato's essentially negative assessment. To counter the common understanding of Plato's treatment of rhetoric, the next chapter will consider what is usually taken to be Plato's most severe attack on rhetoric, his dialogue *Gorgias*. A careful reconsideration of that dialogue will show that, behind the polemical and eristic displays, the dialogue develops a profound consideration of how philosophy, rhetoric, and logos belong to one another.

THREE

The Deep Rhetoric of Plato's *Gorgias*

It may be helpful at this point simply to announce a number of overarching theses concerning the project of a deep rhetoric. Some of these theses have been announced already, some have already received discussion and support, and some will receive discussion and support in this and following chapters. Some others indicate in an outlined and programmatic way ideas that belong to the conception of deep rhetoric, but do not receive central attention here.

Deep Rhetoric: An Overview

Deep rhetoric is not a discipline. Rather, deep rhetoric is in a way metadisciplinary, but beyond that it is a way of understanding not only all language and symbolic activity but also all communication. For a deep rhetoric, "communication" is not simply the sending and receiving of a message already understood. That notion does not capture the profundity of the rhetorical tradition, of Vico's "Wisdom speaking" ([1709] 1990, 89), or of Plato's and Perelman's notion of speech that is capable of convincing the gods themselves (*Phaedrus* 273e; *NR* 7), or of Socrates' famous understanding of *logos* as a power of "leading the soul" (*Phaedrus* 271d, Fowler trans.).

The idea of rhetoric has yet to emerge as the idea it is striving to be: the idea of rhetoric as coincident and interdependent with the idea that philosophy itself has been striving toward. Rhetoric cannot be rhetoric and philosophy cannot be philosophy until their conceptual alienation from one another is overcome. The project of a deep rhetoric is an attempt to begin to develop this idea.

Deep rhetoric does not grasp or possess its objects. It does not generate formal or operational definitions of them. It is always essaying after what it is attempting to speak about. In this way, rhetoric returns to Socratic "philosophy" as a way of searching, a way of affiliating with what it seeks, a befriending of what it hopes to understand. It is a persevering affection and search for the proper practice of its attempts to understand.

Deep rhetoric takes seriously Emmanuel Levinas's critique of the tradition of metaphysics and epistemology and their privileging of ontology over ethics (1998). With Levinas, it finds that something like ethics comes before everything else. However, it understands this ethics as the form of a transcendence toward others and oneself that carries ethical force and generates meaning, and so is a kind of communication. We are messages to each other. Further, we are the messages to each other *out of which* something like our being and identity are called forth. We communicate being to each other; we give being to one another communicatively.

The ethics of rhetoric is not a specific problem that rhetoric faces, and it is not an "area" of rhetorical studies. The good is not grasped or conceptualized or possessed, but sought; it is that for which human existence stretches out. The ethics of rhetoric is constitutive for rhetoric. Transcendence is conflict. This is the tragedy of existence. But conflict is also transcendence, and this is the comic romance of existence, and the hope of a deep rhetoric.

The philosophical, psychological, political, ethical, and communicative dimensions of human transcendence are all implicated in one another.

Argumentation is an attempt to purify reason of violence, and only a deep rhetoric is capable of illuminating the profounder dimensions of this project. However, deep rhetoric sees the goal of absolute nonviolence as a chimera, a mistaken reification or abstraction—a telearchical error. Nonviolence is an important part of peace, but it is not the whole of it. Deep rhetoric reveals both that violence and nonviolence tend to be implicated in one another and that the fuller peace of just relation and creative communication is the aspiration of argumentation. It discovers that nonviolence is a means to another end, not an end in itself.

Human being is transcendence, transcendence is communicative, and communication is meaningful. To be oneself requires transcendence toward oneself and so communication with oneself. Being oneself is an event of deep rhetoric, a communicative giving and receiving of ourselves. To be real is to be created in communication, to be sustained by communication, and to be limited by communication.

————

This is all very abstract and programmatic. One way to sharpen the notion of a deep rhetoric is to show how deep rhetoric has been one strand in a complicated weave of the rhetorical tradition. In this tradition, one can find a wide range of different conceptions of rhetoric. One general way to distinguish conceptions of rhetoric is to divide the philosophical rhetorics (the ones that contribute to a deep rhetorical tradition) from the "disciplinary" rhetorics. The former think of the study of rhetoric as a kind of philosophy or metaphilosophy that seeks something that lies in all communication and is prior to knowledge. The latter think of rhetoric as the study of a particular kind of communication or knowing, appropriate for specific purposes and occasions or in specific institutional settings. A disciplinary rhetoric thus seeks a method of its own, one that is fitting for its own subject matter. So, for example, Plato seems to hold rhetoric to the same standards as philosophy, and in fact Socrates argues in the *Phaedrus* that a complete rhetoric would be philosophy. In this sense, Plato is a major figure in the tradition of what I am calling deep rhetoric. Aristotle, on the other hand, in his *Rhetoric,* develops a sophisticated notion of rhetoric as a discipline, with its own specific methods appropriate for specific occasions.

A few qualifications are necessary at the start. Although the tradition of philosophical rhetoric certainly contributes to the idea of a deep rhetoric, there is something in the idea of deep rhetoric that conflicts with the philosophical tradition itself. For in the twentieth century, deep rhetoric emerged as a struggle with the philosophical tradition, a tradition that had by then been narrowed by a constricted notion of reason. Deep rhetoric emerged in the late twentieth century partly as a turn to rhetoric that had not been philosophical in the modern sense but had been protected by its disciplinary shelter from participating in the reduction of reason that occurred in the modern period. Another qualification is that the contrast between the philosophical and the disciplinary does not capture the sense in which philosophy itself suffers disciplinary cycles throughout its history. Neither does it capture the difference between Plato and the sophists, both of whom develop, in a way, philosophical rhetorics. The difference between them is not that only one of them develops a philosophical rhetoric, but that the sophists seem to hold to a gnostic skepticism while Plato wants to point to a more practical and agnostic eroto-fideism.

Since, as we have seen, deep rhetoric is in some respects a return to philosophical concerns and approaches to rhetoric that are found in Plato's dialogues, it is worth exploring this connection explicitly. Plato's dialogues have been read as attacks on rhetoric, but approached in the light of a deep rhetoric they read quite differently. In what follows, I want to track Plato's wrestling with the possibility of a deep rhetoric, particularly in the *Gorgias*.

Plato and the Sophists

To write about "Plato's concept of rhetoric" may seem futile by now. What remains to be said that has not already been said? Besides, Plato's dialogues explore several conceptions of rhetoric that are incompatible with one another. In addition, the Socrates of the *Phaedrus* expresses the plausibly Platonic view that thoughtful people would never believe that they could express their deepest convictions in writing. And as if that were not trouble enough, Plato's *Seventh Letter* makes it clear that all the means by which we might communicate—names, descriptions, images, conceptual knowledge itself—are inaccurate and unstable:

> For this reason no serious man will ever think of writing about serious realities for the general public. . . . When anyone sees anywhere the written work of anyone . . . the subject treated cannot have been his most serious concern—that is, if he is himself a serious man. (344c-d)

Thus, the idea that Plato has expressed in the dialogues some extractable philosophy of rhetoric seems misguided.

However, the dialogues are provided by Plato for education and formation, not doctrine. He believes that they can, in good circumstances, lead us toward that about which we might hope to become serious. He also believes that if one forsakes argument about such matters, there is no movement at all toward what is best (344e). From the standpoint of deep rhetoric, thinking about rhetoric is a Platonic path, a way of being led, a way of moving forward, as if, in Plato's mythology, one were making an ascent. According to Plato's *Seventh Letter,* names, descriptions, images, and knowledges do not possess what they attempt to be knowledge of, but they can, when we are learning, conduct us toward what we think we want to know. This is exactly the kind of project a deep rhetoric intends to be, always seeking what it is attempting to speak about, always being shaped and formed by what it seeks, without ever quite having it in its grasp.

Plato begins to answer the question "What is rhetoric?" by exploring delineations between rhetoric and philosophy, and specifically by linking rhetoric with the sophists. Two major spokespersons for rhetoric in the dialogues of Plato are Gorgias and Protagoras, and they are both targets of Plato's critique of sophism. Plato explores many objections to the sophists as a group, but I will consider only three major charges here.[1]

First, the sophists seem to have an instrumental, commercial relationship to *logos*, to rhetoric, and to their students. They claim to possess knowledge of an art or technique—a power of some kind—and for them this is a possession that can be sold, one which they are willing to sell to young men wealthy enough to afford it. This is the view expressed by the Stranger in Plato's dialogue, the *Sophist:*

STRANGER: [The sophist's] art may be traced as a branch of the appropriative, acquisitive family . . . which hunts man, privately, for hire, taking money in exchange, having the semblance of education—and this is termed sophistry, and is the hunt after young men of wealth and rank. (223b, trans. in McComiskey 2002)

Probably the first question we should ask here is: What is wrong with this? Why is this part of a critique of sophism?[2] For us, it seems to be a natural entrepreneurship, perfectly appropriate to the changing social and political and legal conditions of fifth-century Greece. Plato's answer is that there is a profoundly ethical dimension to rhetoric, to the power of *logos,* to any relationship between a teacher of rhetoric and a student of rhetoric. The power of *logos* is, according to the Socrates of the *Phaedrus, psychagōgia,* the power of leading the soul.[3] This power is, according to the Gorgias of the *Encomium to Helen,* a power to lead one against one's will. However, for the Socrates of the *Phaedrus,* it is the power to lead the soul toward what is best, the power to lead it, through the interactivity of dialogue, in a way that works in the *logoi* arising between people, a way that Socrates calls "midwifery" at times, to emphasize its acknowledgment of and dependence on the creativity of dialogue. What is at stake in the quarrel with the sophists is whether the commercial, instrumental relationship the sophists have with their students can bear the ethical burdens of rhetoric as Socratic *psychagōgia.*

So important to Plato is the relationship between student and teacher that, in the passage from the *Sophist,* the sophist is *defined* not in terms of the "art" he teaches, which is, on the face of things, the approach Socrates takes with Gorgias and Protagoras, but he is defined instead in terms of his relationship with his students. Plato's view of the sophist's art is that its deep rhetoric operates in the ethical and ontogenetic relationships that the sophist seeks and maintains—and not its more ontic and technical aspects. Thus, it is an art of acquiring and using power over others. It is in some respects an art of hunting down young men of rank and wealth and getting their money from them. It is also referred to in the *Sophist* as an art of conquest, and the first conquest is of the students themselves, for they are said to be sold not even an education but only the semblance of one. The point is not simply that the sophists market a faulty product in a dishonest way or that they are morally worse than other people or that they are in some way bad because they make money. It is emphatically not that Plato wants to return to a previous era where aristocratic and Homeric virtues were taken for granted—after all, Socrates is for Plato the paragon educator. The point is that the most significant way in which the sophists lead the souls of their students— the most determining part of their art of *logos*—lies in the purpose and character of the communicative actions that give rise to their students as students and to themselves as sophists. In many respects, given the characterizations in the *Sophist,* Socrates himself is clearly a sophist, although not in this respect.

In articulating this critique of the sophists, Plato develops an important dimension of the idea of a deep rhetoric. Behind rhetoric's being studied, taught, and learned, a deeper rhetoric has already taken hold in the ethical comportment of teachers and students toward one another and toward *logos* itself. In their transcendence of themselves and toward one another, the ethical dimensions of acquiring, possessing, and dominating have opened up—a structured communicative transcendence that makes the sophist a sophist before he teaches anything at all.

This deep rhetoric also defines the role of the student, for the student has, so to speak, yielded to the deep rhetoric of the sophist without knowing it. He imagines that a commercial transaction is just a commercial transaction, that he is simply trading money for power, power that will allow him, too, to acquire and dominate. However, as the Socrates of the *Protagoras* warns young Hippocrates, he is also committing his soul to the sophist, and yet does not know the ethical character of the man, and does not have any idea of what he believes the sophist knows, and hardly has any notion at all of what the outcome of his education will be. Socrates' intervention in this sophistic recruitment process is to slow down or stop the students by bringing this deeper rhetoric to light.

Logos itself is also at stake in this deep rhetoric. The sophist comports himself toward *logos* itself in a particular way, and in this very comportment leads his own soul in light of the *logoi* he uses of *logos* itself. And the sophist's belief about *logos* is that it is an instrument at his disposal—that it has no end in itself but is a means subordinate to his own ends. However, these *logoi* about *logos* already lead the sophist and make him who he is. In both the *Gorgias* and the *Phaedrus,* rhetoric is examined as if it were an art of *logos,* and in both cases rhetoric conceived this way is shown to be *atelic*—that is, incomplete, or purposeless.[4] The sophist is trapped but also thrives—as a sophist—in a deep rhetoric of instrumentalism, an incoherent because *atelic* project.

Second, as instrumentalists, the sophists have no genuine loyalties, no true attachments, and so cannot be trusted. They are ethical nomads (very different from ordinary nomads), adapting to different cities and situations in just the ways they must in order to gain wealth and power. As the Socrates of the *Timaeus* puts it, "I am aware that the sophists have plenty of brave words and fair conceits, but I am afraid that being only wanderers from one city to another, and having never had habitations of their own, they may fail in their conception of philosophers and statesmen and may not know what they do and say in time of war, when they are fighting or holding parley with their enemies" (*Timaeus* 19e, McComiskey trans.).

It is important to note here that this must be not be taken in the literal sense. The sophists were travelers, but they of course had homes as well. What they did not have were true ethical habitations, dwellings in which they lived with ethical seriousness. For them, all cities were fundamentally alike, ruled by *nomos* and not *physis*. The question for them was how to adapt to and then how to use the laws and customs of the different cities to their own advantage. In our time, we might think of this ethical vagrancy on the model of professional classes who manage for mobile multinational or global corporations, who move from one place to another, and who have merely instrumental relations to nations and peoples as they pursue wealth and power. Again, Plato is not saying that such people are actually morally bad in some way that other people are not. Real people in real situations are much more complicated than characters in dialogues. However, he is asking about the appropriate kind and amount of trust one can properly place in such people when they themselves, as practicing educators, are the effects of such an ethical formation. He is asking especially whether one wants them to lead the souls of the young. He is approaching the question of rhetoric from what I am calling a deep rhetorical perspective, treating ethics not as a matter of judging specific actions as "good" or "bad," but as a reality that gives rise to someone's being one way or another at all.

Socrates seems to have a special kind of objection to this feature of the sophists, for they cannot speak aloud their true views of cities. The cities would not abide the sophists if they came and taught their best young men that the laws and customs of their cities had no special ethical status and were there to be used for personal gain. And so Socrates has his idea of fun with the sophists, getting close to exposing their implicit teachings, the ones they cannot teach in public, and he focuses his elenchus on them when he gets these teachings in view. When, in the *Republic,* Thrasymachus glimpses the strange fact that Socrates has a philosophical way to take cities seriously, he comes up with one of the best philosophical epithets ever devised. He calls the just person, who Socrates describes as being unwilling to take advantage of another just person, an "urbane innocent" (349b). For Thrasymachus, this is as much as to say: "You fool! You take ethics seriously! You believe the moral ideas of your community have some genuine moral status! You soft-headed child of a town! You have no stomach for the truths of nature! You are a weakling!" Whether one has the stomach to override ordinary moral concerns, whether one is too queasy for the work of the world, whether one is man enough to do what needs to be done to dominate others—this is a familiar challenge made to those who take Socrates' position.

The underlying difference between Plato and the sophists in this regard is that the sophist has a knowledge of how things are by nature (how they *really* are) that produces a skepticism about (the ideological formations of) ethics, law, justice, religion, and the "merely" conventional morals and practices of cities. Socrates, by contrast, is represented as professing ignorance at the level of how things really are. And he is deeply interested in the ethical ideas of cities, not as means for gaining wealth and power but as indications of a reality even deeper than conceptions of being and nature, and out of which the latter arise and take shape—a reality I am trying to think as deep rhetoric. Socrates believed that self-understanding was prior to genuinely understanding anything else. He hoped that what he called "philosophy" would enhance this self-understanding, but he also knew that philosophy was dependent for its thriving on civic life of a particular kind. As he is represented in the *Crito,* Socrates knew in the end that his own understanding of himself, as well as his practice of philosophy, was inseparable from his serious participation in the life of the city and his loyalty to its laws—which for Socrates meant hosting a vigorous debate between those laws and justice itself.

Much the same issue is addressed in the *Phaedrus* (at 229c-230a), where, when Socrates and Phaedrus are walking along the banks of the Ilissus, Phaedrus asks Socrates whether he really believes the mythic tales about Boreas and Orithyia which were supposed to have occurred there. Orithyia was a mortal princess who was said to have been abducted by a god. The wise (*hoi sophoi*), says Socrates, disbelieve, and create more naturalistic explanations for what happened. Then they set to work on a complete demythologizing project to substitute rational explanations for all the strange creations of myth. However, it would be ridiculous for he himself to undertake such a vast demythologizing task without first attempting *to know himself.* And this is the point: *we ourselves* are the ones who tell these stories, who create and sustain mythic discourse, on the one hand, and factual discourse, on the other. And we ourselves maintain the distinction between the two. Until we understand *what we are doing when we do this, and why we do it,* until we understand ourselves, what sense could it make to ask whether myth is "really" merely an elaborate distortion of underlying natural facts? We must first understand why and how we produce these discourses and make these distinctions. Until we understand our own motivations for creating and preserving and using myths, or for wanting to show that they are not factually true, how will we understand what we have done, and why, if we succeed at either belief or demythologizing? However, Socrates goes even further than this, and suggests that myth may, like dialectic, be a means (a leading-toward) of self-understanding:

I must first know myself, as the Delphian inscription says; to be curious about that which is not my concern, while I am still in ignorance of my own self, would be ridiculous. And therefore I bid farewell to all this; the common opinion is enough for me. For, as I was saying, I want to know not about this, but about myself: am I a monster more complicated and swollen with passion than the serpent Typho, or a creature of a gentler and simpler sort, to whom Nature has given a diviner and lowlier destiny? (229e-230a, Jowett trans.)

How can one know whether one is a monster unless one has monsters with which to ask the question? In this passage, and despite the pragmatic distinctions Plato seems sometimes to make between myth and *logos,* myth is itself a necessary part of *logos* in the critical sense, a means of leading the soul through well-formed questions. In fact, this may even make it a necessary part of dialectic.

The "wise," like the "sophists," know that myths are not really true. They have an entire science of reducing myth to naturalistic explanations. Myths are fictions, believed by the ignorant. However, for Socrates, the knowledge of nature the sophists believe they have cannot truly be pursued unless one first pursues self-knowledge—that is, a knowledge of how this idea of nature (*physis*) came about and how it was justified, and what motivated it. The testing the sophists undergo in Plato's dialogues is a testing of their self-knowledge.

From these two examples, we begin to see how "sophists" can justifiably be characterized as dogmatic skeptics who are not what they appear to be and why they cannot be trusted in the ordinary ways. They have a dogmatic knowledge of nature that justifies their skepticism about justice, law, goodness, religion, and myth. They are loyal in none of the senses in which common people understand and sustain their loyalties to one another, to their neighbors, to their communities. Sophists restrain their own egos and ambitions, their own desire for power and wealth, by none of the cultural means by which ordinary people do and for only a few of the same reasons. Here it must be emphasized again—so as not to be misunderstood—that these are the sophists who are characters in Plato's philosophical dialogues, where they show themselves in certain ways and not others for the purposes of clarifying ideas and choices that Plato believes are primary. Further, what is important here is that the critique is not so much a critique of rhetoric as it is a deep rhetorical critique of a way of forming oneself or being formed by others. Deep rhetorical patterns of communicative transcendence are the issue—the substance, so to speak, of both rhetoric and philosophy.

Third, as instrumentalists, the sophists could never give an account either of the ethics of rhetoric or of the senses in which it was an art or practical knowledge. These two issues are closely related. In the *Protagoras,* the discussion takes the form of a long examination of Protagoras to see whether he really knows what virtue is. Here, however, I want to begin a more focused examination of the *Gorgias,* for the *Gorgias* hinges on an understanding of the ethical dimensions of rhetoric—and highlights the impossibility of counting rhetoric as something worth teaching and learning unless one has also comprehended its ethical character.

Gorgias

The modern sympathetic reconsideration of Gorgias has been in process since at least Hegel's famous account of the progression from natural philosophy, through the sophists, to Plato and Aristotle. However, it has picked up force since the middle of the twentieth century, beginning with Mario Untersteiner's beautiful storm of a book, *The Sophists* (1954), in which Gorgias is treated at length and credited with developing the philosophical equivalent of Greek tragedy.[5] Laszlo Versényi also develops a sympathetic account of Gorgias in his book, *Socratic Humanism* (1963), which emphasizes the continuities between Gorgias and Socrates, partly by defending the educative power of the Gorgian *logos*. G. B. Kerferd offers an account of the sophists as an intellectual movement in *The Sophistic Movement* (1981), and pays special attention to Gorgias' philosophical arguments. More recently, Susan Jarratt (1991), Takis Poulakos (1995), Robert Wardy (1996), Victor Vitanza (1997), Edward Schiappa (1999), and Bruce McComiskey (2002) have all contributed to a more positive reappraisal of the contributions of the sophists in general and Gorgias in particular, although there are many significant differences among these writers.

All of this work seems to have sparked an unintended consequence: a corresponding reappraisal of Plato's view of rhetoric. The traditional view of Plato on rhetoric is that he is an implacable enemy of all things rhetorical and that philosophy is rhetoric's opposite. The *Gorgias* is often taken to be the primary site of Plato's expression of this judgment.[6] However, if the advocates of rhetoric, the sophists, are much more philosophically sophisticated than readers of Plato have usually taken them to be, then perhaps the case for rhetoric is much more powerful than readers of Plato have usually taken it to be. But even beyond that, perhaps Plato's dialogues themselves are not as dismissive of rhetoric as they have been taken to be. This is my own view, that Plato not only takes the sophists and rhetoric seriously but that he thinks of philosophy as that toward which rhetoric—intrinsically, as rhetoric—is really aiming, and that he is profoundly interested in the rhetoric of something that would be called philosophy. This kind of reappraisal is now taking place among writers on Plato's *Gorgias*. Both Marina McCoy's *Plato on the Rhetoric of Philosophers and Sophists* (2008) and Devin Stauffer's *The Unity of Plato's Gorgias* (2006) discover not only a Platonic sympathy for the project of rhetoric but also a Platonic conviction that philosophy is in important respects continuous with rhetoric.[7]

In what follows, I will explore the ways in which a deep rhetoric comes to shape in Plato's *Gorgias,* and so I will to some extent read against the apparent grain of the dialogue.[8] I will focus first and briefly on the initial exchanges between Socrates and Gorgias. I will set aside entirely the most teachable part of the dialogue on which most attention has focused when the nature of rhetoric is at issue, the famous exposition of the four parts of the counterfeit art of flattery, one of which is rhetoric. That exposition takes place in the context of the silence of Gorgias, the impatience and superficiality of Polus, and the gathering anger of Callicles. Socrates is at that point in the dialogue engaged in taming Polus, who is unruly and quick to jump to conclusions. The famous discussion of rhetoric as flattery is in part serious and in part a kind of bait for Polus. The function of that discussion in the dialogue as a whole is to ask: if flattery is a debased kind of rhetoric, then what is the better kind of rhetoric? That is a question that is indeed raised later in the dialogue. However, much of the work at uncovering this rhetoric, and at discovering the work of rhetoric at a deeper level, is carried out in more subtle ways. In what follows, I will concentrate mostly on the confrontation between Socrates and Callicles, for it is there that Plato gives us the clearest glimpses into the deep rhetorical dimensions of philosophy.

The Gorgias of the dialogue *Gorgias* is clearly the same kind of sophist characterized by the Stranger in Plato's *Sophist*—and so a recurrent type in the world of the dialogues. At the beginning, when asked to define rhetoric, Gorgias seems to speak very openly:

I say it is the power to persuade by speech jurymen in the jury-court, council-men in the Council Chamber, assemblymen in the Assembly, and in every other gathering, whatever political [or public: *politikon*] gathering there may be. And I tell you, with this power you will hold the doctor as your slave, the trainer as your slave—and this money-maker here will turn out to make money for someone else—not for himself, but for you with the power to speak and persuade the masses. (452e, Irwin trans.)

Here is conquest and domination, power over others to the point of making them slaves; here is wealth for oneself—at the expense of others. Here is also, although this is debatable, a potentially expansive conception of rhetoric in which the craft is applicable to any public gathering whatsoever. This is a far-reaching conception of rhetoric, and we shall see that it both aligns with and conflicts with the idea of a deep rhetoric. If we take this as a partially philosophically serious statement about rhetoric, and I believe that we should, then we should also recognize that it is a warrior theory of transcendence. The power of communicative transcendence is a social power that is power-over or power-against. These interrelations of violence, power, and rhetoric are without question a central concern of a deep rhetoric, and they are on full exhibit in Gorgias's definition.

Socrates lets the violence of this statement stand, and then restates a simplified Gorgian position in order to clarify it: so then, he says, the power of rhetoric is to produce persuasion in the souls of hearers—and Gorgias agrees with this restatement. Socrates then points out that just about all craftspeople know this art for they know how to persuade people about that at which they are experts—painting, shoe-making, etc. In what appears to be a casual adjustment, Gorgias clarifies his position by saying that rhetoric is the craft of producing persuasion in certain large public gatherings, for example, in juries, about the just and the unjust (454b). He further admits that rhetoric does not yield knowledge about the just and unjust but only persuasion (455a). He says that the art may be misused by base people, but he says that this misuse may not be blamed on the art or on its teachers (457a-b). In a reformulation, Gorgias says at 459a that rhetoric can make one persuasive about everything. Socrates presses Gorgias on how the rhetor will come to a knowledge about any of these things, especially about the just and unjust, if the art teaches only persuasion. In another casual adjustment, Gorgias says that if his students are ignorant of such things, then they can learn them from him. (This is the point that Callicles will refer to later, where Gorgias seems to mean by "justice" the laws of the cities and Socrates seems to mean a notion of justice that might conflict with those laws.) Then, says Socrates, just as someone who has a knowledge of a medicine is a physician who promotes health, won't his students who have knowledge of justice necessarily be just themselves (460b-e)? And won't that conflict with the earlier idea that someone trained in rhetoric could misuse the art? At this point, Gorgias's answers become increasingly qualified and brief until Polus jumps in to try to defend him.

This exchange again bears directly on the question of what rhetoric is and on the problem of elaborating the characteristics of a deep rhetoric. Gorgias's move from a general rhetoric to a rhetoric that focuses on the just and unjust is the classic move in the disciplining of rhetoric. Quite simply, one way to avoid some of the philosophical challenges of a deep rhetoric is to define rhetoric in a limited way, not as a general art of *logos,* not as a Socratic leading of the soul, and not as Isocrates does, as that which makes us human and wise, nor as the Gorgias of the *Helen* describes the general power of *logos* to overcome souls, but rather as Ricoeur says we will, as an art with a special connection to specific institutions, with a method that is appropriate to a specific institutional function—in this case, for example, in juries and other such large public gatherings, but with specific reference to speech about "things which are just and unjust." Gorgias seems to make this move casually and against his own beliefs. His tacking back and forth on this important issue, as well as on the highlighted issue of whether the rhetor has a knowledge of justice or not, is simply baffling.

It is difficult to believe that Plato's account is an attempt to deal with Gorgias's ideas seriously. Rather, the point seems to be that the character Gorgias himself is not serious about the conversation but is going along and answering Socrates just to keep the crowd pleased. It is this playing to the crowd that seems to be the point. Gorgias is simply taking the path of least resistance, making the natural dialogical adjustments to the questioning. Gorgias need not have answered this way; in fact he should have rejected some of the questions posed to him. He might have done so for any number of good Gorgian reasons. However, it is also Gorgian for him to go along. If, as Scott Consigny argues, Gorgias believes that play and competition generate truths that are warranted by victory, and that the great measure of truth and appropriateness is *kairos,* then perhaps Plato's Gorgias has guessed that, after hours of displaying his rhetoric to the crowd, and confronted with Socrates, it is better at this point to go along with common opinion in the flow of the conversation, and see where it leads. The opening of the *Gorgias* suggests that the battles are over, the passions are already spent, and the games and the competitions of rhetoric are complete, by the time Socrates (philosophy) arrives. Faced with a crowd and Socrates, after the real show is over, Gorgias is not about to begin to explain how there is, in a way, no essential difference between being persuaded of something and knowing something. That conversation would lead into deep seas where Socrates could swim forever and where Gorgias is perhaps not at his best.

Nevertheless, the Socratic questioning here allows the character Gorgias to make a remarkable statement, that rhetoric "practically captures all powers and keeps them under its control" (456a), and to give the speech in which he explains that rhetoric is a power that, like any craft, can be used for good or ill (456c-457c). The latter speech is noteworthy, too, because he uses the analogy of boxing to explain the point. Just because a great fighter *can* beat friends and relatives and enemies alike doesn't mean that he *should.* He was taught the craft of fighting to use "against enemies and those who do injustice, in defense, not in aggression."

This is not an accidental analogy.[9] The character Gorgias sees rhetoric as an essentially overpowering power, similar to violent power. Rhetoric is a fight because human relations are essentially a contest of power. The Gorgian aspires, as a kind of warrior, to be the victor, and to end up as the leader, the master of logos who says what leads to what, the one who subordinates all other powers. Socrates' strategic response to something like this is usually to work *to expose the philosophical character* of the speaker through *elenchus.* When faced with sophists, Socrates enforces a famous "Say What You Mean" rule, according to which people must give sincere answers when they are questioned, and must express their beliefs with a willingness to have them openly examined, and must be willing to change their minds if the discussion leads to that.[10] Socrates enforces the rule on Gorgias gently at 454b-c, and then in an unusual way at 457c-458b, where it is not Gorgias's beliefs about rhetoric as an art that are at stake but rather Gorgias's beliefs about what kind of man he is and what the purpose of their conversation is. Socrates insists that his effort to examine Gorgias is not an attempt simply to be victorious over him in a battle of speeches. He insists that he himself values being refuted in such an examination because then he learns and changes for the better. He wants to know whether Gorgias considers himself this kind of man and also holds this belief about dialogical testing.

Of course, Gorgias is not this kind of person at all, and he holds nothing like this belief about dialogue. However, he cannot say this aloud before a large group. He has already been teased by Socrates about the fact that their conversation together is an opportunity for Gorgias to recruit students from the crowd (455c-d). Socrates knows very well that Gorgias cannot really say what he believes here. In these contexts, Plato is putting the character of Socrates (and so philosophy, and so a certain kind of ethics) up against the character of his sophistic interlocutors (and so sophistic skeptical dogma and the sophistic ethic that both generates and issues from it). There is, for Plato's Socrates, an inseparable unity of the philosophical, psychological, and ethical dimensions of the sophist. They all interact to sustain the sophist as sophist. In this, philosophers and sophists are alike. Their struggle takes place at a deep rhetorical level, where their very identities are at stake. The question is the kind of human being each one is, and this is determined by the way one realizes one's existence in *logos*—whether one comports oneself in and toward it as an instrument of domination or whether one comports oneself in and toward *logos* as something whose most significant power is to lead the soul, in this case, through acquiring self-knowledge by learning that the *logoi* by which one has been conducting oneself are not as fit as one has thought.

In this short exchange, we find complex ways of envisioning rhetoric as transcendence. On the one hand, Gorgias believes—and says—that rhetoric is essentially aimed at conquest. However, rhetoric seems to be pacified and turned into its opposite here, when Gorgias adapts to the situation and says that he would just as soon be refuted as refute, something that is essentially untrue for him, but whose statement is an apparently necessary step toward what he hopes will be an eventual victory—or at least a draw. He realizes that he is in a bind, and so he says that the bystanders are probably tired and don't really want to stay and listen, but they all adamantly deny it. On the other hand, Socrates says that he also would just as soon be refuted as refute, and yet uses this little speech to set the hook in Gorgias so that he can reel him in through the final elenchus. The violence looks like inquiry and the inquiry looks like violence.

This difficulty in knowing what is violence and what is not, what is an attempt to overpower and what is not, indicates an intractable instability in any rhetorical theory of transcendence. Violence and nonviolence seem to be implicated in one another in a way that is very difficult to clarify. This will become evident again in the exchange with Callicles. If the philosophical, psychological, ethical, and communicative dimensions of human transcendence are all implicated in one another, then the *agon* and the testing will go on in all these dimensions in ways that will be difficult to untangle. Testing and refuting abstract ideas and definitions are one thing; testing someone's character is something else, and can generate discursive maneuvering that looks much more like boxing than conversation.

Socrates completes the superficial exposure of Gorgias fairly quickly by showing that Gorgias has said both that rhetoric might be used justly or unjustly *and* that rhetoric can be practiced only by the just, that the rhetor would never do injustice. At this point, Polus jumps in to rescue Gorgias, and Gorgias is pretty much silent for the rest of the dialogue.

Gorgias/Callicles

Gorgias does, however, make a kind of veiled appearance later in the dialogue as Callicles, who speaks for Gorgias, defending him against what he can comprehend only as the shame of defeat by Socrates. However, if the character of Gorgias is a highly stylized and altered version of the actual writer of *Helen, Palamedes,* and *On Not-being,* then Callicles is an at least equally stylized and altered version of that character. More specifically, while the character Gorgias prefers a context for competitive display and refuses to overexpose himself in dialogue, Callicles jumps right into extensive dialogue with Socrates, as if he could use triumphant displays to overpower Socrates even while undergoing Socratic questioning. Even the character Gorgias is more Gorgian and circumspect than that. Further, Callicles seems to have no sense of Gorgian *kairos*. He preaches the dogmas of Gorgian skepticism with little regard for the occasion and audience. Perhaps Gorgias himself would implicitly *perform* these dogmas—in which case their dogmatic character would be relatively inaccessible. The character Gorgias, even if he held these dogmas implicitly, would know that this was no occasion for expressing them openly as assertions. However, Callicles lacks strategic Gorgian restraint, and this permits Plato to explore the Gorgian idea of rhetoric more thoroughly than he ever could with Gorgias.

In a speech beginning at 482c, Callicles explodes with an expression of the very skeptical dogmatism to which Socrates believes Gorgias adheres but which he does not openly express. One of its articles is: there is an essential difference between what is of value according to human custom, convention, law, and ethics, or in general value that is socially generated (*nomos*), and what is of value according to nature (*physis*). According to nature, it is better to do injustice to others than to suffer injustice. According to *nomos*, it is better to suffer injustice. But the rule of *nomos*, says Callicles, is a slave morality, a morality for the weak. Callicles is explicit about his proto-Nietzschean vision of ethics:

In my view those who lay down the [conventional] rules are the weak men, the many. And so they lay down the rules and assign their praise and blame with their eye on themselves and their own advantage. They terrorize the stronger men capable of having more; and to prevent these men from having more than themselves they say that taking more is shameful and unjust, and that doing injustice is this, seeking to have more than other people; they are satisfied, I take it, if they themselves have an equal share when they're inferior. That's why by rule this is said to be unjust and shameful, to seek to have more than the many, and they call that doing injustice. (483b-c, Irwin trans.)

Power is natural justice, and the best are those who are strongest. However, cities "tame" the strong by "spells and incantations," and so "enslave" them. The truly strong, though, will defy all the "writings, charms, incantations, all the rules contrary to nature." And then, says Callicles, "the justice of nature suddenly bursts into light" (484a-b).

Socrates does not ask Callicles whether the distinction between *physis* and *nomos* is a natural distinction or just a distinction by convention. Instead, he is silent while Callicles goes on to denounce the weakness and powerlessness of philosophy compared with the strength and power of rhetoric. Of course, Socrates believes that the power of this Gorgian rhetoric lies in flattery and conformity and so in slavery. The contrast could not be more sharply drawn. The difficulty Callicles faces here is that he has said a little too much. He is no longer speaking in a way that is likely to be attractive to any community. His skeptical view of law and ethics, and his equating of power and justice, are not exactly the principles on which democratic or monarchic communities sustain themselves. And the skepticism that comes from his radical distinction between *physis* and *nomos*, when expressed openly, will undermine his ability to speak of ethics and law in assemblies and in judicial settings. No one will take him seriously. And so, at the conclusion of his speech, Socrates praises Callicles for his knowledge (far more than Socrates possesses), for his goodwill (in his advising Socrates not to become too wise), and for speaking freely (for saying openly what Gorgias and Polus would not).

The character Gorgias would not be drawn into this discussion. He knew that it was not the appropriate time or occasion to debate Socrates. He recognized the limitations offered by the circumstances. Besides, any believable Gorgias, when he spoke seriously about these "philosophical" issues, would engage in performative ironies that would tend to expose, at least for the initiated elite, the impossibility of Socratic discourse. He would play on the multiplicity of meanings without ever stopping to be held accountable for his meaning, for taking responsibility for meaning one thing rather than another, or at least trying to. Plato's maneuver here is to withhold from Gorgias the opportunity to speak at length, the opportunity to take power, to display the elite sophistication that would delight the dogmatic skeptics in his audience. Instead, he is led down the difficult pathways of dialogue with Socrates. Gorgias would go only so far down this path. At the appropriate time, he quits the dialogue, as any good Gorgias would.

Callicles does not. Not only does he violate the principle of Gorgian *kairos* by continuing the dialogue, he also violates by speaking openly the doctrines of dogmatic skepticism at the wrong time and in the wrong place—an occasion Socrates has already identified as a recruitment party. Socrates then sets out on his next elenchus.

A Failure of Transcendence: Rhetoric and Narcissism

Callicles is thrown off balance by his own outburst of openness. On the one hand, he knows that he should not say what he really believes and on the other he cannot help saying it when no one else will because he seems to believe that it is true—and because he cannot lose a fight. He is in a bind. What is being exposed here is not simply the inadequate rhetoric of Gorgias but the inability of any Gorgian to transcend himself toward the other in a true meeting and conflict of *logoi,* a matter of deep rhetoric. The only conflict the Gorgian knows is conflict aimed at domination and gratification. When these aims cannot be achieved, the Gorgian withdraws. He has nothing to learn in *logos.* He is in possession of what he takes to be a deeper comprehension of things than open discussion would allow—and so he cannot test his beliefs. He cannot grow. He cannot learn. He cannot change, except in his own private reflections about what he has lost and how he might dominate better in the next go-round. Socrates' remarks about the different attitudes people have toward argumentation are simple but serious. Gorgian transcendence is power and domination over the other, domination by a self that cannot be questioned by any other, that need not justify itself to the weak.

This incapacity for conflict is implicitly represented as a failure of transcendence, a failure of ethics, a triumph of violence over the freedom of transcendence found in dialogue. Socrates' real charge against Gorgian rhetoric is that *it does not go deep enough.* The Gorgian individual, and the elite Gorgian clique, already have a kind of knowledge that is invulnerable to rhetoric, inaccessible to communicative exploration and treatment. It is a privileged gnosis, and it is not clear how it is come by, or what the source of its authority is, and yet it forms their ethical identities. Socrates will have none of it. His own view is that *communication goes all the way down,* that the unexamined dogma deserves communicative examination, that *logos* leads the soul. He is challenging the Gorgians among us, or in us, to go all the way to a deep rhetoric.

One way of reading the elenchus Socrates executes on Callicles is that it comes down to a *reductio* of the Calliclean ideal of power's being justice. Those who believe this, Socrates shows, are incapable of community (*koinōnia*) and friendship (*philia*) (507e). Their associations are instrumental; others are only a means for the exercise of power. Since no one believes only this, we might read the dialogue to say that to the degree that one sees things this way, or in the times and circumstances that one does, one is incapable of community and friendship. This is deep rhetorical narcissism, in which self-gratification short-circuits the transcendence that rhetoric makes possible. At the level of a deep rhetoric, everything important about communication—and the knowledge and decisions and the perceptions and the ways of life that flow out of it—is cast in a particular way by *the kind of transcendence* at play in the communication. If the desire for power takes hold in a more or less fundamental way, everything will be shaped by that. Socrates' interlocutors in a Platonic dialogue are usually stamped by far simpler kinds of transcendence than the transcendence shaped by the complex personalities of real people. However, from the standpoint of a deep rhetoric, this complexity does not undermine the idea that transcendence is communicative and has an ineluctably ethical dimension.

Deep Rhetorical *Nomos* and the Care of the Soul

What is not often recognized about the *Gorgias* is that it ends in high praise of rhetoric and myth, refusing to find in them any essential distinction from what Socrates elsewhere calls philosophy and here calls simply *logos*. The gathering of this large conception of *logos* that corresponds to a deep rhetoric occurs near the end of the dialogue, in a kind of eschatological avalanche of Platonic rhetoric that comes crashing down on Callicles and culminates in a myth/*logos* about what happens to our souls after death. However, to come to that point, Socrates must first lead Callicles through some difficult *logoi*.

At 504c, Socrates begins to guide Callicles into a discussion of the health of the soul that overthrows the sophistic conception of *nomos* and creates a new one. Just as the body has a state of health and a state of being unhealthy, so does the soul. The soul's health, like the body's, lies in a certain kind of harmony, pattern, or order. However, the health of the soul is not a "physical" state. The harmonies or patterns, or whatever we call those energies that sustain the health of the soul, come from a life in which the soul is in accord with something beyond itself—in short, the soul's health is found only in the ethical accords of community, in *nomos*, not in *physis* (504d). Callicles takes the sphere of *nomos* to be made up of conflicting sets of merely conventional social norms. The intelligent and powerful see through them, know that they are groundless—that they have no reality in nature—and take up an instrumental relation to them. Socrates seems to hold that the soul's very health depends on not taking up this kind of a relation to ethical principles, but instead on giving up one's position at the center of things, giving up one's making use of them to increase one's power and satisfy one's desires, and on letting ethics take a kind of power over one's soul, letting ethics lead even when it comes to one's transcendence toward oneself. Socrates agrees that *nomos* is not grounded in *physis*. In this, he is as "sophisticated" as Callicles. However, he does not seem to believe that such a grounding is necessary for ethics to have a kind of authority, and in this he is quite different from Callicles—and his modern followers, who often seem to believe that the form of ideological critique that denaturalizes somehow at the same time de-authorizes.

Gorgian sophistry focuses on *nomos* only as the specific content of custom, ethics, and law—the culturally variable and often self-contradictory codes by which communities order themselves. However, at a deeper level, it is not the specific content of customs and laws that makes *nomos* what it is, but rather the fact that *nomos* is a kind of accord, an achieving of peace and health in the social body. Further, what is important for the deep rhetoric Socrates is striving toward is not just the accord itself but rather how seriously people take that accord. If one believes that every accord is nothing more than the outcome of a pure struggle for power, then not only is the possibility of social change radically curtailed, but social goods such as friendship and community are made to look like simple covers for efforts to gain power. For dogmatic skepticism, there is no meaningful reflection on power that questions whether there is something better to live for than power. For Socrates, the accords of social life make possible philosophy itself, the pursuit of beauty and justice, the opening up of the freedom of the argument between law and justice, the vision of a good that is not power but which is in fact occluded by its single-minded pursuit. The *con*venings of social life, the *com*munion of *nomos*, can be deformed into means of forcing an old philosopher to swallow poison. However, they are also the habitat of philosophy, the advent of a sense of something more real than the objectified nature of the dogmatic skeptics.

Two Kinds of Rhetoric: A Deep Rhetorical Critique

It is just before this discussion, and as a way of introducing this revolutionary move, that Socrates begins to speak of the possibility of two different kinds of rhetoric. This idea was already common in Athenian speech, and it was made by rhetors themselves to distinguish between the public-minded oratory of former times and the more decadent speech that followed (Irwin, in Plato 1980, 212–13). However, Socrates makes the cut in a different way:

If there are really two types here, I presume one type is flattery, and shameful public oratory, while the other is fine—trying to make the souls of the citizens as good as possible, and working hard in saying what is best, whether it is pleasant or unpleasant to the audience. (503a-b, Irwin trans.)

The question Socrates treats in the section on *nomos* is whether the fine type of rhetoric really exists. Callicles cannot produce any convincing examples of speechmakers who exemplified this type of rhetoric. So Socrates goes forward by reasoning about what it must be like. Socrates begins by asking, "The good man who speaks with a view to the best, surely he won't speak at random, but will look to something?" (503d-e). He looks, as we know, to the health of the soul, which is said to lie in what we might call its ethical pattern, in its harmony and order, its accords, in *nomos*. This in itself is also Socrates' offering of a deep rhetoric: the difference between "shameful" and "fine" rhetoric, or as he also divides them, between "flattering" rhetoric and the "good" kind, is an ethical effect, an effect of different kinds of transcendence. And the ethics that is developed in the discussion that follows is a version of the complicated and surprising Socratic ethic that appears in different forms throughout Plato's dialogues. It receives a really very funny elaboration in the last part of the *Gorgias,* and to comprehend it requires experiencing the humor with which it is developed (since the humor depends on the success of a number of different kind of reductios). However I will try to give a relatively sober summary of it here.

First, however, it is critical to recognize that the issue is not simply that Callicles is an unreconstructed "individualist" while Socrates is a simple apologist for a social self and conformity to social norms. Rather, Callicles is more an "egoist" whose social relations are exhausted in instrumental power relations to other people. This generates the irony that Socrates keeps pointing out, that Callicles is in fact hardly an individual at all, but a "slave" who must conform, who lives in fear of being overpowered by others, who must gratify their desires to preserve his power over them. Socrates, on the other hand, who acknowledges the creative power of *nomos* to guide individuals, is the one who is the individual, who is fearless before the ones Callicles must flatter. Individuality depends on a culture whose guiding ideas allow for and help to develop independence of mind, which in turn subsists only in the cultural matrix that supports it. And this leads us to restraint.

The Ethical Ontology of Deep Rhetorical Decorum

A great deal of the *Gorgias* hinges on the distinction between restraint and lack of restraint, especially toward the end of the dialogue. The soul that lacks restraint (the person who is an *akolastos*) is untrained, unpruned, unchecked. Callicles has already glorified this as a high virtue. Souls that lack restraint (restraint demanded by *nomos* and its social accords) belong to those who act out a natural justice, using others as means to gratify their own desires. To this kind of soul, Socrates contrasts the opposite kind, the soul of the self-restrained person, a "temperate soul" (*"sōphrōn psyche"* 507a). Plato plays on the associations of these words. *Sōphrōn* suggests not only restraint and moderation but also soundness of mind. The opposite of this is of course unsoundness of mind. If one is unrestrained (an *akolastos*), then this may call for correction (*kolazein*), restraint.

However, before we can go further with this, it is necessary to see what restraint is good for. And it comes to this:

> And now the temperate man would do fitting [*prosēkonta*] things toward both gods and men. For surely he wouldn't be acting temperately if he did unfitting things. . . . Now by fitting things towards men he would be doing just things, and by doing them toward gods, he would do pious things. (507a-b, Irwin trans.)

This is a remarkable little passage because it contains one of the guiding concepts of the rhetorical tradition—the notion of the fitting.[11] If one is restrained, then one is not simply in a negative state, a state of restraining one's desires and a state of not using other people as a means for one's own gratification. Instead, *restraint lets something happen that would not otherwise take place;* it allows for a different kind of comportment—one that in some way "fits" the situation. *Prosōkonta* means: appropriate, fitting, proper, meet. In other contexts, it also means "that which belongs," and when used of persons, it means "akin." It can also mean what is "fit" in the sense of one's duties. The word and its extended meanings come from the verb *prosōko,* whose more literal meaning is: to have come to, to have arrived at (a place), to be at hand, to be present.

The word is clearly related to the rhetorical idea of decorum, the idea that one's speech should fit the occasion. As it is used here, though, it is almost a counter-concept to Gorgian *kairos,* which has been exposed in the dialogue as an instrumental use of language to gain victory and power by conforming to the desires of the audience, a "fitting" of one's desire for power to the audience's desire for pleasure. The Socratic idea, by contrast, is that when one no longer allows one's unrestrained desires to dominate and order discourse, then—and only then—is it possible for another ordering idea to arrive, to come to presence. This is the idea of a kind of belonging, one more like being kin, a social event whose order is analogous to health in the body. It is not domination through the power of *logos,* but rather restraint, and it produces justice, a dimension of peace, the accord that can come to be when the sophisticated do not dismiss *nomos* so quickly.

And there is still another level to this. There is an ontological event of the kairotic arrival of something that belongs. The idea of being as a kind of belonging is exactly the kind of non-reifying approach to being that Heidegger was seeking in the essays collected in *Poetry, Language, Thought,* beginning with the "addendum" to the "Origin of the Work of Art" and perhaps most clearly expressed in the essay "Language." There he used the words *ereignen* ("to take place," but also to "enown" or "make to belong") and *Das Ereignis* ("occurrence" but also "enownment" or event of belonging) in place of *sein* ("to be") and *wesen* ("essence" but also "to be present"). The general idea in "Language" is that each of the fourfold of earth, sky, mortals, and divinities receives its being only by belonging to the others. In their mutual belonging, each receives its occurrence as what it is in this more general occurrence (*Ereignis*) of belonging.[12] Heidegger is here on the verge of a Levinasian conversion, but he seems not to be able to escape the domination of the tradition of ontology. *Das Ereignis* is still grasped in terms of its ontological function, even though the way in which it is supposed to be an alternative to the dominion of technology and instrumentalism is fairly explicit. In any case, the point is that Plato is playing in these ontological fields—but in a manner in which the ethics of what comes to be is directly before our eyes and prepares for an event of arrival, for something's being given. And the discussion centers on a distinction between "two types" of rhetoric and the idea of what is fitting. The "fine" kind of rhetoric concerns itself with what is ethically fitting not simply in the sense of adapting to the audience and occasion but in this sense of allowing something to begin to arrive by conducting oneself and one's speech in the proper way, something that otherwise would not begin to arrive.

Perhaps now it can be seen just why the "unrestrained" soul must learn restraint. The Gorgian economy of desire and domination glorifies the unrestrained soul and allows no room for the appearance of the fitting, or of justice, as anything more than someone else's power-ploy. Socratic restraint is not restraint-for-the-sake-of-restraint, but is restraint for the sake of something that can come to pass only in the deep rhetorical space and time opened up by restraint. The education of the soul is both a learning of restraint and a learning of what begins to be given in the clearing opened up by restraint. Ethics gives being—not the being of the beings that can be dominated by speech, but the coming to be of a restrained way of transcendence that in a fitting way gives place to the transcendence of others in dialogue.

This brings to light still another issue, the issue of "correction" or "tempering" or "punishment." If education requires self-restraint, how does one teach someone else self-restraint? What are the hopes of educating sophists? In one respect, the entire dialogue is an example of such tempering. Gorgias, then Polus, and then Callicles all undergo tempering of a sort. This becomes explicit at times, especially at 505b, where Callicles refuses to go on with the dialogue and tells Socrates to question someone else. Socrates responds: "This man won't abide being helped and tempered, and himself undergoing the very thing our discussion is about—being tempered" (505c). The idea is that philosophical dialogue of the Socratic kind *can* help to temper someone but that such tempering can also be refused.

This is no small problem in Plato. In the Allegory of the Cave, at *Republic* 7, the prisoners' lack of restraint in gratification is paradoxically figured by the irons they wear, irons that keep them fixed on the shadowy images they take to be reality. In the allegory, they can be freed only by violence. They must be *forcibly turned around,* turned away from the images that give them pleasure and their only sense of reality, to face the fact that there is something else that can come to pass, something else that can come to be. In the *Gorgias,* where a lack of restraint is also figured as a lack of freedom, a kind of slavery, the threat of violence is on all sides. On the one side, Gorgian rhetoric is openly violent in its forcing of the rhetor's ways on others. On the other side, Socratic education seems to require force, tempering, correction, a violent "turning" of the prisoner. Socratic education, however focused on the individual soul, and on midwifery, is also experienced as coming from without with a kind of force. This troubling persistence of rhetorical violence appears to be intractable. The crux seems to be the relation of the different kinds of violence and nonviolence to the different kinds of justice and peace to which they lead, although this can in no way be a simple causal or means/end relation. Socrates leads as well as he can by dialogue, but at the end of the *Gorgias* he departs from the dialectic of question and answer to engage in an extended *logos/mythos,* which seems to bring together persuasion, myth, *logos,* rhetoric, philosophy, *kolazein,* and *psychagōgia* in a mind-boggling way.

Logos

So let us move toward the conclusion of this discussion of the *Gorgias* with some attention to the way Plato concludes the dialogue. One of the Platonic criticisms of the sophists is that they are demythologizers who have no real comprehension of the work of myth. In highlighting the unity of myth and reason, *mythos* and *logos,* Socrates expresses the universality of deep rhetoric. The event of truth can occur in myth when myths are related in a *fitting* manner. At 522e-523a, Socrates tells Callicles that, if he likes, he will give him a rational account (*logos*) of the fate of the soul after death. "I suppose you'll think it's myth," he says, "but I think it's a reasonable account (*logos*); for I tell you what I'm about to tell you in the belief that it's true" (Nichols trans). Socrates then offers a lively, image-rich story about how after death the soul receives its fitting recompense—ethics gives being—for the life it has led. Socrates does not hesitate to draw direct implications from the story for how one should live. In fact, this is how the dialogue ends. The event of truth, the leading and educating of the soul in such a way that "justice and the rest of virtue" can begin to come to pass—the *dynamis* of *logos*—is all about this. And these events occur not in a narrow kind of dialectical logic but in the storying of myth, too. A deeper rhetoric will notice these dynamics, and will, according to the Socratic view, learn to use them in a way that aligns with a good that both comes to light in the sphere of *nomos* and also comes to be recognized as more real or even more "natural" than the domain of sophistic *physis*.

Whether one turns toward Socratic justice or toward Gorgian ironies is not the issue here. The issue is that the controversy over rhetoric that is played out in the *Gorgias* is not at all a controversy over rhetoric in some limited or disciplinary sense. It is a controversy over *logos* itself, with everything that means for the way we think of rhetoric. Just as in the *Phaedrus,* where Socrates imagines that the work of a complete rhetoric would be equivalent to the work of dialectic and would be the art of leading the soul, so in the *Gorgias,* in the idea of the "good" kind of rhetoric, the kind that is not simply conformity to the audience's need to be gratified, rhetoric also takes the philosophical path. Plato's *logos* of there being no final, absolute distinction between rhetoric and philosophy is a refusal to discipline either rhetoric or philosophy. Neither has a circumscribed domain of entities all its own or a specific method of treating them which would establish its authority as a separate discipline. Instead, there lies in *logos* itself a specific power, and both rhetoric and philosophy are attempts to find ways to live and act in that power, a power in which we are always deeply implicated and by which we are always being led, and which we can never completely objectify.

The Gorgian notion of *logos* is not easy to come by. Scott Consigny says that Gorgias has a negative theory of *logos*—he shows that the common theories lead to contradictions, especially in the case of *On Not Being*—but not a positive one. Yet, says Consigny, a positive theory can be gleaned by looking at his extant writings as a whole, and primarily the *Epitaphios, Helen, Palamedes,* and some of the aphorisms (Consigny 2001, 73). First, according to Consigny, for Gorgias, *logos* is the sphere of the agon, the realm of competitive struggle. This is a very specific kind of *agon;* it is (and here Consigny relies on Nietzsche) a "personal fight" (74). The goal is to demolish opponents, succeed in battles, win wars. Second, all *logos,* all language, is action, and all action is language. The primary Gorgian actions are actions of force—in *Helen,* rape, violence, druggings, but also images of competitive play, such as wrestling, are also frequent. Third, words acquire their meaning from the roles they play in the various agons or games (80). Fourth, inquiry and knowledge begin not in wonder but in social conflict and a struggle for dominance. Knowledge is thoroughly socially constructed in the sense of being entirely immanent; there is nothing "beyond" the agon and its struggles for power (83–84). Fifth, rhetoric is the art of fighting it out in the sphere of *logos,* with the goal, quite literally, of becoming the master of (the power of) *logos* (86). Truth is the result of victory in the fight. The victor wins the endorsement of his *logos.* It is then rewarded by the public with the adornment of "truth," a kind of trophy, the fairest "ornament" of *logos* (89). This is quite an impressive positive account to be given for someone who is said to have only a negative theory of *logos.*

Neither is the Platonic idea of *logos* easy to discover. Plato certainly represents *logos* at least in part as the sphere of the *agon,* but the agonistic struggle in Plato is not only with others but is also with ourselves, as the discussion of restraint with Callicles shows, as the allegory of the cave displays, and as the myth of the chariot and horses in the *Phaedrus* portrays. In addition, the struggle is not simply a personal fight aimed at victory over the other. It is a struggle with one another but for the sake of something else. It has all the dimensions of a personal fight—and can sometimes be much more personal than a mere fight for dominance—but it is focused so little on simple victory that Socrates says it is better to lose an argument than win one because only in that way does one learn and change, and so move along the path on which *logos* can lead the soul toward what is best. For the Plato of the *Republic* and the *Symposium,* there is certainly a wonder and longing that is personally experienced, and which generates the desire for knowledge, but it is also the case that for Plato the desire for knowledge finds its best expression in the agonistic dialectic, or the "complete" or "fine" rhetoric that is sometimes exemplified in the very agonistic Platonic dialogues. So, even in Plato, rhetoric and philosophy are partly the art of struggle and agonistic competition, but they are more essentially the art that corresponds to the *dynamis* of *logos*, the power of leading the soul, by which Socrates pursues his vocation of caring for the soul. And in Plato this is at least in part a power to which one must yield and not simply a power that one attempts to master and use for oneself. One "leads" the souls of others in much more subtle and restrained ways than that. When Socrates could easily dispatch of young Theaetetus in Plato's dialogue of that name, when he could conquer him in a philosophical-rhetorical victory, he instead restrains himself from pursuing a particular line of questioning. He believes that the experience of being defeated in *logos* too often while one is young can lead to a mistrust and hatred of *logos* itself. Much more is at stake than simply Socrates' power and victorious domination, his mastery of *logos*.

And yet despite these differences, and despite Gorgias's uncharacteristic demurral early in the dialogue, both Gorgias and Plato seem to have ideas of *logos* that are vast, and ideas of rhetoric that correspond to this vast idea. They both work with the notion that there is in some sense one art of *logos*, a philosophy/rhetoric that aligns with and uses or follows the power that is in *logos* itself. Since this orientation moves against a background idea of *logos* that includes not only language and reason and speech but also the intelligibility of things themselves, this opens up an unlimited scope for rhetoric.

A deep rhetoric is attuned to this kind of context, and so draws from a dimension of Plato that is too often eclipsed by the lively eristics and dramas of Socrates' arguments with the sophists and all the funny and exaggerated ways rhetoric is portrayed when Socrates is trying to provoke his interlocutors and expose what they would rather keep hidden. It is time for Plato to be read more charitably and carefully, without all the presuppositions that have attached themselves to his name. It is also time for rhetoric to take a new shape for us now, in part as deep rhetoric, so that the resources of the tradition and its recent renewal can be more thoroughly understood, and so that the human capacities and possibilities it carries can be more widely developed.

FOUR

Rhetoric and Violence

From its mythic origins to its resurgence in the late twentieth century, rhetoric has always formed itself in an intimate relation with violence. On the one hand, rhetoric's origin is in its difference from violence, its renunciation of it, its being an alternative to violence, its providing a discursive means to resolve conflicts that would otherwise become violent. Rhetoric is the great other to violence. On the other hand, rhetoric has been widely suspected as being mostly nothing other than violence and domination and trickery disguised, violence masquerading as reason and language, but every bit as coercive and domineering as an armed interlocutor. In some contemporary thinking, language itself is a permanent host of this violence, and so rhetoric cannot help but be the deployment of it. The relation is intimate because rhetoric is defined as the other to violence, because it is suspected of harboring violence, and then also because, even in its defining itself as nonviolence, it claims to be able to accomplish exactly what violence accomplishes. It claims to be able to make language a means of conflict, a medium in which differences can be expressed and in which they can vie with one another, contest with each other, struggle with each other, and in which they can finally defeat each other or in some other way settle accounts. This is the promise of reason—to settle conflicts without violence, to settle them through reasoning that properly appreciates and evaluates the different perspectives that have come into conflict. Traditionally, rhetoric has been studied and taught as the art that can fulfill this promise. But in order to be an alternative to violence, rhetoric must in some way resemble it.

A great deal is at stake in understanding the complexities of the relation of rhetoric and violence. To oversimplify what is involved here would be disastrous on many levels. To distinguish rhetoric and violence in an absolute way would be to shut one's eyes and ears to the testimony of Walter Benjamin, Emmanuel Levinas, Jacques Derrida, Michel Foucault and others that there is a violence in language and sociality that cannot be fully eradicated without eradicating language and sociality themselves. It would be to designate some specific rhetoric as a discourse beyond reproach or criticism, to be in principle blind to whatever coercion or violence it might harbor. Such an oversimplification, which simply defines rhetorical reasoning as nonviolence, might falsely claim to be able to ground a social and political program in which a final discursive solution had been reached, one which could be institutionalized universally in rules and procedures of discourse, and which would be beyond violence.

However, to destabilize or erase the distinction would be no less disastrous. To deny the differences between real physical violence and the contest of ideas in language would be not only madness but also a kind of evil. To deny the difference between consent and coercion would be both to legitimate violence and to make the defense of the violated impossible. Without significant and practicable ways to distinguish rhetoric from violence, violence simply holds sway. Hannah Arendt wrote valiantly in this vein, distinguished sharply between power and violence, and strongly promoted a public, agonistic rhetoric, as well as a kind of thinking that was an inner performance of it, as a way of fighting back the violence.[1] The struggle to reduce violence depends on being able to know the difference between violence and rhetoric. It has long been known that skepticism generates violence as readily as dogmatism and fanaticism do.

In what follows, I will offer an interpretation of the project of rhetoric in the light of the arguments that have been made that rhetoric is indistinguishable from violence. As a focus for this effort, I will pay special attention to some of the main lines of argument of Chaim Perelman and Lucie Olbrechts-Tyteca's The New Rhetoric: A Treatise on Argumentation. The New Rhetoric stands very clearly on the side of those who emphasize the possibility of making meaningful distinctions between rhetoric and violence. However, by pursuing this effort in the light of recent arguments that call the distinction into question, that make the distinction more difficult to make, I intend to offer more than a simple defense of rhetoric. Instead, I intend to provide an interpretation of rhetoric that will hold open the difference between rhetoric and violence and yet not in such a way that rhetoric is ever purified of violence. Instead, I want to hold the difference open in such a way that rhetorical theory and practice are always exposed to the critique of violence and yet never undone simply by this exposure. On the contrary, this exposure allows rhetoric a certain kind of transcendence of itself, an experience of the intimate partner who dwells in proximity to it—that is, an experience of violence, but an experience that neither undermines its claims to be different from violence nor defeats the whole-heartedness with which it pursues the struggle against violence. The movement will be toward a suffering rhetoric, a rhetoric capable of suffering, but capable too of whatever wisdom and strength attend suffering in the best of circumstances. Although in cases of actual human suffering those circumstances are often beyond our understanding or our actions, the circumstances in which we think through the relation of rhetoric and violence are much more amenable to our attention.

This will require more than an exploration of rhetoric as an art or practice. It will require a push toward a deep rhetoric that explores the ontological and ethical dimensions of the rhetorical formations of individuals and societies.

The Rhetorical Origin of Human Sociality: The Great Myth of Protagoras

It is always a good idea to start with a story. As a way of beginning this effort at a deep rhetorical understanding of the relation between rhetoric and violence, here is a story about the origin of rhetoric.

Early in Plato's *Protagoras*, the great sophist is given to offer a story about how human societies could not come into being without the help of rhetoric. The story is wonderful and complex and full of violence and nonviolence. The story begins at a time when there were gods but no mortals. The gods shaped creatures from earth and fire and charged Epimetheus and Prometheus with giving them the powers they would need to survive. So, Epimetheus distributed to these creatures strength, speed, wings, size, fur, thick hides, and so on, in such a way that each kind could survive in the right relation to the others. However, when it came time to give powers to human beings, he had already given them all away. Human beings were left unclothed, unprotected, unarmed, without any powers whatsoever. To save human beings, Prometheus stole divine practical scientific skills from Hephaestus and Athena, as well as fire, and gave them to human beings. And so human beings used these powers to invent and to protect and sustain themselves. And because the powers they had were divine, they also began to believe in gods and to worship.

However, human beings still could not resolve their conflicts or cooperate well enough to live together in cities. As a result, they were scattered. And although they were skilled enough to survive, they were still often prey to wild beasts because they could not organize against them. The reason Protagoras gives for this failure is that, although they had scientific skill and so a limited power over nature, they did not have political skills or power over themselves. When they tried to form cities, they ended up committing injustice against one another, and had no way to resolve their conflicts. And here Protagoras comes to the center of his origin story: "Whereupon Zeus, being afraid concerning our kind, that it might perish utterly, sent Hermes unto mankind with justice (*dikē*) and a sense of shame (*aidōs*), to bring order to their cities and common bonds of amity" (322c). Zeus also tells Hermes not to distribute them unevenly, the way the scientific skills were, but instead:

Let all have them in common. For there could be no cities if but a few had them, as it is with the other skills. And lay down this law from me: if any man be not able to share justice and a sense of shame even as other men do, they must kill him as a pestilence to the city. (322d, Hubbard and Karnofsky trans.)

The mutual advent of human political society and rhetoric lie in a sense of justice and a sense of shame and in their use to resolve conflicts discursively.

However, there is violence along all the borders of this civil peace, the borders of rhetoric. To start with the temporal border, or the border between history and prehistory: before rhetoric, violence rules. There is no peace anywhere. This appears to be the fault of a god who cannot think ahead, cannot think into a truly human time, and so sacrifices human beings to the time of animals, but this is not quite wholly true. If Epimetheus had distributed natural powers more evenly, more thoughtfully, human beings would simply be a part of a deeper ecology of violence, without peace of any kind, engaged in a well-balanced standoff with wild animals and natural forces. Instead, we have here the kind of failure whose addressing forecasts a future that is radically different from the prehistorical time that would have reigned if Epimetheus had been successful. So the first border is the one between a monolithically violent prehistory and a history in which a struggle between violence and peace becomes possible.

However, this border is at the same time the bloody border that marks the front between human beings and wild predators. Protagoras says explicitly that the original human beings could not war against wild beasts because the skill of warfare is itself a political art. One cannot organize people for warfare against predators if one cannot resolve the conflicts among the people themselves. However, once people have rhetoric, a political discourse in which conflicts can be experienced and addressed nonviolently, then they can launch warfare against wild animals. So if the first consequence of rhetoric is peace among people, the second consequence is war against the animals, the nonhuman, those who have no human sense of justice or shame but are still part of the order of natural violence. Those who still prey on people. It is worth asking to what degree this border has excluded all the nonhuman (or more than human), and to what degree it has legitimated violence against them.

There is yet another bloody border here. Zeus lays down a law. Those who do not have the capacity for rhetoric are to be slaughtered as if they were not human but a "pestilence." Such unfortunates would not have even the power to speak for themselves, for they would lack the sense of justice that is a condition for being able to mount a defense. Their offense is in part that they cannot defend themselves! In any case, this border breaks out inside the political order, after the origin of rhetoric and within the political order it founds. Those who would continue the order of "nature," the order of self-interest and injustice and the settling of conflicts by way of violence or flight, are to be killed. Their injustices and violence would destroy the political order. They are still utter individualists, insensitive to the claim of equity, incapable either of transcendence toward the other or of self-transformation by way of learning through the contest of ideas that goes on in the rhetorical order. This bloody border breaks out, perhaps, in crime or madness, or along any of the social fissures that mark the legitimate use of violence against those who threaten a human order. However, it is worth asking whether this border does not also fence out some of the disabled or the strangers with whom one does not share a common language.

The central significance of the rhetoric/violence pair is the most important feature of the rhetorical order—its ability to "substitute" argumentation and reasoning for violence. However, the rhetorical order is also accompanied by a broader pacification of violence. Just as the contest of ideas in argumentation "substitutes" for the violent physical contest of people against one another, so the bloody borders of rhetoric, openly exposed in myth (and in "vestigial" ritual sacrifices such as capital punishment) are, from within the rhetorical order, patrolled not by way of violence but by way of pacified processes and procedures: by education, by imprisonment and confinement, by drugs and therapy. We carry out the command of Zeus in subtle and "peaceful" ways. And just as we puzzle over the nonviolent "force" of reasons, we puzzle also over violence that often seems to be hiding in the ways we inculcate shame and justice where they are missing, or prevent those who are lacking them from disrupting the social order. We want to universalize the rhetorical realm, to establish peace, to recognize the claim of wild animals, either to speak for wild nature or somehow learn its rhetoric, to train and educate the incapable, to cure those whose sense of justice and shame is diseased, *and* we know that this ideal—which cannot be denied or mitigated without yielding to violence—can never be achieved, that the ideal does not belong to history but creates it.

The myth of an escape from the violence of nature in the rhetorical origin of human society is repeated by Isocrates in "Antidosis" (1956), his famous hymn to *logos*, which I offer here once again:

Because there has been implanted in us the power to persuade each other and to make clear to each other whatever we desire, not only have we escaped the life of wild beasts, but we have come together and founded cities and made laws and invented arts; and, generally speaking, there is no institution devised by man which the power of speech has not helped us to establish [15.255]. For this it is which has laid down laws concerning things just and unjust, and things honorable and base; and if it were not for these ordinances we should not be able to live with one another. . . . It is by this also that we confute the bad and extol the good. Through this we educate the ignorant and appraise the wise; for the power to speak well is taken as the surest index of a sound understanding, and discourse which is true and lawful and just is the outward image of a good and faithful soul [15.256]. With this faculty we both contend against others on matters which are open to dispute and seek light for ourselves on things which are unknown; for the same arguments which we use in persuading others when we speak in public, we employ also when we deliberate in our own thoughts; and, while we call eloquent those who are able to speak before a crowd, we regard as sage those who most skillfully debate their problems in their own minds [15.257]. And, if there is need to speak in brief summary of this power, we shall find that none of the things which are done with intelligence take place without the help of speech, but that in all our actions as well as in all our thoughts speech is our guide, and is most employed by those who have the most wisdom.

To be noted in this context is not only what is parallel to Protagoras's myth, but also the extra gloss on transcendence. Rhetoric gives us not only the power to persuade each other, but also the power "to make clear to each other whatever we desire." The idea is that "before" or without rhetoric, the wishes and desires of others were not clear, not manifest, not able to show themselves. They were behind a closed border. Rhetoric opens that border between us, permits a transcendence toward each other in which each other's desires become apparent. In this passage, transcendence is parallel in importance with "persuasion." In Perelman and Olbrechts-Tyteca's *The New Rhetoric*, transcendence is first broached as the contact of *esprits*, and then expanded and elaborated in terms of the "starting points" of argumentation. This idea of transcendence will become a central focus of the next chapter and a central concept in the development of a deep rhetoric.

One can step back from Isocrates here and allow a number of questions about rhetoric and violence to surface. For Isocrates, this transcendence and making manifest occur in speech, peacefully, and this is clearly one of the blessings of logos. However, one could begin to press the question of violence here, too. Opening this border grants not only the power to make known to others what we wish to make known to them; it also opens the possibility that others will find ways, through speech or through direct violence, to make known what we do not wish to make known. One cannot torture speechless animals into confession. One cannot drug them to loosen their tongues. One cannot trick them into disclosing secrets or into other betrayals. Only the blessings of logos allow for this.

However, the question of violence and consent becomes more subtle. This transcendence which allows for persuasion and reason and mutual understanding and peace allows, too, as part of this very possibility, for the philosophical elenchus, the testing of one another by questioning, a means by which we are persuaded or not. This testing of one another is, for Socrates, inseparable from the testing of ideas. Elenchus proceeds through the process of question and answer in which what is "made clear" is either that the one who is being questioned holds inconsistent views, or that an idea that was thought to be a good one is really not, or even that the person being questioned is not reporting beliefs honestly. When the elenchus becomes the process of exposing the inadequacy of an idea or the failure of an interlocutor, it can easily become a simple struggle, a fight, to expose or to prevent exposure. That is, it can become a kind of verbal warring, or violence. In Plato's *Protagoras*, where Socrates is trying to expose Protagoras and some ideas that Protagoras is trying to keep hidden, the martial character of the conversation becomes explicit. Socrates even describes himself at one point as a boxer who has taken a blow (339e). In Plato's dialogues, an interlocutor will sometimes cut off such a process by refusing to go on, falling silent, or rushing off on more urgent business. Or he may become angry and threaten actual violence. Violence is made a kind of comedy in Plato's dialogues, in which characters like Callicles and Thrasymachus threaten violence and seem on the verge of crossing over into it. However, the way in which violence sometimes hovers around a dialogue helps to remind us that a struggle is taking place, that the exposure of our weakness is something we do not just naturally accept. We feel it as a violence, and we often fight back. And in this process we become suspicious of "persuasion" and "making clear" themselves. We suspect that some people really are just warring with words, not transcending toward the other in respect or friendship or peace, but practicing in language (with its justice and shame) a version of the same injustices that afflicted the hyper-individualistic proto-humans of Protagoras's myth.

One threat of exposing ourselves to one another in language is that we may be called on to change. What may be made clear is that the ideas of others are in some sense better than our own ideas. What they desire may be more truly desirable than what we thought we desired. The willingness to change one's mind is often thought to be a condition for genuine argumentation. Socrates even says at one point that he would rather lose an argument than win one because if he loses he learns something new, he changes, while if he wins he is no better off than he was. This willingness is described by Perelman and Olbrechts-Tyteca as a feature of any genuine contact of minds. Without it, one can have eristics, or threats, or demands, or trickery, or any number of things, but not genuine transcendence toward the other, not argumentation. Isocrates seems to have in view the peaceful struggle of transcendence and not the fake transcendence of simple attempts at unyielding domination through language. However the entire history of rhetoric and argumentation and often of reason itself has been afflicted by a sense that the difference between openness to the other found in the substitution of argument for violence, on the one hand, and the continuing of injustice by linguistic means, on the other, is a difference for which one must fight.

Isocrates also describes the transcendence made possible by logos as a transcendence toward ourselves. Just as logos allows public contention over ideas, logos also allows us to "deliberate in our own thoughts," to "seek light for ourselves on things unknown," to debate problems in our minds, to become wise. We can get into conversations with ourselves, debate with ourselves. What we are at one moment, with our present desires and attainments and perspectives, can be challenged by other desires and attainments and perspectives, and the process can be one not of dissonance and fragmentation and psychic violence but one of conversation and transcendence toward our selves. This capacity for being hospitable to a rhetorical interaction of competing perspectives is associated with wisdom itself, and is a kind of peace.

This view of thought and wisdom as an inner version of argumentation first carried out in public between contesting parties is part of the vision Plato has of Socrates. At the end of *Hippias Major*, Socrates refers to his "close relative," a "houseguest," who never leaves him alone but is always challenging his views and engaging in debate with him about the most important matters. He tells the wealthy sophist Hippias that he is lucky not to be so tormented. The implication is clear—the sophist is an individualist who is not engaged in the transcendence that is a condition for wisdom. The idea is similar to Hannah Arendt's concept of thinking, and in fact Arendt refers to the *Hippias Major* in her elaboration of what it is to think.[2]

Chaim Perelman and Lucie Olbrechts-Tyteca treat this internalized argumentation in a chapter of *The New Rhetoric* called "Self-Deliberating," and they amplify the important ways in which inward thought becomes paradigmatic of reason itself. They say that self-deliberating is "often regarded as" the "incarnation of the universal audience" (*NR* 40), and they point out that Pascal, Descartes, Schopenhauer, J. S. Mill, and "a large number of people" seem to hold this idea. Henry Johnstone once distinguished between philosophy and rhetoric by distinguishing between rhetoric's accepting reasoning in which a speaker forces conclusions on an audience and philosophy's insisting that each individual must reach his or her own conclusions "freely." One of the ways of force is for a speaker to conceal the reasons the audience might have for raising objections or developing alternative lines of reasoning. In such a case, it is assumed that disagreements must be overcome and that the audience's desire to reason for itself must be defeated.

And so, two very old issues in the rhetorical tradition surface again: the question of sincerity and the question of whether defeating the opponent and thus ending the disagreement is the measure of success in argumentation. Johnstone insists that, however the rhetorical issues are resolved, "A conclusion has no philosophical use if it is not reached freely. To be philosophically useful, it must represent the unconstrained attempt on the part of its advocate to fulfill his obligation to defend and clarify his position" (1978, 19). Johnstone insists on something like argumentative sincerity, on one's speech being a reflection of one's inward self-deliberating. Without this, argumentation has no philosophical status. In addition, he explicitly rejects the idea that disagreement needs to be overcome, holding instead that "philosophical discussion is, in effect, a collaborative effort to maintain the conditions under which disagreement is possible" (19). Further, he uses the words "freely" and "unconstrained" to clarify what he means. I will return to these words shortly.

Perelman and Olbrechts-Tyteca interpret the valorization of self-deliberating to be related to the idea that one is more often sincere with oneself and not as often sincere with others: "It does indeed seem that a man endowed with reason who seeks to convince himself is bound to be contemptuous of procedures aimed at winning over other people. It is believed that he cannot avoid being sincere with himself and is in a better position than anyone else to test the value of his own arguments" (*NR* 40). However, they call into question both the claim that self-deliberating is somehow a paradigmatic form of reason and also the claim that sincerity is a mark of rationality. They insist that although self-deliberating has its own specific characteristics, it is best understood on the model of reasoning with others. "Agreement with oneself," they say, "is merely a particular case of agreement with others" (41). They follow this with a brief sketch of some of the internal dynamics of reasoning, but they do not get very far with it.

Their primary concern is to show that the success of "depth psychology" in exposing hidden motives and the sometimes unconscious and sometimes conscious insincerity of self-deliberation is no difficulty for a theory of argumentation that wants to defend the argumentative status of self-deliberating. In fact, we adjust our arguments for our internal audiences in exactly the way we adjust our arguments for our external audiences. Our offering one set of reasons to one audience and another set of reasons to another does not undermine the status of our reasoning as argumentation. Argumentation, and its value, remains a function of the audience being addressed (44).

At one point, Perelman and Olbrechts-Tyteca imagine reasoning with one's conscience (42). One wishes that they had developed this section in more detail. One cannot help but wonder about the status of the "self" in self-deliberation when one's self splits into the different personae of an argument. For example, when one's "conscience" is taking the role of the audience, who or what is taking the role of the speaker? And is there a suggestion here that one's self is perhaps not lodged in any of these roles but is in some sense emergent from self-deliberating? Henry Johnstone seems to take this position in *The Problem of the Self* (1970), in which the self comes to be only in the ability to experience contradictory and mutually exclusive perspectives at the same time, to experience the reality of arguing from both sides. In this ontogenetic view of rhetoric, Johnstone is on the brink of a deep rhetoric.

In interpreting the claim that self-deliberation's value rests on an assumption about sincerity, Perelman and Olbrechts-Tyteca have seen only part of what is significant about self-deliberating. Near the opening of their discussion, they quote A. E. Chaignet, from *La Rhétorique et son histoire* (1888, 93): "When we are convinced, we are overcome only by ourselves, by our own ideas. When we are persuaded, it is always by another" (41). Perelman and Olbrechts-Tyteca have already adopted Chaignet's terms "convince" and "persuade" to distinguish between actions that are successful with a universal audience and actions that are successful only with a particular audience. They freely admit that this is an important distinction. However, there is nothing about sincerity in this passage. It is all about coercion and a kind of violence. Chaignet is pretty clearly assuming what many, many people have assumed about reason—that it is a kind of pacification that produces a sphere of freedom from coercion and violence, freedom from being "overcome by another." Johnstone's perspective is much the same. He uses the words "freely" and "unconstrained" to describe the argumentation that has philosophical value, the argumentation in which one is a full participant, reaching conclusions for oneself.

The freedom at stake here is not a metaphysical freedom, a Kantian freedom necessary for reason to have a chance against necessity. Rather, it is a social freedom thought as a freedom from being "overcome by others." It is a freedom from coercion or from a kind of violence. Interpretations of this freedom are everywhere in philosophy, and the attempt to locate the sphere of this freedom are everywhere. The inner sphere of self-deliberating is an obvious choice here. Inwardly, as the stoics knew, one might achieve the most freedom and control. Only by deliberating as individuals, Rousseau believed, could we escape being overpowered by factional interests, and so only by way of self-deliberating could we deliberate reasonably about a common good, a General Will. Even Kant's metaphysical freedom is an attempt to conceptualize our not being overcome by violent necessity. Violence and unfreedom and unreason assail us from without, or at least, if they come from within, they come from our "inclinations," that within us which is not a part of our truest agency, our reason.

There is of course something critical in this recognition that there is a social violence in which one's own reasoning is overcome through coercive communication. And there is something important and valuable in acknowledging that a sphere of privacy can serve as a shelter from this kind of violence. Such spheres themselves need protecting; they serve an important purpose, even if they are not impermeable to all violence, and even if they defeat part of what they are trying to accomplish. For a compelling irony surfaces just here. In Protagoras's great myth, and in Isocrates' hymn to logos, rhetoric makes transcendence toward community possible, which seems to be its reason for being. However, in the valorizing of self-deliberating as a special freedom from social coercion, there is a movement toward closing down this opening created by rhetoric, desocializing discourse, taking all its treasures home, and locking all the doors and windows. This process—the absolute pacification of discourse—is a built-in tendency of the search for reason, for the nonviolent working through of conflicts.

Yet there are two reasons to be suspicious of this process. First, as we will see from the ensuing discussion, there are reasons to believe that all transcendence, all sociality, all discourse—even inward discourse—is inflected by violence. This claim will have to be qualified in very important ways, and the meaning of the word "violence" here is not the only meaning the word has, but still, there is a sense in which a kind of force attends all transcendence and discourse. Second, although nonviolence or pacification is a necessary dimension of the struggle for reason and political community, it is not the goal itself. It is a means, and yet not simply a means; it is also, but in a limited way, a part of the goal. However, absolute pacification and absolute nonviolence is not a goal. Nonviolence is a means for achieving peace, and peace is a kind of sociality or community in which conflict has become one of the means by which individuals and groups are renewed and grow and achieve well-being. The form of this peace is justice, and as we will see, justice is also the form of reason. These ideas have been active in partial ways from the very beginning of the conceptualization of rhetoric. They can be glimpsed in Protagoras's great myth and Isocrates' hymn. And in what follows we will explore some of the paradoxes with which they confront us. Some of these paradoxes have to do with violence and peace.

The question is whether and to what extent violence always accompanies rhetoric and the social formations it makes possible—ways of life in which deliberation and justice give form to peace, more or less imperfectly. Some serious writers have stressed the violence, some the peace. Can a deep rhetoric help to clarify this question?

Rhetoric Is Violence: Walter Benjamin

Why explore Walter Benjamin as a way of coming to terms with the question of rhetoric and violence? After all, Benjamin never addressed the question of rhetoric directly, and his approach to violence was marked in a specific way by the history of the period between the European wars. He was concerned with the problem of the general strike, with Sorel-style revolutionary violence, and in general with the problems of violence that are specific to this period in Germany. However one reason to look beyond this is that Benjamin also developed a kind of philosophy of violence, more properly perhaps, a theology of violence, in which he probes the political order for the violence that creates and sustains it. He identifies historical forms of violence, from whose injustice there seems to be no escape, but he also identifies a divine violence that can put an end—or at least be a limit—to historical violence and injustice. His account of the inescapability of violence is a challenge to the idea that rhetoric can be a substitute for violence. Further, his most important work on violence, "The Critique of Violence" ([1921] 1986), has received close attention from Jacques Derrida (1992), Jürgen Habermas (1979), Beatrice Hanssen (2000), Hent de Vries (2002) and others.[3] Many of these writers explore the philosophical and political-theoretical dimensions of Benjamin's essay, and they do so in a way that has implications for any understanding of rhetoric and violence. A transgenerational, multilinguistic conversation of this depth, focused on this issue, should not be ignored.

One difficulty with approaching Benjamin's "Critique of Violence" and its relation to the question of rhetoric and violence lies in the way that Benjamin conceptualizes violence in terms of its connection with law and justice. In my plan for elaborating the idea of a deep rhetoric, I have tried to keep the analyses of violence and justice distinct. I will continue to do this as well as I can, but justice will begin here to play more and more of a role in the discussion. Derrida's lecture on Benjamin's essay is titled "The Force of Law" (*droit*), and Benjamin's essay begins with the cryptic sentence, "The task of a critique of violence can be summarized as that of expounding its relation to law and justice," so the connections here are deep. Just how deep will become even more apparent in the chapter below on justice. Here, however, the issues will take on some of their most persistent forms: justice is not force, but justice that has no force supporting it is not real justice. Any grounding of justice will be violent and groundless, will occur outside or prior to the form of life it grounds. A sphere of justice must also be defended and sustained by violence. This violence occurs in large part outside of the contexts in which we have controlling rational or ethical or even political power, generated from a different kind of power, one not under our control. And so, justice is implicated in violence; they are in fact interimplicated. All of this presents a challenge to any claim that there is a rhetorical order that offers an alternative to violence. Further, the Benjaminian notion of "critique" has not only a Kantian and Marxist provenance, but it also bears Hegelian and Romantic and Messianic elements in its use of the finite/infinite, historical/divine pairs, and this pushes rhetorical theory's reflections into those "religious" domains toward which it naturally moves but from which it has always distanced itself.

Benjamin's essay begins with a rejection of natural law theory on the grounds that it is incapable of recognizing the most critical issues concerning violence. Natural law assumes the naturalness of violence, and the natural "right" of individuals to exercise violence, and so tends to be concerned with this right only in the contexts of conflicts between the individual and the state, and offers a framework for justifying violence against the criterion of whether it is an appropriate means for achieving a just end. Positive law views violence not as a product of nature but as a product of history, and it is concerned not with justice or the just ends that are the critical center of the approach of natural law, but with the historical legality of violence as a means. One might say that positive law has a derivative concept of justice, one derived from the legal-historical justification of the means. As Benjamin puts it, the theory of positive law guarantees the justness of the ends by justifying the means (through historically specific procedures generated by a legal system). Natural law theory, on the other hand, has a derivative concept of justification that leads back to an idea of justice as an end that is not limited by the legal procedures available in some specific historical context. Benjamin calls the relationship between these two views an "antinomy." The word has a specific Kantian background, and refers here (at least) to the way reason can generate paradoxes when it is applied beyond its range or out of its depth. So although Benjamin finds good reasons to begin the "Critique of Violence" within the context of positive law theory, he also lets us know ahead of time that the critique will lead beyond both positive and natural law: "If the criterion established by positive law to assess the legality of violence can be analyzed in regard to its meaning, then the sphere of its application must be criticized with regard to its value. For this critique a standpoint outside positive legal philosophy but also outside natural law must be found" (1986, 279).

Here Benjamin's circumspection and foresight must be acknowledged. He is as keenly aware as any other Marxist, or as any future poststructuralist or new historicist, of the way natural law theory—or any concept of "nature" or "justice"—can short-circuit and prejudice a critical discussion, reify and absolutize a historical contingency, and remove from any effective agency or political thought the ability to imagine or produce historical change. At the same time, he is aware that historicist and "natural" approaches are in a dialectical relationship with one another, mutually defined and interimplicated. One must begin the analysis with history and law, but the concept of justice as something more than positive law cannot be evaded, has an important critical role to play, and yet will find its limits just as positive legal theory will.

Although Derrida draws a sharp distinction between Benjamin's Jewish ideas and the Greek ideas to which they are contrasted, the Protagorean story of the origin of rhetoric might plausibly be interpreted as "Benjaminian" in these respects. Certainly, violence is "natural" in that the gods created a violent natural order "before history." However, human history has two origins in this myth. One is the origin of the proto-humans, who have language and religion but lack rhetoric and so have no relation to their own violence. The second is the origin of the rhetorical order, of properly human people, who are not simply naturally violent but enter a time in which they do have a relation to violence, in which they have a history of their relation to violence. The first story explains how violence is natural. The second story explains how it is historical and has an essential relation to law. If we carry this one step further, we find Socrates expressing something like Benjamin's recognition of the fact that neither side of this antinomy can be absolutized. In the *Crito*, explaining why he has a relation to Athenian law that prevents him from fleeing his captors, leaving Athens, and saving his life, Socrates shows himself to Crito as an interlocutor with law itself, holding open in the conversation the possibility that justice and law might not be the same. Yet the laws have powerful arguments in this conversation.

There are at least two unsettling Platonic ironies there. Consider the details of the situation again: Socrates is about to be put to death. Crito urges him to take advantage of a plan that his friends have devised for his escape. Socrates replies that he has been convicted in a legal process. He asks Crito whether he should justify an escape on the grounds that the conviction was "unjust" (50c). Crito says yes. A long, imaginary conversation with the Athenian laws ensues, in which Socrates gives profound prosopopoetic voice to the laws. Clearly, the conversation assumes the possible difference between justice and law, and holds open the difference between them. The laws have to defend their justness; they cannot merely define themselves as just. In the end, the laws do deliver powerful arguments for their justness, and give direct refutation of the natural law argument urged by Crito. And yet . . . the laws do not have the last word. The dialogue ends this way: "Then, Crito, let it be, and let us act in this way, since it is in this way that god leads us" (54e). So, the laws do not simply justify themselves; they are also justified because they show the way that god leads us. So much for positive law having the last word. And yet here we are at the Benjaminian moment where what might be a natural law approach (God guarantees a natural justice) is not rightly described as simply naturalistic because there is a (supernatural) divinity involved who is not simply on one side of the positive law/natural law divide. Plato leads us through a positivistic logos only to have the outcome be that we were being led by the divine all along. Law is more than law.

The other irony, however, leads in the opposite direction. Socrates-the-most-law-abiding-man is more outside the law than anyone else in the dialogue. He has been condemned to death. His loyalty to the Athenian laws, at least the ones that can speak, takes him all the way to the point at which almost no one else judges his actions as legal. Crito in some way knows that Socrates' life and actions were "just," but he cannot handle the argument between justice and the law, the argument which Socrates is, and the argument whose final move lies in his willingness to identify with the living, speaking law. His actions lead him straight to the bloody border of Athens and of life itself. Not even the law-loving gods can cure Athens of violence. In the life of Socrates, and in Plato's representation of his trial, the rhetorical order is found to be incapable of redeeming its promise to overcome violence and achieve justice. Beyond all of Plato's persistent efforts to join rhetoric and philosophy, the corpse of Socrates stands, for Plato, as the sign of the (philosophically impossible but politically real) difference between rhetoric and philosophy.

Once Benjamin establishes that the critical conversation must pass through positive law, he announces that he will confine his critique to the European legal tradition. The first feature of this tradition is its monopoly of violence; there is no legitimate violence beyond that which is specifically legally sanctioned. Individuals reserve no right to exercise violence outside the law. The state has divine power. Governmental monopoly of violence knows only one important exception: organized labor's right to strike. Benjamin sees striking as an act of force, or violence (which brings out part of the contrast between the German *Gewalt* and English "violence"). However, this acknowledged right to strike, this use of the power of workers to force employers to raise wages or improve conditions or otherwise grant the demands of labor, is restricted to strikes aimed at specific, local goals. If the strike becomes generalized across industries, it infringes on the state's monopoly of force/violence. It becomes a challenge to the state for legal and political power.[4]

This renewal of violence sometimes breaks out when the established rhetorical order comes to be seen as unjust and violent—that is, when it is no longer seen to be realizing its reasons for being. However, this renewal of violence occurs not only within rhetorical orders but also between them, in military violence between states. Military violence has a predatory dimension, in that it aims at a seizure of power, land, industries, natural resources, wealth, strategic locations, and so on, but as Benjamin points out, it is not simply predatory. Military violence is also creative, and has a lawmaking character. It destroys the previous law, but Benjamin insists that its victories are accompanied by ceremonies of peace and processes of reinstituting new law. In addition, military violence also has a law-preserving character, in which force is used to preserve the legal order. Here Benjamin offers the example of general conscription, the forceful subordination of citizens to the state's projects of legal violence. Law-preserving violence sets no new ends but is a pure means; lawmaking violence is also a means, but also sets new ends, new laws. All valid violence is, Benjamin says, justified as either lawmaking or law-preserving, either creative or conservative.

The fundamental obstacle confronting the "Critique of Violence" is that the justification of violence rests on an argument that violence is the origin and defense and so the condition for the possibility of a nonviolent legal-rhetorical order. Legitimate violence arises not within the rhetorical order but at its borders, where it is threatened from outside, by what has not entered the rhetorical order of peaceful deliberation and the nonviolent resolution of conflict. Benjamin says that the defenders of violence call this uncontrollable, nonlegal, nonrhetorical power "fate." So, the critique of violence faces the reality that violence seems to be the ground and possibility of law and nonviolence, their origin and preservation, their creator and preserver. If this is so, then rhetoric is rooted in violence. How, then, can it be the alternative to and substitute for violence? Not only is violence the origin and guarantor of the rhetorical order, but the justification of violence, the only justification of violence, is that the violence in question is necessary to defend law, to defend the rhetorical order, to defend the peace. The very existence of rhetoric *creates* the justification of violence. It participates in the state's assumption of divine power.

Benjamin is so taken with this justification of violence that he turns his critique around for a moment and asks whether violence is not intractable and whether it is not in fact ultimately the only means for regulating conflicting human interests. Such a question does not follow directly from the discussion of lawmaking and law-preserving violence. If there really are "borders" across which one passes from violence to nonviolence, then it is not a surprise that there is violence on those borders. This does not directly impinge on the rhetorical order's claim to be a sphere of nonviolence and justice. The problems are (1) whether the boundaries of violence have been truly identified, whether there are not parties outside the purported boundaries who really do seek a nonviolent hearing and a just adjudication of their claims, (2) whether the threat of violence is an essential dimension of the rhetorical order, one which stands behind and preserves the integrity of all purportedly legal and nonviolent transactions, and (3) whether the violent creation and preservation of the rhetorical order has not forcefully closed off certain discursive possibilities, forced certain silences and incomprehensions, and compelled idioms and phrases and expressions that forcefully prevent us from communicating what we would otherwise want to communicate.

Benjamin addresses the second of these concerns, and he exposes the violence that continues to back apparently nonviolent legal transactions. The idea of a legal contract seems to be a paradigm of nonviolent law; contracts are binding simply by the force of law. However, Benjamin detects two kinds of violence here. First, there is the intolerable violence that led the originators of contract law to develop and assent to rules that would mitigate the intolerable aspects of the violent resolutions of conflict. Intolerable violence is the motivation for law. If violence were not intolerable, there would be no law; therefore law depends on (the fear of) intolerable violence. Second, the threat of force still stands behind and guarantees contracts. If there were no sanctions for the violations of contracts, sanctions backed by force, then contracts themselves would have no force. Benjamin takes the democratic/parliamentarian amnesia about both kinds of violence to be a factor in democracy's decadence. Unless one bears in mind that the provenance of law is violence, and that violence attends as sanction all legal agreements, one literally does not know what one is doing within the rhetorical order. If legislatures had a clearer idea of the violence that attends all their actions, they would undertake their nonviolent work with deeper and more forceful seriousness.[5]

Benjamin has in mind here the ineffective democratic governments in the Germany of his time, although in light of what followed them their "decadence" may seem attractive. However, this kind of argument is often made by others in a general way, and Benjamin is not reluctant to draw general conclusions from it here. Does it stand at a general level? Most of us would probably want to make a few significant qualifications. If Benjamin is asking whether a "totally nonviolent resolution of conflict" is present in the process of legal contracts, we can, under some readings of "totally," agree with him that "total nonviolence" is never achieved. The rhetorical order has a violent origin. Force, including violence, is exerted when laws are broken, when the rhetorical order breaks down.

From another point of view, though, such a totality-minded critique of violence misses the point. The claim of rhetoric has never been that it can completely overcome the violent historical effects of its origins. In fact, Perelman and Olbrechts-Tyteca frequently insist that this must be remembered, that the alternative to rhetoric is a lapse into the violence that waits for any rejection of rhetoric. Deep rhetoric is in part precisely an awareness of the violence to which rhetoric is a direct and profound response. Rhetoric is the social and historical and personal formation of nonviolence. Further, rhetoric is a way of addressing the continuing effects of its own violent origin. The bloody borders of the rhetorical order come to light as political and ethical issues only within an order in which violence is morally suspect and is supposed to be made unnecessary. Although Zeus decrees that those who are deficient in a sense of justice or shame be violently put to death, the tendency of the rhetorical order is to universalize its expectations, to educate and rehabilitate and understand and negotiate—as well as to substitute drugs, therapy, imprisonment, relocation, walls, and other forceful short-of-death methods to avoid the need for violent putting-to-death. This can lead to projects of education and health care and cultural interaction that increase the understanding of and tolerance of differences and promote a flourishing of human freedom—as well as to discursive and therapeutic and other cultural regimens that cloak their violences in subtle and insidious forms. The critique of violence has been undermined by a failure to make such distinctions, to know the difference between violence and nonviolence, or even, at times, between violence and the worst violence. To say, as Benjamin does, that nonviolence is attended by violence is hardly a revelation to anyone who reads the history of rhetoric; it is an essential part of the story. To say that dimensions of force and freedom, violence and nonviolence, can be uncovered in any communicative action is hardly something unknown. However, to use this as a reason to fail to discriminate between them, a reason to fail to register and acknowledge the freedom and nonviolence that have been achieved in any particular situation, would be to fail in courage and hope. If the origin of rhetoric lies in violence against animals and criminals and the insane, the rhetorical order still organizes itself in large part as a way to mitigate that violence as it goes on with its historical tasks. The exposure of violence and the acknowledgment of freedom are indispensable companions in any liberatory critical project.

In relation to the sanctions that stand behind any contract, the response must be much the same. No matter how peaceful the process of agreeing on a contract, says Benjamin, "it leads finally to possible violence" (1986, 288). "Possible violence" is an interesting concept, and if the issue is simply "possible violence," then it's hard to see how any human transaction doesn't "lead," "finally," to "possible violence." What Benjamin seems to mean here is something like: if a contract is violated, and if it is violated intentionally, and if the violation does harm to one of the contracting parties, and if the harm cannot or will not be addressed by some kind of compensation, or if the contract cannot be renegotiated, or if some other settlement cannot be found, and if the legal means of settling the dispute are not adhered to by the violating party, and if all the formal and legal and informal means of settling the dispute fail, then legal force will be applied to the violating party—a fine or monetary or other kind of settlement will be paid or assessed in some way, or if criminality is involved, perhaps the offending party will be hauled off to prison. "Finally" means something like: if people are intransigent in the violation of the law (law to which they have given express consent by negotiating a contract), and if all the peaceful means of settling the matter are exhausted, then force will be applied to compel the person to obey the law and pay its penalty.

Once again, there can be no real quarrel with Benjamin here, but *a critique of violence must go further than this*. It must explain not only the boundary violence that surrounds the spheres in which we nonviolently make and keep promises; it must also explain the possibility of a fairly huge space of nonviolence and of peace, of the actions that make it unnecessary to go to the extremes of the boundary, the actions that substitute for moving toward the violent apocalypse of the "finally." It must also cut more closely to the violent injustices sedimented in the law itself. The violence/nonviolence pair must be understood together, and the critique must describe both their differences and their interpenetrations more thoroughly and subtly.

As if he knows that he has delivered a somewhat one-sided case, Benjamin asks himself the general question again, in a different form: "Is any nonviolent resolution of conflict possible?" And his answer is clear: "Without doubt" (289). However, this certainty regards the relationships of "private persons" only. The framework within which this communication takes place has not, apparently, been established by violence, and it is not necessarily sanctioned by violence. Instead, says Benjamin, using Hegelian language, its "subjective conditions" are something like virtues:

courtesy, sympathy, peaceableness, trust. This is a short but thought-provoking list, and virtues of this sort would have to be included in any account of rhetorical formation. In Perelman and Olbrechts-Tyteca's chapter on the contact of *esprits*, which explores the conditions for nonviolent argumentation, "courtesy" is captured in the protocols or rules that interlocutors acknowledge as governing their communication—taking turns in conversation, for example. Further, "sympathy" can be thought of as a requirement of any rhetorical formation that emphasizes *controversia* and the ability to argue from different sides of an issue. "Peaceableness" is that virtue which keeps one in the argumentative situation, persevering in the hope and practice of nonviolence and refusing the temptations of force and the *ad baculum*. "Trust" is the practical investing of one's efforts in communication with an interlocutor whom one believes really is interested in a peaceful solution. Without a regard for one's interlocutor, there can be no argumentation in *The New Rhetoric*'s sense. What social formations and personal and political efforts promote these virtues? What social formations and personal and political efforts do they help to produce? With this exploration of the ethical dimensions of nonviolent communication, Benjamin enters the realm of a deep rhetorical critique of violence.

Yet he immediately drops this discussion to enforce a Hegelian distinction: the *objective* condition for the effectiveness of these virtues in resolving a conflict nonviolently is that the conflict concern only goods and not be a "conflict between man and man" (289). It is hard to say what Benjamin means by this. He moves quickly into a new discussion of the "profoundest example" of nonviolent communication, "the conference [or dialogue, conversation, *Unterredung*] considered as a technique of civil agreement." He takes the conference to be wholly nonviolent, and he takes the defining mark of this nonviolent sphere to be the absence of any sanctions, particularly for lying. No external power enforces truthfulness at the conference; the enforcement of truth is entirely discursive and communicative. This is what Benjamin calls the use of "pure means," or "unalloyed means." The idea is that conflicting parties consent to submit to a process (a means) whose outcome (end) is not predetermined but can be determined only through communicative actions, often through argumentation. As Aristotle noted, one does not submit just any conflict to this kind of a process. There are some things about which one just doesn't argue, and there are some people with whom one just doesn't argue. Benjamin is getting at something like this Aristotelian observation in his distinction between conflicts about goods and conflicts between persons.

The critical idea of "pure means" marks off, in Benjaminian terms, that sphere in which rhetoric succeeds in being a substitute for violence, the rhetorical order proper, especially as it is conceived in the theory of argumentation. It is established here by way of distinctions between means/ends (processes/outcomes) and a Hegelian subjective/objective scheme. There are two kinds of critical limitations to this approach. First, Benjamin does not operate with a subtle enough understanding of the rhetoric of means/ends and subjective/objective.[6] This leads to an underestimation of the way in which ends are already constitutive of nonviolent discourse and an underestimation of the extent to which nonviolent processes can be effective in conflicts about ends. Second, there are important critical questions that are ignored here. Even here, in this use of "pure means," are there not forceful exclusions? Are all parties who seek involvement in nonviolent resolutions of conflicts permitted to participate? If not, isn't a kind of force or violence still driving the communication? And what about the power of the discourse itself? Is it the outcome of a violent history? Does it enforce associations and silences and amplifications and diminishments that just further consolidate the violent suppressions of its history? A critique of violence need not have unrealistically utopian expectations of language to point out the possibility of such questions.

Perhaps one of Benjamin's most compelling observations in this section is that violence attends peace in that the failure of rhetoric, the failure of nonviolent discourse, opens a door to uncontrollable violence. The fear of this violence motivates a deep investment in the rhetorical order, helps to encourage the cultivation of rhetorical virtues, and keeps pressure on conflicting parties to resist the escalation of the forceful dimensions of their conflicts. Benjamin believes that the state grants certain uses of force, despite its fundamental insistence on a monopoly of violence, because this concession makes greater violence unlikely. For example, the state grants workers the right to strike in order to prevent more violent actions by workers. However, Benjamin sees this fear at work in relations among individuals, too. The escalation of forceful and violent confrontation brings disadvantages to everyone—a decline of trust and hope and friendship and cooperation among individuals, a weakening of faith in negotiations and contracts and legal processes in civil affairs, an increasing chance that one will be both the victim and perpetrator of violences. In simple terms, life gets more solitary, poor, nasty, and brutish—if not shorter—as the rhetorical order gives way to violence.

Benjamin ends this discussion in a thought-provoking way by taking a large, historical view of this motive for rhetoric. He has just concluded a few remarks on the rhetorical motive for relations among private individuals, which he says are "clearly visible in countless cases." However:

It is different when classes and nations are in conflict, since the higher orders that threaten to overwhelm equally victor and vanquished are hidden from the feelings of most, and from the intelligence of almost all. Space does not here permit me to trace such higher orders and the common interests corresponding to them, which constitute the most enduring motive for a policy of pure means. We can therefore only point to pure means in politics as analogous to those which govern peaceful intercourse between private persons. (1986, 290–91)

This is quite cryptic, but also quite Benjaminian in its joining of massive suggestiveness and a striking absence of political-theoretical details. The picture is of historical and psychological forces outside our ken that threaten to destroy us. I find it difficult to read this passage without thinking of the angel in Benjamin's "Theses on History," who flies forward in time, but with his face turned toward the past, which is all he can see, and what he sees are ruins. We can't control or even understand these forces, yet their indifferent destructiveness threatens us all equally, and this creates a set of common human interests in the preservation of the rhetorical order, a set of common interests that is analogous to the interests we have in maintaining peace in our individual relations with each other.

A complete reading of Benjamin's "Critique of Violence" would take us more deeply into a discussion of Marxist and Romantic defenses of revolutionary violence, but this is enough to set the table for the entry of Benjamin's unexpected guest and to allow us to explore what is unique and strangely relevant about Benjamin's approach. The essential problem for the "Critique" is that from the standpoint of legal theory or political thought human conflict cannot be resolved in purely nonviolent ways, and the available forms of violence cannot produce a peace that is not founded in and attended by violence. Benjamin's question is: are there then other kinds of violence than legal-political violence that must be considered? The question is critical because it is possible that "all the violence imposed by fate, using justified means" is in "irreconcilable conflict with just ends" (293). Notice how far this critique now reaches, even into Foucauldian regions: the exclusion of certain individuals or groups, the residual threats of violence that sustain the rhetorical order, or the fateful discourses that command speech—all this violence is included here. What if, in light of the justice that violence purportedly accomplishes, it is finally unjustifiable? What if violence is ultimately violently unjust?

The global and totalizing reach of this thought does not seem mad if one imagines it coming from the oppressed, dispossessed, enslaved, impoverished, diseased, and hopeless people of the earth who must endure the peace and justice that violence has accomplished in our time. And I would be the very last to deny them or any mortal the religious move Benjamin is about to make here.

And yet . . . Benjamin has once again left the spaces and threads of concrete nonviolence neglected, unclarified. Can injustice and violence be understood if we do not also understand even more thoroughly both the "private" practices of peace (even if we do not call into question the public/private dichotomy so absolutized here) and the diplomatic uses of nonviolence that Benjamin explicitly acknowledges in the "Critique"? And can we understand the unjust effects of violence if we do not also understand how, even in conditions of injustice attended by violence, individuals and groups and even organized political entities expose violence, struggle to mitigate it and its effects, and successfully pursue the work of peace? Do we understand the failure of justice if we do not understand the imperfect justices that are accomplished and have hardly inconsequential effects on the lives of those who suffer fateful injustices? Can we understand the nature of the Ultimate Failure of rhetoric without understanding its hardly insignificant penultimate successes? It is one thing to acknowledge the real limitations of all historical political efforts, of all attempts to defeat violence and achieve justice; it is quite another to mistake those limitations for a vitiating failure. And when a line is about to be drawn between something like history/end of time, finite/infinite, or human/divine, it is an intellectual and moral and political imperative to watch for the ways each is active in the conceptualization of the other, to refuse a victory (of inevitable terror) to one side or the other, and to, as Derrida once put it, practice the interval as well as one can.

Having said that as strongly as seems fitting, it is also important to allow these Benjaminian pairs to emerge and do their work. When the religious is repressed and isolated, it is more likely to grow violent, just as it is when it assumes exclusive power. The same goes for the forcefully antireligious powers of modernity, although their violences are often more successfully disguised than Stalin's. Deep rhetoric understands that philosophical pairs are not simply to be struggled with or undermined or deconstructed; they are formulated because an incompatibility has arisen, and a new pair is rhetoric's way of wrestling with deep incompatibilities.[7]

At first, says Benjamin, the cycles of unjust historical violence and the impossibility of a legal solution may seem discouraging. However, he says, this should discourage us no more than our inability to make absolute judgments about "right" and "wrong" (*richtig falsch*) in languages that are still evolving (*in werdenden Sprachen*). Our problem is that we believe that reason has the answer to the question of justice, but, says Benjamin, "it is never reason that decides on the justification of means and the justness of ends, but fate-imposed violence on the former and God on the latter" (294). Benjamin links this religious idea to what we might call ethical particularism: just ends cannot be the ends of any possible law because justice is incapable of abstract generalization. Situations that require judgments about justice are never exactly alike, and they are dissimilar in exactly the ways that call generalizations about justice into question. God's justice is not an intellectual generalization and probably not articulable in "evolving languages." Human justifications of violence are controlled and circumscribed by the gods of fate.[8]

Benjamin here introduces his famous distinction between mythic violence and divine violence: "Mythical violence . . . is a mere manifestation of the gods" (294). What is at stake in mythical violence is not justice but power (*Macht*). Benjamin gives the example of the Niobe myth. Niobe and Amphion, King of Thebes, have seven sons and seven daughters. Niobe speaks out, and compares herself favorably with the divine Leto, who has only two sons, Apollo and Artemis. No sooner has Niobe spoken than Artemis and Apollo slay her children. Benjamin insists that this is not punishment or a reasoned means to justice. Rather, it is a manifestation of the fateful violence that constitutes the border between gods and human beings. This mythical violence falls on Niobe as violent fate. Power is all on the side of fate. The border between the divine and human is patrolled not by reason or knowledge or discourse but by fateful violence that is not—to any extent—under anyone's control. However, this violence is law-making, creative, because it identifies a border; it fixes a frontier. It is not clear in the case of mythic violence whether the infringement of the border triggers violence or whether the violence creates the border. The nature of fate and of mythical violence is that there seems to be no way of distinguishing these two explanations.

Benjamin carries this beyond myth proper to the sphere of any establishing of borders, and focuses especially on the conclusions of wars and on constitutional law. In all cases, the establishment of borders is seen to be coincident with the violence that (potentially) falls on those who violate them. This is explicit law-making violence, and yet it has no connection with justice, or with reasoning about ends and means. Violence is the establishment of law, and law is the establishment of violence, apart from any such considerations. The unconstrained agent and author here is fate, the executor of mythical violence. Benjamin's next step is extraordinary:

Far from inaugurating a purer sphere, the mythical manifestation of immediate violence shows itself fundamentally identical with all legal violence, and turns suspicion concerning the latter into certainty of the perniciousness of its historical function, the destruction of which thus becomes obligatory. (296–97)

For Benjamin, only a higher violence can fulfill this obligation, only the violence of the God-Who-opposes-all-myth, only the apocalyptic, law-destroying violence of the divine. (And although Derrida and most others read this as a specifically Judaic God, and overall this is preeminently reasonable, it is Shiva who first came to mind for me.) Divine violence is different from mythic violence in several ways: it destroys law, dissolves boundaries and borders, strikes lethally without spilling blood and so expiates, is concerned not with mere biological life (blood) and (bloody) power over it but with a pure power over all (not simply biological) life for the sake of the living. Mythical violence must demand bloody sacrifice; divine violence simply accepts or assumes it, simply takes it into its own service.

The religious and messianic dimensions of this idea play themselves out in relation to history in Benjamin's final paragraph. Here the critique of violence becomes the philosophy of the history of violence, which discovers only cycles of creative and conserving violence, governed by fate.[9] It discovers only a system of violence/law and an obligation to destroy that system. The philosopher who sees this can hope, in the "coming age," to launch an attack on law itself. Radical revolutionary violence is indeed possible, if not obligatory. It is *not* possible, on the other hand, to discover unalloyed violence in particular cases because "the expiatory power of violence is not visible to men" (300). And here we are simply left wondering how anyone could know anything about its visibility or invisibility. What position would such knowledge require?

The real provenance of law and its fate are identified in the conclusion of Benjamin's essay:

All the eternal forms are open to divine violence, which myth bastardized with law. It may manifest itself in a true war exactly as in the divine judgment of the multitude on a criminal. But one must reject all mythical violence, the violence that founds law, and which we may call ruling violence. One must also reject the violence that conserves law, the managed violence that serves what rules. Divine violence, which is the sign and seal but never the means of sacred execution, may be called sovereign violence. (300)[10]

However, this move to divine violence has come in for some rough commentary.

In his Post-scriptum to "Force of Law: The 'Mystical Foundation of Authority', '" Derrida somewhat reluctantly—and after a number of clarifications and qualifications—feels forced to point out that the image of Benjamin's divine bloodless violence is just way too close to the Nazi gas chambers and cremation ovens:

What I find, in conclusion, the most redoubtable, indeed (perhaps almost) intolerable in this text, even beyond the affinities it maintains with the worst (the critique of *Aufklärung*, the theory of the fall and of original authenticity, the polarity between ordinary language and fallen language, the critique of representation and of parliamentary democracy, etc.), is a temptation that it would leave open, and leave open notably to the survivors or the victims of the final solution, to its past, present or potential victims. Which temptation? The temptation to think the holocaust as an uninterpretable manifestation of divine violence insofar as this divine violence would be at the same time nihilating, expiatory and bloodless, says Benjamin, a divine violence that would destroy current law through a bloodless process that strikes and causes to expiate. . . . When one thinks of the gas chambers and cremation ovens, this allusion to an extermination that would be expiatory because bloodless must cause one to shudder. One is terrified at the idea of an interpretation that would make of the holocaust an expiation and an indecipherable signature of the just and violent anger of God. (1992, 62)

The messianico-marxist and archeo-eschatological discourses at work in Benjamin's text seem to Derrida somehow complicit in "the very thing against which one must act and think, do and speak, that with which one must break (perhaps, perhaps)" otherwise characterized as "the worst" (here the final solution) (62, 63). Derrida goes on:

In my view, this defines a task and a responsibility the theme of which (yes, the theme) I have not been able to read in either Benjaminian "destruction" or Heidegerian "*Destruktion.*" It is the thought of difference between these destructions on the one hand and a deconstructive affirmation on the other that has guided me . . . in this reading. It is this thought that the memory of the final solution seems to me to dictate. (63)

The extremity of Benjamin's judgment concerning the omnipresence of violence and its intractable power in relentless historical cycles of violence leads directly to the need for an extreme solution. If history and law and the entire rhetorical order are governed by violence, then the only redress for violence must come from outside the law and from beyond history. If the human order is trapped in mythic violence, then only incomprehensible divine violence offers hope.

These ruling pairs of mythic/divine and violently unjust law/divine justice are so absolute that their eventually violent collision is inscribed in their logic from the start. Derrida seems to be acknowledging the violence of absolutizing these oppositions when he describes the discourse of these pairs as something against which one must think and act, but when he says that it is also "that with which one must break," he adds: "(perhaps, perhaps)." For if one sets up Benjaminian discourse as one side of another potential pair, a side from which one must break, just as Benjamin said that one must break with the historical cycles of legal violence, then one is very possibly setting up another abstract pair that will rule the possibilities of the thought and action it governs, a pair that will warrant another forceful rupture of some kind, another eschatological promise that destroys first and keeps its promises, in whatever way it does, only "in an age to come."

If there is something of this sort that is to occur, says Derrida, it will occur perhaps as the thought of the "difference" between the discursive destructions in question and a "deconstructive affirmation." Deconstructive affirmation is a promise of a kind, too, one that has been hard to redeem, but it is clearly not a simple destruction of one side of an abstract opposition. And it is not simply that Benjamin makes this move to an "age to come," whether in a Messianic sense or a revolutionary one, and not simply that the binaries he is working with seem to dictate such a move. Rather, the issue is that the binaries are formed by way of a neglect or suppression or misrecognition for whatever reason of the vast work of nonviolence already at play in the history of law. Benjamin's claim concerning the extent to which violence holds sway in legal societies cannot hold even on his own account. Perhaps it is the mind-devastating violence of the First World War, or perhaps it is the hopelessness and despair engendered by the continuing violence and disorder of the Weimar Republic, but the social-psychological and historical conditions of Benjamin's understanding of the rule of violence cannot justify his judgment when it conflicts so profoundly with the conditions he explicitly acknowledges but whose significance seems not to register significantly with him.

Deep Rhetoric: Otherwise Than Violence

Where Derrida breaks off, rhetorical criticism steps in, and the approach of a deep rhetoric takes over from traditional philosophy and political theory. The question is whether and to what extent violence constitutes the political-rhetorical order, permeates rhetoric, inhabits our social engagements, determines our reasoned decisions, and forms our individual and social identities. In one very general sense, "violence" describes any force that is exerted without complete assent and participation—physically, emotionally, symbolically, in any way at all—on a person or group or on the things which are valuable to them, or on the cultural and linguistic and symbolic and physical habitats out of which they come to understand what is valuable to them and what is not. Insofar as violence has meaning, insofar as it comes from another and is in some way social, its habitat is the transcendence opened up by rhetoric. Without rhetoric, there can be force but not violence; with rhetoric, the world opens to violence, both the meaningful violence of war and other overtly physical kinds of violence, and the violence whose force does not depend so much on direct physical compulsion as on more purely symbolic power.

Rhetoric, thought as deep rhetoric, is the contact zone for the transcendence of selves toward one another (and toward themselves). As such, rhetoric can never be completely comprehended; this zone can never be grasped as a totality without (forcefully) infringing on transcendence. So something about rhetoric—that sphere in which we strive for peace and assume responsibility for our ideas and actions by reasoning with each other about them—escapes, at least in part, our responsibility and our autonomy and control and our struggles for nonviolence. Rhetoric is, in the story of Protagoras, a gift of Zeus. And Zeus is not exactly a pacifist. On the other hand, rhetoric is the opposite of violence, the great, cultural anti-violence. Its very existence is an attempt to redress the problems of violence, and it is explicitly a substitution of a conflict of ideas and arguments for physical conflict. Rhetoric is awakening from violence. And yet its institution and preservation is, as we have seen, plagued by violence. The force of this paradox will always, to some extent, persist.

This concerted focus on violence and rhetoric is justified not only by the stories of rhetoric's origin, or by the widespread claim in the rhetorical tradition that the right kind of speech and argumentation can both prevent violence and substitute for it, but it is justified also by the challenges made concerning any public sphere's ability to mitigate the violence that attends religious differences, ethnic and racial differences, national differences, class differences, gender differences, age differences, differences in ability and health, and all the other differences that are no longer understood to characterize just individuals or groups but mark the very sphere of transcendence (of violence and justice) that rhetoric is supposed to open up.

The political promise of modernity, of liberal society, of democratic states and their institutions—the university, for example—is partly redeemed through free speech, affirmative action, equal opportunity, and open political processes, but from the standpoint of a deep rhetoric, the challenge is met only partly—though in critically important ways—in the political sphere. Deeper in culture, in the transcendence that takes form in communication—even the communication that occurs in simple perception and thought—the interactions of rhetoric and violence are shaping outcomes that are mostly beyond the reach of ordinary political action.

This is in part why Levinas and others have tried to turn us away from ontology to the much more difficult work of what they call "ethics" in the sphere of transcendence in which we, in Levinas's word, "transgress" against each other before we even know what we are doing, before we understand or are able to take seriously our own transcendence toward ourselves. It is crucial here not to think of ethics as a set of rules or principles or any kind of theory in the traditional philosophical sense. In Levinas's writings, ethics describes the form of transcendence as such. Stanley Cavell has tried to develop a similar idea in his interpretations of Emerson: "In Emerson's teaching . . . the moral is not a separate realm or a separate branch of philosophical study, but one in which each assertion is a moral act (intrusive or not, magnanimous or not, heartfelt or not, kind or cutting, faithful or treacherous, promising cheer or chagrin, acknowledging or denying)" (1990, xxix). (It would be interesting to explore the dynamics of violence and nonviolence in each of those pairs.) Deep rhetoric is an approach to this sphere of "ethics" (rhetoric has always been an issue of ethics), an approach that experiences these deeper actions as communicative, all the way to the event where the communication is what is bringing the self and other into being as the self and other they are.

However, deep rhetoric and its attendant violences and amities are not limited to a prepolitical sphere. Its ethical effects reverberate throughout all political and public spheres. And these are not simply "effects," as if something in a prepolitical sphere were causing something in the political sphere. The ethical is not a place where political problems can be directly addressed or "solved." Rather, the political always has its own deep rhetorical dimensions. Deep rhetoric is a dimension of *all* communication. It is concerned with the overtly ontic and politically manageable aspects of communication at the same time—and as part of the same act of concern—that it is concerned with the less controllable, deeper dimensions of communication.

This grasp of the necessity and limitations of exercises of political power, and of the interimplications of rhetoric and violence, encourages restraint in political ambition without in any way ironizing political hope or undermining the wholeheartedness of political work. An absolutely nonviolent rhetoric to which everyone assents and in which everyone participates fully is a generative and productive ideal, a guide to aspiration and deliberation. However, when it is taken as the absolute goal of a political project, it produces its opposite. History provides too many examples of the failures of this project. Any particular organization of communicative participation, any real, historical polity, falls short of this ideal, and the more various cultures aspire to it, and claim it for their own, and intensify their struggle for it (which is also a struggle against the other cultures who fail to grasp it correctly), the further the ideal recedes from history. The more we believe that we almost have it in our grasp, the *further* it recedes. This knowledge can produce political restraint—it can even help to hold off violence. To understand the ways in which the unmanageable violences and amities of deep rhetoric interact with the potentially manageable violences and concords of political life can help us begin to imagine a political activism that is both wholehearted and properly humble.[11] And understanding more clearly the ways in which rhetoric can be a substitute for violence, the extent to which the ideal is realized in concrete practices, can give us the hope in politics that demands our wholehearted participation. Rhetorical practice is the antidote for the distortions and terror that rhetorical abstractions can produce. And yet rhetorical idealism is the antidote to the violences and distortions produced by rhetorical practice.

The strength of Benjamin's critique lies in its exposé of violence, but, as we have seen, this very effort amplifies and exaggerates the vision of violence, and diminishes and understates the possibilities of peace. The critique also operates with two abstract pairs that distort what a deep rhetoric would treat much more concretely. First, the abstract distinction between the political and the private distorts the way that violence threatens ordinary "private" life and the extent to which peace reigns in political society. Distinctions between "private" and "political" are useful in some contexts but less so in others. It can be useful to distinguish between the "lawful" and, for Benjamin, "necessary" violence of the state or legal-political system and the unlawful violences of private life. However, that distinction can also occlude the violences that permeate private life and its own formations of power and distributions of violence. The physically strong exert force over the physically weak both through threat and through actual violence, without the sanction of law but with a sanction that is often no less effective. Violence organizes itself within many families in such a way that a monopolization of violence is constitutive of family order. Extralegal religious traditions and other kinds of cultural traditions can also carry asymmetrically distributed authority over violence. Criminal organizations, which can gain extensive territorial and financial-commercial power, exercise violence in complex and powerful ways that shape lives and societies sometimes more completely than state power. The list could go on, and could include subtler kinds of force than I have broached here. In all of these instances, there will be complicated interweavings of pacified means of settling disputes and violent enforcements of what is indisputable. A deep rhetorical approach would stay cognizant of the way abstract pairs such as "private" and "political" obscure extralegal formations of violent social authority that is strongly analogous to state authority. Setting up a strict distinction between "private" and "political" prevents a critique of violence from achieving its own aim. Like all theoretical constructions, such oppositions carry implicit ethical judgments about what is worth attention, under what categories, in what relations to other terms, and for what purposes.

Second, Benjamin's concepts of violence and nonviolence are way too abstract to help real human beings deal with the concrete realities they face, even in the conflicts between political orders. The way he opposes mythic to divine violence is an expression of this failure. This abstractness tends to be endemic in some philosophical and critical social and political theory. As I mentioned in the first chapter, deep rhetoric aligns with that strand in philosophy which can be said to act as the prevention of such theory. In its interpretation of "theory" as theorizing *communication*, deep rhetoric situates theory in a rhetorical situation and is itself "critical" of the theoretical entities it produces. It interprets theories as functions of communicative actions that have ethical shape and ultimately pragmatic meaning, in that they lead us to one thing or another—one set of actions or policies rather than another, one set of theoretical terms and relations or another, one disclosure of ourselves and other people or another, one way of letting our environment and its beings come to presence or another. Theoretical entities arise from rhetorical situations, reveal things in a particular way, and lead towards a specific range of new situations.

When Benjamin designates historical violence as mythic violence and distinguishes it from divine violence, he generates unusual theoretical entities that allow him an unusual outside critical perspective on history and its formations of law-governed societies. Most critical theory identifies at least possible historical agents that can redress the relatively specific injustices and violences of social life as it is. Benjamin's radically abstract generation of "mythic violence" as the violence of history itself, and the logical need to generate an equally abstract agent to stand against it, "divine violence," is almost a *reductio ad absurdum* of critical theory, in which the real actions of the real people in the real world are dwarfed and made irrelevant by abstract concepts that have, ironically, once again become the divinities from which, according to Horkeimer and Adorno (1976), they have descended.

The point is to see this kind of critical theory as what it is. Benjamin's account is illuminating and thought-provoking. It offers us new experiences of what happens when we think of history and violence and law together in this very general way. It requires careful consideration, and it explains, partly through example, why writing about "history" or "violence" or "law" so quickly takes on the appearance of theology. The danger lies in reifying (or ontotheologically deifying) these theoretical conceptions and not recognizing that their being is communicative and that their form is ethical. They cannot be reliably transferred into critical theories of society that will provide us with the sweeping vistas and the knowledge and competence to be able to pull the levers and push the buttons of whole social formations to control their futures. This is exactly what the Benjamin of the *Theses on History* warns us of—the critical theory that produces Stalins and moral absurdities.[12]

Kenneth Burke once pointed out a difference between what he called "scientific realism" and "poetic realism." According to scientific realism, one approaches the truth as one's perspectives and theories converge on a single explanation. According to poetic realism, which operates in the humanities, one approaches truth as one's perspectives multiply. One takes a pluralist approach to theories and explanations, as well as to goods and purposes when it comes to social and political thought. Rhetoric has always tended toward the pluralist position, and a deep rhetoric is deeply implicated in pluralism. Rhetoric finds the means of persuasion "in each case," and cases are various. Central rhetorical virtues are copiousness—being able to produce as many perspectives and arguments as possible—and being able to argue all sides, to see from all sides. Only when one has invented copiously, can one try out the perspectives and arguments in the particular case and have a hope of approaching the true complexity of the situation. Deep rhetoric carries these virtues into philosophical and theoretical communication, alert to the oversimplifications of the abstract and theoretical, the reduction or displacement of multiple perspectives with a single one. Does it thereby become a single persperctive itself? This important question will be addressed in chapter 8. However, it can be said now that the reality to which deep rhetoric is attuned is communicative and complex and requires multiple perspectives that are open to one another. This "openness" that is an event of truth is not a theory but a continuing conversation that has both an explicit discursive dimension and an ethical dimension of transcendence. It has the form of justice.

Suffering Violence

It is always too late to get into history without violence. Benjamin's philosophical trauma over this violence helps to produce the extremity of his critique. Historical repetitions of violence do produce a mood of inevitability. Compulsive mythic violence is as real as disease and death, even if it is not as natural. But what response is called for here? We can take direction from many sources, and not just philosophers or critical theorists or arguments. Here are some other sources of direction. First, the *Oresteia* of Aeschylus in some ways confronts the same compulsive historical violence that seizes Benjamin's eye. Blood revenge rules families and peoples, and produces wars, and calls for a divine response. However, the response of Athena, who is called wise, is not to produce ever more sublime violence, but to institute juridical rhetoric and a jury system for adjudicating disputes. She is not concerned with the abstract opposite of violence or the end of history; she is concerned with the justice that will diminish and weaken the forces of violence. She addresses mythic violence not with an equally abstract opposite that will be the absolute end of mythic violence, but with concrete procedures of transcendence that will clarify conflicts and, just barely, lead to resolutions with which the conflicting parties can, with objections, live—although they are transformed in the process. And, by the way, she gives up her divine authority—provisionally—except to authorize human beings to judge their own affairs. I will explore this story in connection with the idea of rhetorical wisdom in chapter 8, but I will say here that everyone speaks in the drama, and the dramatic achievement is to give some justice to all the voices.

Second, I said at the beginning of this chapter that any rhetoric that could claim to address the problem of violence must be a suffering rhetoric; it cannot pretend to abolish violence and its suffering. It must experience and endure it. So this project can also take direction from Les Murray, who, in a poem titled "An Absolutely Ordinary Rainbow," gives us a man simply standing, weeping, on a central pedestrian mall in Sydney. The poem begins with word going around Sydney that a man is just standing there, weeping. People of all kinds hear of this, and drop what they are doing to go and see—and this is what they see:

The man we surround, the man no one approaches
simply weeps, and does not cover it, weeps
not like a child, not like the wind, like a man
and does not declaim it, nor beat his breast, nor even
sob very loudly—yet the dignity of his weeping

holds us back from his space, the hollow he makes about him
in the midday light, in his pentagram of sorrow,
and uniforms back in the crowd who tried to seize him
stare out at him, and feel, with amazement, their minds
longing for tears as children for a rainbow.

The crowd builds. Traffic backs up. The poem tells of the many ways people think and feel and react, and of what they will say in later years. No one can stop the crying. Some tremble and burn. Some "scream / who thought themselves happy." Children "and such as look out of Paradise" draw near, with dogs and pigeons. Many weep, but for different reasons. He ignores them all. Eventually, he finishes weeping, and hurries away. The picture is of pure grief. The man has cried out "not words, but grief, not messages, but sorrow"—and the line ends with sorrow.

I want to say just three things about what Murray shows in this verse story. First, suffering attracts us. The action of the poem begins with "The word" which "goes round" about a weeping man and which draws people from their preoccupations to the street where the man weeps. So, strictly speaking, it is the rhetorical transcendence of the word about suffering that first attracts people, not the suffering itself. The suffering as it is encountered is already meaningful, already a summons of the word. After they hear it, people leave their work and fill the street. The word is this: "There's a fellow crying in Martin Place. They can't stop him."

Why should inconsolable grief attract us, take us away from our work? And what is the nature of the attraction? The poem tells us that some are going out with the intent of stopping him, consoling him—to end his suffering and grief. But the crowds are also simply one of the facts of the poem, a reality. Suffering draws us. Even to deny or neglect suffering requires action and is possible only after it catches our attention. Benjamin's catching sight of the transcendental violence, the necessary suffering that is a condition for history, for the rhetorical-political order, and his philosophical amplifying of the vision of its presence, are examples of the power of this attraction. The amount and intensity of commentary on Benjamin's "Critique" is an encounter with and in part a critique of this attraction itself. The desire to look into suffering, or to theorize it, has many ways of expressing itself, many motivations and purposes, and we have many ways to respond to the fact of this desire.

Second, suffering judges us. It is a mirror. Potentially, it transforms us. This is one possible outcome of discovering that it has attracted us. In the passage above, "uniforms" have tried to "seize" the weeping man, and they "stare" at him. That is, they objectify him in sight as something threatening, and they begin violent actions against him. And this is the image in the first objectifying mirror—human beings who are at first coincident with the strict confines of their uniformed social roles. However, in the process of "staring," which is here not only a seizing with sight but a continuing vulnerability to what is showing itself, they begin to "feel, with amazement, their minds"—and that is the end of the line, an awakening of the mind. But in the next line these awakened minds then also feel their own longing for the ability to weep—"as children for a rainbow." Another man sees, and says "Ridiculous." But he, too, becomes aware of himself, "and stops his mouth with his hands, as if he uttered vomit." Vomit is of course disgusting, but it is also involuntary, automatic, and requires no thought or intent—but stopping one's mouth does. This line is followed by two more in which the narrator sees "a woman, shining, stretch her hand / and shake as she receives the gift of weeping."

Benjamin encounters violence as a philosophical political theorist with powerful messianic religious tendencies. His essay moves not simply toward a critique of violence, as its title suggests, but toward conceptualizing a (divine) violence that ends all (mythic) violence. Intellectually traumatized, attracted by the violence of the early twentieth century, he becomes the theological critic of history itself. However, this leads directly to the third thing I would like to say about this poem. There is no ultimate solution here to suffering. Everything depends on recognizing one's insufficiency, one's finally limited resources, and refusing all theoretical solutions, including ontotheological ones. The crying man himself is the exemplar here. He is not writing a critique of suffering, or a philosophy or theology of suffering. He is weeping. He "cries out / of his writhen face and ordinary body / not words, but grief, not messages, but sorrow." And at the end of the poem, he simply finishes weeping, passes through the crowd, and "Evading believers, he hurries off down

Pitt Street." Believers have answers—sciences, philosophies, theologies—and they have the cures and words and messages that go along with them. The weeping man does not possess these things; instead, he gives "the gift of weeping." There is no "solution," intellectual or political or personal. One weeps. One endures it. Or one undergoes it—this is the meaning of *pathos/pathein*, what one undergoes/to undergo. It is part of what rhetoric is about, what it affirms and does not deny. At the level of disciplinary rhetoric, it is an art of understanding what an audience is undergoing and then being able to adapt to that, or it is the art of getting people to undergo something that will help in achieving an aim. However, from a deep rhetorical perspective, *pathos* as undergoing is also one of the ways we are. There is a level at which we do not control what we undergo, yet it is a dimension of all transcendence—even at the deepest level where there is no obvious, conscious putting of someone into a mood. The man undergoes grief and sorrow and weeping. He is not at that moment believing or not believing; it has nothing to do with belief, which is, compared to grief, a kind of self-sufficiency. His weeping is the practice of an utter lack of self-sufficiency, the utter lack of a "belief" that could correspond to his grief.

From the point of view of the poem, Benjamin's idea of divine violence is only an extreme example of the common tendency to think of a theoretical, ontotheological solution to the problem of violence. And from the point of view of the poem, reflecting on the suffering of violence calls for something else—some practical acknowledgment of an ultimate lack of self-sufficiency and of any theoretical solution or comprehension of the historical suffering caused by violence. Such acknowledgment need in no way be a diminishment of one's efforts to mitigate suffering and reduce violence. On the contrary, it can help to focus one's efforts on the violence and suffering that can be reduced, and so protect them from being drawn away by abstract utopian projects to end all violence, projects which threaten to become blind to the suffering of real people as they pursue goals that grossly simplify and reify violence, suffering, and peace. From a deep rhetorical perspective, the logoi, the theories and policies, that guide our efforts to prevent and reduce violence are all "occasional," all dependent on how fitting they are to a time and place and situation and how defensible they are in light of logoi that would take us on a different course. These logoi are also accompanied by, understood in the light of, and partly motivated by the pathos with which we bear the suffering and violence. Deep rhetoric, as a kind of philosophy, may tend to prevent overarching theories and comprehensive politics and policies, but it also bears the promise of a more grounded and concrete and carefully attuned and humane approach to politics and policies.

A third source of direction comes from another work of Les Murray: his verse novel, *Fredy Neptune* (1999). The action of the novel begins during the first European war and ends after the second, and so it is concerned with some of the same violence Benjamin was concerned with and traverses the time Benjamin was writing his critique. The main character, Fred Boettcher, has a German background. In his travels, and through many turns of events, he ends up serving on both sides in the First World War. He is a witness to cruelties and violences no one would want to witness. Few of them are law-preserving or law-creating, except in the enormously abstract sense that they occur under the umbrella of war and national conflicts, although the conflicts are as much ethnic as political. And many are gratuitous, as they often are in the context of war and large-scale police actions. However, the experience of the Armenian genocide finally overwhelms Fred Boettcher. He witnesses the degradation of Armenian women by Turkish men, who force them to dance as they light them on fire. At this point, Fredy goes literally numb and loses his ability to feel pain. Although it is a gross disrespect to the work and truth of the novel to summarize this way, he recovers, years later, when he becomes capable of forgiveness (although it is no ordinary forgiveness). The substance of the novel is what Fredy undergoes. His name is Neptune because he can survive the depths, never goes completely under or perishes, and yet he undergoes as much as is humanly possible. He does not have the pure catharsis of the weeping man. He does not undergo the intellectualized trauma of Benjamin's "Critique." Instead, he goes so far that he loses the bodily ability to undergo more pain.

Murray addresses violence not as a political theorist, delineating its relation to justice and law, but as a poet, exploring experiences out of which concepts of violence arise and out of which motivations for critiques of violence also arise. Still, in some ways, Murray parallels Benjamin. Fredy serves on both sides in the war, and experiences it from both sides, and so he knows that the cruelties and violences perpetrated in war are endemic. However, Murray is nowhere close to proposing either that there is a revolutionary political-historical solution to violence or that any form of law or nation-state can abolish it. Still, both Benjamin and Murray wrestle with Gods. Benjamin's end of mythic violence requires divine action. Fredy's recovery requires, in part, forgiving God.

The poetic direction here is not easy to simplify. The profound and concrete exploration of what is human and what is humane in *Fredy*

Neptune is in some ways the whole point of the novel—how it is still possible to be human after enduring the first half of the twentieth century. In some ways, we are simply back to the weeping man, and the recognition that there is no belief or theory or theology that could possibly address what one has undergone or witnessed and that whatever intellectual work does come forth must somehow stay faithful to the experience of that lack of self-sufficiency and that inadequacy. One idea here is that it is not possible to endure without losing something of oneself along the way, and it is not possible to recover from that loss without giving up certain demands one formerly made of the world and certain expectations one had of oneself for comprehending that world.[13]

How does one take this direction, which points toward intellectual humility, without stepping down one's overall commitment to reducing violence and suffering? The idea must surely be in part that theoretical and philosophical and theological solutions to the problem of violence have not reduced violence or mitigated human suffering to the degree that any of them have claimed. It is not that these projects should be discontinued. It is rather that they need to be supplemented by more practical, less ultimate perspectives. And they need to be corrected by reflections on the nature of justice and peace. The experience of violence is trauma-inducing, and human thinking about violence bears marks of that trauma. It would be foolish to turn away altogether from thinking about violence, but it would also be foolish not to think just as vigilantly about peace.

To step out of the treacherous, abstract dialectics of violence, it will be helpful to stop thinking of peace as the absence of violence. The abolition of violence, however desirable abstractly, does not have the content of a practical possibility or of the reality of peace. The truth of Les Murray's work is that responding to violence is richly practical and existential in ways that an idea of absolute nonviolence could never capture.

The counter to violence—the projects of preventing, displacing, and stepping aside from violence, and of restitution and restoration for its victims—is the work of justice and peace. To return to the relation of justice and violence takes us back to the ideas with which Benjamin began, but I would like to move the focus to the way a deep rhetoric of reason reveals how reasoning and argumentation can be events of justice and forms of peace. The goal will be to be guided by the call for intellectual humility that issues from Murray's poetry without yielding any reasonable hope for structural change or any degree of commitment to the practical project of diminishing the rule of violence. The critique of the critique of violence will lead to the affirmation of suppressed and neglected experiences and possibilities of peace.

To explain the way in which a deep rhetoric interprets reason and argumentation to be events of justice and forms of dynamic peace requires some additional preparation. From a deep rhetorical perspective, reason is a way of giving justice to each other's *esprits*, the *esprits* that make contact in argumentation. However, achieving the proper understanding of ourselves as the *"esprits"* that come into contact in argumentation is no simple task. It is too easy to jump to ontic conclusions about these *esprits*, and this would derail the project of a deep rhetoric. From a deep rhetorical point of view, we come to be and we continue to be rhetorically, communicatively, in our transcendence: our moving beyond ourselves, and yet toward the selves we are becoming; our moving toward the world and its entities; our moving with and toward the others with whom we are in contact, and with whom we share transcendence. In our transcendence, we have always taken a direction, toward some things and not others, and in some ways and not others. We are ethical from start to finish.

In our transcendence, our being led from one thing to the next, we exist in logos, and find direction in logoi. In this transcendence, we are a continuing revelation and amplification of ourselves and others and what is around us; however, insofar as transcendence takes particular directions and not all directions, these revelations and emphases differ from and conflict with each other. Reason is giving justice to each other's lives, and to the realities these lives reveal, and in terms of which they are the lives they are. Reason is also our capability for leading and being led by others and by the realities we each reveal. Developing and clarifying this will take us through some deep philosophical waters in chapters 5 and 6. We will find shore in chapter 7, where we will continue the conversation on justice, carrying the philosophical achievements of chapters 5 and 6 with us.

FIVE

Through Heidegger: Transcendence and Logos

Deep rhetoric tries to think rhetoric as a form of transcendence, the event by which human beings (but not necessarily only human beings) are not simple entities, enclosed in themselves, but are movements toward and away from each other, movements toward and away from the world, movements toward and away from themselves, and movements toward and away from whatever else their transcendence reveals. Deep rhetoric also thinks this transcendence as being made possible by logos. Taken in terms of its power to "lead the soul," and thinking of transcendence as always having a direction, always being led by or toward something, logos is the medium and path, or route, of transcendence.

Pathos and ethos complement each other in this phenomenon. We undergo profoundly complex modes of attraction and repulsion and indifference toward what we experience. These are forms of transcendence, ways of being toward, even if in a negative mode. Being irritated and so repelled by something or someone is still transcendence, still a way of comporting oneself toward, although negatively. Insofar as undergoing this attraction or repulsion has a specific structure or form in its movement, a direction or path, it is accompanied by logos. Of course, in reality these things are inextricably joined. However, granted that the distinction in any particular case is always a matter of emphasis, it is one thing to see a radically elliptical arch of glass and steel and stone rising above the smaller buildings in the near distance and to feel one's spirits lift. It is another to stop what one was doing and decide to set out on a course to see the structure more clearly, to walk around it, to go inside, to discover its history and uses. That requires logos, a leading of one thing to another. The logos would have no reason for being without the pathos, a motive and energy of transcendence, but the pathos would have no direction without logos, which provides direction and form for pathos. Without the articulation of an intelligible world, without things being distinguished from and related to one another, without the meaningful references things bear to each other, there would be no transcendence, no path for our movement beyond ourselves. Logos is the openness of things to each other, the dynamic web of references that not only relates things to one another but that also constitutes the intelligibility of things and guides the transcendence of Dasein.

This notion of logos may sound reminiscent of the poststructuralist appropriation of Saussurean notions of language, and in some ways it is. However, there are three important differences when one takes the rhetorical point of view. First, rhetoric refuses the *langue/parole* distinction.[1] That distinction makes language into an object for study and theoretical inspection by setting aside the fact that language is the concrete way human beings transcend themselves. There is nothing wrong with making this distinction for the purpose of pursuing a specific kind of linguistic study, but such study will not have access to the event of transcendence, without which there would not be language at all. Second, the Saussurean approach sets aside all questions about the "relation" between language and reality. Poststructuralism tends to radicalize this methodological setting aside by proclaiming that the gulf can *never* be bridged, that the system of signification is free-floating. Deep rhetoric never makes this distinction—at least, not in this methodological and at least implicitly metaphysical way. Its approach to truth and meaning tends to be pragmatic rather than metaphysical. The truth and meaning of language do not lie in some correspondence between what is language and what is not—a breach that is impossible to repair after the Saussurean violence anyway—but rather in the interactive correspondence of language with the future toward which some use of language leads us. Further, deep rhetoric holds an expansive view of logos. Insofar as reality is intelligible, insofar as it can be experienced, it is an event of logos. Logos is in part the references things bear to each other. The being of things lies not in their being detached from all relation to one another, but rather in the internal references that link them to each other. They *are* as their references. Beings are nodes on a web of logos. However, unlike the free-floating signifiers of early poststructuralism, they are historical, with an intrinsically ethical dimension, and they would not *be* at all without the purposeful transcendence of human beings toward one another. They are enmeshed with reality from the start, from the ground up. Third, logos is not confined to language in the strict sense of natural or artificial or formal languages. The visual arts have logos. Music has logos. Skillful, practical action has logos. Contemplation has logos. All transcendence has a direction, is meaningful, and so depends on the references and relations and links that allow meaningful movement from one step to the next. Logos as natural language will be immensely important in approaching the question of justice, but that importance will be experienced most sharply against the background of this more expansive conception of logos.

One way to clarify the challenges facing the project of a deep rhetoric is to focus on a primary exemplary event in the study of rhetoric: someone saying something about something to someone. This event includes most of what we call "thinking," most speech and writing, and a great deal of our intelligible experience. It includes and is never isolated from the influences of character and imitation and attunement and reception. When I notice that the wind is picking up, someone (I) is saying (pointing out, remarking, registering) something (the increasing speed) about something (the wind) to someone (myself). This structure is evident in most intelligible experience, and discovering it makes it possible to hear into the communicative dimensions of experience. Different perspectives on and experiences of reality come from giving priority to different elements of this primary event, or from reducing some elements to others, or from discharging some elements altogether. So, for example, when chemists and biologists debate the properties of plasticizers in polyvinyl chloride, they try to rely on experiments and observations that are repeatable by *anyone*, so that assertions and predictions (saying something) can be made about plasticizers in PVC (about something) without reference to the fact that *someone* is speaking *to someone*. Legislators and policymakers, on the other hand, will want to know *who* is speaking (what are their qualifications, their institutional affiliations, their funding sources), and will be aware that their audience is perhaps made up of labor representatives and citizens who work in factories where PVC is manufactured. On a more theoretical level, there are moments in physics and philosophy, especially, where the *someone* is not a particular someone but a general human being, and where the theoretical difficulty lies in discharging that premise—can one make an observation or conceive a theory that does not bear the specific limitations of an observer/conceiver that is functional only under specific temporal and spatial conditions and whose conceptual, logical, and grammatical equipment is not empirically testable in any ordinary sense?

In what follows, I will confine the focus to something slightly more manageable by thinking through the importance of transcendence for the project of a deep rhetoric in a philosophical context informed by the thinking of Martin Heidegger, as well as the kinds of criticism of Heidegger made by Karl Jaspers, Emmanuel Levinas, Hans-Georg Gadamer, and others. This context is both ontological and ethical, and is centered on transcendence.

Deep rhetoric is an encounter with, a critique of, and a rapprochement with philosophy, and Heidegger is a critical philosophical passage to a deep rhetoric for a number of reasons.[2] First, his persevering critique of the way we ordinarily conceptualize being and beings prevents us from incorporating into rhetorical theory the very presumptions that preclude rhetoric from becoming philosophical—and from becoming as critical, creative, and truthful as it could be. Heidegger's development of the *Seinsfrage*, the question of being, both makes a deep rhetoric possible and carries with it the false trails that a deep rhetoric must avoid. Second, Heidegger's notion of Dasein as the kind of being that human beings are guards rhetorical humanism against a number of errors that could lead it astray. The notion of Dasein can do this because Heidegger thinks of human being not simply as a kind of thing or entity but as transcendence, and transcendence is an essential concern of a deep rhetoric. Third, Heidegger's project is in part a continuing, failed encounter with rhetoric. He confronts rhetoric head on in Aristotle, incorporates features of it into *Being and Time*, but on the whole turns away from thematizing rhetoric because the history of philosophy (and perhaps the history of being itself) has neglected rhetoric in favor of a narrower conception of logos. Fourth, Heidegger's achievements and failures demand of us a critique of Heidegger for the sake of a deep rhetoric. Heidegger develops a profound interpretation of transcendence as equivalent to human existence itself, and this allows deep rhetoric to explore the way this transcendence leads to conflict and its just resolution as events that are constitutive for what we know as human life and society. Ultimately, Heidegger's thought allows us to explore—both sympathetically and critically—the ways in which logos and transcendence work together, and so helps us to begin to survey the range of a deep rhetoric.

Heidegger, Emmanuel Levinas, and Hans-Georg Gadamer were all concerned with understanding transcendence in a far-reaching way, probing beyond and beneath the ordinary theoretical presumptions that tended to grasp transcendence in familiar categories and as concerned with consciousness, intentionality, and epistemology. Yet they each interpreted the primary event of rhetoric in a different way. This exemplary event is: *someone saying something about something to someone*. In general, Heidegger keeps his attention on the *about something* and on the play of being and beings in every *saying something about something*. There are qualifications to be made about this, but in general it is certainly fair to say that ontology is Heidegger's dominating orientation. Levinas tries to stand Heidegger on his head, or rather his feet. He focuses more on the *saying* than he does on the *about something*, and he divides the *saying something* into the *saying* and the *said*, emphasizing the *saying* over the *said*. However, this is only part of a major shift of attention to the *someones* involved, to their infinity, their specificity, and to the fact that their reality is primarily ethical rather than ontological.[3] Gadamer, I believe, tries to accomplish and preserve a balance in describing the interdependence of the elements of this primary rhetorical event. For Gadamer, the elements are at play with one another, and are what they are only in terms of one another. In other words, transcendence *is* their reality, and logos, for Gadamer, turns out to be the only transcendence we know. All of this sets the stage for a deep rhetorical account of what Perelman and Olbrechts-Tyteca accomplish in *The New Rhetoric*—and specifically what Perelman accomplishes in his accounts of the relation of justice and reason. Ultimately, *The New Rhetoric* is concerned with the *justice of transcendence*, understood in light of the primary rhetorical event and specifically within the event of argumentation. Argumentation is reasonable by virtue of its justice, and it is the process by which the violence of transcendence is transformed into peace.

This approach requires a break with some of the traditional ways of thinking of rhetoric as a specific art or discipline, and it requires a deeper and more developed philosophical context for rhetoric. Only a philosophical rhetoric will be able to explain the genuinely revolutionary implications of the new rhetoric project. That project is not simply a rhetoric of argumentation that applies disciplinary rhetoric to the practice of argumentation to show what argumentation is and to explain how to argue effectively. The new rhetoric project aims at a rhetoric of reason that is thoroughly philosophical. It pursues this aim by effecting a rapprochement with philosophy, holding a conversation with philosophy, and launching a critique of philosophy. The new rhetoric project is focused on a theory of argumentation, but it is a theory of argumentation as a theory of reason and of social life itself at the level of Protagoras's great myth of the origin of society and rhetoric. Perelman was trained as a philosopher, wrote as a philosopher, and thought of himself primarily as a philosopher. The new rhetoric project offers an account of reasoned argument as a stand-in for violence, a way to undergo and pass through conflicts nonviolently. Reason is an acceptable way to do this because it is just; reasonable outcomes are justifiable outcomes. The conflicts that are addressed by a rhetoric of argumentation go all the way down to the conflicts that organize individual psyches and all the way out to the most abstract philosophical and scientific controversies. The announced purpose of the project is: "the justification of the possibility of a human community in the sphere of action when this justification cannot be based on a reality or objective truth" (*NR* 514). This project can be clarified and explained more completely by a deep rhetoric, one that is much more attentive to the ethical and communicative dimensions of transcendence and to the theory of argumentation as a theory of justice at the level of transcendence itself. The passage through Heidegger will help to make the break with traditional ways of conceptualizing rhetoric, and the conversation with and critique of Heidegger will provide the context for a philosophical rhetoric.

Heidegger

Martin Heidegger's collected works fill over a hundred volumes and include lectures and writings that were produced over the course of more than sixty-five years. In these works, he draws from the entire Western philosophical and theological tradition. His wrestling with being and beings and transcendence and logos, and his ways of speaking and writing about them, change in important ways over the many years he lectured and wrote. Even in single texts, or a single course of lectures, these notions change shape as Heidegger pursues his questions, following them wherever they seem to lead. My aim here is not so much to capture Heidegger's idea of transcendence and then deploy it for the purposes of a deep rhetoric as it is to follow some of the currents of his thinking about transcendence (and its connection with logos and communication) as a way of filling out the philosophical dimensions of a deep rhetoric with the same questioning consideration that marks Heidegger's philosophical struggles. Only against the background of a philosophical exploration and development of the notion of transcendence will the philosophical significance of Perelman's account of reason as justice begin to appear in its proper light. In what follows, I will concentrate mostly on two stages of Heidegger's thought—first, and mainly, on the later 1920s, the period of *Being and Time*, *The Basic Problems of Phenomenology*, *The Essence of*

Reasons, and *The Fundamental Concepts of Metaphysics*; and, second, on the period of 1936/37, the period in which the *Contributions to Philosophy (From Enowning)* were written and the period sometimes called the shift or turning in Heidegger's thought.[4]

Four central ideas orient Heidegger's thinking during the later 1920s. By way of introduction, I will offer brief explanations of each of them, summarizing from the writings of the later 1920s. First is the question of being. Heidegger believes that we have forgotten this question, and his project is to remember how to ask it, to develop it, and to address it. Asking the question depends on being able to distinguish between beings and being. We have no trouble asking about beings. The trouble is that we tend to think of being as a being—but it is not. It is the being of beings, but not a being itself. Neither is it a kind of supercategory for all beings. We get hints of being when we examine the different ways that a being has been said to be—say, when we think of the difference between what it is (essence) and that it is (existence), or the difference between mind (*res cogitans*) and matter (*res extensa*). We see something like being at work, too, in the differentiation of fields of scientific study, which study beings in their being in different ways: as historical, as mathematical, as living, as sheerly physical, and so on. The sciences seem to presume that being can be differentiated this way—but what then is it that is being differentiated? What allows itself to be differentiated in these ways? The answer is not at all clear. It is not even clear *exactly* what the question is. The continuing difficulty is that when we do start to understand being, we tend to think of it as a being, yet when we stop thinking of it as a being, we seem to find ourselves at a loss, or thinking of nothing at all. Yet, says Heidegger, we do ask this question. We do make the distinction between being and beings. And we do encounter beings in their being, even if our understanding of being is only implicit and indistinct. Heidegger's project is to pursue this question of what he regards as the most questionable matter of all: being itself.

This project has the immediate impact of suspending the credentials of beings. Beings become questionable in their very being, which is usually what is most secure about them. Having specific objects of study—entities with a certain kind of being—and a productive methodology are constitutive for the legitimacy of the different sciences and disciplines. However, Heidegger believes that the ontologies of the sciences have been generated from within the implicit notions of being that are operative in the research projects that make up a science in some place and time. The sciences do not raise the question of being. Going through

Heidegger, even a short way, exposes the field of rhetoric to the question of being, and so undoes the obviousness of ordinary notions of, for example, speaker, audience, speech, violence, reason, and justice because the being of these beings is fundamentally questionable. It also poses philosophical challenges for the range and depth of rhetoric by asking whether and how there might be communicative and so deep rhetorical dimensions in being itself, the question of being, the difference between being and beings, as well as in the being of human being.

The second orienting idea of Heidegger's project is that we discover access to being only because there is a being that already in some way understands being. Heidegger uses the word "ontic" to characterize anything having to do with beings. He uses the word "ontological" to characterize whatever has to do with being. So, a study of beings is an ontic study, and most sciences and disciplines are ontic enterprises. Philosophy, according to Heidegger, is ontological. Philosophy is possible only because one kind of being is both ontic *and* ontological. That is, it is both a specific entity and also an understanding of being. This ontic-ontological being Heidegger calls "Dasein." Dasein is thus the name of the entity, the human being, and the name of its way of being, its being human. "Dasein" ordinarily means existence and literally means "there-being" or "being there." The "there" is the place in which beings have their being, the space in which they can have their differences from each other and show themselves *as* what they *are*. It is also the space where the difference between being and beings occurs. This space is held open by the entity Dasein, which is, in its very being, a holding open of this space, this "Da." In the way Dasein comports itself toward this space and what it holds, it moves with an implicit understanding of being and acts skillfully in interacting with beings according to the kind of being they are. The first part of Heidegger's project, then, is to investigate the being of this entity called Dasein, for it holds in its very being an implicit understanding of being, the only basis on which one can begin to clarify and develop the meaning of being.

Deep rhetorical humanism follows along in this investigation of Dasein. Rhetorical capabilities and actions will participate in and be modes or concrete instances of the kind of being with which Dasein comports itself toward its own "there." Insofar as Dasein is a rhetorical being—and for a deep rhetoric it is—the being of what is rhetorical will have to be articulated in a conversation with the analysis of Dasein as an ontological entity. Rhetorical actions and categories are not simply ontic objects to be studied and improved. They are ways of being of an entity that has an ontological way of being that is a disclosure of the being of entities, the being of others, and its own being. Rhetoric is a way things come to be what they are.

Third, Dasein exists as transcendence. It is not a self-enclosed entity with its being and essence inside of it, in its matter or soul. Its being is to be outside of itself, beyond itself, ahead of itself, transcending itself in a movement toward beings, toward other human beings, and toward its own being—that is, toward a way of being who it is and is becoming. Its being is to be on the way to itself. So, says Heidegger, Dasein does not have "properties" or qualities that serve to define it as an entity; instead, it has ways of transcending, ways of moving beyond itself and toward itself. He calls these ways of existing "existentialia." As Dasein, our ability to be is an ability and competence to move beyond ourselves and into possibilities of being ourselves in a world among entities and with other people. Heidegger calls this ability "understanding" not because it always involves explicit cognition or theoretical knowledge but because it always involves the manifesting of beings and others and ourselves, even if in our skillful competence for moving beyond our currently actual selves into new possibilities of being with others and in the world we have only an implicit understanding of what is happening. This event of transcendence is not simply a matter of consciousness, says Heidegger; it is existential, practical, and this transcendence is in fact the form of all action.

This transcendence also has the character of always being in an attunement or mood of some kind. This implicit mood not only participates in determining how entities show themselves, but also serves as a kind of indicator of how things are going for the Dasein. We care about our own being and the way it is always moving beyond us, dragging us with it into new possibilities, forward in time, and we always have some sense and some attitude about how we are doing. We find ourselves in this attunement to our being, and it shapes the way we find everything else, too. This transcendence also has the form of discourse, or "talk" (*Rede*), which Heidegger calls the articulation of intelligibility. In transcendence, the world is already intelligible, already significant, already, in Heidegger's terms, informed by a kind of talk which is itself a mode of transcendence, a necessary one, without which there would be no transcendence at all. Finally this transcendence exhibits "falling," a tendency to understand and attune and talk in standard, default, accepted, or "inauthentic" ways and so to occlude and neglect its own freedom for "authentic" transcendence.

This all has immense import for a deep rhetoric. Heidegger has taken the scholastic and phenomenological concept of intentionality, according to which all consciousness is consciousness of something, and he has transformed it into an understanding of existence, according to which all transcendence—all speech and action, for example—is existing transcendence *toward something*. We are, in our very being, a transcendence-toward that always moves in the element of talk or speech (*Rede*), some articulation of intelligibility. This will generate core questions for the deep rhetorical passage through Heidegger: how can we best characterize the unity of logos and transcendence? And then also: how can we best characterize logos as it differentiates itself into the different kinds of intelligibility that attend transcendence? It will turn out that Heidegger is aware of a larger notion of logos that would embrace all forms of intelligibility; however, he decides in the later 1920s mostly to confine his use of the word "logos" to describing a narrow range of assertable intelligibility, and so to make it a focus of his critical "destruction" of the tradition—for reasons that we will examine.

Transcendence is also a critical notion because it is the context for understanding how it is that we can come into conflict with each other in our actions and our speech in experiences of *violence* rather than mere brute force. Without transcendence, there can be brute force, but only with transcendence do we have the possibility of violence. Transcendence is also the context for explaining how a *contact des esprits* is possible in argumentation and how we are able to undergo change and growth in the experience of reasoning together. Put simply, this is possible because language is transcendence, a way we encounter and interact with ourselves and other people and other beings—but this means "encounter and interact with" in the context of a deep rhetorical understanding that beings come to be what they are out of the encounter itself.

This characterization of transcendence is also critical for rhetoric because Heidegger has incorporated into it an acknowledgment of something he learned from lecturing on Aristotle's *Rhetoric*: that *pathos/pathein*, undergoing transcendence in an affectivity that attunes us, in one way or another, to our being and to other beings, is a dimension of all transcendence. There is no understanding without *pathos*.

The fourth and final orienting idea here is that the being of Dasein is being-in-the-world. Dasein is not first an entity, a "subject," who then faces the epistemological problem of establishing a relation to another entity called the "world." Rather, our being is not only to be outside of and beyond ourselves but also to be *as* the encounter with beings in the light of their being in an ordered world. According to Heidegger, transcendence is our capacity for experiencing what he calls "the manifestness of beings as such, of beings *as* beings" (1995, 274). This manifestness, says Heidegger, belongs to *worldliness*, which is a feature of the kind of being we have: being-in-the-world. Our transcendence occurs on a web of intrinsically related entities—in a world. Only within a world is a relation to entities as such possible. Heidegger insists that the "understanding of the being of beings is connected with the *understanding of world*, which is the presupposition for the experience of an intraworldly being" (1982, 175), so "world" plays a critical role in approaching the question of being itself. This is all the more important because both the being of beings and the being of Dasein are here connected with "world," and so being itself is encountered by Dasein in an undifferentiated way.

Heidegger's notion of worldliness is very abstract, but very important for taking steps toward the idea of a deep rhetoric. It will lead us into an extensive discussion of intelligibility and logos that will clear the way for a deep rhetoric, and it will require some detailed commentary. The commentary will necessarily be both sympathetic and critical, gathering from Heidegger the philosophical depth and scope a deep rhetoric will need, as it thinks through, step by step, some of Heidegger's central moves, but also abandoning the Heideggerian paths that lead nowhere, the ones that are exposed as missteps in the encounter with deep rhetoric.

World and Logos

For a being to become manifest *as* a particular being is for it to be interpreted in light of its relations to other beings (*somethings*)—for it to be understood as belonging to a *world*. That is, our transcendence toward entities takes place as part of an event that includes a limited kind of transcendence of entities toward each other. This limited and dependent transcendence of entities toward each other is part of their meaningfulness. Both kinds of transcendence are dimensions of the same primary phenomenon of transcendence.

For example, my cell phone *is* a physical object, but also an object designed and produced by other people in a global system of resource extraction, design, manufacturing, marketing, distribution, and sale. It *is* a communication device and has numerous voice and texting functions, as well as *being* a clock, an alarm, a timer, a camera, a video camera, a video screen and player, a voice recorder, a calendar, an audio player, a photo album, an address book, a map, a gps device, a tracking device, and much more. It *can be* some of these things only because it *belongs* to a larger system of relationships of cell towers, land lines, satellites, software, servers, storage facilities, other cell phones, computers, users, content providers—and the entire framework of labor, management, ownership, and physical plants that support these. Further, it *is possible* for me to have experience with this cell phone as a cell phone (*as something*) only because *I also understand*, however dimly, that this cell phone *belongs to* this larger network without which it would not be experienced as *what it is*. That is, only within a culture in which cell phones make sense can a cell phone become manifest *as* a cell phone and be used to accomplish the particular purposes people accomplish in their lives. If we dropped one into the hands of Socrates or Ramses II, the cell phone *would not become manifest as* a cell phone. It would become manifest—to the extent that it became manifest at all—as something else. Clock, alarm, timer, video, and gps only show up for us in the context of a world in which they have the meaning they do. One in which, for instance, specific systems of time measurement and notation and representation exist, or one in which the earth is understood as a globe on which locations can be identified by means of transmissions from spacecraft.

The experiences in which the cell phone becomes manifest *as* a cell phone (*as something*) have the same purposeful temporal structure that human experience has. Only within the context of individual human lives does a cell phone make itself manifest in experience. This happens in different ways in different lives. Some people seem almost to live through cell phones. Some refuse to use them altogether. One person may use his simply to communicate with family members. Another may use hers for everything from shopping to trading stock to consulting with her sister's doctor. However, in each kind of life, the cell phone becomes manifest *as* a being, *as* something unified, and this is true for all entities. In some actions and in some lives, a cell phone's manifestness as a cell phone may be intensified—and in some others diminished. However, the way in which a cell phone is manifest will always have these two very general features. It will become manifest in light of a social world and in light of an individual human life. However, these two features of the manifestness of entities are often missed altogether. Ordinarily, the "world" is in the background, forgotten. It is enough to buy the cell phone and to use it. Much of our understanding of the world is implicit, and has more or less sunk into our skills and habits and predispositions.[5] We "know how" to use the phone in a way that depends on some implicit knowledge of the web of relations that allow the phone to be manifest, but we never step back to ponder the interdependence of the entity and the world that allows it to be what it is. The phone is just there to be used, or, if we think of it at all, we think of it as an object deprived of this background—sheerly present in its objectness. Much the same is true of the individual human life in light of which the phone makes its appearance as a phone. The phone appears to be a simple object (*something*), but it is the human life that carries the world that makes the manifestness of the phone possible, and human life for Heidegger is conceived as temporal existence that always, formally and ultimately, belongs to an individual, a *someone*, even though ordinarily this someone speaks and acts and thinks as a mostly undifferentiated subject and agent of predominant historical and social formations.

Manifestness happens in logos, the intelligibility of beings that is also language, speech, reason, argument—the transcendence of beings toward each other. Heidegger thinks of logos in myriad different ways in different writings, and with marked changes in emphasis over his career. In 1927, in *Being and Time*, he thinks of the practical web of relations in which entities become manifest as a prelinguistic system of references to which words accrue. He imagines these references coming to be in the practical activities of human beings pursuing their purposes. We encounter beings ordinarily as good for something or not, in terms of having a relation to the purposes we pursue. Even having-no-relation-to-our-purposes is a way that beings become manifest, although perhaps only dimly. At the same time, we encounter beings as having references to other people, as being made by or for them, as usable by them or not, as having social meaning of various kinds. These references are indications and representatives of that larger network of references that in Heidegger goes by the name of "world" or sometimes even "being," and, in a deep rhetoric, belongs to logos in the broad sense. The being of beings encountered in this practical way Heidegger calls "readiness-to-hand" (1962, 95–102). In this context, Heidegger is especially interested in emphasizing the implicitness of this network of references and in the implicitness of our comprehension of it. Nonetheless, something of logos articulates itself in the references that are constitutive of this web or network, implicit as it may be.

In 1929–30, Heidegger thinks of the way individual entities keep outshining this network of their being as the "prevailing" of entities. This prevailing becomes manifest in logos: "In the logos, the prevailing of beings becomes revealed, becomes manifest" (1995, 27). The dominant idea here is that logos manifests *the prevailing of beings over being*. Logos, construed in the narrow sense, is the path of applying logical assertion and grammatical predication to everything, including human beings and being itself, because everything is conceptualized and experienced and treated as a being. More specifically, everything tends to be treated not simply as being ready to hand, but as merely *present at hand*—that is, extracted from the background of practical meanings and references in which the ready to hand has its being. In our own time, says Heidegger, everything that is shows itself as a preexistent, independently present at hand being to be managed logically and used as a potential resource according to the technical and scientific capabilities of our time. To the extent possible, beings all appear as susceptible to our control. Where control is not possible, their behavior is at least potentially predictable. What leads beings to have this kind of being is "forgotten," as Heidegger says. We barely have the wherewithal to try to formulate the question about being at all, but the restriction of logos to a narrowly logical use of language greatly exacerbates this inability.

However, even here, the issue becomes complicated in ways that will become explicit later because Heidegger holds two different views of logos. Heidegger puts it this way in 1929 in *The Essence of Reasons*: "The understanding of being (logos in a very broad sense), which from the outset clarifies and guides every way of behaving toward being, is neither a grasping of being as such nor even a comprehending of that which is grasped (logos in the narrowest sense . . .)" (1969, 23). Here, even our preconceptual implicit understanding of being is a matter of logos, logos which is contrasted with the very different idea of logos as explicit and conceptual and predicative. Apparently everything in between these two is also a matter of logos because, as Heidegger says: "There are many stages between the preontological understanding of being and the explicit problematic involved in conceptualizing" (23).

"Logos in a very broad sense" would be *something like* the ancient sense of logos, the broad sense with which a deep rhetoric is allied, in which intelligibility and language are not completely distinguishable, and in which both being and *beings as beings* depend on logos, even before logos becomes conceptual, propositional, and "logical." Gadamer will make this move openly and announce that "Being that can be understood is language" (2003, 474). Later in his career, Heidegger will emphasize something similar to this conception of language in formulations such as "Language is the house of being" and in passages where he says that when we walk into a forest, we are always walking through the word "forest." There, the historical congealing of entities and the development of their relations in explicit discourses become nearly all-determining. However, in the later 1920s and often beyond, Heidegger mostly speaks of and focuses on "logos in the narrowest sense" when he writes about logos. A deep rhetoric will fight its way through this oscillating in Heidegger, and side decisively with being consistently attentive to "logos in a very broad sense."

Logos is transcendence, the condition for the advent of the self and the world and those we are with, which are all ontologically interdependent.[6] It might seem to be an exaggeration to say that human transcendence, the openness of human beings to each other and to the world, is logos. After all, aren't our physical senses an openness to the world? And isn't the very movement of our bodies through space a movement toward other people and objects? And don't we perceive and move in silence? And the answer is, yes. No one would want to deny this. However, our senses would not encounter beings *as* beings, human beings *as* human beings, without logos, without their being to some degree separated from other beings and unified in themselves and related to one another in meaningfulness.

Even in silence, logos gives us access to each other. When, in the middle of the night, in silence, half asleep, my wife turns over and rests her knee on my thigh, we are as far from speech as we can be. Yet, I experience this not as a mere sensation or stimulation of the nerves in my legs. I experience my wife and her knee. Not her hand, not someone else's knee. Her hand would mean something different. She would be trying to wake me, or testing to see whether I was awake. If she moved her knee, instead of resting it, that would also be a sign that she was trying to wake me. Since she merely rests it there, she may be asleep. If she is awake, she may be moving closer because she has had a disturbing dream or thought and wants the comfort of closeness. There are many possibilities, but not every possibility. Her knee is not a brute sensation. It is experienced as what it is—it is given its being as a being—by the web of meanings that relate it to other beings, by logos. Even in the silence of night, things show themselves as such because logos makes them intelligible, connects them with one another, draws them into a world. Two people can encounter each other only in the world that logos opens for them.

A familiar difficulty here is that we tend to think of a "relation" as something that connects distinct entities that are what they are independently of that relation. However, this is not the case with the relations we are exploring here. They are instead an entity's internal references to other entities that allow it to be *what it is*. Entities give being to one another in their giving meaning to one another along these lines of references that permeate beings as such. This giving and receiving is part of what they are, and they would not be what they are without it.

Another difficulty in learning to think with the idea of logos is that, once again, a certain misleading concept of language keeps interfering. We often think of language as a grammatical system and a lexicon that can be studied as an object independently of any questions about the way language is always revealing the things we experience (even at the same time that it may also be hiding them) and working as a medium of transcendence. But that concept of language is gained only by subtracting from language an important part of what it is. There is nothing wrong with that method of subtracting as a way to study certain features of grammar and syntax and morphology. However, that is not language as it actually comes to pass, and it is not logos.

This world made of logos is also temporal, historical. The world one generation inherits has been received from other generations. It is changed through the actions and experiences of a generation, and passed on in time to yet other generations. The logos is in movement in time in this large, historical way. In its particularity, it is directional, steering generations and cultures and groups and individuals in specific ways, leading them. It gives particular possibilities of intelligibility and language and reason and choice to each generation. We exist in the interpretive application of what is past to what is new, which always keeps the intelligibility of the past partly in the future and the intelligibility of the future dependent on the past.[7]

It is helpful, while preserving the larger sense of logos, also to keep in mind a distinction between concrete historical logoi and logos in the larger sense. There are important differences between logos as that which makes possible the intelligibility of anything at all and the historical logoi that *we* inherit and which make up *our* world. In fact, there are three clearly distinct senses of "logos" as the notion works in a deep rhetoric. First, there are the actual logoi we speak and write and think and to which we have an at least partially free and deliberate relation. Second, there is the complete historical world of meaning and significance in which we first find ourselves and in light of which we understand ourselves and other things—this is the logos from out of which we draw the specific logoi we speak and write and think. It is possible to have a partly free and deliberate and critical relation to parts of this world, but there are daunting difficulties and complexities involved in this. Third, there is the larger primary notion of logos as the medium of human transcendence in which it is possible for one thing to lead to another at all. This primary kind of logos gives entities the ability to relate to each other as part of their internal constitution. One of the challenges of speaking about logos is to show how these different senses of logos belong to one another.

Heidegger rarely confronts this challenge directly or clearly. For him, the ontological difference is primary, and elaborating his conception of logos in the broadest sense, as well as the narrower differentiations of different kinds of logoi, is just not a matter he pursues with focus or consistency, although he cannot help coming across the issues again and again. In the face of them, he sometimes asserts that silence is required to move from beings to being and to become capable of experiencing the difference between them. That move lies, in *Being and Time*, in the clearing of Dasein in authentic silence and in Heidegger's later writings in the silent waiting for a new giving of being. In these discussions, logos seems to lie almost exclusively on the side of beings and their logically limited manifestness. However, this is an impossible solution with which Heidegger must eventually come to terms. Here is one formulation of the problem. For Heidegger, being makes possible the intelligibility and manifestness of beings. Without world, there are not beings as such. However, this distinction between being and beings is a distinction *made by way of* logos. It is in fact not only the classic move of a transcendental *argument* but also the classic move of creating a *philosophical pair*, described by Perelman and Olbrechts-Tyteca in *The New Rhetoric*. It raises obvious questions about the nature of the distinction. What domains does it distinguish? What concepts does it distinguish? What do beings and being still have in common and what specifically differentiates them? What are the criteria for making the distinction appropriately? Mustn't one somehow know a great deal about what is on both sides of the distinction in order to mark the difference at all? The intelligibility of the distinction thus depends on logos.

Heidegger fully recognizes the difficulties, of course, and he embarks on a number of maneuvers to prevent the distinction from being understood as simply another distinction among beings. However, this distinction can be made only in language and with the help of logos. Even the apophatic, negative way will be a way of logos. This is why one of Heidegger's best critics, Gadamer, will conclude that "language always forestalls any objection to its jurisdiction" and that "its universality keeps pace with the universality of reason" (2003, 401). Gadamer's inviolate concern is "the indissoluble unity of thought and language as we encounter it in the hermeneutical phenomenon, namely as the unity of understanding and interpretation" (403). The hermeneutical phenomenon par excellence for Heidegger, and in many ways for Gadamer, too, is Dasein. In fact, Gadamer's notion of the unity of thought and language, understanding and interpretation, is developed out of and in response to Heidegger's own account of understanding and interpretation in sections 31 and 32 of *Being and Time* (to which we will come shortly).

So here we get a clear picture of the challenge. Can Heidegger mark the ontological difference by somehow going beyond logos without succumbing to some kind of irrationalism? By "irrationalism" I mean not the idea that reason has limits or that we can undergo important experiences that cannot be certified by reason or that silence both has important meanings and is a way of experience itself, but rather that we can have knowledge that does not depend on language or on the intelligibility made available to us by logos. Think of this irrationalism as a kind of gnosticism—direct knowledge that bypasses logos and is not supportable by reasoned discussion. Heidegger gives every sign that he is aware of the danger he is facing.

Near the very end of his 1929–30 lectures, *The Fundamental Concepts of Metaphysics*, Heidegger skillfully attempts to elaborate this distinction without collapsing it into an ordinary, ontic distinction and without consigning it altogether to silence. First, the goal seems to be to "hear" this distinction, and I take this to be a deliberate contrast to "seeing" it in the sense of grasping it or conceptualizing it: "We constantly *fail to hear* [*überhören*, italics in original] this distinction between being and beings" (1995, 357). And yet, says Heidegger, we continuously make use of it. Further: "It is not *we* who make it, rather *it* happens *to us* as the fundamental occurrence of our *Dasein*" (357). We already understand being—we *must*, "although not conceptually" (357). However, we too quickly convert this preconceptual, undifferentiated being into categories such as essence and existence, which apply universally to entities, and then we think of these as concepts of the being of beings.

That is Heidegger's analysis. But if our understanding of world is preconceptual, and if it is a kind of nonlinguistic whole, inherited but not fully received, directing us, leading us, without our being able to "remember" or conceive of it—isn't all of *that description* still language, logos, making sense of being, although in mostly negative ways? Of course it is, and Heidegger knows this. For all of *that description* is also supposed to be only a "formal indication" of something else. Heidegger wants to push the negative way still further. And yet an "indication," in its referring, is still logos. And moving along a way, from one step which leads to another, is also leading, also logos. In fact, pointing in a direction, "indicating" "formally" without establishing some absolute point of arrival or goal, is almost a definition of logos in the larger sense, as the "leading" of one thing to another.

For Heidegger, one of the problems of ontology in these 1929–1930 lectures is that it is dominated by the logos, but when he says this he means the narrow and forgetful logic of assertion, of subjects and predicates and the truth and falsity of their connection—all of which is determined by an understanding of entities as simply present at hand, without world or Dasein. One might think, then, that Heidegger would redress this problem by speaking of a larger sense of logos—say, one connected with rhetoric, one which might include the way attunements lead to one another as well as to different beliefs and conclusions. Heidegger had given a seminar on Aristotle's *Rhetoric* in the summer of 1924, and he had written in 1927 in *Being and Time*: "Contrary to the traditional orientation, according to which rhetoric is conceived as the kind of thing we 'learn in school,' this work of Aristotle must be taken as the first systematic hermeneutic of the everydayness of Being with one another" (1962, 178). This was said in the context of a discussion of *Befindlichkeit* and the *pathē*. Even in the 1929–30 lectures we are following here, Heidegger says:

> When we said that the history of Western logic, and following from that the science of languages in general, is determined by the Greek theory of the *logos* in the sense of the propositional statement, then it must also be mentioned that the same Aristotle who—under essential influences from Plato—first penetrated to an insight into the structure of the statement, also in his *Rhetoric* recognized and undertook the mighty task of submitting the forms and formations of non-thetic discourse to interpretation. It was certainly true for various reasons, however, that the power of logic was too strong to leave open any genuine possibility of developing this attempt. (1995, 303)

And yet Heidegger very self-consciously chooses to forego an inquiry into a deep rhetoric and into the senses of logos that exceed propositional logic. He himself is unwilling to take up Aristotle's mighty task in the context of his thinking about logos and language and logic.

But why? The whole field of modern argumentation studies (as distinct from logic) still lay fallow in 1930, and Europe was in the middle of convulsions of violent irrationality. The ancient Greek notion of *logos* was stripped down to bare logic. Reason was becoming confined pretty much to sense-data and formal logic. As Heidegger delivered the 1929–30 lectures, Rudolph Carnap, Otto Neurath, and Hans Hahn were publishing *The Scientific Conception of the World: The Vienna Circle*. The ideas of a larger sense of logos or of the tradition of rhetoric or of a study of argumentation that focuses on how people reason in conditions of conflict and uncertainty were at this time already barely conceivable and were about to slip into oblivion altogether. This would seem to have been the appropriate moment to speak for rhetoric, to develop that larger sense of logos associated with rhetoric that, according to Heidegger, did not develop after Aristotle. So why did Heidegger choose to focus his attention instead on a narrow conception of logos and set the agenda for the overcoming of logocentrism? Why not develop, at least to some degree, the larger conception of logos that might be active in a philosophical rhetoric that would take up the project whose development, as Heidegger says, was prevented by the power of the narrow understanding of logos and logic?

Heidegger does have a kind of answer:

> But then why should we investigate this form of discourse [the narrowly logical] at all if, as we admit, it is *not an originary one*, not one that immediately displays the problem? Why do we not directly force the problem of the 'as' into its proper dimension? Because the task is to catch sight of *this dimension* as something *entirely other* [*das ganz Andere*] and this can only occur if we contrast it with that in which we self-evidently move. (1995, 304)

It is difficult to characterize the philosophical method being proposed here. I have somewhat casually described it as apophatic, a negative way of discovering access to something by contrasting it with what it is not, and moving slowly, through the negation, toward it, or at least toward an end to mistaking other things for it. However, it is difficult to defend his move here. First, the method is based on results that have already been achieved—apparently without the method. We somehow already know that the "dimension" we are seeking is *wholly other*. That's a pretty conceptual concept for something that is known preconceptually. In addition, this is a surprising way to describe the ontological difference. Being and beings are here said to be found in different "dimensions," and they are "wholly other" to each other. Most of Heidegger's accounts do not, in fact, conform to this view. Being is usually said to be necessarily the being of beings. And the ontological difference is usually pursued in much more subtle ways.

Second, it is simply not self-evident that "we" "move" in the dimension of propositional logic—or that we moved that way in 1929. Heidegger acknowledged as much when he recognized Aristotle's *Rhetoric* as a "systematic hermeneutic of the everydayness of being with one another." We also move self-evidently in everydayness, but as Heidegger has shown, there is nothing simple about everydayness, and scientific and logical theories about the world are, in his view, derivative and privative in comparison with everydayness, and not at all "everyday." Aristotle's *Rhetoric* was an attempt to interpret the everydayness of his time and place, just as Heidegger is attempting to interpret the everydayness of his time and place, and these moves are in some ways similar to the move that ordinary language philosophers will make in the years after Heidegger's 1929 lectures. Something goes amiss in Heidegger's choice to limit his focus during this period to a narrow notion of logos. One of the consequences is that the possibility of a philosophical rhetoric—a deep rhetoric—is completely set aside, and the possibility never seems to be entertained again.

It is important to get the nature of this failure right. It is not that Heidegger is embracing this narrowing of logos because there is no real historical alternative. After all, he is insisting that, eventually, describing and understanding this fate of logos is supposed to prepare us to glimpse something else, some alternative. It is rather that the project of understanding the narrowing of logos eclipses the project of developing an account of logos in the larger sense and of a rhetoric that might correspond to it. To put it in simpler terms, Heidegger is juggling projects that both complement each other and conflict and compete with each other. First is the project of "destruction," the dismantling of the history of philosophy and the laying open of its ontological unconscious. In this project, "logos" is an object of "destruction," something to be exposed as an effect of ontological forgetfulness. This is, of course, logos in the narrow sense, what he calls *logos apophantikos*. However, Heideggerian "destruction" is not destruction for its own sake. It is rather a "destruction" of something that needs to be dismantled to make way for something else to appear. This "something else" is connected with the second project, the hermeneutic project of a retrieval of what has been obscured and forgotten by the narrowing of logos and the forgetting of the question of being. This project could be concerned with logos in the larger sense and with recovering an understanding of the many ways logos is creative and dynamic outside of narrowly logical discourse, manipulative persuasion, and the gossipy parroting that, according to Heidegger, dominates the daily life of Dasein.

The hermeneutic project is itself dependent on the project of destruction: "*Hermeneutics carries out its task only on the path of destruction.*"[8] The challenge is that the continuing priority of the project of destruction leads to the eclipse and postponement of the hermeneutic project, *and nowhere is this truer than with respect to rhetoric*. Consider again Heidegger's acknowledgment that "Aristotle . . . in his *Rhetoric* recognized and undertook the mighty task of submitting the forms and formations of non-thetic discourse to interpretation"—that is, that Aristotle engaged in something like the hermeneutic project connected with a larger sense of logos (1995, 303). It would seem, then, that Heidegger's hermeneutic project would want to take up where Aristotle left off and recover the neglected possibilities of rhetoric that had been buried by the narrowing movement of logic.

In some ways, this is what Heidegger began to do in his 1924 Summer Semester course on Aristotle's *Rhetoric*, and although I do not propose to offer anything like an analysis of those lectures, it is important to recognize at least the vision that Heidegger caught there of the potential philosophical importance of rhetoric and the causes of his rejection of rhetoric as a philosophical possibility. The subject of the SS 1924 lectures was "Basic Concepts of Aristotelian Philosophy." The approach was not conceptual analysis but a tracing back of Aristotelian philosophical concepts to the basic experiences from which they arose, with special attention to the continuing influence those basic experiences exerted on the concepts and to the interaction between the technical terms and their everyday meanings and ordinary use. The basic experiences are, for Heidegger, even at this point already linguistic. As he puts it: "Living, for the human being, means speaking. Thus this preliminary clarification of *logos* refers to a being-context that is preliminarily described as the life of the human being" (2009a, 16–17). Heidegger expands on this a little later: "In being-in-the-polis, Aristotle sees the genuine life of human beings . . . [sees] that the being of human beings is *logon echein*. Implicit in this determination is an entirely peculiar, fundamental mode of the being of human beings characterized as 'being-with-one-another,' *koinōnia*. These beings who speak with the world are, as such, through being-with-others" (2009a, 33).

Here, according to Heidegger, Aristotle conceives human being as political community-in-logos. These political Greeks are themselves only in the transcendence and sociality made possible by logos. More particularly, they achieve community through logos because "*logos* is that which is able to constitute the having-with-one-another of the *agathon*" (36). For our purposes, this expansive conception of logos is the most important feature of the 1924 lectures, despite the richness of Heidegger's commentary, its importance for our understanding of the history of rhetoric, and its illumination of some of the neglected dimensions of the discipline of rhetoric.[9] For here, Heidegger looks past the narrow theoretical *logos apophantikos*, the logos of "logic," and finds, at a more original level, rhetorical logos, with all its sociality, its pathos, its concern with the beneficial and good, its ability to get things done. In the logos of everyday political life, the Greeks come to be themselves.[10] Here, Heidegger accounts for this community ontologically, as arising in and as a result of rhetorical logos. Rhetoric itself, as a mode of inquiry or discipline, is an awareness of this more original logos of communication, controversy, deliberation, and being-with-one-another—the essential sociality of Dasein.

Almost everyone who writes about the 1924 lectures comes away asking why Heidegger "dropped" rhetoric—especially this rich and philosophically significant notion of rhetoric. If the whole point of the "destruction" is to read beyond the hypertheoretical and narrowly logical senses of logos, and the whole point of hermeneutics is to discover a more original practice and understanding, hasn't that in some sense been achieved by discovering rhetoric at the level of the basic experiences from which theoretical concepts arose? And doesn't this give us a form of access to that broader notion of logos that had been left behind in the narrowing of logos to *logos apophantikos*?

Well, yes and no. On the one hand, Heidegger never lets go of what he discovers about *pathos* in these lectures. In *Being and Time*, we find something much like the *pathē* of Aristotle's *Rhetoric*, but formalized and unified as an essential way in which Dasein exists, under the rubric of *Befindlichkeit*. In *Being and Time*, the *pathē* are in no way connected with pragmatic concessions to an audience of limited intelligence (even in SS 1924, they were already more than that); rather, they are said to be an intrinsic factor in all understanding.

On the other hand, however, Heidegger makes a rather strange retreat from his 1924 discoveries. First, as P. Christopher Smith (1995) has pointed out, Heidegger seems to lose hold of the notion of original rhetorical logos as communicative speech that is heard and spoken and to retrain his focus on the derivative logos that is a matter of something's being brought to *sight* in logos, something's showing itself. Second, Heidegger's conception of a logos that grants *koinōnia* and being-with-one-another comes to fall under the shadow of his analysis of falling, of the tendency for the sociality of Dasein to overwhelm and displace Dasein's capability for authentic existence. This leads to Heidegger's struggle to find an account of authenticity, a way of making one's being one's own—authenticity that becomes increasingly private, individualistic, silent, monological at best, and at some times verges on the irrational. I will investigate this second matter in detail below. First, though, I would like to develop Smith's view and then make a brief acknowledgement of Heidegger's later return to thinking about logos more broadly.

Smith points out that the original rhetorical logos uncovered in Heidegger's reading of Aristotle is primarily oral and acoustical and primarily a practical social interaction. The "someones" are highlighted, and the "saying" is clearly a matter of voice, with all its pathos and attitude and purpose. The "something about something" is not forgotten, but it is not limited to assertion or predication, and it does not occlude the speaker and listener or the speaking and listening. As Smith points out, Heidegger even contrasts this primary "hearing" with the theoretical "seeing" that is derivative from it. "Nevertheless," Smith writes, "Heidegger, even as early as [SS 1924], largely passes over this oral-acoustical nature of fundamental language as speech. Indeed, his single-minded interests actually lead him away from our original experience of hearing someone's call and lead him back to the very *logos apophantikos*, the declarative statement, that was supposed to be exposed as derivative" (1995, 326). Smith suggests that Heidegger is perhaps "misled" by Aristotle in this because he ends up separating voice (*phone*) and *logos*, whereas he had previously united them (327). Smith in fact suggests that Heidegger actually lost track of the notion of rhetorical logos that he was developing (328), and retained only the idea that logos was a kind of revealing. He finds this confirmed in *Being and Time*'s prevalent metaphors of light and illumination. In fact, Heidegger will continue to make a fundamental distinction between logos and voice throughout his later writings, so Smith is certainly on to something here. I would qualify the claim somewhat, though, because Heidegger also frequently highlights hearing and even the hearing of the logos, and sometimes deliberately resists the dominance of vision.

Heidegger's "passing over" the rhetorical logos, with its pathos and its speaking and hearing and its human voice, is also motivated by the increasing shadow cast by what would emerge in *Being and Time* as an apparently negative view of the public-political and of everyday speech. However, Heidegger had already noted in his SS 1924 lectures that the politicized being-with-one-another of the Greeks was a specific realization of being-with-one-another that had its own danger: "For the Greeks themselves, this process of living in the world, *to be absorbed* in what is ordinary, to fall into the world in which it lives, became, through language, the basic danger of their being-there" (2009, 74). It turns out that the basic experience of rhetoric, though more original than the logic of assertion and even the Aristotelian basic concepts, is in fact an "ungrounded" passing along of what has been heard and not a discourse that Dasein has spoken out of its own ability to take responsibility for itself.

The difficulty here, from a deep rhetorical point of view, is not that the Greek public was determined by commonly held beliefs and attitudes that were not fully supported. Neither is it that their being-with-one-another was determined by what Heidegger would call *Gerede*—a kind of ungrounded talk in which one simply passes along what one has heard. Nor is it that Heidegger formalizes the notion in *Being and Time* into an intrinsic way that Dasein exists. The difficulty lies rather in Heidegger's way of addressing this situation. For Heidegger, rhetoric takes place in the domain of *das Man*—the One, the anonymous anyone, the "they," the public, the average, the shared: "The One is the genuine how of the being of human beings in everydayness, and *the genuine bearer of this One is language*. The One maintains itself, has its genuine dominion, in language" (2009, 45). A speaker speaks out of this shared way of being in order to address an audience, which is just as much under its dominion. Being-with-one-another is governed by *das Man*. Even Dasein's own, authentic self is in constant danger of being overcome by *das Man-selbst*, an anonymous "oneself," a kind of all-purpose self to which one ordinarily defaults.

However, for Heidegger, the way out is not through language, communication with one another, questioning, challenging, controversy, thinking things through, deliberation, reasoning, new mutual understanding. The alternative is rather for Dasein to become profoundly its own, to achieve ownness, authenticity. This process involves a modification of *das Man* through a drawing back from sociality into ownness, into the silence of the call of conscience, even into the radical individualization of facing one's death as one's own. A deep rhetoric, while acknowledging what truth there is in Heidegger's account, will not follow Heidegger into this withdrawal into silence and aloneness. A richer conception of logos and a more complex vision of sociality will help us to chart a passage through language and sociality that will allow us to make sense of reason, justice, wisdom, and something like "authentic" sociality in ways that Heidegger could not.

Heidegger returned to logos often throughout his lectures and writings. He never settled on a single definition or attitude when it came to something as challenging as logos, and he never seemed to set a goal of having a theory or even a consistent account of logos. When writing on Heraclitus, logos became the "gathering."[11] Gathering is the collecting and preserving of something that is at first scattered and unprotected and yet somehow implicitly sensed in advance to a degree that is definite enough to give guidance. Even more, the possibilities of collecting and preserving and being scattered and being unprotected themselves guide any gathering. As Heidegger puts it, gathering itself must first be gathered! This provocative account of how logos addresses or calls forth something out of its being dispersed is grounded in the basic experience of harvest and its gathering of something that needs preserving. This is obviously a logos-in-the-broad-sense that goes way beyond the assertion or proposition, and way beyond ordinary speech or writing. However, it diverges radically from a deep rhetoric in that it loses sight of someones saying something to one another. When Heidegger speaks of speaking, it is beings themselves that are "addressed." When he speaks of hearing, it is the logos itself that is heard. Heidegger never returns to the earlier encounter with rhetoric and being-with-one-another in an attempt to draw this larger notion of logos into a connection with human communication or sociality. That opportunity was foregone and then forgotten.

Through the later 1920s and well beyond, Heidegger continued the "destructive" project of focusing on the narrow notion of logos, leaving the rest outside of logos, and so risked the irrationalism of professing philosophical access to something that is beyond discussion. Gadamer would predict that language would forestall that attempt and that some larger sense of logos would have to reemerge. Yet Heidegger continued along his narrow path—and found that the trail narrowed and disappeared. As this happened, he himself forecast Emmanuel Levinas's critique of the primacy of ontology.

Let's return now to the thinking of the 1929 lectures. Since onto-logy is shaped by the logos (in the narrow sense), and logos is instrumental in the prevailing of beings over being, ontology works against itself. Heidegger faces the consequences squarely:

It is nowhere written that there must be such a thing as ontology, nor that the problematic of philosophy is rooted in ontology. . . . Perhaps the problem of the distinction between being and beings is prematurely stifled as a problematic by our entrusting it to ontology and naming it in this way. . . . We must unfold this problem still more radically, with the danger of arriving at a position where we must reject all ontology in its very idea as an inadequate metaphysical problematic. . . . Ontology too and its idea must fall, precisely because the radicalization of this idea was a necessary stage in unfolding the fundamental problem of metaphysics. (1995, 359)

This is a rather stunning outcome to the project of fundamental ontology that was announced in *Being and Time*. There the problem of the "prevailing of beings," of seeing from an ontic point-of-view, as if everything that could be experienced were simply an entity, was supposed to be overcome by pursuing ontological understanding. This was made possible through the recognition that the being of human beings was Dasein, an ecstatic transcendence in time in which an understanding of being took place. Dasein was an entity that was both ontic and also ontological—that is, a being that was an understanding of being, even if that understanding was implicit and indistinct. Heidegger's idea was that a truly fundamental ontology would be possible only by way of an analysis of Dasein. However, Dasein is mostly subordinate to the prevailing of entities and the forgetting of being. Heidegger does chart a (mostly negative) path for Dasein to clear its being of ontic obfuscation, and this path is laid out in *Being and Time* in the way Dasein takes hold of its being authentically, as its own. This "clearing" of Dasein of the distortions caused by the oblivion of being and the prevailing of entities is supposed to prepare the way for a "fundamental ontology." However, by 1929/30 Heidegger is risking the idea that the project of ontology must be given up.

What is strange is that "the problem of the distinction between being and beings" is still to be pursued—but not as ontology—and the reason is that ontology is too dominated by "logos" in the narrow sense of a kind of propositional logic and grammar. It is ultimately this narrow notion of logos that is distorting everything here—and yet it is precisely this notion that Heidegger will not yield—at least not yet—for something more responsive to "the problem." This is a result of his wanting to keep to the path of destruction. It makes for an interesting and dramatic philosophical tragedy, but one has to wonder what kind of more lithe and renewing philosophical comedy could have been achieved if the *hubris* of the narrow logos had not been granted at the start and if the writer had not anticipated the necessary and fated outcome so strictly.

To understand the basic insufficiencies of Heidegger's approach, and the way they are addressed by a deep rhetoric, it will be helpful to stay focused on the earlier writings for a little longer, for some of the main tactics Heidegger employs in this regard throughout his career appear most clearly in *Being and Time* and other contemporaneous lectures and writings, and those analyses are a good way to gain entry into the difficulties of the later Heideggerian approach. A further look into these efforts will expose the consequences of forsaking a serious philosophical encounter with the rhetorical tradition.

The essential and continuing error and neglect of Heidegger's path is his choice not to develop an interpretation of rhetoric as the alternative to the narrow notion of logos and so to narrow logocentrism. I say his "choice" because Heidegger knows that this is the alternative. He says explicitly—and I repeat the quotation above—that the alternative to "logos in the sense of the propositional statement" was developed by Aristotle in his *Rhetoric*. He then says falsely that "the power of logic was too strong to leave open any genuine possibility of developing this attempt." This is simply false because it neglects the entire tradition of rhetoric. It is a profound error because it continues the philosophical unresponsiveness to that tradition and so the alienation of rhetoric from philosophy and thus the continued narrowness of philosophy itself. The alternative to this failure is deep rhetoric—to achieve a rapprochement of philosophy and rhetoric by developing a philosophical rhetoric according to the larger sense of logos at work in both philosophy and rhetoric, a sense of logos that Heidegger acknowledges but forsakes because of the historical hegemony of propositional logic. This forsaking is by no means necessary or fated.

Within the context of an errant philosophical path, and a severely restricted role for logos,[12] Heidegger attempts to describe a way that Dasein is nevertheless able to step back from this mostly fated and necessary misunderstanding of its own being and so of being itself. This occurs, as we have seen, in Dasein's taking hold of its being "authentically." In what follows, I will explore this possibility in the context of a larger idea of logos and with a critical perspective provided by the project of a deep rhetoric. Let's first step back for a moment and summarize a little in light of this larger idea of logos that includes *any* reference and significance (*any* leading of Dasein from one thing to another) and in light of an effort to place Heidegger more clearly in a deep rhetorical framework—against some of his own proclivities.

In and from the world of logos, human individuals and groups take their own directions, their own paths in time. Heidegger thinks of this transcendence toward other beings in time as what we *are*, and so he thinks of it not simply as action but as the possibility condition and the form of whatever action we take. We are a movement in time, transcending ourselves toward other entities and experiencing them as such, within the logos that makes such experience possible. This transcendence, this movement forward and its direction, is experienced as something about which we care, and so it is something we have feelings about, always—boredom, anxiety, joy, anticipation, some way we find and experience ourselves in our transcendence. This transcendence is always moving forward in time, and so is defined and given shape by our pursuits and purposes. Entities show up as entities in connection with these pursuits and purposes. The cell phone shows up as useful and significant for some task or not. My wife's knee shows up in the context of a long marriage and my love for her and my concern for her sleep and the day ahead of her. Things show a whole range of relevance to our purposes, and it is human purposes that establish the framework in which entities can be experienced as entities. Ultimately, Dasein transcends itself toward what it is trying to be or become, some particular possibility of its own well-being, some formation of a purpose for itself.

For Heidegger, understanding logos and transcendence from within this understanding of Dasein requires distinctions that highlight the difficulty of comprehending logos and transcendence at all. One main problem is the difference between the way logos works historically to form a shared world and the way logos works to make possible our living out our individuality and our choices. These two ways of logos sometimes move in conflicting directions, and they rely at times on different senses of the word "logos." Both of these ways are ways that human beings exist. They each have their own special kind of priority. The general logos we inherit has an everyday priority. It forms the social world in which we live through our social roles and live out our everyday lives of work and citizenship and so on. It provides the implicit agreements on the basis of which we able to cooperate and even understand and deal with disagreements.

The way we live out our individuality in logos has a different kind of priority. One difficulty with the general logos we inherit is that we tend to live in it relatively unconsciously, half-awake, and this is our default mode. It is what connects us with everyone else, and it provides us with shared ways to understand and speak about and live out these connections. Questioning their ultimate justifications or choosing to alter them in radical ways does not seem easy to combine with living well with others and accomplishing one's purposes. Besides, it can produce anxiety and even unhappiness to question too deeply. This is especially the case when one begins to think of one's own death, of one's solitude, of one's unpreparedness for taking responsibility for one's existence. This leads, says Heidegger, to a dominance of living through the general worldly logos one has inherited, and it leads to a kind of neglecting or even avoiding the possibility of taking one's own individual capacity for logos seriously. When the world is dominated by a powerful and unified way of organizing experience and knowledge that is successful for achieving short-term prediction and control of a narrow but privileged range of events, and when other ways of existing in time and other events that fall outside that range have grown dim in social life, then the dominance of that general inherited world and its specific paths of logos becomes almost unquestionable.

In *Being and Time*, Heidegger calls the counterforce to this domination of one's Dasein *Eigentlichkeit*, or "ownness," which is usually translated as "authenticity." It is activated by honestly facing up to one's lack of self-sufficiency and one's death and becoming answerable for one's existence. It is not a violent withdrawal from living through the social logos. Rather, it is a different way of living through it. Heidegger has difficulty formulating exactly what this different way is, or how one achieves it, and he has difficulty describing authenticity without giving it a positive value, which he says he does not want to do. However, it is very clear in the more technical parts of his analysis that authenticity is necessary for pursuing philosophy in the way he wants to pursue it—as an existential phenomenology that will clear the way for a fundamental ontology—because the existence we are trying to understand, the existence in which beings show themselves as such, is in each case our own. Without "clearing" our existence of the forgetfulness of our individual capacities for becoming answerable for ourselves, we would not be able to see into ourselves and take hold of our responsibility for ourselves—and philosophy depends on this.

A central requisite for accomplishing this "clearing" is to face the possibility of one's death—the end of one's transcendence—and to allow that experience to free one from anxious attachments to one's anonymous social identities and ways of understanding. Death can do this because it is, of all possibilities, one's "ownmost," although the default social mode of existence always neutralizes this fact, partly by acknowledging so facilely that, of course, everyone dies. When one turns to face one's death, one frees oneself from the hold of that anonymous default way of understanding and achieves a clearer insight into oneself as a specific, individual finite transcendence—because death is unsurpassable. Transcendence is what we are and what we cannot help being, and yet we cannot go on being ourselves as transcendence in the face of death because death is the limit to our transcendence. We either flee from this and become reabsorbed in social life, in which "everyone dies" (but not me, or at least not now), or we come to terms with the fact that we ourselves will die and social life will fail us. Our ceaseless transcendence will never find its fulfillment but will simply come to a stop.

This forces the question of what I am living for (transcending toward), of whether and in what sense my life is my own or not. As Thoreau put it in his own way of being toward death: "I went to the woods because I wished to live deliberately, to front only the essential facts of life, and see if I could not learn what it had to teach, and not, when I came to die, discover that I had not lived." "Going to the woods" is, in *Walden*, the outward form of something like what Heidegger envisioned far more abstractly as authenticity. However, in both cases, transcendence toward death utterly individualizes the Dasein that risks it, and allows it to become the specific, individual "I" that lives and transcends.

Heidegger's attempt to understand human existence as transcendence, and his critical resistance to prevailing ontic and ontotheological approaches to ontology, are useful guideposts for a deep rhetoric, and they will be essential in giving an account of deep rhetorical justice. A deep rhetoric cannot just launch itself on the basis of a world taken for granted in which individual human entities transmit messages in symbols to other individual human beings, either well or poorly, and do so with a number of techniques and in a number of media that can be studied and taught. The project of rhetoric is not deepened by simply emphasizing the ways people do this as members of groups on the basis of shared assumptions and beliefs, or by describing and criticizing the way new media environments shape agencies and outcomes. These and many other ways of pursuing rhetoric and rhetorical theory are increasingly important and must be supported more strongly than they are. The shapes of communication are changing much faster than the disciplined study of their emergence and their forms and their impacts.

However, such studies and the rhetorical capabilities they enhance always proceed and develop on the basis of some understanding of what a deep rhetoric pursues—a philosophical understanding of communication, which demands the most searching questions about logos as the medium of human transcendence and so involves the study of rhetoric in the breadth and depth and the seriousness with which Heidegger pursued his own attempt at understanding logos and human transcendence. Besides, when it comes to the question of justice, we will find that the only justice that can support the challenges and demands of reason itself—as well as the other forms of justice we seek—is the justice of transcendence. In all conflict, we come into conflict with each other's transcendence. Since logos is the medium of transcendence, we need to pursue the justice of logoi in a rhetoric that follows such justice all the way down to the logos of transcendence itself. Heidegger has tried to take this plunge into an understanding of deep transcendence, so we are riding his back into these depths.

I have already identified the central failure in Heidegger's project: the abandonment of rhetoric and its tradition as an alternative to the narrowing of logos in the history of philosophy. Heidegger saw very clearly the potential of rhetoric in his 1924 summer session lectures on Aristotle's *Rhetoric*. It is obvious that *Being and Time* not only contains fairly explicit incorporations of Aristotle's treatment of *pathos* in the development of the notions of *Befindlichkeit* and *Gestimmtheit* and *Stimmung* (sometimes translated state-of-mind, attunement, and mood), but also thematizes, in the vague and indistinct understanding of being that marks Dasein as an ontic-ontological being, the nonpropositional comportment toward being in which Dasein cannot help but to "discourse." "Discourse" (*Rede*) is the pre-propositional experience of meaning and signification. In fact, it is in the section of *Being and Time* on discourse and language that Heidegger comes again to the brink of a deep rhetoric—and again turns away.

Understanding, Interpretation, and Meaning

Before moving ahead with a deep rhetorical critique of Heidegger, I would like to press this point again because it explains why the encounter with Heidegger is so important for a deep rhetoric. In *Being and Time*, discourse (logos) is said to be "equally original" with state-of-mind (pathos) and understanding (transcendence, which can be either authentic or inauthentic and so a kind of ethos). These three "fundamental *existentialia*" together constitute the unity of the transcendence of Dasein in its having a "there." If they are equally original, then they are each equally fundamental and never found without the other. They are intrinsic features of a single, unified phenomenon. They are distinguished only for the purpose of analysis and not to determine which one is the ground of the others. This is tantamount to having the larger notion of logos at work right in the very being of Dasein, though again Heidegger is anything but systematic and consistent in the sections on understanding and discourse in *Being and Time*. It will be well worth our while to go into more detail here.

In his discussion of understanding (1962, 182–203), Heidegger offers a three-part account that moves from more implicit to more explicit: understanding (182–88), interpretation as a developed mode of understanding (188–95), and assertion as a "derivative mode of understanding" that executes an "explicit restriction" (195–203).

Understanding itself is simply our being in the world as a transcendence. In our everydayness, our transcendence toward beings is in skillful practical activity. I reach for the doorknob to open the door and step out onto the porch. I walk down the driveway to the car, and I use my remote to unlock the door. I use the handle to open the door, and I climb inside with my keys in my hand. I am on my way to the arboretum, to take a long walk. I am competent to move in this world of doors and keys and cars in which each leads to the next and all lead, for now, to the arboretum. I do not explicitly think or say: "Here is the key. The key is metal. The key starts the truck. These things are entities." Nor do I live through anything like the equivalent of those assertions. The world that includes these things as well as the roads and other people and other cars and the traffic lights and laws and all the rest, as well as the "relations" among them, is something I "have" already without thinking about it, and it helps to make these things accessible for me. I transcend understandingly toward a walk in the arboretum, a possibility of my own existence. For a deep rhetoric, the meaning and significance involved in this worldly understanding is already a matter of logos, even when no word is heard or spoken, no writing read or written. The way things can lead to one another and to a purpose is made possible by logos. However, Heidegger is silent about logos in the section. The web of significations that allows entities to be understood and interpreted, and is part of what they are, belongs to us "before" any explicit interpretation or assertion. We interpret and assert "out of" that background, which is also part of—or an event occurring in—our own being. Heidegger is reluctant to describe this "relation" between ourselves and our being as one of logos; however, he does insist that the "significations" that allow entities to be are part of this background itself. It is just that they are somehow not yet "explicit" or "expressed."

In this implicit wholeness of the background that belongs to us, we have the interesting challenge of thinking of the implicit logos of an implicit whole. We follow such a logos in our engaged, practical activities, and it accompanies and makes possible all explicit understanding; however, when we attempt to understand it, we make it explicit, and reduce it to a kind of entity.

Interpretation is a developed kind of understanding that concerns itself with the "as" of entities in an explicit way. We are familiar with the "as" structure from the example of the cell phone. The explicit "as" constitutes what Heidegger calls "interpretation." We experience something as something when we are concerned with it in light of its purpose and its place in a network of relations. In interpretation, the cell phone shows up *as* a cell phone—the way it could not for Ramses II. For Heidegger, this interpretation includes what he calls (1) *Vorhabe*—already having a world in its wholeness with all its implicit significations, (2) *Vorsicht*—a view toward some particular purpose that allows the practical and skillful discovery of the relevant features of that whole, and (3) *Vorgriff*—a preliminary conceptualization of what is discovered or brought out of this whole. The point is that transcendence is finite not only in the face of the unsurpassibility of death but also in that it is dependent on the inheritance of a world out of which all understanding and interpretation and experience of beings as such take place. This means that there is nothing autonomous about understanding. We understand on the basis of understanding that has been passed on to us from the past. However, this does not mean that understanding simply repeats the past. The past in the present is no longer the past but the past in a new situation. We are capable of reflection on the fore-structure of understanding, and we are capable of using the past in new ways in relation to new situations and new purposes.

This hermeneutical account of understanding has important consequences for a deep rhetoric because its perspective on the way understanding is historically conditioned leads to a judgment that knowledge is more practical, probable, and occasional than it is theoretical, certain, and timeless. These distinctions are traditional ways of distinguishing rhetoric from philosophy. We understand in historically specific situations, drawing on an implicitly understood but ordered world of logoi and their entities, selecting from it according to the demands of the situation, and preconceptualizing what we understand in a way that adapts it to our purposes. These are some of the outlines of a rhetorical situation and rhetorical action. They contrast with the modern philosophical picture of understanding as the reception of isolated sense-data, the application of categories and logical connectives, the inductive accumulation of knowledge, the scientific testing of hypotheses, and the development of theories. Heideggerian hermeneutics aligns almost precisely with a framework for rhetorical reasoning.

Meaning (*Sinn*), too, becomes something new from this perspective. Meaning is usually taken to be a property of propositions, and is often taken to be related to the conditions of their truth. Rhetoric has been more interested in the practical meaning of utterances than in their sheer theoretical meaning, and so speech-act accounts of illocutionary and perlocutionary force would play a role in meaning for most rhetorical approaches. Heidegger, however, approaches the question of meaning from a completely different angle. He raises the question of meaning in *Being and Time* before he develops his account of explicit assertion, while he is still concerned with interpretation and the way in which entities are what they are only because of the implicit background in light of which they show themselves. Meaning, he says, is "that wherein the intelligibility of something maintains itself" (193). What this means for entities is, of course, the referential whole, from which Dasein draws in its preunderstanding of entities in the prepossession, foresight, and preconception that give "structure" to entities. But this interpretive structuring is the way Dasein exists, and not a property of entities. So, says Heidegger, only Dasein can be meaningful or meaningless. The idea does not even apply to entities. However, although meaning is not a property of entities, it *is* part of their being-in-themselves. Their being-what-they-are happens in the being-there of Dasein, in the referential web in terms of which they are what they are.

The question concerning the meaning of being, says Heidegger, is exactly about this:

It asks about Being insofar as Being enters into the intelligibility of Dasein. The meaning of Being can never be contrasted with entities, or with Being as the 'ground'
[*Grund*] which gives entities support; for a 'ground' becomes accessible only as meaning, even if it is itself the abyss [*Abgrund*] of meaninglessness. (194)

This is Heidegger's unmistakable position in *Being and Time*: (1) The question of the meaning of Being (*Sein*) can be pursued only in the context
of the conditions for the possibility of anything's being meaningful at
all—the existence of Dasein and its structures of understanding and interpretation. (2) Being is accessible only as the being of entities, the being of
beings. Both of these principles will suffer some weakening in Heidegger's
later writings; however, they are so essential here that Heidegger places
his own effort at fundamental ontology into the famous hermeneutic
circle. We pursue even the question of being in a "circular" way because
all understanding of entities and their being is circular. We draw from our
implicit understanding of the referential totality—all the implicit logoi
in which entities have their being, all their references to each other—to
make sense of what is before us, and we do this even in posing questions
for inquiry, such as the question of being. Without our having inherited
a world of some kind, beings could not show up as such at all and the
question of being could never be posed. The task for philosophy and
other serious work is not to imagine that one can get access to beings
independently of their being—that is, independently of a specific framework of intelligibility—but to illuminate the implicit frameworks within
which our understanding functions, to question them, to examine them
in light of what is happening with beings, including Dasein. The point,
says Heidegger, is not to escape the circle, but "to get into it in the right
way" since it holds, after all, any possibility of meaningful understanding
or experience or criticism.

Assertion

Heidegger brings this entire analysis to bear on the concept of assertion,
or judgment (*Aussage, Urteil*). Heidegger treats assertion as a "derivative"
mode of interpretation. This is very different, he says, from the way philosophy has interpreted assertion and judgment. Philosophy has interpreted assertion in terms of a narrow notion of logos, according to which
logos is a present-at-hand entity found in words and sequences of words,
which are also taken to be present-at-hand entities. Assertions manifest
the ontic unity of an entity through their own ontic unity as assertions.

They do this through a grammar of subject and predicate that reflects the logic of the entity and its properties. Assertions include positive judgments about the unity of an entity and its properties and negative judgments that separate an entity from what it is not and what does not belong to it. Assertions can serve as premises or theses. In fact, the logic of assertion can be formalized and systematized.

Heidegger acknowledges that this approach does indeed give us the entity "as" what it is—say, the cell phone in the assertion "the cell phone is a hand-held electronic device." He calls this the *apophantic* "as," and he says that it is produced by subtracting from the cell phone almost all the meaning it has in relation to its being worldly and reducing its meaning to sheer predication as it appears to mere observation. Heidegger does not believe that there is anything wrong in itself with developing a theory of the apophantic "as" and the kind of assertion that belongs to it. The problem is that this derivative notion of assertion and the stripped down "as" come to be taken as the primary and original building blocks from which something like a "world" is constructed by collecting enough assertions about things and getting them all in the proper logical and grammatical relations to each other. From this point of view, logic and grammar give proper form to the world, and rhetoric has no place in this. Communication, too, is incidental. Dasein and the structure of its transcendence are altogether neglected.

Heidegger believes that this obscures the genuine being of assertion and leads to a suppression of the implicit understanding of world that would have to guide any reconstruction of the world out of assertions and their relations. The project would literally make no sense if it were not guided beforehand by some knowledge of what a world was supposed to be. He contrasts the *apophantic* "as" to the *existential-hermeneutical* "as" that preserves the whole web of references in which entities have their everyday being and out of which one abstracts the present-at-hand entity of the apophantic assertion. Assertion in general is characterized by three features, but primary among them, insists Heidegger, is "pointing out" (*Aufzeigung*). "The cell phone is broken" points out the cell phone in its brokenness, but it does point out the cell phone. The second feature is predication, in which the cell phone is made determinate. Predication is a reductive pointing out in which the cell phone's being broken is highlighted and the cell phone and its many other possible meanings are overshadowed. A third feature of assertion is communication. For Heidegger, this communication is a way of being in which we share our *being toward* whatever is being pointed out. It is a form of co-transcendence. Assertion in general must also be understood as grounded in understanding and interpretation, and so must have all the structures of interpretation: the implicit grasp of the whole background of significations and a view toward a goal—some way of being that lies ahead, and in light of which it can identify the entity and select the relevant predication.

Heidegger's ontological account of how assertion is grounded in Dasein's transcendence is an important move in opening the way to a deep rhetoric and a new understanding of argumentation; however, it is also a critically unsatisfactory account of the sociality of transcendence and the place of communication in assertion. Returning to the primary rhetorical phenomenon can help illuminate the failure here. An assertion is *someone saying something about something to someone.* To say that the *something about something* is the primary feature of assertion is itself an unjustifiable assertion that is already halfway down the road to stripping assertion down to something present at hand. If we keep the primary phenomenon in focus, the *someones* are at least as important as the *something about something.* Heidegger's being taken by ontology and his own preoccupation with beings certainly skew his vision here. We do not think up assertions and then look for someone to assert them to. Assertions arise in the transcendence of Dasein's pursuing its projects, and they are social in a much more complicated and profound way than Heidegger's account implies.

The main failures here are: (1) Heidegger himself succumbs to propositionalism; (2) the account neglects to note that assertions take place in a complex process of questioning, claiming, and giving reasons; (3) we not only "share" being toward entities but we also have conflicts in our being toward them; and so (4) assertions are claims on the transcendence of others. Let us take these in order.

(1) *Heidegger himself succumbs to propositionalism.* "Propositionalism" is a term used by Michel Meyer (2009, 32–33; 1994, 10–14ff.; 1995, 130–200) to describe the dominant tendency in philosophy to suppress the question and emphasize only the answer or result, and so to see logic and reasoning only as the linking of proposition to proposition. Although Meyer believes that Heidegger's question of being is a persevering attempt to keep the question in play in philosophy, and in many ways it is, Heidegger certainly does not persevere with the question when it comes to engaging with assertion, logos, and reasoning. Meyer insists that a proposition is *always* the answer to a question and that the interrogative dimensions of logos have been neglected, that the meanings of assertions cannot be grasped except when they are understood as the answer to some question.

Gadamer, too, has insisted on this conversational, dialogical origin and ground of the assertion. There is a wonderful moment in an interview with Ricardo Dottori when the hundred-year-old Gadamer recollects his last meeting with Heidegger. Gadamer says: "I saw Heidegger himself just a few days before his death. I was in Freiburg, and I visited him at home. He came downstairs with his wife to greet me, and later we drank a marvelous wine (he was always receiving very good wines as gifts from his devoted admirers, and was no longer allowed to drink as much). But, philosophically speaking, he definitely did not think too highly of me." Dottori is patient, and then asks, understandably: "What did he say to you when you saw him for the last time?" Gadamer replies: "Well, he began like this: 'You say that language is a conversation, no?' 'Yes,' I answered. It began like this, but it didn't go much further." And Gadamer explains that the reason was that he himself simply did not have the talent for such a conversation with Heidegger![13]

This could not be more illuminating. Heidegger enacts and so justifies Gadamer's account of the priority of the question and the centrality of conversation and dialogue. The disappointing irony, however, is that Gadamer, the philosopher of questioning and dialogue, cannot sustain the conversation. Perhaps most notably, though, Heidegger is interested, a few days before his death, in the idea that language is a conversation, and he wants to talk about it with Gadamer.

Gadamer's notion of dialogue is built on his understanding of the primacy of questioning, and this primacy could not be more radical: "The structure of the question is implicit in all experience," he writes. "We cannot have experiences without asking questions" (2003, 362). What Gadamer means is that we cannot have experiences from which we learn unless we are able to question. In order to learn that the water we see on the road in the distance is not water but a mirage, we must be able to ask implicitly: was that water or was it a mirage? One can never learn that x is really y unless one has the ability to experience the question of whether x is really x or y. The experience of the question, he says, is the experience of Socratic ignorance—the knowledge that one does not have knowledge—a condition in which it is possible to learn. Before one can learn anything from an assertion, one must have the question to which an assertion is the answer; without a question, the assertion is practically meaningless. The most difficult part of learning is learning to ask questions.

The structure of interpretation—the fore-having or prepossession—that Heidegger finds in the assertion, Gadamer finds in the question

(363ff.). The question directs us toward a place of inquiry; it "opens up" the being of the object, he says, and establishes a place of indeterminacy. It also limits the inquiry by establishing a horizon and foregrounding what is important. Thus, it discloses a "world" to support the inquiry, identifies the questionable thing, and selects the important issues to foreground. The assertion is guided by the question, and can come about at all as a meaningful assertion only because it is guided by the question. Inquiry and learning and knowledge come about not by stringing together assertions but in a process of questioning and answering, in a dialogue, a conversation. Gadamer, too, finds something like propositionalism to be an occlusion and distortion of the true phenomenon of assertion, which has its meaning only in a conversation.[14]

(2) *Heidegger's account neglects to note that assertions take place in a complex process of questioning, claiming, and giving reasons.* When it comes to reasoning, and not a formal logic of assertions, this conversation can be described in more detail because there are specific constraints on it. In outline form, the assertion is not a mere assertion at all; it is a *claim*. First of all, it is a claim made *by someone on someone*. It attempts to direct someone else's transcendence in a specific way. It is a claim on someone else's attention, and so implicitly a claim that giving such attention is worthwhile and relevant. Such claims not only answer questions, but they also provoke questions, because explicit claims are essentially questionable. As answers to provoked questions, assertions take the form of reasons, which can *be* reasons as such only in the context of conversation. Arguments themselves are processes of questioning and answering and giving reasons.[15]

(3) *We not only "share" being toward entities but we also have conflicts in our being toward them.* Because assertive transcendence is a matter of transcending into someone else's transcendence, assertion is a matter not only of "sharing" but of misunderstanding and conflict. Heidegger speaks of "world" in a very abstract way as a transcendental structure that must be in place for Dasein to be as it is. However the traditions we inherit, and which are active in all transcending, are shared and not shared in many different ways and degrees, and this generates mis-understanding and not simply sharing. In fact, to try to establish the possibility of sharing at a transcendental level is to empty "sharing" of any meaningful content. Gadamer has wrestled with this issue in his hermeneutics in a far more helpful way, struggling to establish the possibility of a fusion of horizons and insisting on the constant possibility of translation. Further, even with a shared tradition, assertive transcendence is often a matter of conflict. If someone asserts: "Contemporary popular culture is not a le-

gitimate field of research and study in a university," or "Sports Marketing is not a legitimate field of research and study in a public institution," or "The history and theory of Rhetoric is not a legitimate field of research," then it must be that there are someones to whom these claims are unacceptable and objectionable, someones who find the projects to which these assertive transcendences are attached to be in conflict with their own projects. In co-transcendence, we are in the ur-contact zone of what Emmanuel Levinas calls "proximity," encroaching on one another, "persecuting" one another. Transcendence is an ethical phenomenon from the ground up, ethical in these challenges and sufferings of proximity and ethical in whatever responsibility we manage to take for one another out of that condition.

(4) Ultimately, *assertions are claims on the transcendence of others*. It is difficult to see why the misunderstanding and conflict implicit in this conflict of transcendence did not receive more attention from Heidegger, but once again it is probably attributable to his primarily ontological orientation. His ultimate concern is with being and beings, with saying something *about something* and not with the *someones* who say it and hear it—and not even with the *someones* whose beings are in conflict about beings in their being. Here it is not only propositionalism that rules over the question and dialogue but ontology that rules over ethics. For all his resistance to attributing an "inner" domain to Dasein, Heidegger nevertheless treats the difference between authenticity and inauthenticity as an inner struggle that goes on in privacy and solitude in the individual Dasein. But what about sharing transcendence authentically? What about exploring misunderstandings and resolving conflicts in a way that aligns with a deep acknowledgment of and a practical reconciliation with the fact of our finitude and mortality and limitations? Is there any dimension of true sociality in transcendence? For Levinas, the *someone* to whom we speak has a face and must be approached as an infinity. This must happen in the context of an acknowledgment that our transcendences have already violated each other so deeply that we must work toward transcendence out of the failure of transcendence, which requires a restraint on our transcendence. For Levinas, it is not only the *saying* that has a priority over the *said*, but the *someones* who have infinite precedence over the *something*.

Gadamer tries to bring the entire phenomenon to light in a balanced way in his account of a true conversation:

This is not an external matter of simply adjusting our tools; nor is it even right to say that the partners adapt themselves to one another but, rather, in a successful conversation they both come under the influence of the truth of the object and are thus bound together in a new community. To reach an understanding in a dialogue is not merely a matter of putting oneself forward and successfully asserting one's point of view, but being transformed into a communion in which we do not remain what we were. (2003, 379)

Here we have the *someones* and the *saying* and the *somethings* all in balance with one another, at play with one another, as Gadamer says, and the being of each unfolds or is transformed in the process.

In fact, if we think differently here, we could say that this is a deep rhetorical account par excellence, not only because the different participants in the primary rhetorical event are held in balance, with each given its due and none being foundational, but also because they *give being to each other* in a process of *communication*. They communicate being to each other. Being is an effect of communication; this is the event toward which a deep rhetoric directs its attention. Ontology comes on the scene only afterward, and sees only the result, and that not clearly—that is, all too clearly.

For Gadamer, the notion of play is the critical passage for understanding how being can be given by communication and how the assertions of partners in a dialogue can be transformed when something else asserts itself, something in the process, the play, of dialogue itself:

The players' actions should not be considered subjective actions, since it is rather the game itself that plays, for it draws the players into itself and thus itself becomes the actual *subjectum* of the playing. The analogue is . . . the play of language itself, which addresses us, proposes and withdraws, asks and fulfills itself in the answer. (490)

Gadamer explains that the players, insofar as they are in the game, *cannot hold themselves back*. Understanding in the Heideggerian-Gadamerian sense is a transcendence that we *are*, not an action to which we may or may not be committed. Instead:

Someone who understands is always already drawn into an event through which meaning asserts itself. . . . The fact that in such knowledge the knower's own being comes into play certainly shows the limits of method, but not of science. Rather, what the tool of method does not achieve must—and really can—be achieved by a discipline of questioning and inquiring, a discipline that guarantees truth. (490–91)

The discipline of questioning and inquiring is not a natural or social science or a specific field of humanistic study. It is not a method or a logic or a theory of rationality or a calculus of probability or a cognitive science or a decision theory. It is the conversation of reason itself understood as argumentation, something on which every field of study depends, originally and ultimately and pretty much all along the way, too.

A true assessment of Heidegger's achievements and his failures can provide an important avenue to a rapprochement between philosophy, which almost loses touch with reason in the twentieth century, and rhetoric, which resurges in the middle of the twentieth century in a new theory of argumentation and reason. In the new rhetoric project of Perelman and Olbrechts-Tyteca, argumentation is the occurrence of language's asserting itself in the form of justice, and the only guarantor of truth is the justness of the conversation, the fairness and respect shown in the conflict of transcendence. But we are still only on the way to a discussion of deep rhetoric and justice.

Logos and Discourse

Only after Heidegger has developed his account of assertion's being a derivative development from interpretation does he go back to talk about language and its ontological grounding, even though it has been assumed all along. It turns out that "discourse" or "talk" (*Rede*) is a basic way that Dasein exists and transcends, just as fundamental and primary as understanding (transcendence) and state of mind (pathos) and not, like assertion, a subordinate development. Not everything Heidegger says about discourse is consistent, but the notion is perhaps as close as he gets to logos in the largest sense, so it is worth some attention.[16]

Intelligibility lies in meaning and overall in the totality of significations in light of which beings have their being. However, this intelligibility is completely implicit, and so I have called it a few times implicit logos. Significations lead to one another, and this leading is logos in the largest sense, implicit or not. However, says Heidegger, the totality of significations is the *articulable*; significations are the *articulated*. In the first instance, we have a web of implicitly or potentially rich and indefinite possibilities of meaning. In the second instance, we have something more like the actual following out of specific references and significations within that web. *Rede*, or discourse, is the articulation of intelligibility, the way we move from articulable to articulated, the way we transcend along particular lines of logos, or meaning, in time, and not all at once.

These significations are articulated primarily but not solely by our practical engagement with things as we pursue our purposes. We may begin with significations brought out by our practical engagements, but we can extend meanings through practical imaginative acts even without using language. And language interacts with these significations in all kinds of complicated ways. However, Heidegger says that language is the explicit "outspokenness" of *Rede*. This means that in some sense *Rede* does come "before" language, at least in this formulation. In any case, Heidegger says that this phase of logos is a way of being of Dasein, a feature of its transcendence that can never be absent. It is the active reception of logoi as the medium of transcendence, so even hearing is a mode of discourse because it follows articulated intelligibility. Hearing is an experience of meaning. Keeping silent, too, can be a mode of discourse, in that sometimes the richness of meaning is better articulated through well-timed restraint than a rush to say too much, too poorly, all at once.

As a mode of transcendence, *Rede* has being with others as its kind of being, too. In listening there are something like implicit illocutions such as "following, going along with, not-hearing, resisting, defying, and turning away" (206–7). Once again, however, the sociality of this transcendence is drastically attenuated in Heidegger's discussion. This can perhaps also be seen in his account of the structure of *Rede*, which includes (1) what the *Rede* is about, (2) what is said, (3) the communication, and (4) the making known. Different theories of language give emphasis to one or another factor, says Heidegger. One can see here something like the primary rhetorical phenomenon: (1) about something, (2) saying something, (3) someone(s); however, the fourth item shows where the emphasis is for Heidegger. Against all his efforts, an epistemological bias and a diminution of communication (and ethics) is at play.

Heidegger seems to realize how close he is here to "logos in the larger sense," and so he concludes his brief discussion of *Rede* with some explicit attention to logos. He believes that the Greeks (Plato and Aristotle) focused on logos as assertion, and so narrowed the notion, and that grammar and logic developed on the basis of the assertion. However, he says, a true account of language would rest on understanding how signification is rooted in the ontology of Dasein. That would have to be at least in part the account he has just given, but then it would also have to be carried out in light of "logos in the larger sense." He then projects a liberation of grammar from a narrow logic but says almost nothing about this. It is hard to see how this liberation of grammar for a greater logos of more manners of signification would not be exactly what a deep rhetoric could make possible: accounts of the many ways one thing can lead to another as an account of Dasein's transcendence, its rhetorical being.

Transcendence: Grounds and Reasons

For all his concern about logos and assertion and logic during this period, Heidegger almost never writes about reasoning or argument. However, Steven Crowell (2007) has made the interesting case that Heidegger does address the question of reasons and reasoning—not in *Being and Time* but in *Vom Wesen des Grundes* (published in 1929 and translated as *The Essence of Reasons* [1969] and also as *On the Essence of Ground* [1998]). This piece was originally published in a festschrift for Edmund Husserl on the occasion of his seventieth birthday. It is worth close attention here.

Heidegger introduces his subject by going back to Aristotle's discussion of "Grounds" in *Metaphysics* Delta/V at 1013a33, where Aristotle describes what *archē* means in the broadest sense as something from which something else follows, the "beginning" or "ground" of something—in some respect and in some context and not in an absolute way. Aristotle follows this opening with a discussion of different kinds of causes, as well as other related notions such as nature, necessity, substance, prior and posterior, potency, and what it means to come from something. Heidegger uses the word "ground" in this same very abstract sense. In this sense, ground functions in an essential way in logos because "ground" is Heidegger's name for the possibility of one thing leading to another, for the unifying of a world into a world, its being ordered by the references each part bears to others. "Grounding" is the name of logos as it occurs in the transcendence of Dasein.

Crowell's interest is in the sense of "ground" as reason. So he is careful to distinguish two senses of "ground" in Heidegger. In the first sense, "ground" is that which is beyond our reach, out of our control. There are causes for things that are just beyond us and about which there is little we can do. The justifications of this kind of grounding can seem obscure to us. Crowell mentions nature, history, and God as some ways of thinking about ground in this sense. However, with Heidegger, we immediately think of Dasein's worldliness and the totality of significations in light of which entities show up. Dasein "grounds itself" in this sense in its very being by being the handing down of possibilities to itself. Dasein's transcendence is always transcendence in light of the possibilities potentiated by what it has inherited in its implicit understandings. Insofar as this is out of our control, we have grounding in the first sense. As we have seen, Heidegger believes that in its everyday life Dasein typically exists in the roles and according to the expectations it has inherited, grounded in this first sense in a way for which it is not accountable and subject to forces that tend to prevent it from achieving a position of accountability. As Crowell points out, post-Heideggerian thinkers often interpret this "ground" as sensibilities or practices or discourses or structures of thought or forms of an unconscious that distribute power asymmetrically, even before we know or will it. In this sense, we are subjected to these unthought forms of power, and most notions of agency or subjectivity or reason are therefore naïve. We are subjects and victims of deep rhetorical power, persuaded and directed even before we have achieved the ability to be ourselves. Probably no one has developed this approach as extensively as Michel Foucault.

Nevertheless, the possibility of *becoming* accountable, responsible, and not merely subject to this grounding is part of what it means to be Dasein. So, says Crowell, there is a second sense of "ground" in Heidegger, and this involves each individual's own freedom to take over being a ground— something from which something else follows—and so to become accountable, responsible. One does this in shaking off the anonymous self that is grounded only in the first sense of having inherited background understandings which ground one's interpretations and actions and *transforming* what one has inherited into possibilities. One can do this because, as transcendence, one is always projecting oneself into a future version of oneself, always seeking some kind of well-being for the sake of which one chooses and acts. That notion of something worth seeking—some future version of oneself—allows one to understand one's situation in light of the different opportunities it offers for moving beyond oneself and into that way of being. This, says Heidegger, is transcendence:

> Transcendence is explicitly expressed in Plato's *epekeina tēs ousias* [beyond being]. . . . The *agathon* [the good] is that *hexis* [powerful capability] that is powerful in its making possible of truth, understanding, and even being, and indeed of all three together in their unity. . . . It is no accident that the content of the *agathon* is indeterminate, so that all definitions and explanations of it must founder. Rationalist clarifications fail in the same way as the 'irrationalist' flight to 'mystery.' . . . The essence of the *agathon* lies in its sovereignty over itself as *hou heneka*; as the 'for the sake of . . .' it is the source of possibility as such. And because the possible lies higher than the actual, *hē tou agathou hexis* [the capability of the good], the essential source of possibility, is *meizonōs timēteon* [even more to be honored]. (Heidegger 1969, 93 [trans. Malik]; 1998, 124 [trans. McNeill])[17]

Here is a convergence of Plato, Heidegger, and American pragmatism that unveils an agreement behind all their numerous and essential differences. For Heidegger, however, Dasein is capable of the good not in the sense that it may or may not become good or in the sense that it may gain some good toward which it is aiming, but in the sense that it *is* a *transcendence toward* and a disclosing of something that counts as good and so functions to make things interpretable as leading toward what is good or not. This capability for a good, and so the occurrence of goods, is Dasein's transcendence, whether Dasein knows it and wills it or not. We are the ways beings show themselves as leading to a good or not; however, we do not for the most part exist in full acknowledgment that this is the case. For the most part, we are not accountable for this event.

When we take over being-a-ground in an authentic way, we take over responsibility for being a ground, and so, says Crowell, "possibilize" the grounds that have been determining us. This involves, he says, transforming grounds that had been functioning as causes into grounds that can function as reasons. If we are *caused* to act a certain way, then we could not have acted otherwise. Once we know the cause, there is no sense in asking why we acted the way we did rather than some other way. Causes are matters of necessity, not possibility. When a ground becomes a *possible reason* for acting, then we ourselves experience ourselves as (1) questionable—as facing the question of whether to exist one way rather than another—and as (2) capable of acting on reasons that are the answer to the question of why one should exist one way rather than another. First, though, we must experience the reason as a good (or bad) reason for acting in some particular way. We can do this because we are a transcendence beyond the current state of our existing and toward some future state of our existing at which we are aiming. A reason is a good reason because it helps to lead to a way of being ourselves that is a good way of being ourselves—at least, as good as possible. We can also do this because Dasein is our own being, something we ourselves have to handle and take on as a task. The transformation of causes into reasons is always in some sense first-personal. To be answerable, accountable, responsible for oneself is to be able to give answers to the why questions—and these answers are reasons.

What makes some way of being a good one? Heidegger is not directly concerned with that question. He is concerned, however, with defeating two common kinds of answers to that question. First, we don't simply decide in an arbitrary way what is good. We don't just place value on some things and not on others. This view is sometimes called "decisionism" or "voluntarism." The world of significations we inherit is already threaded through and through by goods that arose in and informed the experience of the Dasein that was there before us. We are already part and parcel of a morally and ethically and socially and economically and politically significant world from which we cannot completely separate ourselves.

Second, however, we do not simply follow the norms and rules and social roles and the ethics that have been handed down to us. They are neither simply causes nor dogmas. We do not just discover a good way of life that comes complete with a set of guidelines that will instruct us on how to act in all the specific situations we will face. To take over being a ground is an event of transcendence and of being-in-the-world. It thus requires both a morally and ethically significant context in light of which it experiences itself and others and other beings *and* an achievement of freedom in the way it stretches out toward the good and so selects and conceptualizes and interprets and acts in light of the past in a new way, in a new situation, for itself and the others with whom it shares Dasein. At this point, we are on the threshold of a rhetoric of argumentation rather than a logic—that is, a kind of reasoning that is free of the compulsion and necessity of a formal system of logic or a complete ethical theory but that preserves the constraints of reasoning that lead to justifiable outcomes. Crowell rightly points to Heidegger's use of the word *Rechtgebung* or legitimation, when it comes to saying what is required of Dasein's being a grounding (2007, 61).

However, Crowell's reconstruction exposes some failures in Heidegger's account that only a deep rhetoric can address. What is distinctive in Crowell's interpretation is that he awards the call of conscience (from *Being and Time*) a role in *The Essence of Grounds* as the agent who calls Dasein to account for itself and so generates the why-questions, even though conscience discourses in silence. In this case, I believe that Crowell's reconstruction is also repair work—and it is just what is needed.

He goes even further by giving conscience the responsibility for both hearing and answering, which of course requires logos and even dialogue and reasoning. He is led to this because of the surprise ending Heidegger gives to his essay on *The Essence of Grounds*. After developing a pretty much utterly solipsistic account of the way Dasein is a grounding, Heidegger suddenly, out of nowhere, concludes:

In *transcendence*, the essence of the finitude of Dasein discloses itself *as freedom for reasons*. . . . And so the human being, existing as a transcendence that exceeds in the direction of possibilities, is a *creature of distance*. Only through originary distances that he forms for himself in his transcendence with respect to all beings does a true nearness to things begin to arise in him. And only being able to listen into the distance awakens Dasein as a self to the response of the other Dasein in whose company [*Mitsein*] it can surrender its I-ness in order to win itself as an authentic self. (Heidegger 1969, 131 [Malik]; 1998, 135 [McNeill])

This is striking on several accounts. Transcendence opens up a space and time for Dasein in which it can encounter itself, others, and beings. But this transcendence is *a freedom for reasons*—that is, a freedom to transform mere grounds and causes into reasons for being one way or another, a freedom to lead the soul. This is the primal scene of rhetoric itself. To be capable of this transforming is to have the faculty of seeing all the available grounds of persuasion *as grounds of persuasion, as reasons* for being one way rather than another. The world is a world of possible arguments by means of which we can persuade and lead ourselves and others, and in turn be led by others. Discovering and giving reasons is not only a mode of transcendence, it is the mode of transcendence that corresponds in a special way to the freedom of transcendence. This capability of interpreting grounds *as* grounds of persuasion is a deep rhetorical capability. It is what makes possible Aristotle's more concrete conception of rhetoric: the ability to see, in any given case, the available means of persuasion.

Even more striking is the sudden appearance of "the other Dasein" and the announcement of an event that takes place "in its company" (*Mitsein*): Dasein's surrendering its I-ness (*Ichheit*) and attaining its authentic self. This is announced without any preparation or explanation. Crowell's extensive reconstruction concludes with this passage. For him, this other Dasein is the one to whom Dasein must account for itself, the one to whom it is answerable. However, given how cryptic the comment is, it could mean many things. It could, after all, mean that a form of *Mitsein* with myself occurs in the Dasein that is always my own when I take responsibility for myself, when I take up a resolute relation to myself and hold myself accountable. The "distance" mentioned here could be the distance that opens up between me and my authentic self when I stretch toward myself in an authentic way. This interpretation would without a doubt be more consistent with what has preceded this passage in *The Essence of Grounds*. One of the problems with *The Essence of Grounds* is that it borders on being solipsistic. The references to *Mitsein* and the references to "other beings like myself" receive no development. They act almost as formal placeholders, simply reminding us that Heidegger has a notion of *Mitsein*; however, these others have no agency, no capability of their own, until perhaps in the last sentence, but that is where the account ends.

So it will prove useful to follow Crowell's lead, but then to move further toward a critique of Heidegger and to push toward a more robust notion of *Mitsein*, letting Emmanuel Levinas do some leading, too. According to Heidegger, we are called to accountability by conscience, by ourselves. For Levinas, we are called to account by others. It is in the encounter with the other that the "I" first experiences itself as "called" and feels the need to account for itself. Here is the mythical primordial call to accountability of the kind mentioned by Hans Robert Jauss—the original question and the original encounter with the other: "Adam! Where art thou?" (1989, 52). It is this responsibility/accountability that calls us to an "authenticity" which is not authenticity (*Eigentlichkeit*, "ownness") at all but ethics—a demand for an authentic response *to another*. The logos of this "authenticity" is dialogue, and so *auth*enticity cannot be the right word. The call of the other, the imploring, perhaps has no discursive content except, as in Levinas's account of the encounter with the face of the other: "Thou shalt not kill" (1990a, 7–10).[18]

Perhaps the call to accountability expressed by the other *is* the purely formal call of conscience to take responsibility—but for justifying oneself not to oneself *but to the other*, and perhaps at the same time to *oneself as the other*, oneself as the new self who has taken into consideration the imploring other and speaks on his or her behalf. This is a giving place to the other in a new way of being oneself that emerges in response to a call in which the event of conscience and the encounter with the other are the same event, the same advent of a new way of being oneself. The other is an interruption in the self that becomes constitutive for any self insofar as it is capable of questioning itself, changing, growing, transcending itself toward a better way of being, which is at the same time transcending its *Ichheit* toward becoming responsible for others.

As Levinas puts it: "Does the subject arrive at the human condition prior to assuming responsibility for the other man in the act of election that raises him up to this height? This election comes from a god—or God—who beholds him in the face of the other man, his neighbor, the original 'site' of the Revelation" (1990b, 63). This human condition must be *achieved*. It is the *human* condition of the *humanism* to which a deep rhetoric aspires. The call of the other is a call, and so it is the advent of the call and response that make up dialogue. The dialogue will be the dialogue of reason, in which Dasein is no longer grounded in mere grounds but rather in the shift of ground, the *Abgrund*, opened up by the transformation of grounds into reasons in the response to the call of the other: Where are you? Why are you existing this way rather than some other way? And assertions will not be simply assertions. They will be, as Michel Meyer has very patiently tried to teach us for many years now, the answers to questions. Giving reasons, or "grounding," is a form of transcendence that is, as transcendence, a complicated co-transcendence involving questioning each other, answering each other, and giving reasons to each other. It is a way we interfere in and intrude on each other and a way we care for each other and call each other into a human condition.

We also have in this deeper rhetoric a reversal of the priority of ontology over ethics and a new context for asking the question of the meaning of being. If we follow Crowell's lead toward thinking of conscience as a call to be accountable to the other, and if we follow, too, Levinas's insight that making ourselves accountable to, responsible for, the other is tantamount to arriving at a human condition, then Heidegger's entire ontological project appears to be grounded in ethics, for authenticity is an essentially dialogical project that involves making ourselves accountable to one another. In *Being and Time*, the whole purpose of the analysis of authenticity is to "clear" Dasein of the thoughtless, conformist way it has been captivated by beings and has forgotten being, so authenticity is the portal to the meaning of being. Only by achieving and sustaining ourselves in authenticity do we maintain the appropriate condition for understanding the being of entities and the meaning of being. Yet authenticity is a specific ethical formation that is constituted by a specific comportment toward others. We hold ourselves accountable and responsible to them. In a way, we yield our selfhood (our *Ichheit*, I-ness) to their guidance and participation. The other is co-responsible for the authenticity of Dasein.

Further, meaning is always a function of the for-the-sake-of-which, which is a good, *agathon*—either the good in which one is already ensconced without thinking about it, or the good on which one stakes one's existence. This future condition of an authentic being-a-ground stays in the dialogue that attends the transformation of grounds into reasons: Why so and not otherwise? Why this and not that? Why something at all and not nothing? The call and response and question and answer are all part of a dialogical process *out of which* the being of being and the meaning of being can show themselves in a clarified way—in light of a background world but also in light of some good that Dasein is tilted toward. *This dialogue is prior to and so conditions* whatever clarification of the being of beings and the meaning of being can be achieved. Ontology has its ethical origin in the encounter with the other, its ethical form in question and answer, its ethical materiality in logos, and its ethical telos in the for-the-sake-of-which, or *agathon*, some state of well-being toward which Dasein cannot help but to stretch and in light of which the being of beings comes to pass.

———

At this point, we have overshot Heidegger by a long stretch; however, we have clarified both the way in which philosophy itself develops toward a deep rhetoric and the way in which a deep rhetoric might be developed more completely in light of Heidegger's achievements and failures. We have also greatly developed and clarified the reality of transcendence, its connection with logos, and the way it works in understanding, interpretation, meaning, assertion, discourse, and reasoning. In chapter 6, I would like to consolidate the philosophical ground that has been gained here, and advance further by surveying even more critically some of Heidegger's false trails, then sympathetically rereading the aims of his project, and moving the analysis forward toward Heidegger's very different work from the mid-1930s, which will lead to more hard-won gains for the project of conceptualizing a deep rhetoric.

SIX

Beyond Heidegger:
False Trails and Re-readings

The encounter with philosophy, the critique of philosophy, and the rapprochement with philosophy are constitutive for a deep rhetoric. The encounter with Heidegger's philosophical project, certainly one of the most comprehensive and far-reaching philosophical projects of the twentieth century, helps to give definition and guidance to the project of a deep rhetoric in several ways. The critique of the ontic prejudice of modern thought and the rethinking of the being of human beings as transcendence are accomplishments without which it would be hard to imagine a deep rhetoric at all. Heidegger's struggles with larger and more restrictive conceptions of logos map a field of concerns for any project that wants to take logos in the larger sense seriously. Heidegger's glancing and oblique encounter with rhetoric as an alternative to narrower philosophical conceptions of language and reason also helps to form an agenda of unfulfilled opportunities for a contemporary philosophical rhetoric. In addition, Heidegger's thinking creates a fertile context for comprehending how philosophically profound the new rhetoric project of Perelman and Olbrechts-Tyteca really is—and how far down the road toward a deep rhetoric it moves us.

However, there are essential weaknesses in the Heideggerian project, and the encounter with Heidegger must also be a critique of Heidegger. Heidegger's radical isolating of Dasein in its individual authenticity neglects the sociality of authenticity. His diminishment of logos throughout, but especially in his valorizing of silence in authenticity and at times in the attempt to think being directly, is also an exaggeration that obscures the ineluctable need for logos in all transcendence. The absence of others as authentic agents is also mostly absent from Heidegger's account of sociality. The ghostly other of *Mitsein* has nothing like the concreteness of the Dasein that is in each case my own. Finally, Heidegger's attempt to move beyond the limitations of his accomplishments of the 1920s and the Dasein-analysis project and to think being directly exposes him to the charge of irrationalism. However, his failures are not simple failures. They are instructive and capable of giving direction because they map the misleading trails one faces on this difficult philosophical ground. Heidegger's errors are indicative of the dangers any philosophical project will encounter on this terrain. If a deep rhetoric is a rapprochement with as well as a rejoinder to philosophy, it will have to test its capability in negotiating these same dangers. Heidegger was fond of Hölderlin's lines from "Patmos" (Hölderlin 1966, 462–63):

Wo aber Gefahr ist, wächst
Das Rettende auch.

But where danger lies, grows
what rescues, too.

By surveying Heidegger's false trails, one finds the sites of philosophical challenges that define the need for reorienting with a deep rhetoric. The opportunities for a deep rhetoric to make a contribution are greatest where Heidegger falls silent or misspeaks or leads us down a false trail.

There is one false trail that will not be explored in detail here: Heidegger's speeches and writings and actions during and in the years immediately following his infamous rectorship of the University of Freiburg, his membership in the Nazi party, and his support of Hitler and National Socialism. There is now a voluminous literature on this catastrophe, and this is not the place to summarize or judge it. What is clear is that Heidegger's political speeches and actions and writings of this period show an inexcusable attempt to find common ground with Hitler and the Nazis. Heidegger showed himself to be a prime example of the naïve "unpolitical man," with little understanding of the larger political realities he was facing. He deluded himself into thinking that he could steer National Socialist thinking in a philosophical direction and preserve some autonomy for the university. He was willing to make disastrous compromises to do so. He foolishly projected his own interpretation of contemporary crises of thought onto certain movements in National Socialism, and he tolerated the evils of Hitler's coup beyond what anyone can think is justifiable. His period of extreme self-deception and collaboration lasted only ten months, from May 1933 until February 1934, when he resigned his rectorship, but there are reliable reports and indications of his continued sympathy for at least parts of the movement, and the damage he did during that time was immense.

Having said this, it is also the case that no close study of Heidegger's philosophical writings of the 1920s can discover philosophical support for or elaboration of any of the central notions of Hitler or National Socialism—especially the biological racism that became such a core doctrine. There are reports that Heidegger showed indications of vague anti-Semitic attitudes, but these are difficult to verify. It is certain that his philosophical work not only has no indications of racial anti-Semitism but that it is essentially incompatible with it. Dasein is free transcendence from an inherited world of meaning toward future possibilities. To conceptualize Dasein in terms of race would be one more ontic misinterpretation of transcendence, the ontological character of human being.

Heidegger's actual political speeches and writings of the period are weirdly obscure, finding the most remote and nearly incomprehensible connections between contemporary events in Germany, ancient philosophical ideas, and a future Heideggerian philosophy. They exhibit on their face the strain of trying to combine the question of being with the practical challenge of leading the university under Nazi supervision. The kind of technical philosophical work with which we are familiar from *Being and Time* and the lectures of the period are nowhere to be seen in these speeches and writings. Not only is there little philosophical work in them, but there is no *political* philosophy in them at all. Heidegger is very obviously uninterested in political philosophy as such, or anything we would consider political philosophy. He offers no analysis of liberal political theory. He provides no readings of Marx, no serious reading even of Hegel's political thought. He shows every sign of being provincial when it comes to serious political thought or to facing up to the dangers that finally overwhelmed Germany. His nationalism and his German exceptionalism never received the philosophical attention he lavished on other subjects.

His failure is in part a specific example of the abstract and unworkable notion of approaching politics "philosophically" in the sense of trying to force abstract philosophical ideas onto very specific historical and political events and actions. His primary failure is not a failure of his philosophical work but of his judgment that the work in fundamental ontology had some direct application in the concrete political context of his place and time—a context of which he had no solid grasp at all, at least none that went beyond the German universities, although even there his grasp was quite weak. It is one thing to understand the general ontological framework within which contemporary thinking is confined overall; it is an entirely different thing to know what to do given that context, especially when powers within that context are moving in ways that can cause immense suffering and death for millions of people.

Much more can, of course, be said about the particular dimensions of Heidegger's political failure—how his provincial past, his nascent notions of the history of being and the essence of technology, and the experiences of war and of Weimar collapse might have provided the context for this failure; however, there are other failures that will concern us here. Though not as humanly catastrophic and as politically consequential and dramatic as the failure of 1933–34, they are nevertheless philosophically important, and it will be critical for the project of a deep rhetoric to discover the missed opportunities in these failures.

Solus Ipse v. Logos

First, Heidegger over-individualizes authenticity. Authenticity requires a collapse of the everyday self that exhausts itself in its social identity and an emergence of an authentic self that is capable of experiencing anxiety before death without fleeing. This experience of the possibility of death is, says Heidegger, one's ownmost (*eigenste*) possibility. That is, it belongs only to oneself and no one else. There is no dying together, no social death; all social roles and relationships fail at death. For this reason, he also calls facing one's death "nonrelational" (*unbezügliche*). This suggests a dissolution of world and *logos* along with a breakdown of being with others. This individualization in the face of death is supposed to reveal a human being's authentic being in a true way, without the cover-ups of social life in which our radical solitude and finitude are obscured. One does not need to be actually dying, or even thinking about one's actual death, to be facing up to death in this way.

There is of course truth in Heidegger's analysis, which is much more complex than I can relate here. Anyone who has read Tolstoy's *The Death of Ivan Ilych*, to which Heidegger refers, recognizes what Heidegger is trying to say. So do many of those who have suffered closely with the dying, come close to dying themselves, and those who have experienced the way grief seems to reveal an utter aloneness. There is without a doubt important insight in Heidegger's account of the way we experience this first-personal truth. However, it is very important here to ask whether there is a social way of being authentic, a way of being with others that allows us to stay true to the realizations Heidegger mentions even while we pursue projects that demand sympathy, shared understandings, and mutual help. Heidegger's accounts of such a way of being are tenuous at best. He contrasts two positive modes of being with one another. In one, we intervene in each other's existence, stepping in for one another, and taking over for each other. This is, says Heidegger, our everyday way of being with one another. Within limits, we are ordinarily interested in others in connection with our own concerns. At worst, this can mean simply using one another as a means for our own purposes. In the other way of being with one another, we help to open up a place for others to find themselves and their own projects. We are concerned not so much with what someone else will do as with their self-understanding and clarity in the face of what they will do.

However, this is an extremely oversimplified and abstract result for an existential phenomenological ontology. There does seem to be a way in which each of us can die only our own death, and there does seem to be a way that we can discover dimensions of that truth and incorporate it into our existence by engaging in a kind of philosophical-existential honesty with ourselves. However, these actions are also made possible in any determinate sense by our sociality and by the logoi in which we find ourselves. Our relations with one another permeate the interpretations we make of our own death and the way we comport ourselves toward the possibility of our death. If we live in a culture in which immortality is taken for granted, and our conceptions of death and the rituals in which we move toward it define our relations to ourselves and to our families and friends and neighbors, then to say that facing one's death is *unbezügliche*, i.e. unconnected with or unrelated to others, is to obscure the truth of death. One can face death honestly, in full practical acknowledgment of one's insufficiency and the reality that one's death is one's own, only because being toward death is also a way of being-with the others with whom one has lived and in whose company one may well die. Being toward death inevitably *depends on* the logoi that one shares with others in a time and place, whether such logoi sustain a belief in immortality of some kind or not. Even when and where they do not, death is hardly *unbezügliche*. In fact, we could say that it is meaningful to call it "nonrelational" only because it is in its essence (as Heidegger would say) relational. Then "nonrelational" would describe a specific and stripped down way of realizing a possibility that is "in its essence" relational, social. The same thing is true of our experience of individuality—our individual capacity to take responsibility for our existence, in the face of death. The achievement of such individuality varies greatly depending upon the logoi that make such a capacity for individuality intelligible in a place and at a time. Whatever individuality and capacity for deep responsibility one achieves is never simply one's own doing. Its possibility is built out of language and culture, families, friends, experiences of work and education, and much else. To be toward one's death is to let certain logoi concerning death lead one into an understanding of death. Logos is our being toward, the leading of our souls, and death is intelligible to us at all only in terms of the logoi that make it intelligible.

Ultimately, I am in a dispute here with Heidegger's temporal fundamentalism. He believes that human transcendence is fundamentally a stretching out in time. Time is the meaning of being, its absolute phenomenological horizon, the foundation of ontology. From the standpoint of a deep rhetoric, this temporal fundamentalism is one more logos, one more way to lead the soul. It conducts us somewhere, and illuminates some things and not others. One must consider the logoi for it and the logoi against it. For a deep rhetoric, transcendence is stretching out in the light of logos, and it is logos that "gives time," whether it is clock time or kairotic time or time understood in spatial logoi or the time that structures the narratives of Leslie Silko's amazing *Almanac of the Dead* or the timelessness of trance and contemplation or the theological eternities of the divine. These times are given to us by the logoi of the worlds into which we are thrown, and we live in them according to the logoi in terms of which we lead our lives. A deep rhetoric in no way denies the importance of temporality and history; it simply denies their independence of logos and the claim that they are more fundamental than logos.

The point here is not that facing one's death does *not* have an individualizing force. The point is that Heidegger exaggerates and absolutizes this force into the essence of being toward death, at least in some passages of *Being and Time*. Overall, he wants to have it both ways. On the one hand, he says that any authentic being oneself is a *modification* of the social self that lives and moves in the given logoi it has inherited. This would imply that being toward death is a modification of our usual way of being with others and sharing a world, and not a complete collapse or destruction of it—though it may, for an Ivan Ilych, be close to that. But even there, Ivan is helped toward his own being toward death by a servant. And his capacity for at last dying his own death is achieved in the same act with which he seems to attempt to ask forgiveness from his wife and son. On the other hand, however, Heidegger insists on the nonrelational essence of authentic being toward death, and thus, in an important sense, on the nonrelational essence of authenticity itself. The truth is that a single seeing of the essence of death or authenticity will not give us everything we need to let these phenomena show themselves. Being toward death can be radically individualizing at the same time that it makes use of and even energizes social logoi. These things show themselves most truly only in interpretive explorations that highlight them in different ways at different times and for different purposes.

Finally, if we are to give Tolstoy's *Ivan Ilych* the last word about being toward death, then being toward death is deeply rhetorical and very much a matter of logos. In fact, logos-rich being toward death gives time in a way that makes time itself seem to be the servant of logos. Near the end of the story, Ivan is lying on his bed, dying, regretting having devoted his life to utter superficialities, wondering if there is anything left to do to set things right. He opens his eyes and sees his son and his wife, and he feels profound sorrow for them, trapped in a world of dishonesty and impoverished meaning, a world that he has helped to construct and reinforce. He wants to say something, but even more he wants to act, to do something, and so he speaks in a special way. He says that he is sorry, and then the last words he tries to speak are "Forgive me." However, all that he can manage to speak, in the English translation, is "Forego . . ." It is difficult to imagine a more deeply rhetorical or more logos-dependent action. This is not a mere statement; it has illocutionary force. It is a performative, an attempt to act, to set his life right, and to aid his wife and son. He acts out of an ethos that is invisible to those around him. In this light, it could be they who are experiencing nonrelationality and Ivan who is, at last, experiencing profound sociality and relatedness and even intimacy. In the face of his long inward attempt to be toward his own death, in the light of the fitting, the most truly revealing logoi, out of a mood of compassion for his wife and son and for their suffering, he speaks. In terms of the outward reception, however, his ethos is determined by the familiar world in which this familiar man was known to others and by the fact that he is now irrelevant—diseased and dying and demented in speech.

This man is a *someone* who is saying something about something to someone. The saying is a plea for forgiveness, at least as Ivan speaks for himself. From the standpoint of the "to someone," however (thought of as the wife and the son), the "saying" may indeed appear to be a request ("Please forego"), but it may also appear to be a command: "Forego!" And it may also seem to be simply the meaningless word-sound of a deranged and dying man. Ivan himself realizes the truth that Heidegger tries to express in his notion of nonrelationality. He is losing the ability to share logoi with others in any ordinary sense of sharing default meanings that allow the world to function effectively. He is slipping out of that world, alone. And yet not alone, for Tolstoy and Ivan, because there is also a religious dimension to this speech. After failing to speak the words "Forgive me," Ivan (in the English translation) "waves his hand, knowing that He whose understanding mattered would understand." For Ivan, the struggle to be toward his own death is also understood as a struggle to be toward God—that is, to be toward his death as a way of projecting himself into logoi concerning God which also lead toward God and toward the fitting logoi concerning death. "Forgive me" is the speech act in which Ivan achieves his *metanoia*, his transforming turning away from and turning toward. For Heidegger, this is an achievement of solitary self-understanding, existence calling to itself, and turning toward itself honestly, resolutely, and hearing and receiving the call in silence. From a deep rhetorical point of view, these are once more competing logoi, ways of leading one's life and making it intelligible.

The "something" that is said is also important here, and it indicates once more the thickly linguistic and deeply rhetorical death that Tolstoy gives to Ivan. *What* is said—the saying of *something about something*—is strictly limited by the conditions of reception and by the way the some-ones take up the *something about something*. On one level, Ivan is saying something about himself: I, Ivan Ilych, am asking you to forgive me. At another, he is saying something about them: You, my wife and son, are urged to forgive me. At yet another, he is saying something about forgiveness—that it is fitting to be requested and to be given in this situation. In any case, at all these levels (and there are more), forgiveness is at stake because the world that Ivan has helped to form as the world for his family is a dangerous fabrication of meaningless superficialities. He is sorry for having done this to them, and he asks for forgiveness. He has come to this realization only by following certain logoi that concern his living and dying, logoi he was more or less forced to follow because his death was imminent. However, their deaths are not imminent, and they have not followed these logoi, and they are not receptive to his speech. Tolstoy allows them to hear, at most, in the English translator's words, "Forego." Is Ivan's call understood then to be a call to forego this life of acquisition and status-seeking and default living and half-conscious fleeing from what is most meaningful? Is it heard even as an unwelcome command, a kind of "Thou shalt not"? Some logos from the dying man *does* come through. They *are* being asked to give something up, and that is enough for them to hear, to bear. They do not have the receptivity for more. This is a valiant attempt by the English translator to make meaning of a very dense moment in the novel and a very difficult passage of language.

However, this last logos is very different in the Russian. Ivan does indeed attempt to say *prosti* (forgive), but manages only *propusti* ("let it pass" or "let me pass").[1] This is all that can be heard, and it answers no questions. To whom is this request being made? If "it," then what is to be let pass? Ivan's speech? Ivan's thought of forgiveness? If "me," then who or what is preventing his passing? From one angle, we might have here once again evidence for Heidegger's thesis about the "nonrelational" nature of death and the collapse of language. At Ivan's moment of greatest solidarity with his wife and son and himself, in his most honest and compassionate action, he is most alone and falls unintelligible. Yet Tolstoy does not tell the story this way. Instead, Ivan waves his hand, knowing that (in a more literal translation) "the one who needs to understand will understand." There is reception after all, understanding after all. We do not know whether Ivan, having become wise, is conducting the inward speech of wisdom, or whether G-d is attending, or whether we ourselves are the receptive or unreceptive ones, who at least get to "hear" Ivan's intended word. In any case, Ivan's dying is guided by logos in some of the most complex ways imaginable. The very action that is required by Ivan in death is a speech act, a performative. It is logos that leads right through the end of Dasein.

In Tolstoy's narrative, this event of logos and all that attends and follows it has a *priority* to time, and in fact transforms it. Time is leading to death and the confirmation of the meaninglessness of his life. When Ivan looks at his wife, he thinks:

Her dress, her figure, the expression of her face, the tone of her voice, all revealed the same thing. "This is wrong, it is not as it should be. All you have lived for and still live for is falsehood and deception, hiding life and death from you." And as soon as he admitted that thought, his hatred and his agonizing physical suffering again sprang up, and with that suffering a consciousness of the unavoidable, approaching end. And to this was added a new sensation of grinding shooting pain and a feeling of suffocation. (1960, 153)

Ivan has a logos here: "Go away! Go away and leave me alone!" (154). This logos gives time. It is the time of Ivan's hell, the time of the voluntary nonrelational. It is mythically a three-day descent, and it is also without time. "*For three whole days*, during which time did not exist for him, he struggled in that black sack into which he was being thrust by an invisible, resistless force" (154). This force is moving him not in time but in a direction made possible only by a new logos that is taking shape for Ivan: "And every moment he felt that despite all his efforts he was drawing nearer and nearer to what terrified him" (154). Ivan is terrified not of death but of the logos that death is revealing: that his life had not been a good one, that it could not be justified, that it had been all wrong.

Toward the end of the third day, Ivan's resistance breaks down, and his experience of truth takes the temporal form of a series of "suddenlys." "Suddenly" a force strikes him in the chest and side, "like the sensation one sometimes experiences in a railway carriage when one thinks one is going backwards while one is really going forwards and *suddenly* becomes aware of the real direction" (154). The direction here is not a temporal one, although it makes its own time that intersects with part of the clock-time that is counting down the hours to Ivan's death. Accepting the truth had appeared to Ivan to be going backwards, and so he resisted it; yet now it "suddenly" shows itself to be a moving forward after all. Movement in logoi and movement in clock-time are not only moving in, so to speak, opposite directions, but the movement in logoi is also giving time its shape. Its "from that point on," its "for three days," its "suddenly." After this realization, Ivan "suddenly grew quiet" (155). This "suddenly" occurs "at the end of the third day, two hours before his death" (155). His son enters the room, and begins to cry. "*At that very moment* . . . it was revealed to him that [his life] could still be rectified." This is the moment when he looks at his wife and son, and tries to say, "Forgive me." Immediately after, the narrative continues: "And *suddenly* it grew clear to him that what had been oppressing him . . . was dropping away *at once* . . ." (155).

Ivan comes to his final epiphany—"In place of death there was light" (156). "So that's what it is," he *suddenly* exclaimed aloud. "What joy!" (156). After this moment, the two temporalities diverge more sharply. One is the clock-time which moves inexorably toward death, death which, to all appearances, finally triumphs over all logos. The other is the time of moving toward life, in which death disappears:

> To him all this happened *in a single instant*, and *the meaning of that instant did not change*. For those present his agony continued for another two hours . . .
> "It is finished," said someone near him.
> He heard these words and repeated them in his soul.
> "Death is finished," he said to himself. "It is no more!"
> He drew in a breath, stopped in the midst of a sigh, stretched out, and died. (156)

When the two temporalities diverge, they take the meaning of beings with them. "It is finished" could, in the clock time of "at the end of two hours," mean that Ivan's life and dying are finished, that he is in fact now dead. However, for Ivan, in his eternal instant, what is finished and is no more is death itself. Ivan repeats this logos "in his soul," almost as if he had just read the section of the *Phaedrus* in which Socrates and Phaedrus speak of the logos written on the soul. In the end, he is stretching out not in clock-time toward death, though he indeed dies, but through logos, toward his life.

Once Heidegger reduces logos to a narrow form of logic and grammar, and shows that beings and logos are both trapped in a historical structuring by time, logos becomes forever subordinate to time, and mortality is capable of forcing nonrelationality and logos-less experience. It is strange that Heidegger chooses to bring Tolstoy into *Being and Time* at the very point at which he is trying to show that time and death are definitive for ontology and that nonrelationality is definitive for authenticity—because Tolstoy is very clearly telling a story in which logos gives the being of death and time itself, and in which intimacy and communication are constitutive of authentic being toward death. Tolstoy's narrative is itself an exposition of the way deep rhetoric goes further than ontology, both in accounting for the ways in which being and time are given and received and in illuminating the ethical-spiritual dimensions of such communicative giving and receiving. It is not time or temporality that temporalizes, but logos.

Silence and the Diminishment of Logos

This takes us to the second weakness in the Heideggerian approach. Authenticity discourses in silence. In *Being and Time*, Dasein is described as lost in the anonymous idle chatter of everyday talk. This endless and prolific talk in the most superficial language about ultimately nothing of significance is Dasein's everyday existence. In fact, just about every effort to speak authentically gets drowned in the superficiality of the way we ordinarily speak and listen. The call of conscience, according to Heidegger, calls us out of our everyday superficiality and conformity to this chatter by calling us to our authentic potentiality for being ourselves—finite mortals who have our being as a task and who understand ourselves most clearly when we exist honestly with ourselves in the light of our deaths. In order to avoid getting reduced to just more chatter about death, the call of conscience takes the form of keeping silent. Heidegger is quite consistent about this throughout *Being and Time* as well as the writings that come after it, and he goes to some lengths to defend this view against objections to the idea that neither conscience nor authenticity can have any relation to language—there can be no authentic discourse except for keeping silent—or any relation to deciding between conflicting views of how we should live or which actions are better and which worse or which party's account of reality is to be given more credence. The consequence is that it seems impossible to be reasonable about deciding how to act and impossible to justify actions—at least in any authentic way. So we may well ask, where does this leave us when we come into conflict with one another? How are we to use language to resolve issues when there are conflicting sides with competing arguments? Is there any orientation toward or concern with authentic justice in Heidegger's project?

To be fair, Heidegger is focused on something he believes is prior to justice and determines both the abstract and the concrete conceptions of justice that we produce and use in judgments about what is just and unjust. If we carry out "justice" without understanding that our judgments are governed by logoi that are themselves the means by which a specific prevailing of beings takes place, and that the specificity of this prevailing is linked to an epoch of being in which all entities are potential resources for the exercise of power over the things we have some potential for controlling for the sake of gaining even more control—well, then, our notion of justice will never be able to address the most profound questions about justice that are emerging in our time—whether human and animal bodies and organs and genes are in their being resources like other resources, whether the biosphere itself falls within this same framework, what kind of legal standing nonhuman entities might have in a more inclusive system of justice, and so on.

However, the question is whether there is in Heidegger's project any forward movement *at all* in thinking of justice in a new way. The importance of Heidegger's profound questioning of the reigning ontology that undergirds judgments of justice cannot be denied; however, to expose the insufficiencies does not in itself show how questions of justice might be better addressed. As important as Heideggerian considerations are, it is not clear that justice itself is best understood in terms of its being grounded in ontology. Given Heidegger's views on silence, it is difficult to see how he can treat questions of justice in a philosophically serious way, and it is easier to understand his lack of resources when it came to shedding light on ethical and political issues.

Heidegger's insistence on the ontological inadequacies of logos and the superiority of silence became if anything stronger after *Being and Time*, and it is worth looking briefly at his recasting of the issue in the

1936–38 *Contributions to Philosophy (On Enownment)*.[2] Here Heidegger follows up on the idea that ontology may itself be misleading philosophy, even in its attempt to respond to the distinction between being and beings. However, the way in which he follows up is to pursue the misdirected path of believing that since logos is the way that beings prevail, logos is the problem and silence is the answer. In a very helpful discussion of this issue, Francisco J. Gonzalez (2008) traces the development in Heidegger's thinking about language and silence from *Being and Time* to the *Contributions*. Gonzalez claims that in the 1933–34 version of *Vom Wesen der Wahrheit*, Heidegger begins to speak of silence as *"the origin and ground* of language" (2008, 360 n. 5). Here is Heidegger: "Being silent [*Schweigen*]: the gathered openness [*Aufgeschlossenheit*] for the overpowering surge [*Andrang*] of beings as a whole" (GA 36/37:111, Gonzalez 2008, 360).[3] To keep silent in the right way is to have freed oneself from the prevailing of beings that happens in logos, to have found a way to undergo one's being an understanding of being with a more primal openness that is not determined by beings. In a way, there is a kind of logical argument underlying this move: there is no other way than silence to receive language itself and beings as a whole because language and beings cannot precede themselves.

However, what kind of an "undergoing" is this, and what difference does it make? For Heidegger, this is not simply a recognition of a logical necessity; he is trying to describe a new kind of thinking that preserves this truth in the way it speaks. It cannot speak of being directly or even indirectly; it can speak only in silence if it is to escape the prevailing of beings and the reduced notion of logos as assertion that performs that prevailing. By 1936–38, this becomes a central focus of Heidegger's effort to imagine a new kind of thinking. This thinking must be "in itself sigetical [*in sich sigetisch*],[4] precisely remaining silent in the most explicit reflection [*in der ausdrücklichsten Besinnung gerade erschweigend*]" (GA 65:58). Or, as Heidegger puts it later in the same text, "What remains to thinking is only the simplest saying [*Sagen*] of the simplest image in the purest silence" (72). This is an interesting expression. Here silence is both opposed to logos and identified as a way of saying. It is not a way of saying something about something, at least not in the mode of assertion or predication. We keep silent in the act of speaking by foregoing assertion for something else. For what? For a reflection on a "naming" that does not assert, and so does not fall captive to a logos that is handcuffed to the prevailing of entities: "'Logic' as the doctrine of correct thinking is transformed into meditation [*Besinnung*] on the essence of language as the founding naming [*stiftenden Nennung*] of the truth of Being [*Seyns*]" (GA 65:177).

However, it is difficult to hear in this anything "beyond logos." First, there is the intelligibility of the naming as a naming. Naming names. It leads us in some way. It may not bear reference in this case to simple entities, things, in the sense of pointing to them and picking them out as things. The reflection on naming is supposed to allow naming to name being, the giving of beings rather than the beings themselves, the openness to being rather than what appears in the open. However, to do this, the naming must be capable of leading us *toward* being. It must have the power of logos, the power of being able to *be toward* something, to lead toward something, even if just to lean toward it. Naming, too, is logos. And one must also wonder here whether naming also asserts something. It is difficult to imagine how there could not be in any naming an implicit assertion that the name was appropriate, that it really did lead—at least potentially and experienced in the right way—toward the named, that it was not senseless or utterly arbitrary. Even Heidegger's neologisms are made of familiar words, carefully chosen. Is silence so far from logos?

In fact, silence is significant and is a kind action. It follows from something, some experience, some language, some thinking. It is an action in the face of something before which it is silent, and it leads to something—some new experience, some different language or attitude toward language, some new thinking or experience of thinking. It is not the opposite of significance or language; it is an intrinsic feature of it. Silence is a dimension of logos and one might even argue a necessary and essential dimension. This is easier to understand when one keeps the larger sense of logos in mind. Heidegger finds an a-logical silence to be an alternative to the narrower logic and its predominant entities only because he lacks this larger sense of logos as the referentiality that allows for any kind of connectedness and significance, which are themselves *internal* to entities and constitutive for them in a way that Heidegger sometimes sees but often fails to fully acknowledge.

Rhetoric has always kept this truth in mind. Moods follow from and lead to one another not simply in time or as a matter of strict causality, but in logos. Hurt can lead to anger, and anger can lead to regret, and regret can lead to a mood of reflection, and being reflective can lead to calming. None of this leading is necessary or strictly causal. Growth in character or progress in a life means that one phase of life and self-understanding can lead to another; one repertoire of actions and manners of utterance can follow from another—not simply in time, but in light of a hope of growth or of a vision of where a life is leading. In music, one note can follow from another and lead to another. One chord can lead to another, one passage can lead to another; one movement can follow from another. One verse of a song can lead to another. In a narrative, one action or event can lead to another and follow from another. Narrative and music and any kind of growth or progress in life depend on logos—the capacity of one thing to lead to another, to bear a reference to it within the larger logos in which each makes sense. "Logical" relations are only one narrow kind of reference of this sort. And relatively few of these references are simple subject-predicate relations, or relations of essence and accident. Yet they all depend on logos—the possibility of things bearing relations to one another in an intelligible world. Certainly, causalities and temporalities play a supporting role in this, but this kind of leading is, as Plato allows Socrates and Phaedrus to discover, an essential virtue and power of logos.

Metaphors and figures of speech, all tropes, also depend on a kind of silence. They all say, implicitly: this does not mean literally what it says, or does not mean it in the usual way. There is instead a keeping silent about what is said. There is also, in addition to this silence, another kind of saying, one that reorients and redefines what counts as saying something about something, but it is a saying that preserves a kind of silence. Perhaps this is not the case when one can produce a perfect paraphrase, but it has for a long time been a question whether the poetic as such is paraphrasable.

One way to interpret Heidegger's notion of *schweigen*, then, keeping silent, this active kind of silence, a meaningful silence, though not meaningful in the ordinary sense, is to see that poetry is an exemplary case of keeping silent. Poetry lets images and resemblances appear and come to presence, and the emotional apprehensions that occur in rhythm and tone and line, and yet what poetry allows to appear is not what the poem is ultimately about. Poetry uses metaphor and imagery because what it intimates cannot be conveyed directly, certainly not in a series of logical assertions about known entities.

The nonliteral uses of language and the myriad ways in which language can be figured and reshaped syntactically and semantically have long been a concern of rhetoric, in whose tradition one can find elaborate lists of figures and tropes and complicated schemes for categorizing them. However, Heidegger pursues these uses of language under the heading of the "poetic," and although he develops no theory of figuration or philosophical account of tropes, he clearly believes that the power of imagery and of something like metaphor is one great alternative to the restricted kind of logos that is limited to assertions about entities. And yet in his writing about poetry, he is clearly not speaking about silence but about logos.

This is especially clear in his essays on Hölderlin's poetry, where he does not simply interpret or comment on the poems but rather thinks along with and through them.[5] He takes Hölderlin to be a partner in the project to say the unsayable, to speak being through something like "naming." In one of Heidegger's most careful treatments of Hölderlin, "As When on a Holiday . . . ," he tracks Hölderlin's attempts to name what cannot be experienced immediately, what Heidegger sometimes calls Being (*Sein*), but what during the mid and late 1930s he sometimes calls *Seyn* and *Ereignis*. The poem is formative for Heidegger, and much more consequential for his thought than I can begin to say here, but the point about naming and imagery can be made relatively briefly. The essay is also written, apparently, within a few years of the *Contributions to Philosophy* discussed above, so the texts can be understood to cast light on each other.

As Heidegger reads the poem, the issue is how to name something that is not a thing at all. He believes that poetry is the power by which naming can change the time in which we exist.[6] Naming allows for something to become present and to endure in time, which allows for change to have its own temporality, instead of being intensely rapid and constant. The difficulty is that if naming is too "successful," what endures does so simply as a being that is taken for granted. The poetry by which it was called into presence, into history; the tenuousness of its existence in time; its dependence on the time and history and language and circumstances that made the calling successful—all these are forgotten. In such cases, the poetic, by which, as Heidegger and Hölderlin agree, we "dwell on this earth," is forgotten.

In the first two stanzas of the poem, Hölderlin begins by using the word "Nature" to name that which is not simply a being. A countryman, as when on a holiday, goes out at morning after a rain to see a field. The lightning has passed. The thunder still sounds in the distance. Everything is green with life, and the trees and grapevines shine in the sun. Wonderfully "all-present" is the gentle educator of all: "The powerful, divinely beautiful nature." In the third stanza, she is still called "nature," and is said to be "older than the ages," and "above the gods," but is also, at the end of the stanza, called "Inspiration [*Begeisterung*], the all-creative." As Heidegger points out, the shift from nature to inspiration, to spirit, is an attempt to prevent nature's being thought of as separate from spirit

(2009b, 163). Hölderlin is trying to name a unity, an "all," and the narrator realizes the difficulty of this: "Holy be my word" is the second line of the third stanza. Saying the "all" will require a special kind of language and a special relation to language. Here, it is called "holy."

In the fourth stanza, the gods appear. They clearly have something to do with the divine and holy, but they seem not to be what was first named "nature." The powers of nature had at one time been servants who "tended our fields for us." Now, though, because "a fire has been kindled in the souls of poets," the powers of the gods become known. The powers of the gods are called "the all-living," and Heidegger identifies these with the powers of nature. That is, the gods are given their powers by what Hölderlin is calling "nature." The naming of the gods helps to bring these powers to presence. Their spirit blows "in the song" and "drifts between heaven and earth and among the peoples." The song is the song of the poet, and in it, says Heidegger, the holy comes to presence as that which is coming, arriving, and not as an object (2009b, 168).

This song, or poetry, spans and so connects heaven and earth, and what makes this mediation and mutual advent of heaven and earth possible is what is called here the "holy." Heaven and earth, gods and mortals, need one another in order to come to presence as what they are: "The word-work that originates in this way lets the belonging-together of god and human appear. The song bears witness to the ground of their belonging together" (2009b, 170). Poetry allows the holy to appear in a way that is bearable for humans—not as an infinity, or an overwhelming power, but in words. Heidegger points out the lines: "And hence the sons of the earth now drink / Heavenly fire without danger" (171). It is "fire" that now stands in for the holy, as the poem exemplifies the process it describes. Heidegger explains it this way: "The shock of chaos that offers no support; the terror of the immediate that frustrates every intrusion; the holy is transformed, through the quietness of the protected poet, into the mildness of the mediated and mediating word" (171).

And yet the poets themselves are not as fortunate as the ordinary "sons of earth." Hölderlin follows the lines above with these: "Yet us it behooves, you poets, to stand / Bare headed beneath God's thunderstorms, . . ." The poet is exposed to the dangerous power of the holy in order to mediate it for others. Here the experience of the holy seems to be not yet fully mediated, and yet—of course—it is, in the image of "God's thunderstorms." These thunderstorms return us to the opening of the poem, where, after the thunderstorms have passed, "nature" comes to presence. Heidegger remarks that with these thunderstorms we are also returned to the powers of the gods, whom he names the "higher mediators" who give inspiration to the poets. Without these higher mediators, there could be no mortal experience of the holy.

The danger, once again, is that the mediations will substitute for and eclipse what they are mediating. One is faced with being destroyed by an immediate that cannot be put into words or with putting the holy into words that will profane it with images and so obscure it. The very idea of "poetry" seems here impossible. It seems prohibited by what is elsewhere in the poem called the "firm law" according to which "nature" awakens. Heidegger's interpretation of this law is that it is the law of the holy itself: "that 'strict mediatedness' in which all relations of all real things are mediated" (173).

However, Hölderlin's poem ends in an interesting way. He is still addressing the poets who are willing to stand bare-headed in God's thunderstorms. He tells them "To grasp the Father's ray, itself, with your own hands / And offer it to the people / The heavenly gift wrapped in song / For only if we are pure in heart / Like children, are our hands innocent." Once again, we have the mediated immediate in the image of a poet being able to "grasp" the "Father's ray," which is an image of the ungraspable. The poem culminates with an explanation of this impossibility: "The Father's ray, the pure, does not sear it / And deeply shaken, sharing a god's suffering, / The eternal heart yet remains firm" (173).

What we have in the poem is a quick succession of names and images that are powerful but ultimately inadequate. The poem is a kind of narration of the process of poetry itself. The poem begins with "nature," but leaves that naming behind, and moves toward the "holy." Heidegger believes that this is because "nature" once called in the form of *physis*, which, among the Greeks, had named not only the opening in which things came to be but also the "opening into the opening"; that is, *physis* named the access to the "prior" and "primordial" that allowed natural things to come to emerge and come to pass. With the Latin translation of *physis* into *natura*, Heidegger believes that this relation to the primordial was lost, and the word came to name a specific category of beings. The "holy" is an attempt to recapture the ungraspable origin, a naming that will in one sense necessarily fail but will also call out in a way that awakens us to what is not captured, that about which the word keeps silence. In the end, though, there seems to be too much of the gods in "holy." The gods, after all, come to presence in a mutual advent with the humans, and so holiness is something beyond them, more primordial, that which gives humans and gods to each other.

At the very end of the poem, we have the phrase "eternal heart," which is, as Heidegger tells us, unique to this poem. It appears nowhere else in

Hölderlin. This "heart" is now the eternal, that which endures without being compromised, but endures not simply as an existent thing but as a remaining with the primordial origin, the beginning, which belongs to both the "pure in heart / Like children" and to "eternity."[7]

The question, from a deep rhetorical point of view, is to what degree this progression through names speaks for the importance of silence as not-logos and to what degree it speaks for the inescapability of being led by logos. The "keeping silent" that occurs in Hölderlin's poetry is not logos-less. It is logos and rhetoric par excellence. We are led from nature to the holy to the eternal heart as a way of moving toward what Heidegger sometimes calls here the origin or the primordial—that is, the event of *Ereignis* in which the realms of humans and gods and earth and sky open up and come to belong to one another. This is one of the most important ways he comes to treat the question of being in the later 1930s. We are led by means of a kind of negative path, where each name shows its insufficiencies in light of the impossibility of naming being itself, and yet we move toward a naming that is in some sense better, for our time, our place, our situation—even if the situation is "simply" a poem—than the name that came before.

Names lose touch, inevitably, with that which they call; however, the response to this is not to stop being led by words, but to find better words. Heidegger makes very strong statements on this at the end of the essay. He is speaking of the role of the word in Hölderlin's poetry, but he is himself also thinking along with Hölderlin, trying to track the way language speaks being and also remains silent: "The holy bestows the word, and itself comes into this word. The word is the primal event of the holy. . . . Hölderlin's word conveys the holy, thereby naming the singular space of time, time of the primordial decision for the essential structure of the future history of gods and humanities" (176).

Certainly there is a sense in which the logos of Hölderlin's poetry involves a "keeping silent" in the way any *via negativa* does. However, there is an old saying that all determination involves negation, and there is no question here that the negations involved in Hölderlin's namings are determinate negations, to say the least. They proceed in an order, after all, and they lead somewhere. But they are also more than that. They are an attempt to find that "singular space of time" for their own time, or, to put it in rhetorical terms, they are an attempt to be kairotically responsive to a situation in which names are in question, and so an attempt to speak in a fitting manner, a way in which, as in Plato's *Gorgias*, the appropriate things can come to presence in the appropriate way.

Heidegger's overriding concern is with being, and his concern with language and silence is a concern with how either can point to or indicate or refer to or have anything to do with something that seems to be ungraspable in the language we have. This makes the fact that we do have an understanding of being all the more remarkable for him.

———

For a deep rhetoric, though, the cause for wonder is not the question of why there is something rather than nothing, or what the relation of that something is to language, but why there can be questions *about* something at all, or why the word "something" can lead one to the word "nothing," a leading in light of which "something" and "nothing" become more intelligible. Without that specific intelligibility, the question of being would make no sense. For a deep rhetoric, the cause for wonder is that the syntax of a sentence is even possible, these grammatical references of words to each other, not to mention the semantic web of references on which all words depend. All these possible leadings, this logos. Or to go a step further, the cause for wonder is not, as Kant says, the starry heavens above and the moral law within, but the fact that the starry heavens can have anything at all to do with wonder, or with the moral law, that they are capable at all of this leading from themselves to something else, including leading to an awareness of this power of logos that they share with everything else of which we have any inkling.

Beyond Reason

This leads us to the third weakness of Heidegger's way: the tendency to flirt with an immediate experience of being as well as to flirt with the irrationalism that would have to attend claims about such experiences. Heidegger wants to say that being can be said neither directly/immediately (*unmittelbar*) nor indirectly/in a mediated way (*mittelbar*). However, most of Heidegger's energies are turned against the idea of a mediated, indirect saying of being. The turn to silence is an attempt to gain a more direct saying of being, one that arises out of a move toward being that does not go through, is not mediated by, beings. Gonzalez collects a number of passages from the *Contributions to Philosophy* that show this as a consistent focus of Heidegger in 1936/37. Here are two. "The throw-open [*Entwurf*]: that man casts himself off from beings, without beings being already disclosed as such, and into Being" (GA 65:452). "This [the truth of being] therefore can no longer be thought from the perspective of beings [*vom Seienden her gedacht*], it must be thought up from out of itself [*es muss aus ihm selbst erdacht werden*]" (GA 65:7). Heidegger makes a number of such statements throughout the *Contributions* (as well as other writings—see Gonzalez 2008); however, he has a difficult time, as we have seen he must, describing what kind of *saying* can accomplish the work of this kind of silence.

At times, Heidegger turns to tautology, which is a way of speaking without asserting—for example, "the enownment enowns" (GA 65:463) and "Being is" (*das Seyn ist*) (GA 65:472). Heidegger insists that tautologies such as these are to be taken not as assertions or predications of subjects but as sayings that regard the things in themselves (GA 65:473), that is, as that special kind of naming-saying that we have already seen is difficult to distinguish from assertion and impossible to think apart from logos in the larger sense. At other times, he turns to the language of giving "indications" (*Anzeige*); at yet others to Aristotle's *Categories*, which are said to say without combining but instead to give direct sight (GA 18:400); and also to the language of *Gleichnisse*—analogies images, likenesses—which seem to function in a way that is similar to "indications."

The problem is that although Heidegger is trying to bypass the epistemological paradigm for a relation to being, he cannot quite give it up, despite his denying it. Simply to use the language of mediation and immediacy is to stay within its frame. Simply to say that one cannot think being by way of beings but that one must think it from itself and even in itself (GA 65:473) is to reactivate the framework of epistemology, with its direct intuitions as well as its ways of organizing and connecting them with each other. This is certainly not what Heidegger intends, and he acknowledges the difficulty by calling this language only transitional and still dependent on metaphysics in a way that is perhaps for now impossible to avoid.

However, the deepest difficulty with this flirtation is the irrationalism that hovers around it. I use the language of "flirtation" and "hovering" because Heidegger never settles, in the *Contributions*, on a single attitude or position. Since philosophy is a matter of indication and pointing-towards and *Gleichnisse*, and not assertions, one cannot make a judgment about these as if they were arguments or theories or even instances of saying something specific. As Gonzales puts it: "There appears to be in the *Beiträge* a constant oscillation between a characterization of thinking as always transitional and a characterization of it as transitional only now, as well as, correspondingly, between the view that Being always withdraws before or behind beings and the view that this can be overcome in a saying of Being that does not need the detour of beings" (2008, 376).

Nevertheless, Heidegger does sometimes swing to the irrationalist pole of this oscillation. A central notion of the *Contributions* is the "leap" (*Sprung*) that is required for the new beginning in which beings will carry with them the enowning clearing in which they come to be—that is, they will carry their being with them into the clearing instead of appearing in such a way that that their being is necessarily eclipsed and forgotten (1999, 162). But how will it be possible to *say* this? "Raising the essential swaying of be-ing [*Seyn*] into the grasping word—what venture [*Wagnis*] lies in such a projecting-open?" (170). This risky venture is the challenge of saying being that often, for Heidegger, calls for silence. Here he goes a little further:

> The knowing [*Wissen*], such unpretentious boldness, can be born only in the grounding attunement of reservedness. But then it also knows that every attempt to justify and explain the venture from outside—and thus not from within what it ventures—lags behind what is ventured and undermines it. But does that not then continue to be arbitrary? Certainly. The only question is whether this arbitrariness is not the utmost necessity of a distressing distress—that distress that forces the thinking saying of being into word. (1999, 171)

The leap, the new beginning, cannot be justified or explained. Justification and explanation would require reasoning and explaining on the basis of beings, and that could never be a leap into another beginning. So it will have to be without reason or explanation—arbitrary, irrational. And yet if this arbitrariness is a result of the highest necessity—the kind of necessity that is the mother of invention—and it can manage to force a "thinking saying" into word, then it is apparently a tolerable kind of arbitrariness. However, it will still be impossible to explain or justify any statement about whether "thinking saying" has indeed found language. There's just no talking about it that way with anyone else. We are back to the "nonrelational" isolation of authentic existence that was also central to *Being and Time*.

This isolation is also a consistent theme of *Contributions*. It has been said before that this period of Heidegger's thinking was characterized by a withdrawal that was caused by the political failure of his rectorship at Freiburg in 1933–34. One might add to this his earlier feeling of being abandoned by the Church.[8] *Contributions* makes it clear early on that politics is ruled by propaganda and Christianity by apologetics (1999, 29). One can almost hear a kind of bitter disillusionment in some of the ways Heidegger expresses himself there. However, philosophy itself shares this same tendency toward a totalizing worldview that has grown incapable of questioning. The "other beginning" Heidegger seeks will of necessity be a lonely affair. In this context, he completely rejects the idea of a philosophy of a *Volk* (29–30). He even has one section titled "For the Few and Rare," those who have the "utmost courage" for the "solitude" that is demanded for this other beginning (9). This section includes explicit disgust and bitterness toward the people who have taken power:

People of today, who are hardly worth mentioning as one turns away from them, remain excluded from knowing the pathway of thinking. They flee into "new" contents, and, with the construction of the "political" and the "racial" [*Rassischen*], construct for themselves a hitherto unknown façade for the old trimmings of "school-philosophy." (1999, 14)

Yet Heidegger's withdrawal—however motivated by his own experiences and failures—is also justified by his conception of philosophy and of the insufficiencies of logos and communication themselves. His "rare and few" are solitaries consigned to silence. Heidegger can go to extremes in drawing conclusions from this. These rare and few thinkers who are capable of making the other beginning "know that their questioning and saying is *not intelligible* [*unverständlich ist*] . . . not just because those of today are not smart enough and not informed enough for what is said but rather because intelligibility already means destruction of their thinking. . . . Making oneself intelligible is suicide for philosophy" (1999, 306–7). Heidegger makes himself an easy target here, and it is difficult not to take the cheap shot regarding crude irrationalism. I will try not to do that; however, there are important matters at stake.

The Ghostly Other

In his efforts to account for Dasein's taking responsibility for itself, Heidegger isolates Dasein in its mortal individuality to enable it to have a more immediate encounter with its own being and so possibly with being itself. The guiding presumption is that the pressures of Dasein's social being are so purely conformist that others cannot figure in Dasein's transcending toward its own freedom. However, this claim is at least partly belied by its own exposition and by the argument in support of it. The very writing of *Being and Time*, a work of philosophical literature, is an attempt to lead us into an analysis of Dasein—which is in each case one's own—that will clarify it of the social and conformist distortions of its being and allow us to encounter its capability for freedom. That is, the

Mitsein we experience in reading this work, our co-transcendence with Heidegger toward the phenomenon, is supposed to be a clearing of the way for us to act in our own freedom. However, we are guided to this by this work of philosophical literature, by a writer who is someone who is not ourselves, by Heidegger, with whom we have some serious differences but by whom we also allow ourselves in some respects to be led.

If *Being and Time* is to make any sense as a philosophical project, then the *Mitsein* of reading must be one of the modes by which Dasein comes to take hold of its freedom authentically. If we must actually take responsibility for ourselves by our own act, the responsibility and the act itself are understood and interpreted and sighted at all only in the logos (the leading) provided by this philosophical literature, and this is hardly a matter of the self alone wrestling with its own death in and on its own terms. The complicated ways we deny and misrepresent our own freedom and responsibility—we have profound motives for doing so—almost require that others help us in this disclosing of ourselves to ourselves. Although Heidegger is not supposed to be writing as a psychologist or psychoanalyst, he does identify some of the dynamics of self-evasion as having ontological status, and the way to face up and cut through the self-disguises at work here also seems to require a very interesting kind of guidance by others—here in the form of philosophy that is conducted through reading and writing. Others are thus primary agents in anything like what Heidegger calls authenticity, yet this agency is altogether neglected in *Being and Time*.

However, once again, this is in some respects to oppose Heidegger on his own behalf. He himself provides the grounds for this critique not only in his act of writing but also in his account of authentic *Mitsein*, in which he distinguishes between, on the one hand, interfering in each other's transcendence by directing someone else to our own conception of what is good for that person and, on the other, helping to clear the distortions and obstacles from someone else's path and so helping to create the possibility of an authentic freedom for someone else. Heidegger's false trail is the path that leads to the self-alone, pure agent of its own authenticity insofar as it faces death in solitude. True as it is, in some respects, it neglects the agency of others and allows the notion of *Mitsein* to evaporate into abstractness.

Something similar is true in Heidegger's analysis and valorization of silence. We meet in logoi, implicit or explicit. In the significant resting of a knee against a thigh, in the transcendental arguments of the *Daseinanalysis*, in the iconographic calligraphy of a mosque—we are always meeting in logoi. And we not only meet, but we challenge, threaten, teach, adore, insult, befriend, betray, love, and reason with each other by way of these logoi. In his recognition that worldliness bears conventional significations that allow us to share our being toward entities with others in a common way of life, Heidegger acknowledges that we are, ontologically, being-with. Others are "there-with" us in our very encounter with buildings and roads and other artifacts, or even in a solitary walk on public or private land. They allow understanding and interpretation and communicative assertion to be possible for us as individuals. However, as individuals, they not only make this possible in their being-with us; they also realize their own individual possibilities in their own interpretations and assertions that in fact impinge on us just as ours impinge on them. Our co-transcendence can serve as a guide toward authenticity, or allow us to jump in and interfere with one another, but it can also—at an ontological level—open up a space for reasoning, a space for freedom in which we experience each other's choices and goods and weigh them. We open ourselves to the agency of others insofar as they are willing to give an account of themselves when we come into conflict.

Heidegger ignores this entire realm of reasoning in which we encounter each other's transcendence and the goods that ground it as offering invitations to or making claims on our own transcendence. This happens, for example, when we experience conflict—when our transcendence is interrupted in its showing itself to be incompatible with the transcendence of others—when our good, the for-the-sake-of-which that guides our transcendence, conflicts with the good of others. This conflict can lead to violence, something else Heidegger ignores, when we cannot create a mode of co-transcendence within which to pursue these goods. However, it can also lead to the development of logoi within which the conflict can be contained, explored, understood, and in some cases resolved. This can occur when we make explicit in explanations and assertions the logoi of our transcendence, the meaning of our goods and of our moving toward them, and when we use reasons to show why such transcendence and such goods are worth pursuing. This means, though, that others are no longer ghostly presences that occur in the very presencing of entities. Neither are they simply the ones whom we either ontologically aid or with whom we ontologically interfere. They are the ones with whom we ground our existences, with whom we understand and interpret and with whom we reason about goods, including the goods of understanding our being and even awakening the question of the meaning of being itself.

The new rhetoric project of Perelman and Olbrechts-Tyteca develops a theory of argumentation as precisely this kind of sociality—one that shapes the possibility of peace and reason and a community of freedom. To understand the new rhetoric project in this light, to see that it is not just a disciplinary rhetoric but in fact a transcendental argument with ontological stakes, requires this Heideggerian passage, as well as the deep rhetorical account of violence that preceded it.

These are some of the weaknesses, then, in Heidegger's approach, which opens up an understanding of transcendence that is very helpful in developing a deep rhetoric but which shuts down that possibility with its extreme individualism, its narrow understanding of logos, its faith in silence itself, its fixation on the possibility of direct knowledge of being, its flirtations with irrationalism, and its own inability to move outside of what still remains in important respects an epistemological and gnostic framework.

Re-reading Heidegger

Before leaving Heidegger and going forward with an interpretation of the new rhetoric project and its conception of justice, I would like to conclude this two-chapter passage through philosophy with a conversation with Heidegger that will bring out more explicitly the deep rhetorical approach to the issues with which he has such difficulty. What would happen if we found a way that avoided these missteps that draw us away from what we are trying to draw toward? What if we persevered with a more radical conception of logos in a way that were to break down the remnants of the epistemological framework from which Heidegger could not quite twist free?

Philosophy as a Way of Life

In order to open up a rereading that will take the most from Heidegger before we move on to the new rhetoric project, let's start with a practical acknowledgment that Heidegger's writings, especially the *Contributions* of 1936/37, are perhaps not best approached as philosophical writing in anything like a modern, conventional sense. After all, the whole point is to escape the dominance of a logos that is chained to the prevailing of beings and the oblivion of being. It would be thoughtless to do this in a conventional logical manner, in a system of assertions and arguments that led in a valid way from true statement to true statement. One alternative to this approach is to place these writings in the tradition of "spiritual exercises" that Pierre Hadot (1995) has identified as the key to understanding ancient philosophy. Hadot argues that ancient philosophy was understood first of all as a way of life and not as a body of writing or doctrines or arguments. Spiritual exercises are a way of practicing that way of life and of keeping oneself fit for that way of life. The "exercises" involved are intellectual and ethical and emotional, and they involve all of a person's capacities. Ultimately, they lead to a transformation of a person and of his or her experience and vision of the world.[9] They are not systems of statements that are supposed to reflect some way the world is independently of the way we communicate. Instead, they are deep rhetorical actions and disciplines that affect us in a manner that leads to our experiencing the world one way or another. In the Heideggerian case, this deep rhetoric we undergo with ourselves makes it possible for the difference between being and beings to come about in a way that reinforces the oblivion of being or in a way that allows us to become capable of experiencing the belonging together of being and beings. Our communication with ourselves, at this deep rhetorical level, is prior to and determines the character of the beings that show up as possible objects of knowledge. Spiritual exercises develop the habits and dispositions that support this kind of communication with ourselves as a philosophical way of life.

Heidegger himself speaks throughout his career of philosophy as a way of life, so this approach aligns with his own understanding of philosophy. Daniel Dahlstrom (1994) describes Heidegger's early efforts as focused on the discovery of a countermovement to the way we are pushed into a world of present-at-hand entities in light of which we misunderstand what it means to be. Philosophy's project is to attempt the difficult task of saying what it means to be against this powerful current that carries us away from ourselves. "To carry out this task is, in Heidegger's eyes, to live the philosophical life," Dahlstrom explains, and then quotes Heidegger (1985, 80) from his 1921/22 lectures on Aristotle: "Philosophy is a fundamental manner of living itself, such that philosophy in each case authentically re-trieves life, taking it back from its downfall [Abfall], a taking back which, as a radical searching, is itself life." The same general conception is also at play in Being and Time, where Dasein must be cleared of its having fallen into misinterpretations of itself as an entity among other entities. This happens when it takes hold of itself authentically. The Dasein under investigation, however, is not just any Dasein. It is in each case my own. Thus I myself must clear my own Dasein in order to execute that countermovement that will allow me to understand myself authentically. Only then can I pursue the *Daseinanalysis* without being misled, and it is only the *Daseinanalysis* that can, in *Being and Time*, open the way to a fundamental ontology.

In the *Contributions*, too, Heidegger is still pursuing something like philosophy as a way of life. Philosophy is for "the few who from time to time again *ask the question*, i.e. who put up anew the essential sway of truth for decision" (1999, 9). It is for "the rare who bring along the utmost courage for solitude . . ." (9). Philosophy is possible only on the basis of a particular way of life: "It is only through the ones who question that the truth of be-ing becomes a distress. They are the genuine believers, because, in opening themselves up, to what is ownmost to truth, they maintain their being to the ground . . ." (10). Most simply, philosophy requires self-transformation: "In philosophical knowing a transformation of the one who understands takes place with the very first step . . ." (10).

This is the smallest sample of the ways in which the life of the person who pursues philosophy is transformed in the pursuit. Also required is the development of a capacity for certain moods: startled dismay, distress, reservedness, deep foreboding (11–15). These moods are forms of attunement that are intrinsic dimensions of the capacity for another beginning, for asking the question, for experiencing the truth of being.

Since philosophy calls for this kind of personal transformation, since it is a way of life, it is plausible to read the *Contributions*, at least some of it, as a guide to practicing that way of life—that is, as spiritual exercises that will help draw one away from the prevailing of beings over being and re-attune and train one's attention toward being. If we are on the right track here, then Heidegger is leaning toward the ancient idea of philosophy—perhaps even the Socratic idea of philosophy as a search, a love, a stretching toward, instead of as the arrival that his writing about a direct saying of being suggests. For the Socrates of the *Phaedrus*, this stretching out is made possible by logos and its essential power of *psychagōgia*, of leading the soul, whose own being is to move beyond itself, to transcend itself, to desire and stretch toward what it thinks it desires. Socrates' aim is to turn that stretching longing away from the immediate objects of desire, and, by way of logoi that are aligned with the essential power of logos, to ask about desire itself, about the love that stretches us beyond ourselves, and whether there is anything that could possibly satisfy that longing. He contrasts this way of life with "writing"—that is, with the writing that produces a kind of written wisdom to be objectified and admired and enjoyed and believed. That, he says, is not a serious pursuit.

The serious pursuit underlies this effort, and it is the pursuit and love of wisdom as a way of life—that is, a life of pursuing and loving that stretches out toward wisdom but never arrives at it as a possession or a set of propositions or arguments or stories that are the sum of wisdom. That way of life is philosophy, and it is supported by dia-logos, by moving though logoi, by the leading of the soul by the logos. This transcendence across logoi occurs in actual dialogue—as well as in the "internal" dialogues which Socrates is always carrying out with himself, and which can exhibit at least as much transcendence as social dialogues. To stay in the loving stretching toward wisdom through logos is itself the goal of the way of life called philosophy, which is a practice of a deep rhetoric—a practice of persuading oneself, leading oneself, in this essentially transforming way. Or, as Heidegger writes: "Seeking itself is the goal [*Das Suchen selbst ist das Ziel*]. And that means that 'goals' are still too much in the foreground and still take place ahead of be-ing—and thus bury what is needful" (13). This seeking can also be characterized as a way of paying attention—a way of not allowing one's attention to be drawn off to beings but instead a way of keeping one's attention in the search. Spiritual exercises develop this kind of attentiveness. One learns to attend to the silence in the proposition and not simply the "said" in the assertion. One learns to look toward (in a searching mode) where the formal indications and the *Gleichnisse* are pointing. This means looking away from things, and toward what cannot be seen or grasped but which is a direction nonetheless.

From the Via Negativa through the Analogia Entis to Deep Rhetoric

How is this possible? First, there is a *via negativa* here. One is not searching for a being. One is not searching for a set of propositions or beliefs or a worldview on which one can settle. In fact, there is no possibility of settling at all. To search is to stretch out toward—and one cannot even say toward *something*. This is the *via negativa*—a *leading* that is identified primarily by what it is not—and so it is not at first evident that it leads anywhere at all. This seeking is not a seeking of a knowledge of being in any ordinary sense. We are seeking the seeking itself, which, if it succeeds in finding itself as a goal, has not found itself because it is no longer an active seeking that it has found. One trains toward being in the seeking for being and nowhere else. If one arrives at the goal of *finding* the seeking, one has not found it because one has stopped seeking. The way is a negative way—and yet it points *toward*. What we are trying to do in this seeking then is not to arrive at an intuition or judgment about being, but *to be ourselves as seekers*, to stay in the seeking, to stay in questioning and openness, instead of losing ourselves in beings, and so losing the question of being, and our own being as seekers of being. The point is to follow a negative way so that we can come closer to being ourselves—as the ones in whom being becomes less eclipsed and forgotten as we come closer to being ourselves. In seeking for seeking, we are seeking *to be* seekers, capable of seeking, capable of not being bewitched and distracted by beings, but capable of another kind of attentiveness toward what allows for beings at all. We are trying to become more intelligible to ourselves by being ourselves in this more attentive way that develops along the *via negativa*. Socrates calls this ignorance, and says in the *Apology* that it is his only wisdom. The Thoreau of *Walden* is just as keenly aware of this: "How can he remember well his ignorance—which his growth requires—who has so often to use his knowledge? . . . The finest qualities of our nature, like the bloom on fruits, can be preserved only by the most delicate handling. Yet we do not treat ourselves nor one another thus tenderly" (1971, 6).

This is difficult territory because we are attempting to understand a searching questioning that does not seek anything that exists as a being. Obviously, this can seem foolish, a waste of time, impractical. It is just impossible not to catch the similarity to traditional theological problematics here. Like being, G-d cannot be grasped in concepts, and is "uncreated" (not a being). This generates all the familiar difficulties that make theology seem like less than a respectable intellectual enterprise and even a bizarre waste of time. However, the way that Heidegger is forced to follow is analogous to the formal intellectual moves that theology has had to make in its history, and it is possible for these two different attempts to inter-illuminate each other.

Augustine tracks this kind theological reasoning in *De Trinitate*. He calls any purported faith that is grounded in a *knowledge* of God a "feigned faith" because God cannot be directly known by the human mind. Still, although God cannot be known, Augustine insists that God can be worshiped and loved in faith. However, this creates a serious difficulty:

But who can love what he does not know? . . . What I am asking is whether something can be loved that is unknown, because if it cannot then no one loves God before he knows him. And what does knowing God mean but beholding him and firmly grasping him with the mind? For he is not a body to be examined with the eyes in your head. (8.3.6; 1991, 246)

So here he we have a few steps along the *via negativa*. God cannot be known in any ordinary sense, so how then can God be loved? Well, God cannot be known by sight, so perhaps God can be known by the mind.

Yet it turns out that God cannot be known by the mind on its own, either. Instead, Augustine turns to scripture, and tells us that "the pure in heart" can "see God," and hearts are purified by faith, and so hearts "see" God by way of faith first and not primarily by knowledge.

And yet this will not achieve the goal either: "But naturally the spirit which believes what it does not see must be on its guard against fabricating something that does not exist, and thus hoping in and loving something false" (8.3.6; 246). Here is the short version of Feuerbach and Freud, and it is part of the negative way. Augustine follows with a fascinating discussion of our compulsion to fabricate images in our imaginations, a compulsion which is natural, sometimes helpful, and also dangerous, for faith is not directed to those images of bodies but "directed to something else" (8.3.7; 246). He allows for images that may be likenesses of "the apostle Paul" or "the virgin Mary," but not of the Trinity itself:

What then do we know, either generically or specifically, about that transcendent trinity, as though there were many such trinities and we had experience of some of them, and thus could believe according to a standard of likeness impressed on us or in terms of specific and generic notions that that trinity is of the same sort, and hence could love the thing we believe and do not yet know from its likeness to what we do know? . . . [W]e have never seen or known another God, because God is one, he alone is God whom we love by believing, even though we have not yet seen him. What we are asking, though, is from what likeness or comparison of things known to us we are able to believe, so that we may love the as yet unknown God. (8.3.8; 248)

Augustine is now beyond the pure *via negativa*, in search of what Heidegger calls *Gleichnisse*, images, resemblances. These cannot be strict likenesses such as falling into the same category or having the same differentia because there is no category of God, just as in Heidegger there is no category of Being. However, these likenesses are supposed to be "indications" of some kind, pointing us in a direction that is not purely negative. "We are asking . . ." as Augustine says. We are questioning *toward*.

Trying to steer from the *via negativa* toward a positive direction, the last part of *De Trinitate* makes a theological move that Heidegger cannot make. Augustine finds likenesses of the Trinity in the human mind and its workings. He finds images of trinities everywhere in human psychology—in perception, memory, thought, contemplation, knowledge, and language. *And these images of the Trinity are positive likenesses because human beings are made in the image of God.* In fact, the highest trinitarian image is in the mind's remembering, understanding, and loving not just itself, but God. In loving God through the likeness of the triune *imago dei* in our own psyches, we connect with the love the members of the Trinity have for one another. The likeness has conducted us into the reality. The further culmination of this comes "after the judgment," when we see God face to face and the image of God in us is further perfected by this direct encounter.

Although he flirts with the idea more than once, Heidegger has scheduled no direct apocalyptic encounter with being either in historical time or beyond. Neither does he have anything like the notion of an "image of God" that will guarantee the relation of *Gleichnisse* to being. He has simply the fugitive understanding of being that belongs to our being itself. This is in a way an analogue of the *imago dei* because, after all, it is our access to Being and it lies in our very being. Yet, as we have seen, the *Daseinanalysis* fails to deliver what a fundamental ontology had hoped for, and Heidegger set out on new paths.

However, there is another Augustinian move that is available to Heidegger, and it comes without resort to the *imago dei*. After Augustine raises the question of whether he can know that the God he loves is the true God—and he is raising this question after over what amounts to thirty chapters of work aimed at explaining the Trinity—he comes to the following very interesting development:

Let no one say "I don't know what to love." Let him love his brother, and love that love. . . . Embrace love which is God, and embrace God with love. (8.5.12; 253)

God cannot be known by the mind, but can be loved. We cannot *know* whether the God that is loved is the true God. However, we can know that God is love, and this includes the love with which we love each other. And therein lies our way to loving the true God. We can *love the love* with which we love because that love is God—God is in the very love with which we love one another and with which God is loved. (This turns out to be one of the trinitarian processions in which Augustine is most interested. In the Trinity, God is the lover, the beloved, and the love between the two.) Love the love, says Augustine. The "goal" of love is the love itself. This is not like knowledge of an object or a being. It is much more like *participating* in something that is no longer experienced as an object or goal or any kind of simple action. The "goal" is present in the action itself. The "access" to "knowing" that the God one loves is the true God requires a redirecting of attention and a change in one's expectations about the experience of "knowledge" when it is not knowledge of a being.

Heidegger makes a move of the same form. In the questioning seeking of a new beginning, a more direct experience and saying of being itself, he follows a primarily negative way, saying no to every intervening mediation of beings that would condition the experience of being. He faces a difficulty that is similar to Augustine's. How do seekers of being know whether they are seeking being or not? How do they establish a positive direction for their search? And Heidegger has an Augustinian answer: "Seeking itself is the goal" (13). "Love the love" becomes "seek the seeking." The goal is not in a being or in an accomplishment in which one's activity comes to rest. It is in transcendence itself, prior to knowledge or beings. I would not hesitate to say that it is in the ethics of transcendence, in the way that transcendence conditions what we might draw toward as a goal, or beings, or God, or love, or seeking.

So Heidegger's concern is to somehow develop and strengthen our capacity for seeking itself by seeking our seeking. And, as in Plato and Augustine, this happens by way of logoi that can be understood as spiritual exercises and which require conversations with oneself that lead to ethical and intellectual and other kinds of transformation and which take place at the level of a deep rhetoric—a level that determines how beings will show up in the world. That is, all of this requires deep rhetorical experience that is attuned not only to practical persuasive goals but to the leading of ourselves into an ethical formation that is attuned to that very leading, that very event of logos in the logoi that are our way of being.

In these formal intellectual moves to direct oneself toward what is not a being, working with resemblances is transformed into developing *an awareness and practice of participation*, and the issue is not so much what we can know or do as what we are or can be. At the intellectual level, we are following, in an abstract and formal way, some of the same logical challenges that the theological tradition explored under the rubric of the *analogia entis*. However, this tradition becomes most radical where it forgoes the epistemological concern with likeness and the way one thing might be a "sign" for another and turns instead toward a way of life, or a habit of attentiveness, that participates more openly in what it is seeking. This move distinguishes between thinking or believing by way of a sign (*sēmeion*), on the one hand, and participation in logos, on the other. However, as we have found, it is difficult for Heidegger to write helpfully here not only because of the intrinsic difficulties and the paradoxes involved in *writing* spiritual exercises, but also because of his narrow notion of logos and his predilection for silence, even in the face of the obvious fact that all these moves, and all transcendence, require stretching out across logoi, as well as the fact that the demands of philosophy in particular require participation in a deep and open way in logos.

For these reasons, this is as far as a deep rhetoric can follow Heidegger in his own rehearsal of these formally theological moves. Instead, a deep rhetoric will follow through on what Heidegger began, but only in light of what his critics have insisted against him—again, perhaps on his own behalf. One step on this following through will be to strengthen this attention to participation in what one is seeking and to try to avoid or disarm the language of immediate and mediated, direct and indirect, or—to the extent possible—any other epistemologically inflected language. Another will be to keep attention on the way logos keeps making everything possible—the way, as Gadamer puts it, being that can be understood is language, language which persists in any attempt to think against it or to experience meaning without it.

So consider briefly the judgments of some of Heidegger's better critics. Richard Polt makes the point about participation this way. He is writing about the difficulties that face Heidegger in his attempt to name being directly: "I suggest that we should think of this not as a leap onto a wholly other plane, or a symbolizing of the unseen by the seen, but rather as a rediscovery of a happening that is already at work in our experience of beings themselves" (2001, 97–98). What we are seeking is already at work in us. The point is to learn how to detach at least some of our attention from beings and train it toward what is "at work," what allows them to come to presence in all their ontic allure—and then to participate more fully in what is "already at work in us."

Jaspers, too, tilts toward thinking of something like participation as a way to address the impasses in other ways of pursuing ontology. Gonzalez has very helpful accounts of Jaspers' critique of Heideggerian thinking: "To the concept (*Begriff*) of Being sought by ontology, Jaspers opposes a multiplicity of ciphers that allow of no clear demarcation between the symbol and what is symbolized" (2008, 381). He cites Jaspers: "Since speculation is always in contact only with ciphers, transcendence cannot become any kind of ontological content [*Seinsgehalt*] for it. Transcendence in its relation to speculation is only nearer and farther in its symbol" (Jaspers 1994, 1:136, in Gonzalez 2008, 381).[10] The idea is that the symbol *participates in* what is symbolized; transcendence is more than can be contained in a concept. However, we transcend in terms of logos, here in the form of the ciphers by which we try to capture transcendence. The ciphers and symbols are what they are only because of the transcendence that is moving through them. They participate in this, reveal this, by showing themselves this way or not. As Emerson puts a related point:

"All symbols are fluxional; all language is vehicular and transitive, and is good, as ferries and horses are, for conveyance, not as farms and houses are, for homestead" (1987, 238). This captures the deep rhetorical experience of logos—the medium of transcendence that in the form of specific logoi actually leads somewhere.

This participatory movement through language is intensified and made more transparent in the extreme case of trying to think of being. Jaspers writes: "Wherever I grasp [*fasse*] Being [*das Sein*], it is relativized through a Being [*ein Sein*] that I do not grasp. . . . Where genuine Being is at issue, the maximum of vacillation [*Schweben*] is attained, since it is present [*gegenwärtig*] in the most evanescent manner" (1994, 3:162, in Gonzalez 2008, 381). Jaspers calls this the fundamental experience of determinate knowing. Gonzalez's gloss takes this in a dialectical direction: "This is because it is present only in the interpretation of ciphers: an endless interpretation in which what is signified by a cipher can never be isolated and where what one cipher indicates is continually qualified and put into question by what other ciphers indicate" (2008, 381–82). For Gonzalez, this establishes the case for dialectic, over against Heideggerian *Sigetik*.

However, for a deep rhetoric, this logos of moving from cipher to cipher is probably not best described as dialectical because it is not fundamentally logical or even epistemological (an attempt to capture the whole truth, the totality) but ethical and communicative. The ciphers communicate being to each other in that each is what it is—not empty but significant—not in itself but in its leading to others. This astonishing process of significance is logos—the participation of each cipher in each other by way of leading to one another. Each is what it is, and means what it does, not in itself (in itself it is empty) but only by way of all the others. If there is an ontology of deep rhetoric, this is it; things give and receive being to and from each other communicatively, in the process of their becoming intelligible in logos. This process of being and meaning, in its actuality and in the humanistic, deep rhetorical experience of things, is itself simply human stretching out on logos, human *epektasis* taking place in logoi.

The dialectical move from cipher to cipher is, from a strictly epistemological viewpoint, an attempt to get the whole, but, in terms of a deep rhetoric, this is an ethical effort, since the whole is not attainable, and since one must make a choice in the here and now about which "part" of it—that is, which leading from cipher to cipher—one will follow. This often requires reasoning, but not necessarily with simply logical or epistemological expectations or standards. For example, one must in the pursuit of knowledge make at least a choice about what is worth knowing now, at this time and in this place. And one is always making choices, projecting, in light of some good at which one is oneself aiming, as one takes over being a ground. In this case, it is perhaps the good of knowing something. This reasoning is not directly concerned with knowledge, but is instead practical reasoning, which forever goes on in conditions of uncertainty and requires commitments and all the considerations to which the rhetorical tradition urges us to pay attention, including character and imitation and attunements and emotions but not just those. Knowledge is only one of the purposes for which we lead lives and follow the meanings of things. Because we are constantly choosing among and combining purposes in different ways, reality and our understanding of it is always more primarily an ethical issue than it is an epistemological one. In its severe separation of ethics and epistemology, and in its subordination of ethics to knowledge, philosophy has disciplined itself into a blindness to what a deep rhetoric draws us toward: a truer acknowledgement of the complexity of transcendence and logos, of the communicative and ethical origins of knowledge, and of the fact that all transcendence is seeking a good that both is and is not found in beings.

If epistemologically oriented dialectic is not the best alternative to silence, it is still important not to give up on what gives life to any real dialectic—dialogue and communication, that is, rhetoric. Gonzalez's offering of dialectic as a cure for Heidegger's isolated monological silence is on the right track. Once again, he draws from Jaspers in a helpful way:

A charge frequently repeated in Jaspers' *Notizen* is that Heidegger's thinking is "*komunnikationslos*" (see 35–37, 51, 60, 90, 175). How serious a charge this was for Jaspers is shown by the following passage from *Philosophie*: "Essential truth, truth that concerns being arises only in the communication to which it is tied. . . . Therefore, true philosophy can come into existence only *in community*. A philosopher's inability to communicate (*Kommunikationslosigkeit*) becomes a criterion of the lack of truth in his thinking." (1994, 3:113–14, in Gonzalez 2008, 387)

Jaspers makes the case even more strongly in *Notizen*: "We cannot think without speaking. We become sure of transcendence necessarily in the forming and hearing of ciphers. But speech and ciphers are for us the only way of becoming certain of the inexpressible in communication. Only through language do we arrive where language becomes more a being-silent" (1989, 253; see also 209; in Gonzalez 2008, 386).

When it comes to exposing and correcting the oblivion of communication in Heidegger, what Jaspers calls his *Kommunikationslosigkeit*, one finds a convergence among Gadamer, Jaspers, Gonzalez, and the deep rhetorical critique. Where there is meaning, even where there is meaningful keeping silent, someone is saying something about something to someone, even if the *someones* are members of the internalized community in the conversations we hold with ourselves. A deep rhetoric follows this rhetorical event wherever it leads, tracks its many *someones*, *its sayings*, *its somethings*, its many ways of making things "about" each other. And it tracks the way we ourselves and the world and our sharing of it arise from this communication. We not only communicate about beings, but we give being to beings and to each other communicatively, in the deep rhetoric of communication.

Some of the aims, then, of a deep rhetoric will be to stay alert to the omnipresence of communication in logos and to participate more fully in what is happening in us in a way that learns from Heidegger's accounts of transcendence and freedom without getting diverted onto the false trails of an essentially solitary notion of existence, a valorization of silence and immediate experience, a neglect of the agency of others in our own fullest participation in what we are, and a default tilt toward unreason. The new rhetoric project's theory of argumentation, interpreted in light of the sounder understanding and fuller participation toward which a deep rhetoric stretches, is precisely an account of argumentation as a mode of authentic discourse and sociality. It not only repairs a gaping hole in Heidegger's project, but it also transforms that project in all its dimensions—especially the lonesome idea of *auth*enticity.

SEVEN

Reason and Justice: The Deep Rhetorical Dimensions of the New Rhetoric Project

This chapter will take up challenges left by the three preceding chapters. It will show that Perelman and Olbrechts-Tyteca's new rhetoric project is a philosophical enterprise that both develops themes and approaches found in Heidegger's philosophical work and also addresses the primary failure of that philosophical project: the absence of any genuine elaboration of the communicative dimensions of human existence and a consequent absence of any affirmative account of reason. It will also show that the new rhetoric project is a philosophical response to the problems of violence identified in chapter 4 in that it offers an account of the peace of rhetoric as the justice of argumentation. The outcome of chapter 4 was that violence would not be disarmed by an opposing absolute nonviolence but rather by the work of justice and peace—understood in a deep rhetorical way as means of experiencing and conducting conflict through argumentation. The theory of argumentation is a theory of the practice of peace and justice as dynamic activities of shared transcendence in logos.

This is by no means a new idea. Not only has rhetoric formed itself historically in an intimate relation with violence, but the rhetorical tradition has also connected rhetorical reasoning with justice in a way that is just as de-

finitive of that tradition. The tradition is often said to have arisen in the
legal reforms of ancient Sicily. Aristotle locates its institutional origins
in legislative and in juridical reasoning. In Roman times, rhetoric was
the core of training for the law. As we have seen, this close connection is
also reasserted strongly in the late twentieth century. Stephen Toulmin
claimed that logic was "generalized jurisprudence." Gadamer found a
key to understanding reasoning in the event of applying existing laws
and precedents to new situations. As we shall see, for Chaim Perelman
and Lucie Olbrechts-Tyteca, the relationship between reason and justice
is even more profound. Reason is not only grounded in justice, it is also
a process of justice, and has justice as its aim.

Deep Rhetoric and Justice

Deep rhetoric can help to explain the senses in which this is so. It is not
simply that rhetorical reasoning is especially useful and appropriate in
legislative and juridical contexts, or that the procedures of different rational enterprises are analogous to juridical procedures. It is rather that
human transcendence can itself take a just form and that reasoning is
reasonable by virtue of the justice of transcendence. Justice in argumentation is not only familiar social justice—it is justice that addresses transcendence itself. We seek justice not only in relation to our property and
our bodies and the compensable damages others do to us; we seek justice
also in relation to the human capabilities that shape our transcendence.
Our experience and understanding and interpretations of the world deserve to be treated justly. The truths we experience and live by and assert in our expressions and explanations and justifications also deserve
justice. We are a being-toward some good in light of which beings and
others show up in the way they do and as what they are. We seek a just
respect for what our own existence reveals and for that on which it is
staked. We seek a similar respect for the ways of being and for the goods
revealed by those groups to which we belong and with whom we share
our existence—our families and neighbors, our communities, those who
share our watersheds and air basins, our schools and parks and roads, our
food sources, our cities and states and nations and, increasingly, the earth
itself and the systems and laws that have a global range. Our way of moving toward a good that opens up a way of life may overlap and interact
with all of these in many congruent and many conflicting ways.

The conflicts we face concerning territories, borders, natural resources,
religions, languages, educational policies, currencies, trade, the prices of

goods, human rights, democratic political participation, climate change, contamination and pollution, the prevention and treatment of disease, access to health care, and so on are expressions of and concrete instances of conflicts in our transcendence toward the goods that open the world and give meaning to beings. This truth is lost in the managed world of entities that are comprehended only in their mere detached presence in terms of some monetary or sentimental or other kind of value that is assigned to them. What we are trying to acknowledge when we use the superficial notion of "value" is the meaning entities have in their belonging to a world of entities and in their leading toward good for the people who lead their lives in terms of them. Without these beings being in the way they are, without their having the meaning they do, individual lives and the communities in which they flourish could not be what they are.

If one takes the idea of transcendence seriously, then our lives and hopes and the meaning of our existence itself are, so to speak, manifest in the being of what is around us, but this means that that the concepts of subjective and objective, internal and external, or even body and world, can be misleading when it comes to thinking seriously about justice. Our being is not a "property" of our bodies or souls, but is transcendence, a being beyond ourselves, a capacity for transcending toward the transcendence of others, for co-transcendence, for stretching toward something out ahead of us, something we seek as a good. The beings around us show up in these illuminating projections. Their meaning comes to be in a way that is not detachable from the meaning of our own existence. The meaning of our lives is thus spread out around us, some of it ours alone, or shared with those close to us, and much of it shared with all those others with whom we live. But it is the being of the beings themselves in which we have invested ourselves as individuals and in common. Our bodies (or minds) do not somehow carry this "value" and meaning inside of them, although our bodies help to generate and form and sustain it, and they are adapted to it and capable in relation to it.[1]

The issues that are the usual concerns of talk about justice often fail to register this. The reason "things" have the possibility of being "valuable" at all is because their being is what it is in light of transcendence. If being is being-in-the-world, then justice must be essentially concerned with the ethical and political and material and linguistic *habitat* of transcendence, as well as with the capabilities that belong to transcendence itself. In ordinary, small-scale ethical and legal and political conflicts, this philosophical background may or may not make a significant difference. Conflicts among people with a common way of life who disagree about the amount due for a compensable damage are usually resolved in a way that is acceptable to the community without activating these larger philosophical concerns.

However, they are important in a theory of justice, and they do play an important role in many conflicts, especially those among peoples with different traditions. They certainly play a role wherever a people is moved off the land that has been its habitat. This is one reason why the forced migration of human beings almost always involves intense and often long-lasting suffering. In his account of the Western Apache culture of naming and storytelling in *Wisdom Sits in Places* (1996), Keith Basso clarifies why this is so. For the Western Apache, places in the landscape have names, and those names belong to and tell about a history of that place. Those names and that history also inform the stories from which the people learn to live as the people they are. Those stories are also used to give people guidance when they seem to have lost their way. To walk on the land and remember the names of the places is to be reminded of who you are and how to live. If you show that you have forgotten the story of a place, you will be corrected by actually having it retold to you in public. The ethics of the Western Apache are written in the land, and learned and remembered by means of the land.

Only when he came to understand this could Basso comprehend what Annie Peaches (seventy-seven years old when he interviewed her in 1978) meant when she said: "The land is always stalking people. The land makes people live right. The land looks after us. The land looks after people" (1996, 38). Or what Ronnie Lupe (forty-two in 1978), Chairman of the White Mountain Apache tribe, meant: "Our children are losing the land. It doesn't go to work on them any more. They don't know the stories about what happened at these places. That's why some get into trouble" (38). Or how Wilson Lavender (fifty-two in 1975) could say:

One time I went to L.A., training for mechanic. It was no good, sure no good. I start drinking, hang around bars all the time. I start getting into trouble with my wife, fight sometimes with her. It was bad. I forget about this country here around Cibecue. I forget all the names and stories. I don't hear them in my mind anymore. I forget how to live right, forget how to be strong. (Basso 1996, 38–39)

The being of these people transcended toward the good by way of the logoi-places on the land. These places held the meaning of their lives, the logoi that allowed one thing to lead to another, allowed particular actions to follow from particular situations.

A theory of justice or rationality that conceptualizes human beings as completely detached and autonomous entities whose most important features are somehow carried around inside of their heads or who are identified only with their bodies and who can arbitrarily be moved from place to place and function to function will fail to be a theory of *justice* or *reason*.

This is not to say that people cannot survive cultural devastation, the subject of Jonathan Lear's *Radical Hope* (2006). Lear gives an interpretation of the challenges faced by Plenty Coups, a chief of the Crow nation who lived through the period that saw the ending of the traditional Crow way of life. In Plenty Coups' time, that way of life was largely ordered around nomadic hunting and warfare and competition with other tribes. It ended definitively when the Crow moved to a reservation and ceased nomadic buffalo hunting. However, before his death, Plenty Coups spoke at length to Frank Lindemann and told stories of Crow life as it was. Yet, says Lindemann, he refused to talk about anything after the move to the reservation. Instead, he said:

> I have not told you half of what happened when I was young. . . . I can think back and tell you much more of war and horse-stealing. But when the buffalo went away, the hearts of my people fell to the ground, and they could not lift them up again. After this nothing happened. There was little singing anywhere. Besides . . . you know that part of my life as well as I do. You saw what happened to us when the buffalo went away. (Lear 2006, 2)

Lear urges us to take Plenty Coups as literally as possible: "After this nothing happened." This should not, says Lear, be interpreted psychologically as expressive of the chief's depressed state, but it might plausibly be interpreted as referring to the collapse of the world within which it was possible for things to happen at all. The practice of "counting coups," so definitive for a Crow warrior, was no longer possible. Hunting buffalo and all the associated virtues were no longer possible. Most of the things the Crow people did as Crow people were no longer available to do. As Lear points out, the social roles in light of which it was possible to excel and so develop acknowledged virtues and become a certain kind of person—say, a great chief or warrior or hunter or maker of teepees or clothing—these were gone, and so were the virtues, the standards of excellence, the concrete conceptions of something being done well or poorly. There was no good way of life and so no looking forward or working toward it. The temporal structure of transcendence, moving from an inherited world of significance and toward a future good, a way of being for Dasein, was stripped of all its logoi, all its definition. Lear describes the consequences of this and the profound challenges it presented for the Crow at every level and in every domain of life.

Cultures do not typically prepare their young people with the capabilities they will need to persevere through this kind of devastation. The virtues we teach are shaped to a specific cultural context. However, Lear interprets Plenty Coups' actions and words toward the end of his life as produced by a courage rooted in Crow religious tradition. Lear calls this courage "radical hope." It is not optimism or any calculation about likely outcomes. He reconstructs Plenty Coups' reasoning this way: The devastation is a fact. Our way of life and the goods toward which it leads are gone. We do not know what to hope or seek, but it must be more than survival as mere biological beings, mere bare life. There must still be a good to seek, and there must be a good that will come, because *Ah-badt-dadt-deah* (the one who made all things) is good. So, the good will come back, even if it is not the same as in the old way of life. In a dream, Plenty Coups is told to find guidance in the Chickadee, who listens and learns. So Lear finds Plenty Coups standing in the devastation and yet with a foot forward, drawing on the traditional icon of the chickadee and the traditional authority of a dream and the traditional notion of a creator to take courage and be prepared for something good to happen, something to which the Crow past still has a relation and for which it gives hope.

Discussions of justice and injustice are too frequently carried on in terms that make the experience of the Western Apache or the Crow incomprehensible. However, goods and injuries and virtues and equity and compensation and fairness have no meaning outside of human transcendence from within significant inherited worlds toward future ways of being that are informed by some sense of what is good. This may become most clear in examples of the sort I have given here, but the truth is not limited to these examples. The members of a twenty-first-century professional class may not depend on storied rivers and hills and rocks and canyons, or horses and rifles and hides, as the entities whose meaning makes up a path to the goods toward which they aim. However, they still stretch out toward their goods through professional organizations and conferences and processes of certification and licensing and professional recognition and all the other entities that make it possible for them to do their business. Those who move from place to place almost at will and for whom frequent travel is a necessity still need a world of airports and aircraft and other modern transport and communication and navigation systems through which they reach toward the good. If the conferences and meetings, the hotels and conference centers and airlines, the sponsoring institutions, the internet, were all suddenly gone, the way of life they were seeking would have to change radically.

Discussions of the nature of reason and reasoning are also too often carried on outside of a philosophical understanding of this context of transcendence—the being of human beings. To understand the new rhetoric project as part of the development of a deep rhetoric requires thinking of both justice and reason in this philosophical context. Reason itself is an attempt to resolve conflicts of transcendence justly. This occurs in the explicitly juridical and political contexts in which justice is thematized, but it happens just as much in the process of argumentation that *The New Rhetoric* describes.

The theory of justice and reason that a deep rhetoric offers will have to persevere with a full acknowledgment of two truths that too often have a tendency to diverge. One is the good of the free transcendence of individuals and peoples capable of something like the freedom Heidegger describes in his account of authenticity but who also seek to live out this freedom socially and concretely. The other is the fact that this freedom is only possible in a world that is given and not chosen, a world that is already shared with other individuals and peoples who are also seeking to live out their freedom socially and concretely. These two truths together lead to the acknowledgment of a third: conflict is not only inevitable but is the substance of theories of reason and justice. Our transcendence collides and interacts with that of others, just as it proceeds in a worldly way through entities and through logoi and through time. In fact, conflict is, for human beings, *intrinsic* to transcendence itself. This is what being-in-the-world means. Reason is the just articulation and conduct of this conflict, and argumentation is the process of reason. Interpreted in light of the concerns of a deep rhetoric, this is exactly what the new rhetoric project is about. It describes a mode of discourse, itself a form of transcendence, that makes possible a practice of potentially authentic sociality and speech that were impossible to conceive within the confines of Heidegger's project.

The notion of Heideggerian *auth*enticity is no longer fully functional once conflict is understood to be intrinsic to transcendence, but the development of a deep rhetorical conception of argumentation is continuous with Heideggerian concerns about authenticity, and to emphasize this continuity the word will not be altogether abandoned. Some of the continuing questions are: Can authentic *Mitsein* be shared? Can the solicitude that "clears the way" for someone else's freedom of transcendence take the form of dialogue in which the transparency of each participant is implicated? Can we clear the way for each other in some cooperative process of reasoning? This would be Dasein-with, transcendence-with of a special kind. The conditions for the *contact des esprits*, discussed once more below, begin to identify the form of this sharing of transcendence, which is based on a kind of equity or fairness. This is different from either the simple egoism or the simple deference to the good of the other found in *Being and Time*. Here the realization is that goods do come into conflict, and so here the deference is to justice.

And yet this advent of justice is in no way *ex nihilo*. It is continuous with the social peace and cooperation and ways of resolving conflict that have been inherited and shared among the members of a society. As we saw in the chapter on violence, societies are rhetorical, and they have, as societies, already achieved a rhetorical order that is guided by some conception of justice or another, to some degree or another. They have already found ways to mitigate violence through discourse and customs or codes or law of some kind, something to which they can appeal, if only to a sense of shame and to a sense of justice. Argumentation, as an ideal of discourse and of justice, is built on what is already held in common and on the experience of already having achieved some form of shared transcendence that is a workable, if always limited, resolution of freedom and historicity. The deep rhetorical conception of reason and argumentation as justice does not begin with atomic individuals in conflict with one another. It begins with social beings who share a world and some sense of what is good who must nevertheless resolve the conflicts that inevitably arise in their free transcendence toward what is good in changing and uncertain situations. In the course of this resolution, they are guided by a shared conception of justice that is equivalent to reasonable process, one that defines the realm of argumentation. Argumentation is thus a dynamic process of justice that is a practice of peace. Peace is the social experience of conflict in conditions of justice that succeeds in reconciling sociality with freedom.

Since different cultures have different histories, different cultures will have different traditions of justice and different kinds of peace, different ways of resolving the conflicts between history and freedom. Some cultures face conflict more openly, as it arises, and valorize social spaces that are hospitable to conflict. Others have more developed ways of anticipating and preventing conflict, resolving it, so to speak, before it occurs, by way of intricate and sophisticated social awareness and alertness, highly developed social codes, and socially complex language and practices and institutions. Such cultures may valorize social solidarity, or belonging to family, community, or a people more than they valorize social spaces that are hospitable to conflict. All cultures treat conflict both ways, and in fact having success along both lines is a condition for the possibility of argumentation. Whether a culture tilts one way or the other is a matter of degree. Without sufficient social solidarity, there is too little common understanding and trust for argumentation to take place. Without sufficient social space for undergoing conflicts openly, it is impossible to achieve the conditions of equity that allow for a just process of conflict, one that will be a practice of peace.

A deep rhetorical approach to comprehending reason as justice will also address another of the problems to which the resurgence of rhetoric has given rise: the problem of explaining standards for evaluating arguments. If the standards are not logical, then what are they? Psychological? Sociological? Cultural? Institutional? Ultimately groundless? This is the most fundamental question pressed against the new rhetoric, usually but not only by philosophers. This is the ground of the attack launched by van Eemeren and Grootendorst against Perelman (1995), that the "anthropologism" or sociological nature of the rhetorical standard for judging arguments reduces reason to a crude relativism. However, this charge neglects the profound understanding of the relation of reason and justice embedded in the new rhetoric. A deep rhetorical reconstruction of the new rhetoric project can illuminate the way in which justice is an essential measure of the strength of the arguments, and can bring to light, too, the ways in which justice interacts with other factors in the evaluation of arguments.

Reconstructing *The New Rhetoric*

The new rhetoric project was conceived out of the violence and devastation of war in Europe. European culture had failed to preserve and develop the capabilities necessary to conduct conflicts peacefully. As an assimilated Jew (the phrase does not capture the dynamic interaction between Perelman's Judaic and European heritages!), Perelman suffered both the devastation of the holocaust and the physical and cultural devastation of European society. The new rhetoric project was born out of this devastation. One will never understand the deep rhetorical dimensions of the project unless one reads the *Traité* in this light. It is a philosophical treatise with a profoundly concrete aim: establishing the possibility of a just peace, a possibility that might ground hope and the practical efforts that follow from it. It was written in a context in which this hope had been shattered. If we read it from relatively comfortable cocoons as a merely speculative effort to develop a theory of argumentation, then we fail to comprehend it altogether. For Perelman, philosophy is an attempt to actualize something in communication. It is a way of transcending with and toward one another in logos (discursively), a way of moving beyond our isolation and particularity and achieving a specific kind of receptiveness to each other, a receptiveness in which peace and justice are practiced. This practice of philosophy produces universalities of varying ranges and degrees, shared ways of being receptive to each other's discourse, each other's experience and hopes for a good life.

The aim of the treatise is: "The justification of the possibility of a human community in the sphere of action when this justification cannot be based on a reality or objective truth" (*NR* 514). This is a philosophical aim. To determine the conditions for the possibility of something sounds like a Kantian project. There is also a Kantian aura here around establishing what we may hope, whether we may hope for reasoned accord in the sphere of action—that is, whether we may hope for peace. The project also involves developing an identity between freedom and reason, another Kantian theme. There is in fact a consistent philosophical project going on throughout *The New Rhetoric* and Perelman's other writings. However, it is *not* a project of Kantian transcendental philosophy that is fundamentally epistemological in its orientation. Instead, it is transcendence itself that is at issue—and the conditions necessary for having community in our transcendence when we encounter conflict and when there is no acknowledged absolute to which we can appeal. The concern is not with a "subject" who experiences "objective" nature under conditions that make that experience possible. The concern is rather with what any such philosophical project presupposes: someone saying something about something to someone else in a situation in which the someones are attempting to reason together about something in conditions of uncertainty. The question is: what makes this "to reason together" possible? Once we take this question seriously, we can also see that the concern is not with a subject that is *simply* subjected to objective historical discursive powers. Instead, transcendence itself is at issue as both complement of and competitor with those historical powers. The quest, again, is for justice, understood in part as an acceptable balancing of the historical world on which we depend and the freedom with which we stretch toward a future good.

The Bounds of Argumentation

We are now ready to fill out the account we began in chapter 1 in the discussion of rhetorical capabilities, but with a specific focus on justice and transcendence. The first part of *The New Rhetoric* is called "The Framework of Argumentation," *Les cadres de l'argumentation* (11–62), which can also be translated, "the bounds of argumentation." Identifying the bounds helps to distinguish between what is argumentation and what is not, first by distinguishing between demonstration and argumentation. The exemplars of demonstration are mathematical and logical proofs. The formal systems of rules and symbols on which demonstrations depend allow for valid inferences and undeniable conclusions. This is logos in the most restricted sense, in which the principle of restriction has almost completely erased that for the sake of which the restriction was developed, the need for a reasonable way to understand the world, to make choices, and to navigate conflict. Argumentation, on the other hand, occurs in an open system, and the exemplar here is natural language, in which the definitions of terms are open to challenge and in which argumentative forms do not produce strictly valid arguments or undeniable conclusions. Rather, an audience has a choice when presented with competing arguments, and must make a judgment about the strength of the arguments that are offered.

As Perelman and Olbrechts-Tyteca explain it in "On Temporality as a Characteristic of Argumentation" (2010, 325ff.), demonstration goes on in empty time (*temps vide*), while argumentation goes on in full time (*temps plein*). Empty time is sealed off from history. For demonstration, time does not pass. The meanings of terms do not change. Demonstrations do not grow stronger and weaker in light of new knowledge or in relation to changing contexts because the symbols and rules on which they subsist are insulated from any exposure to such external change. In contrast, the full time in which argumentation occurs is historically dense, and arguments are fully exposed to inevitable and unforeseeable historical change. Most importantly, the historical context of an audience will strongly influence its receptivity to arguments. This is especially true because of the way the principle of justice influences receptivity. The principle holds that what was considered to be an appropriate rule or judgment or principle or argument in the past will be considered to be appropriate in similar situations in the future. This is due to what Perelman and Olbrechts-Tyteca call the force of inertia, and the prototype here is the legal notion of precedent. We all inherit a world in which necessarily, and for better and worse, a great number of precedents have already been established. Without this world of precedents and the force of inertia, we would not have our sense of reality. We could not reason from old knowledge to new knowledge. However, inertia is not the only force operative in *temps plein*. Time also generates new conditions, new situations, and these sometimes demand novel applications of precedents, imaginative reinterpretations of them and of the past situations to which they were applied, and sometimes they demand even the overturning of the precedents and a denial of their continuing applicability. Finally, it is possible, too, that even the past legitimacy of laws and precedents can be overthrown and that the principle of justice can work retrospectively. In any case, the full time of argumentation not only makes argumentation vulnerable to history but also makes history vulnerable to the retrospection of argumentation and its guiding principle of justice.

Michelle Bolduc and David Frank (2010) are surely right and very helpful when they expand on Perelman and Olbrechts-Tyteca's discussion of Bergson's notion of *durée* and Eugène Dupréel's concept of *intervalle* to explain the source of their conceptions of time. However, it is also a little uncanny how the concept of *temps vide* calls to mind Walter Benjamin's notion of a "homogeneous empty time" in his "On the Concept of History" (2001).[2] Benjamin's essay/fragments/notes were first published in French in 1947 in *Les Temps Modernes*, and so Perelman and Olbrechts-Tyteca are almost certain to have seen Benjamin's article. (They cite other articles from *Les Temps Modernes* of those years.) I would not stake a case on a direct influence or an intentional application here, but it is interesting to consider the possibility that Perelman and Olbrechts-Tyteca may have had Benjamin's ideas in the back of their minds. Benjamin's primary distinction in his "Theses" is between homogeneous empty time and the "instant" (*Augenblick*) or "now" (*Jetztzeit*, or the "stop" or "standing still" of time) that has the potential for releasing the past from the grinding machinery of empty time. The issue is that history is the history of the victorious, of the ruling class, and so it is a narrative of progress. This narrative runs roughshod over the silenced, the victims, the forgotten, the buried possibilities. An ideal correction might be, instead of narrative, simple exhaustive chronicle, in which everyone and everything was recognized, regardless of their place in the narratives of the historians. This would do a kind of justice to the past. Benjamin is concerned with the weak messianic power we have in relation to the past, the weak redemptive power to do what his famous angel of history would like to do but cannot: "to pause for a moment . . . to awaken the dead, and to piece together what has been smashed." The angel cannot *pause* because " a storm drives him *irresistibly* into the future. . . . That which we call progress is this storm" (Thesis IX; Benjamin 2001). This progress that makes us helpless before the suffering of the past takes place in homogeneous empty time. In fact, this kind of time buries the past in irretrievable oblivion, driving us further and further from it. We are blown away by its inexorable progress.

The only hope for doing justice to the past is a different kind of time, what Benjamin calls a Now, in which homogeneous, empty time is brought to a standstill. The Now is an interruption in the inexorability of empty, automatic time through which it is possible to have a different relation to the past. It is, for Benjamin, a revolutionary moment. It is also a historically unique moment, indescribable in terms of empty time, too full of possibilities for its narrative of progress. Thinking itself stops in this moment because the theoretical armature that drives historical progress stops turning. Suddenly, a past of lost possibilities springs into view. History is not simply "how it actually was" (*wie es denn eigentlich gewesen ist*), but also how it might have been. One's own time is brought into a living connection with the past. There is a glimpse of what it might mean to awaken some of the dead or piece together what has been smashed in a new practice of remembrance, one that does not idolize a future toward which history is inevitably working, but rather one that strips the future of that kind of magic. In this Now, one fights for an oppressed past and attempts to give justice to its forgotten and misremembered. This not only fundamentally alters the content of history but also fundamentally alters us in our very receptivity to history.

The parallels with the new rhetorical account of the temporality of argumentation are fairly clear, even given the important differences. Benjamin's empty time of inevitable causal connections between independent events that chain together to produce historical progress is analogous to the empty time of demonstration in which discretely meaningful propositions link together according to rules that drive them inexorably forward toward the inevitable and undeniable conclusions of a proof. Just as the empty time of the progress of narrative must be sealed off from what has no relevance to the story, so the formal language of a demonstration must be sealed off from the full time of speakers and audiences and languages that are susceptible to change and in which there is thus indeterminacy.

Benjamin's Now is analogous to the *intervalle* of Dupréel, on which Perelman and Olbrechts-Tyteca place so much importance when establishing the possibility of argumentation:

Even when we reason about causes and effects, motives and reasons, time intervenes; time is only full time [*temps plein*] when the modifications it introduces are both inevitable and contingent, or at least unforeseen, and cannot be described completely by means of an existing vocabulary and contemporary knowledge. Time is effective because it creates what Eugène Dupréel (1933) has called the interval [*intervalle*], an indeterminacy separating the terms that constitute an order. In this way, the order in which arguments are situated is the result of the orator's action, and this order understood as a construction, a system, or a necessary determination, gains its importance from the fact that it always includes an interval. (2010, 325–26)

Bolduc and Frank have a helpful gloss here:

The notion of *intervalle* is the indeterminate wedge between cause and effect, the space between items in a hierarchy. . . . Dupréel does not deny cause and effect reasoning, nor the need for order, but insists that causes and effects must be separated. . . . If there weren't an element of indeterminacy in causation or the construction of order, there would be no space for liberty, creativity, or evolution. Perelman and Olbrechts-Tyteca import the notion *intervalle* into the new rhetoric project to chart a course between demonstration and aporia in argument. In so doing, Perelman and Olbrechts-Tyteca . . . acknowledg[e] the existence of logical patterns and the necessity of order. However . . . they do not place patterns of logic and order beyond human time. . . . (2010, 314)

As in Benjamin, then, the *intervalle* opens up a transformed relation to the past, different from the non-relation of demonstration, and different, too, from the similar relation to the past expressed in the notion of the argumentative inertia that allows for the power of precedence that structures part of the rhetorical conception of justice. That principle guides us to judge the present and future in light of precedents set in the past. This is a matter of justice. However, the *intervalle* also opens up the possibility of a kind of retroactive agency—first, simply in the application of laws and precedents in new situations which changes their meaning and force, but further in the overturning of the precedent itself:

If inertia can transform the patterns of argument into models, this does not mean that these models, notably argumentative models, are immune to modification. The precedent in law provides an understanding of what we mean: it is a model, an example that one follows until a new fact challenges the precedent. But it is a model that can be changed. A reason that, in a particular society, or in a particular discipline, seemed strong will lose its power in new circumstances, in the same way that a precedent in law can be replaced by an unconventional decision that will, in turn, form a precedent. Time might offer new conditions, encouraging the modification of a court's opinion or means of discovery. (2010, 327)

This means that the *intervalle* not only stops the inexorable grinding of empty time and prevents its automatic rule over the present time, but it also undermines its authority over the past and opens up the possibility of doing new justice to the past, to its victims, to its forgotten. The *intervalle* corresponds very closely to the Benjaminian Now.

For Perelman and Olbrechts-Tyteca, however, this *intervalle* is not a flash of vision, but the event of argumentation. Rewriting history, if it is not to be simply another history of the conquerors, places a special burden on the ones who are the agents of the change:

> The burden of proof always belongs to him who wants to change something, which in law produces rules for advocacy. More generally, every change must be justified, whether a change of behavior or a change of assessment. Change must be justified, because if it is true that the change of time and circumstance can challenge precedent, bearing with it the unforeseen, it is necessary that this change be a recognized act, so that it can justify other changes. . . . (2010, 327)

Argumentation is an intermittent transformation of the authority and legitimacy of power, or, in Benjaminian terms, a Now that interrupts history's effortless and automatic "progress."

Argumentation draws on the past but also appeals to a change of conditions that reveals the more complete meaning of the past and its precedents. When the U.S. Supreme Court overturns historic precedents, one can see this process in action and on a large scale. In 1954, in *Brown v. Board of Education*, the Supreme Court overturned *Plessy v. Ferguson*, which had stood as a precedent legitimating racial segregation since 1896. This action was backed by a plethora of arguments at many stages of the process, but at its final written stage it was supported by new findings in psychology, the cumulative history of the reality of segregation, the specific case of Linda Brown (the third grader who was refused admission to her neighborhood school), and growing agreement that the science supporting racism was bogus. The decision and its arguments set a new course for the future of the U.S.—but also transformed its history. In appealing to the Fourteenth Amendment's Equal Protection Clause, the Court was saying that racial segregation had *always* been inconsistent with the Constitution, that history would now have to be viewed in a new light, that an entire people had been unlawfully wronged once more, and that there was a new history of struggle to be narrated that was a core part of the history of law and justice. Time for weak redemption, with its sorrows and its joys.

There is, however, one important difference between Benjamin's orientation toward time and that of Perelman and Olbrechts-Tyteca. Benjamin is wary of any orientation toward the future. Perhaps this is because the historicism that narrates progress imagines that it has a knowledge of the future that supports its injustice toward the past. However, it is worth asking whether Benjamin does not simply invert this injustice in his blistering attack on Social Democracy:

The struggling, oppressed class itself is the depository of historical knowledge. In Marx it appears as . . . the avenger that completes the task of liberation in the name of generations of the downtrodden. This conviction . . . has always been objectionable to Social Democrats . . . [who] thought fit to assign to the working class the role of the redeemer of future generations, in this way cutting the sinews of its greatest strength. This training made the working class forget both its hatred and its spirit of sacrifice, for both are nourished by the image of enslaved ancestors rather than that of liberated grandchildren. (Thesis XII; Benjamin 1969, 260)

Benjamin's writing, with its prophetic and messianic challenges, sometimes amplifies itself with these radical reversals to force us into new recognitions, but this particular reversal deserves some comment. There simply must be a justice that looks toward grandchildren as well as toward ancestors. This is truer than ever, given our current powers to condition their futures on a planetary scale. And it also seems just wrong to say that the strength of an oppressed class is nourished by a past and not a future. One need simply think of Martin Luther King Jr's "I Have a Dream" speech to remember how much courage and strength can be drawn from feeling and thought for one's grandchildren.

Perelman and Olbrechts-Tyteca's account of argumentation conceives temporality in a way that preserves this hope for justice in the future. This is not a known future of certain progress, but a precarious future toward which argumentation charts an uncertain, revisable, but reasoned path. Perelman and Olbrechts-Tyteca are concerned with arguments that will lead to new actions and dispositions to act in new ways. Argumentation is, for them, a potential break with the past, and a potential weak redemption of the past, but also a way of moving toward a future about which one is making a choice—not an arbitrary choice, but a choice guided from what has been drawn from an inherited world, interpreted anew in new conditions, in light of a future worth living in, and deliberated over in the best approximation of conditions of justice one can manage, which may well include a universal audience partly comprised of one's grandchildren.

———

This distinction between demonstration and argumentation and their different temporalities is only one way of marking the bounds or framework within which it becomes possible for argumentation to show up. There are other conditions that are necessary for argumentation to occur. Again, these have received preliminary attention in chapter 1, but here they will be examined in light of deep rhetorical concerns and more specifically in relation to the question of justice.

The first condition is that there must be a meeting of minds (*contact des esprits*; *NR* 14–17). In fact, as we have seen, all of argumentation is a continuous and specific kind of *contact des esprits*. In some ways, this contact already occurs in our very being. We are from the start an exposure to each other's presence in language and practices and institutions and in the meaningfulness of beings that are what they are only in terms of their place in a shared world. Levinas sometimes calls this a kind of trespass or persecution because it has happened even "before" we have become ourselves. We become ourselves in terms of the way others have already become themselves in the world we inherit. However, *le contact des esprits* goes beyond this. It is a first step toward what Heidegger might call an authentic sociality, a taking over of responsiveness to and responsibility for one another as well as ourselves. What Heidegger describes briefly and abstractly, and what Levinas radicalizes as a first, unrealizable, infinite ethical task, *The New Rhetoric* approaches more modestly and concretely by simply setting forth a few conditions for the possibility of argumentation.

So what is the deep rhetorical conception of *le contact des esprits*? *Esprit* is *The New Rhetoric*'s word for Dasein in its rhetorical transcendence, and *contact* is the word for our encountering one another *in our transcendence, as transcendence*. In this contact, lives meet one another in their capacity to lead and be led. We draw from our pasts and project our futures and share the presence of beings that arises from this moving contact, this openness to one another. As Heidegger would say, we have Dasein *with* one another in this contact. Unfortunately, Heidegger has very little to say about this kind of contact. Perelman and Olbrechts-Tyteca take it to be the first condition when it comes to describing what will be an alternative to violence and a practice of justice and peace. In fact, the account of "contact" offers the first sketch of the *justice* of reason. The requirements of this contact are similar to the requirements for a "meeting of minds" in contract law. Without such a meeting—an explicit mutual understanding in contract law—a contract is not valid. Perelman and Olbrechts-Tyteca are attempting to specify similar requirements for a *contact des esprits*. To the degree that such requirements are not met, argumentation and its results are vulnerable to criticism because the reasoning has not proceeded justly, fairly.

This meeting of people in their transcendence is made possible and sustained by sharing the logos that makes any transcendence possible. So the first requirement for a *contact des esprits* is that we must have a common language in which to meet one another, because otherwise there can be no way of being Dasein together that could be called "argumentation" or "reason" (*NR* 15). Language does not have the being of an ordinary entity; it has the being of Dasein, and *this is why we can meet the being of others in it*. We con-vene in language. However, having a common language is no simple matter. What counts as a common language? If we use a translator, do we share a common language and so have a contact of *esprits* in the required sense? If so, to what extent? If one person's fluency substantially exceeds that of another, is the language truly common to each? How much of it? If one person speaks a prestige dialect and the other a vulgar dialect, do they share a common language? What about the specialized vocabularies that people use in technical disputes? How much of this language must be shared? What about educational issues and the cultural allusiveness of language? If two people differ greatly in culture and education, do they employ a common language? Insofar as people do not share a common language, there is no *contact des esprits*, and there is thus a lack of argumentation and reasoning. There is instead an interruption by something else. If one considers the way language use divides along the familiar lines of race, class, gender, age, and ability—as well as the pressing issue of different language groups—then one can begin to understand the complexity of this first condition for argumentation. If one considers the ways in which learning another's language is a sign of respect that wins trust, then one can see the ethical power of this requirement.

This is not at all to suggest that we never have a truly common language. A language is always a "common language" to some degree. Wittgenstein has very convincing philosophical arguments against the idea of a private language. Stanley Cavell's famous essay "Must We Mean What We Say?" argues that people have a kind of natural rational need to mean what they say and so to acquire an education in the way their language has been and is being used by others and to get into some productive relation to those uses and to the language's tradition.

The point here is that this simple precondition for argumentation is a deeply complicated requirement for justice; any answer to the question of whether people have a common language in which to reason will always be a matter of degree. To the degree that we do not have a sufficiently shared language, we are not truly arguing with each other. This is essentially a concern for justice because if the argumentation is carried out in a language or dialect at a level of fluency and competency and cultural density and allusiveness and technical precision for which one party has more capability and the other party less, then the process could well be deficient in fairness, in the justice that grants each party equality in making manifest the beings with which the argumentation is concerned, the world from which they draw their meaning, and the good in light of which they are in the way that they are.

Argumentation is not concerned simply with the abstract meanings of propositions or their logical relations. It is concerned first with ensuring that there is mutual acknowledgment of the interlocutors in their freedom and in their dignity; it is concerned that there be "contact" between two beings who have transcendence as their way of being. The contact will be in the logoi that conduct people in their transcendence, logoi that lead in one direction or another by offering reasons (grounds). If all parties involved have the capability for this, then something called argumentation can come to pass. Insofar as contact is not achieved, it cannot. To that degree, something else will happen instead.

I am not at all suggesting that in argumentation the formal logoi are independent of what have been called the other "persuasives." The specific effect of the logoi in question will be influenced by the pathos, or emotions, in light of which the logoi are put forth. Against a background of fear, a specific argument may be experienced as weaker or stronger than it would against a background of confidence and trust and hope. And ethos, or character, will also play its role. A specific argument may also appear stronger or weaker depending on the character of the one making the argument, the claimant. So although it is the logoi in which contact is made and through which we conduct ourselves and one another, these logoi do their special work only through their interactions with the other energies of rhetoric in the process of transcendence. Arguments also appear strong in light of the good to which they lead, and that good must make a claim on our own attitudes and feelings.

Ethos and pathos themselves can also be the means of a direct leading of one person by another, or even of groups of people by unknown or overdetermined agents. Fear can spread immediately, without arguments, through different kinds of media and by different means.[3] Emotions can be contagiously viral. People can also inspire immediate imitation simply by their serving as a kind of model. This kind of imitation, without arguments, can guide action directly. Celebrities are often imitated directly. All of this can have a vast influence on the strength and effects of arguments and even on the power of argumentation itself. However, when the discourse in question is argumentation, the contact in question is usually the contact that occurs in logoi. And even in the direct action of pathos and ethos and other rhetorical forces, there is logos, a leading of one thing to another, and this can be questioned, and it can become the subject of arguments. In any case, *The New Rhetoric* limits itself only to what it calls the "discursive means" of persuasion, and this leaves aside a number of important matters concerning these other persuasives and their interactions with logos, as well as important questions about visual arguments.

Second, there must be a reason to argue, a goal that has a plausible chance of being achieved through argumentation (*NR* 15). This goal arises out of a situation of impasse or conflict in which the ways we transcend have become incompatible or impracticable.

However, the issues and conditions must be such that a third condition must be met: the parties must all be receptive to argumentation and to some degree willing to change their minds. This follows from the fact that to achieve contact one must listen and be listened to, one must give and receive attention. Without listening and without giving and receiving attention, there is no *contact des esprits*. And, as *The New Rhetoric* conceives it, simply "by listening to someone we display a willingness to eventually accept his point of view" (17). Listening is involved in all argumentation.

The very need to give a reason for making a claim is generated from the fact that the claim is questionable, that the someone who is being spoken to does not simply accept it but questions it. The speaker must be capable of listening to this question. By giving an answer to it, a reason that responds to it, the speaker implicitly acknowledges that the claim is indeed questionable in the way the question suggests and therefore needs support.[4] This very willingness to argue with one another means having sufficient respect for each other *as* people whose transcendence brings beings to presence in light of a way of life. This condition of respect and willingness to change because of the way another person leads in logos is a condition of justice—in this case, of symmetry. If one party is arguing with no willingness to change, then the required "contact" has not been achieved, the requisite just conditions are not in place. Perelman and Olbrechts-Tyteca use this example to illustrate that truth:

When Churchill prohibits the English diplomats from even listening to the peace proposals German emissaries might try to convey or when a political party makes known that it is willing to listen to proposals that might be presented to it for forming a ministry, these two attitudes are significant because they either prevent the establishment or accept the existence of preliminary conditions for the argumentation that could follow. (1958, 22, my translation)

Without listening, the symmetry required for argumentation is not available; however, with listening, and with the respect that listening embodies, one acknowledges that one might eventually be persuaded by the reasoning of the other party.

This may, at first, seem to be far too strong a requirement. However, like the other conditions for a *contact des esprits*, this one, too, will always be a matter of degree, and in practice will have to be judged by the participants in argumentation in some particular situation. The question is always whether there is good enough justice for the argumentation to proceed as argumentation. Yet it does seem important to acknowledge that this requirement will disqualify some speeches that many people would count as arguments. Imagine speakers who are absolutely unwilling to change their minds who nevertheless present claims and supporting reasons to someone and so appear to be engaging in argumentation. We might ask whether that apparent audience is truly listening or is just being forced or coerced into hearing the speech. If we followed *The New Rhetoric*, we would not, insofar as coercion was involved and not genuine listening, judge this to be genuine argumentation. We might also ask whether, if speakers were absolutely unwilling to change their minds, we would consider their speeches to be argumentation. We might instead consider a speech to be simply a concluding report on how the speaker had come to make a decision. It is not unusual sometimes to discover that though people appear to be inquiring or deliberating they may actually already have made up their minds. Or such a speech might be offered more as an epidictic performance, to strengthen commitment to shared goals or antipathy toward an enemy. It does little good to continue to inquire or deliberate in such a situation. The conditions for argumentation are not in place because the speakers are not willing to change their minds. *The New Rhetoric*, in its insistence on a *contact des esprits*, builds a framework in which minimal conditions of justice must be in place because argumentation's legitimacy depends not on its compelling logical form but on its conforming to the requirements of justice.

If a discourse does not meet the condition of argumentative justice, of a good enough equality of respect, that does not mean that the discourse is thereby devalued or is somehow *intrinsically* unjust. It is simply not argumentation as *The New Rhetoric* conceives it. There are forms of reasoning and dialogue that increase mutual understanding and lead to clarity about what is at issue and what is not, and about what is arguable and what is not, and these kinds of communication may be very important, even if they do not meet the conditions of justice required for argumentation. And argumentation is not always a good that should be achieved. *The New Rhetoric* acknowledges that it is by no means good to enter into argument with just anyone about just any issue (16–17).

A fourth condition of justice is that the parties must agree on the rules for the discourse—rules that govern how argumentation should begin, how it should be conducted, and the point at which it should end (15). This includes rules for how long arguments should be, how turns will be taken, and so on. Argumentation is orderly and not a matter of one party introducing advantageous rules either beforehand or during the process of argumentation, either implicitly by action or explicitly by stipulating rules. Insofar as these rules or procedures are not agreed on, the discourse may not be argumentation because it may not have met this condition of justice, of equity, of mutual full participation in consenting to the rules. So, the rules themselves structure the discourse in a fair and orderly manner, and the rules are legitimated justly, though the agreement of the different parties.

A fifth condition of justice is the renunciation of coercion and violence and a commitment to appealing to the other person's freedom: "Recourse to argumentation assumes the establishment of a community of minds [*esprits*], which, while it lasts, excludes the use of violence" (55). This includes threats of force, which constitute the famous *ad baculum* "fallacy" in informal logic, which is here not a "fallacy" but rather not argumentation at all. This condition prevents the more powerful from coercing the less powerful, and so aims toward equity and justice and peace in the process of argumentation. It aims at a focus on the logoi themselves. It also establishes, once again, concrete and practical and embodied respect for the freedom of the other person: "The use of argumentation implies that one has renounced resorting to force alone, that value is attached to gaining the adherence of one's interlocutor by means of reasoned persuasion, and that one is not regarding him as an object, but appealing to his free judgment" (55). The renunciation is not only a constraint, not simply a negative. It is instead a positive and respectful realization of the free transcendence of others and of ourselves. It is the justice of the dynamic and often challenging peace that is the alternative to violence.

This becomes even clearer in the following passage: "One can indeed try to obtain a particular result either by the use of violence or by speech aimed at securing the adherence of minds [*esprits*]. It is in terms of this alternative that the opposition between spiritual freedom and constraint is most clearly seen" (55). Argumentation and violence here have the same aim: to resolve a conflict or impasse. The way forward can be determined by force—unjustly and violently—or by argumentation—justly and peacefully. Argumentation is presented directly not as some abstractly rational or logical way of meeting a standard but as a fair and just and peaceful way to undergo a conflict. In fact, peace and justice *are* this conduct of conflict. Peace is dynamic, and it bears conflict and transcendence by means of this "contact" that is structured by a concern with justice—even though this contact can be challenging and distressing and transforming as well.

Argumentation is not only a flourishing of peaceful and just social life, it is also a deepening of that life: "'Every justification,' writes Dupreel, 'is essentially a moderating act, a step toward greater communion of heart and mind'" (*NR* 55)—and this can be true even if these acts and steps also require sacrifice and suffering, which they surely very often do. This peace is in no way the same as contentment. Written out of the experience of holocaustal violence and the collapse of justice and respect, *Traité de l'argumentation: La nouvelle rhétorique* offers a theory of argumentation as a practice of justice and peace that undergoes the truth of difference and otherness and conflict without offering any hope of final or ultimate resolutions. It offers instead a hope that we can undergo our conflicts with peaceful dynamics and in conditions of good enough justice and so achieve resolutions that will do justice for a time.

Another condition for stepping within the bounds of argumentation is the coming to presence of a speaker and an audience (*NR* 17–23). Argumentation occurs only in a discursive space opened up in, by, and between what *The New Rhetoric* calls a speaker and an audience, that is, in an event of discursive activity and receptivity. And here we come to an important issue—noted already by Allen Scult (1976) and John Arthos (2004). How are we to understand these notions of speaker and audience, these modes of human being, within this domain of argumentation? We no longer have the ontically prejudiced option of thinking of them as objects, as human beings as they are known by any of the scientific disciplines. They are not simply biological entities or a group of historically and culturally specific people. Nothing like that is available to us. Rather, speaker and audience do not exist as such outside argumentation. They take shape at the same time as argumentation, and they subsist, so to speak, on the event of argumentation. They are Dasein, esprits, transcendence, in a specific formation, but all we know at the start of the analysis is that they are possibilities of discursive transcendence and co-transcendence that can be just and peaceful.

When *The New Rhetoric* says that the transcendence must take the forms of speaker and audience for it to fall within the bounds of argumentation, then we learn that transcendence must develop and actualize the capability of both giving and receiving logoi. However, this does not lead to the conclusion that the "speaker" is one entity and the "audience" another, because the treatise devotes an entire chapter (40-45) to our capability for arguing with ourselves, being speaker and audience for ourselves, without which we could not reason thoughtfully about how to act or live. Instead, "speaker" and "audience" name ways of being for human beings who enter into argumentation, even with themselves. As we have already seen, the initial general conditions for getting into argumentation are not especially easy to achieve, and neither are the ways of being called "speaker" and "audience." It is critical to keep this in mind because the language of speaker and audience just naturally leads us into picturing this in ontically rigid ways as a standing person speaking aloud to seated people who are not speaking but listening. *The New Rhetoric* uses this picture often enough to support this natural drift; however, the treatise also explicitly contradicts this picture, and in fact provides most of what is needed to do away with its centrality altogether. Given a charitable reading in a deep rhetorical light, *The New Rhetoric* provides an account of argumentation that supports not only reasoning with oneself but also reasoning dialogically and between groups and in different media that produce different spaces and temporalities and forms of logoi, implicit and explicit. It would require further work to show this concretely, but one aim of the approach taken here is to give a philosophical account of a deep rhetoric of argumentation that will give the philosophical background needed to guide this other work. How are the preliminary conditions of justice articulated in the structure of online spaces? In social networks? When groups speak to individuals? When animals are involved? When one tries to imagine how one's great-grandchildren would speak and judge?

In addition, this outlining of the conditions for entering into argumentation is also a sketch of a critical rhetoric. The conditions for entering into argumentation are never achieved perfectly as measured against some independent standard. They are always realized to a degree, and though argumentation is achieved when participants reach agreement on the formation of a community of *esprits*, one can always—either as a participant or not—step back and focus on the degree to which the conditions are *not* achieved. The means of understanding how justice and peace are achieved are also the means of understanding the extent to which injustice and violence prevail. The discussion of rhetoric and violence in chapter 4 led to the conclusion that the goal of some absolute justice or absolute nonviolence is not a goal that can be concretely sought within history without producing a kind of terror. However, this does not mean that a critical rhetoric cannot in any particular case interpret the extent to which the conditions for argumentation are and are not realized against goals that are more far-reaching than the goals of the participants who have decided that, for this occasion, the conditions provide good enough justice.

The conditions for the formation of a speaker are also the conditions for ethos in a deep rhetorical sense. Ethos in a disciplinary sense is something like the persuasive force of a speaker's self-constructed persona within a discourse, a persona that immediately impresses an audience with its knowledge and good will. Ethos in the deep rhetorical sense is, however, a form of transcendence that makes it possible for there to be a "speaker" at all and so for argumentation of any kind to occur.

For there to be a speaker, not only must the basic conditions of "contact" be met, but someone must also draw someone's attention and activate someone's receptivity. Only then can that someone emerge as a speaker. This is no simple matter. Richard Lanham has devoted an entire book to *The Economics of Attention* (2006) in which he argues that the great scarcity of our time is a scarcity of attention and the great competition of our time is a competition for attention. Being listened to, especially if one is offering arguments, is not simply a given—especially when one is in a very competitive situation or when one is trying to win the attention of people who have exacting standards for giving their time and attention. This kind of ethos is often external to the speaker, in social institutions and practices. As *The New Rhetoric* puts it: "It is true that in a large number of fields—such as those of education, politics, science, the administration of justice—any society possesses institutions which facilitate and organize this contact of minds" (18). And yet this external ethos is not enough because it is also true that: "Under normal circumstances, some quality is necessary in order to speak and be listened to" (18). External ethos makes it easier for the way of being called "speaker" to come to pass; however, it also introduces all the hierarchies and asymmetries in communication that give privilege to expertise but that can also come into conflict with the demands for justice in the *contact des esprits*. This conflict is part of the field of study of a critical deep rhetoric. Aside from the institutional ways of receiving the attention of an audience, there are also the publicity and attention markets and all the attention-trapping that is bought and sold to those who wish to win the attention of others. In addition, there are all the other formal and informal qualities and qualifications for winning attention, many of them catalogued in the rhetorical tradition, and all worthy of attention, including critical attention.

What is essential for a deep rhetoric is that when it comes to *being* a speaker, one *is* a speaker as such because an audience has *given* this attention and the speaker has *received* it. That is, the being of the speaker is given by an audience. The speaker's being circulates, *is*, in this process of giving and receiving between audience and speaker. And this process is continuous in argumentation. It is not only a preliminary condition, but a sustaining condition, "equally necessary if the argumentation is to develop" (18–19).

For both a deep rhetoric and a critical rhetoric, an important issue is that our attention is *taken* as well as given—even beyond the way it is shaped by biological patterning. Powerful organized social forces compete for it and keep it in some channels and not others. Attention is to some degree organized by our social roles, but it often tends to drift and to be taken by whatever or whomever comes along. Beyond that, the endless chatter and noise in all the communicative media keep it dispersed and fragmented. In *The Economics of Attention*, Lanham provides very important accounts of the culture and crisis of attention in the age of an attention market.

Genuinely *giving* attention is always a matter of degree, and the dialectics involved in taking/being taken from and giving/receiving are complicated. There will be important differences between tracking the emergence of the speaker and audience in the psychological formation of self-deliberation and in the social formations of more public argumentation. *The New Rhetoric* insists only that an audience must give attention to a speaker and acknowledge the speaker as the speaker for argumentation to emerge.

Who is the audience that is the source of the being of a speaker? *The New Rhetoric* defines it this way: "*The ensemble of those whom the speaker seeks to influence by his argumentation*" (19). Thus, being an audience is a kind of being that is given by a speaker and received by an audience. If no one seeks to influence, no audience emerges. If no one is receptive to argumentation, no audience emerges. However, these modes of being can be activated in many different ways and need not be assigned to obvious "speakers" and "audiences." This dimension of the new rhetoric has not been worked out very thoroughly because the deep rhetorical dimensions of the project have never been fully recognized—specifically, the fact that speakers and audiences are ways of being that require achieving co-transcendence and come to presence and pass in very complicated interactions of agencies and receptivities that were never fully recognized in *The New Rhetoric* or in Perelman's and Olbrechts-Tyteca's other writings. Some of these issues have been further worked out in reception theory that follows Heidegger and Gadamer—for example, in the work of Wolfgang Iser and Hans-Robert Jauss and others, however not in relation to argumentation.

There are many issues. If I read an argumentative text by an ancient author, am I the audience and is the author the speaker? That author could not have sought to influence me. Are the contemporary translators, then, the speaker? They may well be trying to influence a contemporary public with the arguments. Or is it I who construct arguments from the text and then use them to influence myself as author and speaker both? Or is this kind of reading some convergence of the agency of these three in a new way of being speaker? If we believe that films make arguments, the issues become even more complex. Producers, directors, actors, and many others may all seek to influence the audience's reception of an argument. And studios and distributors and everyone who intends to make money from the film will force a convergence of market and audience considerations that will condition whatever "argumentation" might take place. Which audience is it, then, that a speaker wishes to influence and that gives the right kind of attention to a speaker? Or just think of how rapidly arguments spread and evolve as they traverse online spaces, generating new speakers and audiences as they travel. *The New Rhetoric* gives us here only one limit: the audience is not just anyone; it is limited to those someone wishes to influence by way of argumentation. Argumentation is addressed *by someone to someone*, and it is not argumentation outside of this context. If an argumentative text of some kind becomes detached from this context, it is no longer argumentation, and it can *be* argumentation again—it can cross back within the bounds of argumentation—only in the context of there being a speaker, someone making a claim, and an audience, someone receptive to it in one way or another. Argumentation is a specific form of human co-transcendence and becomes argumentation only in acts of transcendence, even if that transcendence is socially complex. And even if it is the complexity of a single person.

In section 4, titled "The Audience as Construction of the Speaker," *The New Rhetoric* says simply that the audience can be seen, in a limited way, as a "construction" of the speaker: "The audience, *as visualized by one undertaking to argue*, is always a more or less systematized construction" (19, emphasis added). This does not mean that the rhetorical audience *is* some kind of psychological construction of the speaker; it means rather that speakers always have specific and often methodical ways of conceiving of their audiences. This leads *The New Rhetoric* into an overview of the different kinds of knowledge at play in profiling an audience with the goal of understanding how to influence it. These are very important concerns of traditional disciplinary rhetoric. *The New Rhetoric* treats some of these concerns by distinguishing among different kinds of audiences with different profiles who must be addressed and appealed to in very different ways if one is to succeed in arguing.

However, this distinguishing among types of audience also has deep rhetorical dimensions because these different kinds of audience are also different ways of being receptive to reasoning. This means that they hold different standards of reasonableness and make different judgments about the strength of arguments. What counts with some audiences as a reason *for* may be with other audiences a reason *against*. This generates a profound challenge for the new rhetoric project because the essential claim of a rhetoric of reason is that the aim of argumentation is to call forth or intensify an audience's adherence to theses or claims—what Heidegger would call assertions and what we are thinking of as co-transcendence, a sharing of a way of being and a form of life. Argumentation develops in terms of the receptivity to which it is addressed. The quality of an argument is a function of the receptivity of the audience that would be convinced by it. Many people find this to be an unacceptable framework for understanding reason and argumentation. They believe that if the standards for evaluating arguments are not logical or formal, then they must be sociological or psychological or cultural, but in any case radically relative or ultimately groundless. They often believe that *The New Rhetoric* has conflated effectiveness with validity.

There are several responses to this charge. However, most importantly, it betrays an unnecessarily low view of receptivity, of the many possible ways of being receptive. Receptivity is a kind of rational agency that involves judgments that support different forms of life. This is why Perelman and Olbrechts-Tyteca emphasize that the project has a special interest in philosophical argumentation and its analogues in more everyday argumentation. They very deliberately aim for Plato's dream: "When Plato dreams, in his *Phaedrus*, of a rhetoric which would be worthy of a philosopher, what he recommends is a technique capable of convincing the gods themselves" (7).

This paragon audience is a projection of a way of being, a desirable and worthwhile way of being—in this case a divine one. To participate in the "divine" is to have a particular form of receptivity to arguments. To put this in light of the discussion of grounds, reasons, and transcendence from chapter 5: audiences are capable of transforming *into reasons* the beings and logoi that are shared with a speaker and that usually function as *causes*. Causes can be transformed into reasons, which means good reasons or bad reasons, because of the relation they have to a good, a state of well-being or a form of life that an audience seeks in its transcendence, a potential future that partly structures its current receptivity. An audience of the gods themselves would presumably aim toward a higher and better good than those at which mere mortals would aim. *The New Rhetoric* calls this a "universal audience," and this is right because, insofar as it is a paragon or "divine" audience, its sense of what is good is not the ordinary sense of good that belongs to people in their particularity as they seek their individual or group goods. Instead, this "universal" audience aims toward something that might plausibly be a good for human beings as such. When we are able, together, to agree on an audience, we are agreeing on a shared form of life that we believe will follow from that audience's receptivity and judgment. A "form of life" is thus generated and sustained and transformed by the ongoing receptivity of an audience—by, for example, its drawing from its world, the patterns of its deliberations, its adapting and applying and modifying and overturning precedents, its responses to argumentation in all its dimensions, and its making of choices.

As *The New Rhetoric* puts it: "Since rhetorical proof is never a completely necessary proof, the thinking man [*l'esprit*] who gives his adherence to the conclusions of an argumentation does so by an act that commits him and for which he is responsible" (62). If one cannot commit to a receptivity and what follows from it, then argumentation will not succeed. There is no independent, absolute resolution of argumentative conflict that will succeed in completely eliminating all the choices but one. Only a commitment of some kind decides the issue. However, the commitment is not arbitrary. It is based on reasons and it comes with a responsibility—a continuing responsibility to do justice, to continue to act consistently with this commitment in similar situations.

Perelman and Olbrechts-Tyteca imagine a kind of challenge that might be made to the way someone has decided an argument:

Whenever it is necessary to refute the accusation that our desires have determined our beliefs, it is essential that we furnish proof, not of our objectivity, which is not possible, but of our impartiality, and that we indicate the circumstances in which, in a similar situation, we acted contrary to what might appear to be our interest, specifying, if possible, the rule or criteria we are following, which would be valid for a wider group comprising all the interlocutors, and identifiable, at the limit, with the universal audience. (62)

The standard of rationality here is a principle of justice—that we decide cases in a fair and consistent way, a way that is recognized to be fair by our interlocutors and audiences as well as ourselves. This commitment to justice, to taking responsibility for our choices in an ongoing way, gives arguments their strength. Only the arguments for which we are prepared to make this commitment and take on this responsibility can attract our full adherence. This means that arguments are not evaluated once and for all, but that the commitments and responsibilities that undergird them are subject to review, just as in law, where existing laws and precedents hold force, but are not absolute. There are processes and procedures according to which they can be modified or overturned. In argumentation, these processes and procedures are not as specific as they are in law; instead, they develop out of our unfolding conception of justice—justice to the past, the present, and the future—as well as our unfolding sense of the good we are trying to achieve.

Argumentation and World

It is one thing for the minimal conditions of argumentation to be in place, to have crossed the bounds within which argumentation is possible; it is another to have a shared world of logoi on the basis of which one can actually begin to speak and argue. Part 2 of *The New Rhetoric* is titled "The Starting Point of Argument," and it describes the worlds in terms of which *esprits* exist, worlds that they carry with them into argumentation. These worlds are largely shared; otherwise argumentation would not be possible. We have already considered the idea of "world" in the discussion of Heidegger's notion of world in chapter 5. We have furthered that discussion in this chapter in the opening focus on how the concept of justice must be inflected with the idea of being-in-the-world if it is to describe the issues at stake in the experiences of the Crow and Apache peoples. Now, considered in terms of its entering into play in argumentation, a world and its order provide all those features of language and its use that fall within the bounds of argumentation, including potential premises and forms of appeal, though the treatise does not at all neglect other verbal persuasives.

The first chapter of part 2 is titled "L'accord," agreement, and runs through some of the constituents of a shared world: facts organized by theories and other systems of beliefs that are generally held in accord (67–70), values ordered in hierarchies that are held in accord only by particular groups (74–83), presumptions that are generally held in accord but not in all cases (70–74), and general forms of argument acknowledged to carry varying degrees of weight in different times and places and circumstances (83–110). This overall accord varies relative to special audiences and occasions. It is significant here that this general agreement is ordered into what, following Heidegger, I am calling a world, a network of interrelated accords in light of which individual entities and facts have their significance. Simple invention from isolated facts or values is misconceived. Certain facts are held in accord because of their relation to other facts in a "theory," or a "truth" in *The New Rhetoric*'s terms, although these "truths" may sometimes be micro-theories compared to what we usually think of as theories. Facts held in accord in one theoretical context may not be held in the same accord in a different context. For example, something may count as a fact in a psychotherapeutical setting that would not count as a fact in a courtroom. Similarly, a value may be held in accord, but it will not carry the same force in all argumentative situations because different hierarchies of value may be at play. A person may have a strong adherence to truth-telling, and it may overrule most other considerations, but it might also fail on an occasion when saving a life seems to require a lie. Invention on the basis of such accords is complex, but this is because, as we have seen, a world is by its nature complex.

The complexity of the accords that make up a world, and that offer the starting point for argumentation, has practical importance. Acknowledging such complexity is in fact mission critical for constructing artificial intelligences. One cannot simply load isolated fact and value propositions into a database and expect a machine to apply argumentative schemes and then come up with anthropomorphic results. As human beings, the facts and values to which we adhere are what they are only in relation to the wholes to which they belong—the theories and systems of significance and belief and the organized forms of life that give coherence to our experience and action. These forms of coherence do not always cohere well with each other, and this creates interesting effects in the ways we try to reason with ourselves and each other. Modeling this is not an easy task. The project of engineering artificial intelligences that are anthropomorphic enough to be helpful to human beings has evolved into work on multi-agent systems, in which machines that are programmed differently are taught to "argue" with one another. This is at once a dramatic and unsurprising outcome because in manifesting our ability to reason by constructing a mimesis in machine form, and so creating a mirror in which to understand ourselves, we are simply rediscovering what we have long known. Inward reasoning has the form of outward social dialogue. Recall Isocrates: "The same arguments which we use in persuading others when we speak in public, we employ also when we deliberate in our own thoughts; and, while we call eloquent those who are able to speak before a crowd, we regard as sage those who most skillfully debate their problems in their own minds" (*Antidosis* 15.257). And, as Vygotsky (1962) insisted millennia later, we learn to think by internalizing the multiple voices we have witnessed in conversation with each other (51). We reason from out of and in terms of ordered worlds—in which we have achieved whatever coherence or integrity we have.

Out of a world, when rhetorical exigencies press, invention happens. Something is given for argumentation. However, once again, this invention is not simply an isolated, deliberate act. Situations invent arguments. Worlds are not inert systems. They are active and historical. They exist in time, and they change. They are not isolated from the situations through which they act and change. Invention happens when worlds move into new situations, and much of what rhetorical invention is about is watching what is happening in the particular situation—which constituents of the world are coming into question and being put to action at this time and in this place. Invention happens without any practice or teaching or theory of invention. It happens "by nature," as people used to say. And part of invention therefore requires being attuned to what is already happening, the forces already at play that are producing arguments.

Becoming aware of what invention is already happening, and guiding and participating in it, requires additional capabilities, and these can be added to the list we discovered earlier, in chapter 1. First, one must be acquainted with the world in play and with its constituents. As the tradition would put it, one must have a capability for "common sense." This requires a coherent and fairly comprehensive formation through a broad education. Second, one must have a sense for what is happening in the particular situation. It is one thing to know that there are hierarchies of values; it is another to have the capability to sense or recognize a hierarchy as it actually comes into play in a situation. Third, one must have good judgment, first to organize everything one is sensing in a situation into a form that will guide discursive action, and then practical judgment to decide which among the available discursive actions is the most appropriate one. These are capabilities that are acquired in a broad education that involves both knowledge of the world and repeated practical experience with arguments that arise in real situations.

Argument: Understanding, Interpretation, and Presentation

There are yet more capabilities required at the starting point of argumentation, and they are covered in chapter 2 of part 2 of *The New Rhetoric*. Out of a world, the arguer retrieves and adapts what is to function as "given" in a particular situation. Much is potentially given in a world, but relatively little is actually received into argumentation, and what reception there is requires rhetorical invention, deliberate or not. In *The New Rhetoric*, this involves capabilities for selecting, bringing to presence, interpreting, qualifying, and categorizing (115–21). Acting through these capabilities generates the specific starting points for a process of argumentation. *The New Rhetoric* says a great deal about these actions. For categorizing alone, there are many ways we can stretch and contract categories, and many ways we can clarify and obscure by means of them. These actions are taken in order to adapt what is given to the particular challenges of the argumentative situation. These actions take shape only in relation to the coherent world which gives the given, the audience which will receive the given as given, and the situation as a whole. These different agencies are active in argumentation, and each comes to presence as what it is only in the circulation of agency in the process of argumentation.

Chapter 3 of part 2 of *The New Rhetoric* treats the actual presentation of what has been selected, interpreted, qualified, and categorized. All actual coming to presence in argumentation happens in some form. It takes some amount of time and some number and order of words. What is held in accord must be arranged; some agreements come first, some later. Some are elaborated and repeated and amplified; some are merely mentioned. The language in which they are expressed must have a certain style, a particular register, and the specific words must be appropriate for the purpose. Any presentation will make use of the available grammatical possibilities in one way or another. All of these choices have argumentative functions. They serve to increase and decrease presence, to direct and intensify and reduce attention, and in general to amplify and diminish the impact of what is already to some degree acknowledged. Figures of speech can in themselves produce a change of perspective, and, together with a prudent choice of dialect and commonplaces, can, say Perelman and Olbrechts-Tyteca, create a sense of communion or solidarity between a speaker and an audience. By providing this control, form and style make possible what an audience will judge to be either a judicious and fair-minded manner of presentation or a prejudiced and unjust one.

In short, style has an argumentative function and is a vast field of invention.[5] Arguments succeed or fail in this respect not only because they do or do not give aesthetic satisfaction, but more importantly because they do or do not call attention to the right thing in the right way. Form allows things to come forth out of the implicit and undifferentiated background world, to stand out as themselves, and to have their impact in an argument. In this respect, form accomplishes some of what Heidegger describes as the prevailing of beings. Any account of argumentation that neglects this fact, or that draws a strict distinction between style and argumentation, will fail to be true to the reality. Once again, we are encountering implicit capabilities here. Mastering form and style is difficult enough on its own, and requires complex skills. Becoming proficient in its argumentative function adds another layer of difficulty. Then, being able to recognize what is most formally appropriate for some particular situation requires rhetorical sense and judgment that is not simply congenital. A capability for appropriate form and a style that directs attention and increases the presence of the right things at the right time and in the right way are necessary for producing and considering the best available arguments.

Audiences make judgments about these matters, and they are judgments about justice, about whether the presentation of what is held in accord is a fair one, whether justice has been done to the facts. A paragon audience may forgive a speaker for infelicities, but it will not tolerate an unfair presentation of the facts of the case and the goods toward which the speaker and audience together are supposed to be moving.

The Argumentative Logoi: Topoi

Part 3 of *The New Rhetoric* considers argumentative forms themselves— the *techniques* of argumentation that allow for one idea to follow reasonably from another. They are not necessarily truth-preserving, like the rules of the formal proofs of logical systems, but they are supposed to preserve or even increase adherence as an argument moves from the starting points to the claim. In *The New Rhetoric*'s terminology, they are something like presumptions that are generally effective, but not universally so, and whose effectiveness is variable from situation to situation. Every argument requires speaker and audience, operating within the bounds that define argumentation, drawing on a shared world, shaping starting points into discourse, and then moving toward a claim in a way that has an identifiable form associated with an argumentative technique. In the conclusion of *The New Rhetoric*, after explaining the philosophical purpose of the treatise, in the very last sentence, Perelman and Olbrechts-Tyteca write, about the new theory of argumentation they have elaborated: "And its starting point . . . is an analysis of those forms [*formes*] of reasoning which, though they are indispensable in practice, have from the time of Descartes been neglected by logicians and theoreticians of knowledge" (514). End of treatise.

Before the end, the authors analyze over fifty different argumentative forms, frequently with a counter-form that leads reasoning in an opposite direction. The forms include arguments regarding incompatibility, definition, identity, analyticity, reciprocity, transitivity, comparison, probabilities, causality, parts and wholes, ends and means, interactions between persons and acts, groups and members, symbolic relations, analogies, metaphors—and that is just a partial sampling that also ignores the subforms under these rubrics. Perelman and Olbrechts-Tyteca have certainly realized the virtue of copiousness. And this is in the reduced version of a manuscript that was originally several times its published size.

It would be impossible here to explore this extensive and endlessly interesting rhetorical topography. I would like instead to offer three lines of approach to understanding the more general importance of *The New Rhetoric*'s accomplishment. First, Perelman and Olbrechts-Tyteca are presenting a rhetorical logic, an interpretation of the persuasive force of rhetorical logos. This is not logos in the restricted sense of the logic that Heidegger analyzed. Neither is it logos in the largest sense in which any instance of one thing's leading to another might be understood as logos, or in which the very possibility of significance is constituted by logos. Rather, this is rhetorical logos restricted to acts of argumentation that have a claim to being, at least potentially, reasonable. The forms of argumentation allow one thing to follow from another according to a pattern. From a certain starting point—that is, given certain facts and theories and values and hierarchies of value and presumptions—one can, following a form, lead an audience to "adhere" to certain logoi. As *The New Rhetoric* puts it, "Our treatise will be concerned only with *discursive means* of obtaining the adherence of minds [*l'adhésion des esprits*]. . . . Only the technique that uses language to persuade and to convince will be examined" (8).

This conception of logos bears a close resemblance to the conception of logos in Plato's *Phaedrus*, the logos with which rhetoric is concerned. There the special power of logos is said to be "leading the soul" (*psychagōgia*). One leads the soul by way of logoi, speeches, language. In *The New Rhetoric*, one leads *esprits* from adherence to some logoi to adherence to others. The work of rhetorical logos is leading the soul, leading *esprits* to adherence, to keeping faith with certain logoi. The "means" of doing this is to use the forms or techniques that allow certain logoi to follow from others. However, the power of these forms to succeed in this leading varies depending on the situation and the audience and a whole host of factors. Rhetorical logos is not simply getting the formal relations among the logoi right. The forms are necessary but in no way sufficient.

In *The New Rhetoric*, argumentation always involves choice and commitment and considerations of justice.

It is critical here to understand the priorities at play. Language, insofar as it is logos, does not have its meaning or even its being in some autogenic way. It subsists, so to speak, in transcendence, in our *ekstasis*. Its power to signify is rooted in our own "referring" ourselves toward beings, to the world, toward others and ourselves. Language as logos is an explicitly articulated form of our transcendence. Language is meaningful, ultimately, only in light of transcendence. Since transcendence is always in a world, and moves in terms of its world, it moves in terms of one worldly thing leading to another. There are certainly ways of studying language that can more or less objectify language, and consider language in its mere uselessness—as Heidegger puts it, its mere presence at hand; however, the linguistic practice of linguistics, the study and teaching and communicating of an abstract knowledge of language, will necessarily continue to depend on this power of language to "lead the soul," to give form and direction to transcendence. It is not a system of language that has priority; Derrida's "writing" does not precede all speech. Neither is it speech itself that has a prior and more fundamental presence. And it is certainly not the entities that prevail that somehow cause themselves to prevail. Rather, the source and condition of all of these is that with which rhetoric is ultimately concerned, the *dynamis* of logos, the power to lead the soul, a power at play in the very transcendence that makes human existence what it is. This is a power that empowers all the lesser worldly powers that make up our being-in-the-world and that lead our souls in specific ways. Of course, the "power" that empowers is a very different kind of power from the power that is empowered.

A disciplinary rhetoric analyzes the empowered powers, all the worldly alloys of logos that have the power to persuade. It strives to name and systematize them, to develop theories of them, to teach people how to get some of their own power over them—yet another kind of "power," one that, as Plato pointed out, often means a kind of slavery, too. Disciplinary rhetoric also seeks to develop a critical awareness of them in light of competition among powers, and so to engage in the actual rhetorical critique of (some of) these powers. This is obviously immensely important work. However, a deep rhetoric does something different. It steps back to take a larger perspective by pressing questions. It asks about the power of logos itself, whether it can be conceived the way other things are conceived. It asks about what our "relation" to it is. It asks about the "process" by which it is "translated" into actual power. What "power" accomplishes this? Is it possible to "have a say" in this process? To take responsibility for it? Is our conception of what it is to be human inextricably bound up with these issues? Is the warring interdependence of philosophy and rhetoric just as inextricably tangled up in these questions? Is the globalization or expansion of the discipline of rhetoric an effect of uncovering some of the same questions that a deep rhetoric tries to uncover? Can a deeper rhetoric, one that is burdened with these questions, better explain how fundamental the power of violence is in rhetoric and yet how rhetoric can still be understood as a practice of peace and justice? Is there then something like a wisdom in rhetoric?

Second, *The New Rhetoric*'s account of "techniques of argumentation" is not just a profound reinterpretation of rhetorical logos, it is also both an example of and an argument for the rhetorical virtue of copiousness. Since no single argument yields compelling truth (because choice and commitment always play a role), there is a need to develop as many arguments as possible from as many perspectives as possible in order to measure their relative strength, in order to examine all the possible choices and commitments involved, and to consider where they may lead. This requires the old rhetorical capability of copious invention, a capability for imagining and developing the different arguments that shape the different perspectives on an issue. And so a deep rhetoric gives a new and specific importance to another part of the discipline of rhetoric, one of the traditional "offices" of rhetoric: invention.

In some ways, this kind of an argument for the importance of invention is not new. Vico ([1709] 1990) long ago exposed the inertia and narrowness in the modern critical enterprise and its search for certainty. "In our days . . . philosophical criticism alone is honored. The art of 'topics' . . . is utterly disregarded. . . . This is harmful, since the invention of arguments is by nature prior to the judgment of their validity . . . so in teaching, invention should be given priority over philosophical criticism" (14). Vico's premise is unassailable: the invention of arguments is by nature prior to the judgment of their validity. The critical evaluation of arguments depends on there being arguments available to criticize in the first place. Without someone's having invented some arguments, there would be no arguments to criticize. However, Vico notices what is most significant about this obvious logical necessity. Criticism is not only made possible by invention, it is also limited by invention. Criticism can make judgments only about arguments that have been invented by other means. Criticism might judge an argument to be better or worse, but it does not know if there are still other arguments to be discovered, and it does not know how to discover them. Criticism is limited by the work that has been accomplished through invention. The quality of criticism's results will be a function of the quality of the arguments with which invention has provided it. Rational criticism and analysis can never exceed the excessive gifts of copious invention.

Therefore, says Vico, invention should be given priority over criticism in teaching. And here he means not only priority in the sense of its being cultivated before criticism is taught, but also priority of importance in the rational enterprise itself and in the amount of attention directed toward it in education. From its logical priority to criticism, he derives priorities of invention in the process of formation and in its status in relation to the different aspects of reasoning itself. In this context, invention requires copiousness for its significance to become clear. If invention invents prior to criticism, then it invents in some respects independently of criticism, outside of the limits it would impose. And if the value of critical results is dependent on the comprehensiveness of the set of arguments placed before it, then this is exactly what is required: as many arguments from as many sides as possible. Thus we have also activated that other idea of its being a virtue to be able to argue from each side. The more arguments we have, from the more perspectives, the better chance criticism has of producing valuable results. Of course, this is part of what the *topoi* were for, copious invention.

In the new rhetorical context, and in light of the concerns of a deep rhetoric, the case is even stronger. The goal of modern criticism, to strip arguments down to their epistemological bedrock and assent only to those that yield unassailably certain results, is no longer at play. It is no longer a question of compelling truth. One will discover no argument that yields a certain answer because argumentation does not compel but offers grounds for making choices. The more arguments we develop on the different sides of an issue, the clearer we become about how many perspectives and choices there are, about what guidance is available for making our choices, and about what commitments may be involved. This kind of transparency, this "seeing" of the relevant facts and concerns and the possible arguments, transforms the rhetorical situation. This transparency undermines the conditions in which one might be restricted to a narrow band of arguments or might face a forced choice between limited alternatives. Rather than narrowing the field of reasoning, it opens it up and expands it. Part of the power of the "truth" of argumentation, or its "validity," or whatever ground determines the trustworthiness of an argument, is transferred from the form and conclusion of the argumentation to the comprehensiveness of the process of invention. If one does not consider all the relevant arguments, one may well fail to find the strongest one. Invention is prior to judging the strength of arguments not only in time but also in importance because judgment will always be limited by the choices between which it judges. However, the strength of an argument has other sources, for justice plays an even greater role in judging the strength of arguments than we have seen yet.

Assertion and Argumentation

Just before we move on to that final consideration, I would like to present the third line of approach to understanding the importance of *The New Rhetoric*'s conception of rhetorical logos and its relation to considerations of justice. This regards the nature of assertions, of what *The New Rhetoric* calls "theses" when it speaks of argumentation's presenting theses and of audiences' "adhering" to them. Most of what needs to be said here was developed in the section on assertion in chapter 5; however, it has not been brought into connection with justice. Doing so will distinguish a deep rhetoric from the projects of both Heidegger and Levinas, even though it will at the same time show how it draws from them. The usual understanding of an assertion is that it is a judgment or proposition in which one thing is predicated of another and that this predication reflects a true or false state of the relation between entities and properties. However, according to Heidegger, assertions are misunderstood if one believes that it is possible to assemble them, by themselves, into anything like an understanding of the world. Assertions succeed in picking out entities, but only on the basis of an implicitly understood world in which they are already meaningfully related to other entities. Predication can be successful, but only when it is understood as a selection from many possible predicates that has been made on the basis of a good toward which one is aiming, a purpose. Further, assertions are asserted to someone; they are a communication that requires a being-with one another in relation to what is being asserted. So far, so good, but, as we have seen, Heidegger's more comprehensive account is still severely limited.

Although Heidegger acknowledges that assertion is communication, he isolates assertion from the larger processes of questioning, claiming, and giving reasons within which assertions play a role in rhetorical logos.[6] Most importantly, though, he fails to register that in assertions we do not simply "share" the way we encounter entities but that we also make claims on others. We implicitly assert that our encounter with entities is also capable of leading others in their encounter. Our assertions are claims on the transcendence of others, and so transcendence is a site of conflict. A deep rhetorical reading of *The New Rhetoric*'s account of argumentation departs from Heidegger by focusing on this conflict and the way argumentation addresses it and so articulates a social ontology that Heidegger never explores. It follows Levinas in orienting itself with the recognition that in this conflict of transcendence ethics is prior to ontology; however, it departs from Levinas in going beyond the infinite deferral to the other to seek a more particular good: justice in particular cases of conflict. Argumentation is the practice of giving justice to each other's transcendence in situations where a conflict of transcendence presents incompatible judgments or courses of action between which a choice must be made.

Assertions, then, are the explicit speaking out of particular instances of transcendence in which entities and their properties, relations, and meanings take shape in particular ways, as a result of the differences in individual experience, the different ways of drawing from an inherited tradition, the differences among traditions, and the different goods being sought. One can of course isolate assertions from this context to consider their grammar or their narrowly logical relations to one another, but that is not the way a deep rhetoric or *The New Rhetoric* treats assertions. The concern is rather to find a way to do justice to assertions, while fully recognizing that they are rooted in forms of life and in human transcendence. When they come into conflict with one another, there is more at stake than simply the formal relations between propositions. Since assertions are logoi which structure and give direction to transcendence, and thus to human life, when one chooses between assertions, one is choosing, at least to some degree, to give a certain structure and direction to transcendence, to one's life. This is no longer a matter of the logic that works itself out in empty time; it is a matter of rhetorical logos that involves a speaker and an audience drawing from the past in light of a future, attempting to do justice to the past and present, justice to all interlocutors by staying within the bounds of argumentation and making a commitment to which they will be expected to do justice in the future.

In argumentation, assertions do not simply stand; they are questionable and so in need of support. Assertions usually become questionable because they come into conflict with other assertions—that is, the assertions of others.[7] The other makes us questionable, and generates the questions to which still other assertions, reasons, are the answer. These assertions—claims and reasons—require connection to each other by way of a "technique" of argumentation, a "form" of reasoning that allows one assertion to lead to another. They require rhetorical logos.

However, this logos is never decisive on its own. The argument also requires judgment by an audience. The conflict of assertions that articulates the form of a conflict of transcendence, or a conflict of human lives, requires just adjudication and not simply logical analysis, formal or informal. The concern is justice, to do justice to each other's experience and each other's attempts to lead a life. This is why the bounds of argument are so important. They establish the conditions of respect and equity that allow for a just interaction of two people who have come into conflict but are nevertheless willing to endure an openness to each other in argumentation that may lead to an end neither party had anticipated. Passing through this conflict in a just and peaceful way requires logos but also requires more than logos. It requires a choice concerning the future, and choices require attitude, pathos, emotion, feeling, being moved. The choice is between which logoi will have more power in giving form to our transcendence, our future lives. So the question is also how to do justice to and for the future, which means in part the future course of the resolution of conflicts. Any judgment of an audience has at least a small presumptive power of precedence, especially for those who made the choice. Adherence, *The New Rhetoric*'s term for the aim of argumentation, is more than intellectual assent. It involves commitment, and this requires heart. It is a shared commitment to a shared form of life that has been decided on in conditions of justice, one that makes peace possible and one that is itself a dynamic and often difficult practice of peace.

This reconstruction of *The New Rhetoric* in light of a deep rhetorical perspective highlights how profoundly a conception of justice informs the treatise as a whole. In what follows, I will try to show that comprehending justice and its relation to reason is at the heart of the entire new rhetoric project—and not just the treatise—from Perelman's early work in justice in the 1940s until well after the publication of *The New Rhetoric* itself. The entire project addresses the concerns raised about rhetoric in chapter 4, and provides a way of understanding sociality that corrects and complements the more partial work of Heidegger and Levinas.

Reason as Justice: The Justification of Rhetoric

It is fairly well known how Chaim Perelman's theory of justice was changed by his study of actual reasoning. Perelman began his career as a formalist in matters of justice. He believed one could be rational about formal justice, but that disagreements about the application of formal rules to concrete cases could be settled only arbitrarily. Perelman's study of argumentation convinced him that we could indeed reason about questions of concrete values. His "new rhetoric" provided a way to what was for him a much more satisfactory and complete theory of justice.

Perelman often told the story of his recovery from positivist skepticism, and the story has often been retold. I want to begin with the story as Perelman tells it in "The Use and Abuse of Confused Notions" (1980):

It was in 1944 that I undertook my first study of a confused notion, the idea of justice. . . . In my positivistic analysis of the notion of justice, I identified a structure . . . which I designated *formal justice*, according to which it is necessary to treat situations which are essentially the same in the same way. . . . But this principle cannot be applied, in concrete cases, without the intervention of value judgments: in effect, it is necessary, in each case, to answer the question, "are the two situations being compared essentially similar or not?" In order to answer, it is necessary to determine the similarities and differences, thus bringing to bear judgments of value and importance. (1980, 99–100)

However, says Perelman, these judgments cannot be supported by reason. When he published the outcome of his study in 1945 as *De la justice*, he concluded: "As for the value that is the foundation of the normative system, we cannot subject it to any rational criterion: It is utterly arbitrary and logically indeterminate" (1963, 56).

Part of the problem as Perelman sees it is that the idea of justice is an essentially confused notion. Although the formal rule of justice enjoins us to treat people in the same way, the idea of justice contains several incompatible notions of what the essential consideration should be. In *De la justice* Perelman identified six different meanings of "justice":

1. To each the same thing.
2. To each according to his merits.
3. To each according to his works.
4. To each according to his needs.
5. To each according to his rank.
6. To each according to his legal entitlement. (1963, 7)

These six conceptions of justice share a notion of formal justice, but they also conflict with one another in regard to what consideration is the most important. The judgment that one consideration or another is the most important one, or more important than some others, is, says, Perelman, a value judgment, which must in the end be "utterly arbitrary." Thus, his skepticism about the possibility of reasoning about justice in a logical positivist framework—values are grounded neither in logic nor sense experience, and so cannot be justified.

Then comes the next part of Perelman's narrative, this from the Genoa lectures: "It seemed to me that before accepting the theses of positivism about values, someone should make a renewed effort to elaborate a logic of value judgments based not on the reasoning techniques of modern logic but rather on a detailed examination of how men actually reason about values" (1967, 58). And so we come to the next part of the story, and to the twist:

> I undertook to do this work with the collaboration of Madame L. Olbrechts-Tyteca. Ten years after the beginning of our project, we had not found the logic of value judgments that we were looking for. . . . Our research convinced us that there exists no specific logic concerning values; rather, the same techniques of reasoning which we use to criticize and to justify opinions, choices, claims, and decisions, are also used when it comes to criticizing and justifying statements that are usually qualified as value judgments. . . . Losing sight of argumentation . . . and discursive means of convincing not founded on formal logic or experience . . . one could not even imagine what was specific to the process of justification, much less specify its relationship to the idea of justice. (1967, 59)

I want to try to specify this relationship of justification to justice, for it plays a central role in Perelman's thought, and I am not certain that he ever elaborated it in the philosophical depth he could have. Argumentation provides the possibility of reasoning about justice, but what makes argumentation capable of justification in this strong sense? The answer is that a concept of justice lies at the core of *The New Rhetoric*'s idea of argumentation, and only because it does can *The New Rhetoric* provide a response to positivist skepticism about justice. We have already established that justice is a consideration in every part of *The New Rhetoric*. However, this core relationship of justification and justice in Perelman's work can be clarified only by getting a crucial part of the narrative of his intellectual transformation correct.

The New Rhetoric depends on implicit conceptions of justice throughout, as we have seen. However, it also treats justice explicitly. First, the "rule of justice" is itself included as an argumentative technique. The strength of the rule stems from the principle of inertia, from the power of precedence. The rule is the one we are familiar with: give identical treatment to beings or situations of the same kind. However, beings and situations are never identical, so "in every concrete situation a prior classification of the objects and the existence of precedents as to the manner of treating them is indispensable" (219).

This may sound like a repeat of Perelman's earlier skepticism, but it is not. In *The New Rhetoric*, when the rule of justice is applied, one need not justify a value judgment. In every concrete situation a prior classification *has already* been made. Earlier cases *have already been decided*. The rule of justice makes it possible to pass from these earlier cases to future ones. The difference is critical. The world of the positivist skeptic in search of foundations for a system of justice is a world that imagines itself without precedent, without prior classifications of people, without history, a world in which everything is in question, a kind of empty world—or better, a worldlessness that corresponds to *temps vide*. In *The New Rhetoric*, on the other hand, the world and time are full, full of history—of classifications, facts, values, precedents—and full, too, of an anticipated future that structures experience. Only in such a world can the rule of justice have concrete application.

Justice makes another important explicit appearance in *The New Rhetoric*. Perelman and Olbrechts-Tyteca note that the strength of arguments is not something that can be measured psychologically or through social-scientific research. Rather, the idea of the strength of arguments is created by a distinction between two viewpoints—the normal (or usual) and the norm (the normative). This distinction allows the dissociation of effectiveness from validity. Effective arguments may be effective without really being strong; they are normally effective with some audience as a matter of fact. Valid arguments, on the other hand, are strong ones; they have their strength not *de facto* but *de jure*. Perelman and Olbrechts-Tyteca do not pursue the idea that we might be able to exorcise this normative factor from the idea of strength. According to *The New Rhetoric*, there can simply be no doubt that a practical distinction is made between strong arguments and weak ones. The distinction is a fact, a starting point for the analysis, even though, according to *The New Rhetoric*, there can no *logical* ground for this whole framework of distinctions. Rather: "The normal, as well as the norm, is definable only in relation to an audience whose . . . adherence is the foundation for standards of value. . . . The superiority of the norm over the normal is correlative to the superiority of one audience over another" (463).

One might imagine, then, that *The New Rhetoric* would just stop the analysis there, and refer back to the earlier discussion of the universal audience. However, Perelman and Olbrechts-Tyteca repeat the question, as if they were starting the analysis again: "What guarantees this validity? What provides the criterion for it?" I take it that they are asking: what is the criterion by which a universal audience recognizes the strength of arguments?

This is a strange question for them to ask. Earlier in the book, they developed a highly relativized concept of the universal audience. As they say, "Everyone constitutes the universal audience from what he knows of his fellow men, in such a way as to transcend the few oppositions he is aware of. Each individual, each culture, has thus its own conception of the universal audience" (33). However, here they say: "Our hypothesis is that . . . strength is appraised by application of the rule of justice: that which was capable of convincing in a specific situation will appear to be convincing in a similar or analogous situation" (464). This is the only passage I know of in *The New Rhetoric* in which the universal audience is identified with a particular argumentative technique—the rule of justice. If this is so, then the idea of justice has another uniquely essential status in the theory. Since it is the rule of justice that allows a universal audience to judge the strength of arguments, this idea of justice lies at the core of Perelman's theory of argumentation.

Let's summarize for a moment. Perelman's early analysis of the notion of justice led to an impasse because he believed that value judgments were utterly arbitrary. He set out in pursuit of a logic of value judgments that would be grounded in an examination of how people actually reason. He did not find a strict "logic," but he did rediscover argumentation and rhetoric and rhetorical logos—ways to reason and ways to understand reasoning about values. We might imagine the completion of the narrative in this way, then. After discovering this grounding for value judgments, Perelman returned to his 1944 analysis of the confused notion of justice, employed the newly discovered techniques of reasoning about values to the five kinds of value judgments he had earlier identified, pronounced a winner, or at least established a hierarchy, and completed a theory of justice. Of course, this is a ridiculous idea. But why?

The fact is that Perelman's question changed along the way. From the positivist position, the question is: how can one, without belonging to any tradition, without acknowledging any precedents, without adhering to any values, operating in empty time, ground those value judgments which would complete the task of constructing a rational theory of justice? Perelman's answer to this question is not simply that one cannot. His response is that the question betrays misunderstandings about what reasoning is, misunderstandings about what makes the question itself possible. The question is analogous to asking someone to build a house simply by thinking about it, without using any of the available materials that have been used to construct any houses that actually exist.

The new line of questioning can be seen fairly clearly in Perelman's 1964 Genoa Lectures. They bear very strongly on the question of how the new rhetoric project as a whole develops rhetorically conceived argumentation as an alternative to violence, a practice of dynamic peace and justice. In the lecture on "Justice and Justification," Perelman describes how the problem of justifying values connected with justice is handled through the political process, and by executives, legislators, and judges. Ordinarily, "The laws, customs and regulations of a community will be assumed to be just by the mere fact of their existence" (1967, 67). The only condition is that they correspond, in general, to the wishes of the community. However, legal positivism, even in a democratic context, is not sufficient for Perelman, and so he departs from Maneli when it comes to legal positivism and insists on a philosophical approach. He believes that *the essential objection to democratic legal positivism is that it is violent*—and what this means, essentially, is that it abandons the process of struggling for universality:

Bending to the beliefs, aspirations and values of a political community . . . would mean . . . that we allowed force and force alone to settle conflicts between political communities whose aspirations and values turned out to be incompatible. By giving up the search for criteria and norms which transcend those of politically organized communities, we would give up the traditional role of ethics, of legal and political philosophy. Incapable of fortifying justice, the practical philosopher would by his skepticism limit himself to justifying force. Force would become the criterion and ultimate judge of values and of norms. (69)

And so, Perelman formulates the question of justice in a new way. No longer are we searching for a logic of value judgments in a domain where no values are supposed to be in play. Instead, we are in an organized political society, with established precedents, and with laws that correspond roughly to the desires of the most powerful factions in the society. However, there are conflicts—either between this political society and another, or between the dominant factions and the less powerful ones. Legal positivism confronts this situation squarely and insists that it is in fact power and its capacity to use force that establishes the context for law. This is the fact that Benjamin, too, faces so unflinchingly. However, for Perelman to accept this judgment would be simply to return to his earlier skepticism, so he ends the lecture on "Justice and Justification" by posing new questions: "In what sense can we affirm the reasonableness of values, criteria, norms? Is it possible in the practical realm to transcend the aspirations of a political community?" (70).

In the final Genoa lecture, on "Justice and Reason," Perelman connects this last question to the question of whether or not there is such a thing as a philosopher's mission. Perelman takes his definition of philosophy from Husserl, who wrote that "philosophers are the civil servants of humanity" (72). Legislators and judges have to make and apply law in a way that conforms to the aspirations of the political community, but philosophers, says Perelman, must formulate just laws and judge according to those laws not for a given society or group but for the whole of humanity.

What we find in the work of philosophy, according to Perelman, is "a progressive universalization of our moral principles," and this is exactly what Perelman takes the role of philosophy to be: to propose principles of action that could win the assent of all reasonable people (78). However, he rejects any kind of formalism, and makes some very specific objections to Kantian formalism, a formalism of which his own previous positivism was a version. "I do not believe," he says, "that a philosopher should limit himself to the formulation of a purely formal law comparable to the rule of justice." Instead the philosopher should make proposals, make assertions that express "the systematic formulation of an ideal." And he must test these assertions not simply for their logical consistency and their conformity to some notion of experience, but against all opposing points of view. "In philosophy, opposing points of view must be heard, whatever their nature or their source" (80). This, says Perelman, is the only available test of universality.

And so, the philosopher, the theorist of justice, understood within the framework of *The New Rhetoric*, addresses the universal audience. However, Perelman's description of this audience is a little different, a little more forthright, in the Genoa lectures on justice than it was a few years earlier in *The New Rhetoric*. In the lectures, Perelman says: "I do not see [reason] as a faculty in contrast to other faculties in man. I conceive of it as a privileged audience, the universal audience. . . . It is this audience, *with its convictions and aspirations*, that the philosopher wants to convince" (82, emphasis added). It is this audience, he says a few sentences later, that the philosopher is obliged to imagine. "The characteristic of rational argumentation is the aim to universality . . ." (83). This universal audience dwells in the fullness of time, a time with a past in which convictions were gained and a time with a future opened up by its aspirations, especially the aspiration for a justification of justice and of the moral principles and judgment that make justice a concrete reality and not just a formal principle.

This hope for justice is never completely fulfilled, says Perelman. Since the universal audience is always an audience with particular hopes and aspirations, since it is operating with certain starting points, within a tradition of particular commitments, it is always known not to be absolute and eternal. "That is why," says Perelman, "philosophical reasoning implies the philosopher's freedom of judgment as well as his responsibility.

The philosopher who judges commits himself; in judging a philosophy, we are also judging the man who is identified with it." That is, we are judging the philosopher's commitments. And we judge the philosopher's work against some very specific criteria, and they are essentially criteria of justice. As Perelman says: "It will be for others, who will come after him, to continue his efforts for more rationality and justice, and less violence, in the relations of men" (86).

So the question becomes: Can we affirm the reasonableness of values? Is it possible to justify actions by appealing to values and commitments that may transcend the aspirations of a political community? And the answer is: yes, it is possible as long as we share practical aspirations to universality. Yes, it is possible as long as we continue to struggle against violence. Yes, it is possible if we can join our thinking and our actions to a historical community that shares these aspirations. Rhetoric, as Perelman sees it, is motivated by an ethical aspiration. Its boundaries are drawn by ethical aspirations. Its history is the history of an ethical aspiration. Rhetoric is in a very important sense a branch of the study of justice. It is, finally, the study of the application of the rule of justice to utterances, both in particular contexts, and in contexts where there is an aspiration to universality. And in the case of philosophical utterances especially but also in many other cases, these judgments about utterances are indistinguishable from judgments about actual forms of life. Ultimately, they are all judgments about beings that come to presence in human transcendence and its movement through logoi and time. We are ultimately seeking justice for human beings and their experience and their lives.

Let's be blunt: there is some obviously circular reasoning going on here. The final account of how strong arguments are distinguished from weak ones makes an appeal to the rule of justice. Thus, the effectiveness/validity distinction that makes the new rhetoric different from ordinary relativistic rhetorics rests on an ideal of justice. The theory of argumentation seems simply to assume what it was supposed to provide. Quite simply, one can reason successfully about justice because there is a universal audience who is the judge of what is just. One could extend this challenge to all the occurrences of justice we have noted in this chapter, because, in the end, whether in establishing the framework of argumentation or applying the rule of justice, one appeals to a more or less universal audience who rightly judges what is just.

The judgment is never made simply on the basis of the formal rule of justice, as Perelman points out. Instead the universal audience is a participant in argumentation. It operates within the bounds of argumentation, and it shares certain starting points with the other participants in the argumentation. The term "universal audience" is thus, again, somewhat misleading. Although the universal audience is constructed by way of universalizing techniques that tend toward the quantitative—one begins with a particular audience, and then adds more and more people to it until eventually one has arrived at an audience which represents the whole of humanity—it is also constructed by way of qualitative judgments about which people are eligible to be members of this audience—people who are not sufficiently rational or competent, who are not "disposed to hear" the argumentation, or have not "duly reflected" are disqualified (*NR* 31–35).

The general presumption of justice is equality—to treat people who are relevantly similar and in relevantly similar situations in a similar way. And the difficulty in applying the rule of justice is to know when people are relevantly similar. This same challenge arises in constructing the universal audience—include everyone, the whole of humanity, but exclude those who are not relevantly similar, not equal in respect to how "reflective" or how "disposed to hear" they are. Thus, judging prospective members of the universal audience requires making value judgments about which characteristics are the most important, how they should be placed in a hierarchy, and so on. This is a task that, in *The New Rhetoric*, falls to the "undefined universal audience"—the audience that judges the way in which the universal audience is constructed (35). That is, the undefined universal audience does not just adhere to abstract values, or to the formal principle of justice; rather, it is an audience that is committed to concrete values. An audience that knows what justice is. Wherever we look, it is possible to redeem the hope of reasonable inquiry into justice only because at the heart of *The New Rhetoric* rests the assumption that there is someone who already knows what justice is—or at least cares about it enough to endlessly pursue it.

Now this interpretation of the universal audience, although it is explicit in the Genoa lectures, does conflict with some passages of *The New Rhetoric*. For example, In *The New Rhetoric* Perelman and Olbrechts-Tyteca say that facts are what gain the assent of a universal audience, while values are those things to which only a particular audience gives assent. Thus, there is a rhetorical way to distinguish the domain of the real from the domain of the preferred.

However, other parts of *The New Rhetoric* tend in a different direction. Let me point out two ways in which, even in *The New Rhetoric*, the universal audience is better thought of as a "paragon audience." First, the universality of the universal audience is always limited by the good that one can achieve by way of participating in argumentation in a particular situation. Universal audiences arise only in actual argumentation—they are a feature of the argumentation, not something which exists outside of it, waiting for an argument to come along. As such, the universal audience shares an interest in the outcome of the argumentation—it values a nonviolent, mutually satisfactory rapprochement among the participants in the argumentation. It takes this outcome to be a concrete good. In situations in which such rapprochement is not possible, it is because a universal audience that adheres to the concrete value that is needed is not available—it is beyond imagining.

Second, Perelman and Olbrechts-Tyteca admit that "each speaker's universal audience can from an external standpoint be regarded as a particular audience" (31). This has important consequences for the rhetorical version of the fact/value distinction. For viewed from an "external" standpoint, perhaps from a yet more universal position, what is thought to be a fact may be recognized as a value, what is thought to be a universal audience may still be a particular one. In fact, from far enough "outside," most facts would show themselves to be values. And, as *The New Rhetoric* says, and as Perelman repeats in the Genoa lectures, one can *always* take the external view. Thus, all universal audiences begin to appear more as embodiments of a concept of what is good than of what is simply true, or factual. Since any universal audience can be understood to be partly constituted by an agreement on certain concrete values, the universal audience is actually better described as a paragon audience. And so, the circle of reasoning holds just as strongly for the theory set forth in *The New Rhetoric* as it does for the more explicit result of the Genoa lectures on justice. One can find in the proper account of argumentation a way to reason about values and so about justice only because at the heart of this account is an assumption that there is an audience that knows what concrete justice is.

However, a charge of fallacious circular reasoning is largely out of place here. Perelman is rejecting the model of reasoning that searches for external grounds for "value judgments" by methodologically setting aside anything that could be called a "value." He is rejecting the form of the question he posed earlier, the question grounded in such a model of reasoning. The issue is not somehow to discover a logical or epistemological-metaphysical ground for value. It is rather to discover a satisfactory process for conducting conflicts about incompatible choices we face—choices that bear on issues that cannot be decided in a positivist framework but that are in fact issues that are of significant concern and about which we often must make a choice. According to Perelman, the satisfaction we seek is to be satisfied that we have done justice in the process of reasoning and argumentation—justice to one another and to each other's lives, to each other's experience of and perspective on what is and what we hope will be.

I want to end this chapter by placing Perelman's own narrative of his reasoning into the framework provided by his theory. Perelman set out to answer a question that was formulated within a positivist framework: how can one justify value judgments by starting from a position in which one is strictly uncommitted to any values? Is it possible to develop or discover a logic of value judgments which would allow assertions of value to be logically justified? Perelman and Olbrechts-Tyteca failed to discover such a logic, and Perelman abandoned the question. This is the critical moment in the narrative. For Perelman is not simply abandoning a question. He is making a new judgment about which rhetorical community shares his basic aspirations and what the nature of a universal audience really is.

In the early part of his career, his rhetorical community was made up of logicians and philosophers—people committed to universality in a very strict sense and in a very admirable way, an enlightened way. However, they tried to position themselves as thinkers, as philosophers, outside of any tradition, apart from common sense and everyday practices, as thinkers who would attempt to construct the world rationally, from the ground up. Perelman shared their aspiration for universality because he saw the achievement of this universality as the primary alternative to violence. The renunciation of violence and the desire for justice and peace were his most consistent principles and desires. However, he came to abandon the narrowness of this intellectual community, and its specific form of receptivity—of rational agency—because it achieved what universality it did only at the cost of forsaking any reasoning about those issues concerning which human beings really do come to violence.

It is significant, I think, that *De la justice*, which runs sixty pages in its English translation, contains references to only eight other writers, and a few more titles. The only citation which is more than fifteen years old is to Proudhon—1868. Except for one reference to C. L. Stevenson and one to a German writer, they are all to French-language writers. In the first sixty pages of *The New Rhetoric*, we find one hundred sixteen citations. We find Descartes, Mill, Pascal, Leibniz, Richard Whately, Aristotle, Plato, H. L. Hollingworth, Lewis Carroll, Cassirer, Bacon, Bruner, Cicero, Quintilian, Sterne, Vico, Demosthenes, Petronius, Husserl—and these are not even all the names from the notes on the first twenty-six pages. Neither are those the most citation-dense pages of the book—those lie in part 3, where the reasoning is almost strictly by example, and where there are two hundred forty-four notes in the second chapter alone.

The New Rhetoric is a very different kind of work from *De la justice*—but that is the point. It is true that there is a powerful cause for the earlier book's not being citation rich in a scholarly sense: Perelman was under virtual house arrest when he wrote the book. However, an examination of his earlier works confirms the shift in the style of argumentation. It is not an accident that *The New Rhetoric* argues by example. Perelman is not simply in search of techniques of reasoning that can be described in a quasi-formal way and presented as parts of a discursive system. He is in search of new fellow-aspirants, a new form of receptivity, and so a new form of rational agency. Remember that, for Perelman and Olbrechts-Tyteca, argument by example is used not simply to clarify or support a preexisting assertion; that is the role of illustrations. Rather, examples are used to establish a rule. The wealth of examples in *The New Rhetoric* is meant to establish the entire case. The examples as a whole represent the tradition to which Perelman turned when he abandoned the positivist question. It is a tradition of people who are receptive—to a degree, and on some occasions, and in light of a good to be achieved—to arguments that are not logically compelling but still have some strength. It is a tradition of philosophers and rhetoricians who understand such receptivity as a kind of reasonableness that can be cultivated and judged.

Perelman rejected the claim that the rule of justice could not be applied since precedents could not be justified. He came to see that a method that adopted the stance that there were no precedents, no already existing agreements about values, was something of a chimera, a figment of the imaginations of a community that misunderstood itself—in other words, a view to which only a very particular and rather peculiar audience would adhere, and only in a narrow range of situations. He awakened himself to a tradition in which there was a rich store of values and precedents. It became for Perelman a fact that people simply *do* often settle their disputes nonviolently, through reasoning. They *do* succeed in coming together by way of a common conception of what is reasonable, for a time, and for a situation, and sometimes perhaps more broadly.

And the fact became that there was also a transcultural, transhistorical tradition of people who tried to account for how this happens—and who aspired for agreement with one another, too. Both of these groups deliver Perelman and Olbrechts-Tyteca's examples in *The New Rhetoric*. The examples are themselves representative of a community of aspirers: people who aspire to communities of action in small and large ways, people who understand reasoning as a branch of justice, a domain in which speakers and their logoi are treated fairly. The real story is that Perelman decided to keep company with these new interlocutors and their forms of receptivity and rational agency.

Our judgment about whether Perelman's circular reasoning is vicious or not, would, if we accepted his own account, be based on a judgment about whether the circle was drawn widely enough, whether the argumentative community for which he abandoned positivism was inclusive enough, whether it could answer the objections that might be made about its exclusiveness, whether we could ourselves aspire to some solidarity with it and with the forms of reason and justice it has passed down to us. The particular character of *The New Rhetoric*'s aspiration to solidarity, its particular conception of the universal audience, may be found in its examples. They establish the case. If they are taken to represent an excessively narrow range of interests, then one may see the circle from the theory of justice to *The New Rhetoric* and back as a vicious one. Or, in pursuit of better justice, one might take it on oneself to draw a wider circle and expand that store of examples and see what theoretical challenges ensue.

I believe that Perelman would admit that he is aligning himself in a strong way with a community that aspires to human solidarity and hopes progressively to minimize violence by channeling conflict through what he calls "argumentation." His theory of argumentation is not *simply* a generalization based on examples taken from the past. It is also a late-twentieth-century interpretation and application of the examples and the theoretical work of the rhetorical tradition to completely new situations. Beyond that, it is also a projection of a future for that tradition, an account of reason and argumentation that might inform concrete practices of justice and peace. Perelman's recovery of the rhetorical tradition is one of the great intellectual achievements of the twentieth century. However, in all this talk of realigned allegiances, it should also be recognized that Perelman never did truly abandon logical positivism's fundamental aspiration: to seek for a rationality that could make a claim to universality. Instead, he expanded it to a concern for those things that people care most deeply about and concerning which they also often come to violence. This concern took concrete shape in his pursuit of a deeper understanding of justice, in his vision of a dynamic peace of controversy and change, and of course in his work with Lucie Olbrechts-Tyteca that retrieved the rhetorical tradition and gave birth to *The New Rhetoric*.

EIGHT

Rhetoric and Wisdom

This book pursues a conception of rhetoric that resists the disciplinary compulsion for philosophy and rhetoric to define themselves in mutually exclusive ways. The project of a deep rhetoric seeks instead to reveal the philosophical dimensions of rhetoric, especially as rhetoric has come to be understood over the past century. At its beginning and in its etymology, philosophy's relation to a conception of wisdom is one of its essential traits. Although the discipline of philosophy has in the modern period perhaps not generated much discussion of wisdom, there has been more lately a renewed interest in practical reasoning and in virtues and in how to reason as a pluralist, and these are some of the concerns one finds in historical discussions of wisdom. In this chapter, I would like to explore the connections between the emerging conception of a deep rhetoric and some traditional conceptions of wisdom, and so further define some of the interactions and interdependencies of rhetoric and philosophy.

However, it is probably not wise to write about wisdom. First of all, one risks offending the gods, who seem to have a corner on what is for mortals the hubristic claim to wisdom. Further, not only does the word come to us with linguistic and cultural lineages that stretch way beyond any mortal's ability to track and master, but the idea is partly defined by its own resistance to definition. Wisdom is not a technique or a body of knowledge, although it is partly dependent on knowledge. It is not a predictable result of any specific amount or kind of experience, but it is dependent on experience. Wisdom is not simply theoretical understanding, or knowledgeable practical activity, or creative innovation, and yet wisdom has been explained in all three of these ways, as well as many others.

Wisdom in the Rhetorical Tradition

When it comes to the relation of rhetoric and wisdom, the literature is extensive. Some of the earliest rhetoricians, the sophists, were named after the wisdom (*sophia*) they professed, and have long been associated with a transformation of the idea of wisdom from a knowledge-wisdom of nature to a practical wisdom that is effective in social and political life and is associated with ethical development and in some cases identified with specifically political virtue.[1] Plato's writings that treat rhetoric and the sophists are in large part explorations of arguments about the new wisdom—whether it is something that can be possessed and whether "philosophy" is not a better name for an appropriate comportment toward wisdom. Although Aristotle disciplines rhetoric and makes it a specific art, he also attempts to repair this limitation by developing complicated connections between rhetoric and practical wisdom. In Eugene Garver's brilliant reading of Aristotle's *Rhetoric*, these connections become definitive of rhetoric as a civic art, at least in the context of the ancient *polis*.[2] Cicero's *De inventione* begins with his famous judgment on the relation of wisdom (*sapientia*) and eloquence, and his *De oratore* is a lengthy and winding discussion of the relations among eloquence, knowledge, wisdom, and prudence.[3]

In the Christian thinking of what we call the early middle ages, wisdom became an attribute of God, but in Augustine it also came to name the knowledge of divine things, as distinct from the knowledge (*scientia*) of human things. This knowledge-wisdom of God was a contemplative worship and not an ordinary kind of knowledge. In Augustine, practical wisdom was overshadowed by faith, hope, and especially charity. The danger in pursuing traditional forms of wisdom and education was pride—a sense of superiority and self-sufficiency. Charity, on the other hand, was a gift of God—in fact, charity was the giver, the giving, and the gift. Although the two kinds of wisdom, temporal and divine, provided the main framework for thinking about wisdom for hundreds of years, wisdom also had a background Christological theme in which Christ was the wisdom of God. And though this idea was often explicitly linked to the prologue of the Gospel of John, in which Jesus is identified with the logos that is said to be directed toward God (*pros ton theon*) and at the same time to be coming into the world, this apparent apotheosis of something like communication (logos) was occluded by ontic assumptions about *ratio, scientia, sapientia,* and God that led to a focus on epistemology and metaphysics rather than communication. In Augustine, this left rhetoric out of any close relation to wisdom (although in *On Christian Doctrine* it was clearly not wise to be a Christian teacher with poor rhetorical skills). Instead Christian rhetoric was a technical skill that was valuable to learn—as long as one did not succumb to pride. It was capable of absorbing and subordinating Cicero's rhetoric, and it focused on clarifying the truth about God as revealed in scripture. These Augustinian orientations were enormously influential in European history, especially for their first thousand years. They were reasserted in some Reformation thought, and they have never entirely disappeared.[4]

A different movement of thought from the fourteenth through the seventeenth centuries brought wisdom and rhetoric closer together again, and led to a resurgence of interest in classical rhetoric. This swing of thinking moved from a conception of wisdom that focused on the wisdom of God and the knowledge of divine things to one that focused on human wisdom about human things. Wisdom became a virtue that could be perfected through the right kind of educational formation. It also moved out of the realm of contemplation and became a practical knowledge of how to make choices and of how to act. In this movement from divine wisdom to human wisdom and from knowledge-wisdom to practical wisdom, what we call the Renaissance does indeed, in a way, repeat the movement associated with the origin of rhetoric in fifth- and sixth-century Greece. This ricorso is evident in Lorenzo Valla's early-fifteenth-century re-identification of rhetoric and philosophy on the grounds that the philosophical tradition was diverted by overintellectualization and passive theoretical orientations, as well as a neglect of the way experience is animated by desire and of the situatedness of all intellectual and linguistic action. Rhetoric's practical attunement to the reality of time and place—reality itself—led Valla to claim that "philosophy is under the command of rhetoric . . . rhetoric rules . . ." (Grassi 1988, 81). Wisdom is ultimately practical wisdom, the ability to act in a specific situation. As John Arthos (2007) insists, Renaissance wisdom was also a specifically civic wisdom, "political" in Aristotle's sense.[5]

The Renaissance Humanist exploration of the relation of wisdom and rhetoric achieves a late culmination in Giambattista Vico's famous dictum: "Eloquence is nothing more than wisdom speaking." Vico's thinking about wisdom moved from a contemplative knowledge-wisdom to a conception of wisdom as a practical virtue, retracing in a new way both the Greek development from natural philosophy to the sophists and the

Renaissance development that precedes him. Vico also came to identify wisdom with law itself, an external social wisdom, and with the historical course of achieving jurisprudential equity in human societies. For Vico, eloquence, or rhetoric, was the active practice of this jurisprudential wisdom, and so also its substance.[6]

So well into modernity and up to the threshold of what is often thought to be the modern decline of rhetoric, rhetoric and wisdom were believed by many to have an intimate and essential connection, even to the point of an identity that is supposed to inter-illuminate the nature of both rhetoric and wisdom. Certainly a deep rhetoric will have a significant relation to this tradition.

Yet it is not at all clear that rejoining this history is the only or the best way to highlight the features or the significance of an emerging philosophical rhetoric. Different conceptions of wisdom develop in different contexts. Wisdom plays an important role in many religious traditions. It is also an intrinsic part of many so-called secularization processes. The idea of wisdom sometimes functions as a check on the further differentiation of independent expert social authorities with their specialized knowledges, and so a return to an authority that goes beyond specialized knowledge. New philosophically informed rhetorical theory will emerge in an intellectual milieu of transnationality, religious pluralism, proliferating communicative media, and forces of globalization, even if this happens at the same time in a practical milieu of continuing aggressive war, violent ethnic/religious conflict, extralegal seizure, imprisonment and torture, and surveillance and security measures that threaten human liberty and dignity. This book is a prolegomena to the development of that philosophical rhetoric. Though the attempt to elaborate a deep rhetoric is essentially a philosophical one and so has few immediate practical implications, informed practical efforts always take shape in terms of a particular philosophical context. I have no new light to shed on the theory-practice dialectic except to insist on it once more in this context and to refuse both the deduction of practical actions directly from philosophical considerations and the claim that such considerations have no consequences for practical decisions.

What, then, would be a helpful context for exploring this relation between rhetoric and wisdom? Holding in mind this long tradition of literature about rhetoric and wisdom, and our own contemporary concerns, I would like to explore how Kenneth Burke and Chaim Perelman have conceived the relation of wisdom and rhetoric. Moreover, I would like to approach the issue through a version of Kenneth Burke's perspective by incongruity—bringing apparently incongruous elements into relation with each other to see what new light they can shed on one other. I would like to contribute some brief considerations of the thinking about wisdom that occurs in the Buddhist Prajnaparamita Sutras and in ancient Hebrew wisdom literature, as well as a reconsideration of the role of wisdom in Socratic "philosophy." These relative incongruities will offer a context that moves outside the more traditional narrative and historical approach and illuminates some of the religious and philosophical dynamics of the relation of wisdom and rhetoric that are sometimes shadowed in historicist accounts. Burke himself claims that such an approach reveals the "dramatic" relations of ideas, and it is the dramatic, dialectical, and contemporary appropriateness of these ideas in which I am most interested.

However, I would like to develop the question and give some preliminary definition to both rhetoric and wisdom by beginning with an origin-of-rhetoric myth found in the *Eumenides*, the third play in Aeschylus's *Oresteia*. Every philosophical advance is by definition a re-originating, and although rhetoric has many origins, Aeschylus is certainly a father to be claimed or slain—or, at least, in Burke's lexicon, transformed.

The Origin of Rhetoric in the *Oresteia* of Aeschylus

Recall that Orestes is the latest in a line of killers in the house of Atreus. He has killed his mother, who has killed his father. His mother, Clytemnestra, blames fate for her action. The god Apollo has moved Orestes toward his. The divine Furies are now pursuing Orestes; they want yet more blood, so that the endless cycle they rule can continue. The gods have had their way with the house of Atreus for a long time. Orestes flees to Athens, to Athena, who is there because her wisdom and desire for peace were manifest in her offering of an olive tree to its citizens, in contrast to Poseidon's war horse. The Furies find him there, and their first speech in Athens is a chanting hymn to Hades and a demand for blood, lots of blood. Orestes replies that he has been taught when to speak and when to remain silent, and that this is the moment for speech, and so he begins his appeal to Athena by telling about his absolution and his sacrifices, his having lawfully followed what the gods have ordered. The Furies respond with threats to eat him as a sacrifice, and then chant some more about the power they hold and the terror they spread.

When Athena asks for arguments, the Furies say that Orestes has committed matricide. When Athena asks what cause or motivation there was, the Furies say that *there can be no justification* for matricide. Athena replies: "Here are two sides, and only half of the argument" (428).[7] The Furies ask Athena to explain what she intends, to speak out of her wisdom. Athena says that she seeks justice and not a triumph of wrong. The Furies yield to her wisdom (or perhaps to her connections with Zeus), and they allow her to judge Orestes. She then turns to Orestes and asks for an answer to the charges. He says again that he knows that there are rules for speaking, and that a man who has killed must remain speechless until he has performed rites of absolution, and that he has done so. He then tells his story.

Athena concludes that the case cannot be decided. When there is no obvious right, and when the gods themselves cannot decide, then, says Athena, a jury must decide—a jury of the finest Athenians. She says that she will establish a court now and for all time. This is (mythically) the first manifestation of Athenian wisdom. She creates an institutional space for democratic reasoning, the site in which judicial rhetoric will have its home, its generative seat, as Ricouer calls it. Wisdom institutionalizes rhetoric. The first appearances in court are by divinities—who nevertheless have to recognize the authority of a human Athenian jury. Rhetoric is replacing political religion and establishing a kind of humanism. Athena's wisdom also recognizes the place of controversy, but she anticipates that wisdom will nevertheless be possible for the mortal judges, that they will achieve a standpoint that will let them judge the arguments and not simply see from each perspective. Further, Athena's wisdom is connected with justice, and it is justice and wisdom together that seem to lead the Furies to yield. Finally, Athena's wisdom is expressed in procedure, and she seems to have confidence that procedural wisdom will lead to a substantive wisdom, a sound judgment. She recognizes Orestes' careful and pious submission to procedure, and she herself determines the specific procedures for the trial.

The Furies then chant a wonderful hymn to themselves as the ones who use fear to defend justice, who put fear into human hearts and so make them lawful, and who produce, out of human suffering and pain, something like practical wisdom for human beings.[8] This is not the only connection between the Furies and something like wisdom, but it is a critical one, and a continuing support for their claim to importance.

The court is then assembled. Athena opens the trial, declares who should speak first, and says why. The arguments from 610ff. are about procedure, speech, and oath. At times, Athena is addressed; at other times, the jury; at other times, the Furies, or Apollo, or Orestes. The procedures are not strict, but there is order. The actual arguments, however, are strangely comic. The gods end up arguing or maybe bickering about themselves and their behavior and their powers, and about whether mothers are true parents or fathers are. Orestes is hardly the focus. Orestes' defense rests simply upon the facts that his mother murdered his father, that Apollo ordered her killing, and that Apollo also purified Orestes.

However, Athena's eyes are on the future, and she introduces her judgment by announcing that henceforth the Athenians shall judge from the place where she stands, the hill of Ares. She then lays down rules for judging rightly. Judgments must be made in light of history. The citizens should be reverent and just. Neither anarchy nor despotism should reign. There should be a place for fearful awe—and here Athena repeats the speech of the Furies, and acknowledges their work in cities. The court itself should be free from the corruption of money, and should be a watchful protector and guard for the city, always alert. That, she says, is her logos.

At this point, the Furies break in and threaten Athens, and the end of the trial almost becomes a shout-and-threat match among the gods. The Furies begin to portray the trial as a struggle between the old gods (themselves) and the young (Apollo). Athena listens to this exchange, but takes the issue to be not age but gender, and declares that since she was not born of a mother, if there is a tie vote, then her side is with the male.

Athena has already decided that the case cannot be resolved by the gods—and we hear testimony that is itself good evidence that they would solve the case only on the basis of age or gender or some other divinely unconscious power that cannot fully be brought under human control or law. Their criteria are clearly inappropriate. They are, after all, gods and not human beings. They have no human stake in the outcome.

Yet, the human Athenians have no clear grounds for a decision either. Blood revenge should cease, and Orestes is not a danger to anyone; however, matricides should not go unpunished, and the fear of doing wrong must not be weakened. So the vote splits: six to six.

This is the dilemma that creates a need for rhetorical wisdom. There is no way to decide a case in which each side has equally compelling arguments. There is no general perspective from which each perspective can be judged. One can judge only from one side or the other. There is no divine justice here, says Athena, so human beings must decide for themselves. She can give them institutions and procedures and even something like an ideal speech situation where money and violence have no place, and in which the best people deliberate according to rules, but this does not mean that they have the standards by which to judge. And so they come up with equal numbers on each side, unable to reach a judgment. Rhetoric—in this case, the arguments and deliberations of speakers trying to persuade a jury—fails to achieve wisdom.

Here the contrast between rhetoric and wisdom takes a form it will often take. We have two perspectives—"two sides" as Athena says—that of the Furies and that of Orestes and Apollo. We consider both sides—both perspectives, both sets of arguments—and we try to find a standpoint from which we can judge between these perspectives. We try to get a perspective on the perspectives, but we cannot. We have two conflicting kinds of knowledge. First, the knowledge of the Furies. They have divine knowledge and divine roles, and their justifications for their actions rest on their divine natures. However, they also have arguments, usually causal ones, about what would happen to cities and to justice if the Furies did not pursue the unjust, and about the vengeance they will take on Athens if they are defeated (although the latter might be said to be more an *ad baculum* than an argument as such). And then we have also the knowledge of Orestes, grounded in his arguments that his action was in obedience to a god and that he followed all the divinely commanded rites of absolution. What the jury needs is a knowledge of these different kinds of knowledge, some ground for judgment. But it is exactly what they lack.

This is one powerful way to conceptualize wisdom: wisdom is the knowledge of knowledge that allows one to decide controversies where no simple standard of knowledge is sufficient because the available standards conflict with one another. Rhetoric seems to promise this wisdom—as judicial deliberation, it seems to be this wisdom—and yet it also seems not to deliver.

Against the background of this unstable framework for comprehending the relation of wisdom and rhetoric, which nevertheless issues the basic challenge to any conceptualizing of wisdom, I would like to explore and juxtapose a Buddhist conception of wisdom, an ancient Hebrew conception of wisdom, and a Socratic conception of wisdom—all with an eye toward explaining the relation of wisdom and rhetoric. This will of necessity be a set of forays best described as explorations and juxtapositions because a responsible scholarly treatment of these traditions would be impossible within the scope of this project. However, it is possible to offer a general outline of some conceptions of wisdom in these traditions and to press our own questions on those conceptions. Again, I will follow these explorations with a direct treatment of the work of Kenneth Burke and Chaim Perelman and a discussion of the results of all of this for our understanding of rhetoric and wisdom in the context of a deep rhetoric.

The Prajnaparamita Sutras

Within the confines of a subsection in a chapter of a book, it is of course impossible to give anything like a scholarly account of Mahayana Buddhism or the reception and meaning of the Prajnaparamita texts in this tradition.[9] However, it is not impossible to describe some of the general contours of the notion of wisdom that informs these sutras. In any case, for me it is not historical Buddhism that creates a context for articulating a deep rhetoric, but rather Buddhism as it has come to be thought and practiced on the West Coast of the United States, the Buddhism that has been lived and expressed by poets and critics such as Gary Snyder and Jane Hirshfield, by the writer of speculative fiction, Kim Stanley Robinson, and by numerous others—especially my friends who have become practicing Buddhists at the same time that they continue to be observant Jews and Christians, as well as nontheists of many kinds. Elements of this form of Buddhism have become partly naturalized in my own thought and vocabulary, and it is so surprisingly common that, when I mentioned to some friends that I was reading the Heart and Diamond Sutras, two of them told me that they chanted the Heart Sutra as a discipline.

The field of Buddhist studies has recently come to focus more on Buddhism as a religion and on Buddhist practices and less on Buddhism as a kind of philosophy expressed in abstract ideas in texts.[10] However, for my purposes here I will be focusing on some very general ideas from the Heart and Diamond Sutras. Although these Sutras have played and continue to play important roles in Buddhist practice, and although they are highly condensed and allusive in their treatment of received Buddhist ideas, I will be focusing only on some general intellectual tendencies found in them—and especially on the idea of a process of going further, going beyond whatever presents itself (as less than the whole, though even the "whole" is a category that one must eventually "go beyond"). Let me give some brief background to the Prajnaparamita literature and then offer some general characterizations of the idea of wisdom found in them.

The Prajnaparamita sutras developed between 100 BCE and 600 CE, and belong to a genre of writings that are usually taken to represent the oral teachings of the historical Buddha. The Sanskrit word *prajna* is commonly translated as "wisdom," and usually has the special meaning of an intuitive realization achieved by contemplation—of being freed from delusion, of purifying one's understanding. *Paramita* carries the additional meaning of "gone beyond," and qualifies the special wisdom of the Prajnaparamita Sutras as a wisdom that has surpassed all the usual limits of conceptualization and the usual boundaries of experience. The fundamental orientation follows from the teachings of the Buddha as they have been received. Suffering pervades life, and suffering is produced by desire that results from the temporary convergence of a body and the other material realities it encounters. This convergence occurs in feelings and sensations, perceptions, thoughts, beliefs and habits, and, of course, consciousness. In all of these, there is a grasping and clinging to the object of experience, intensified by will. When wisdom is achieved—when one "sees" how the phenomenal world is produced by desire, and when one separates oneself from desire and its illusions through a practice of detachment—then one achieves a knowledge of all knowledge that culminates in an intuition of what lies beyond all knowledge. Disciplined meditation earns release toward wisdom. This much is a general account of common Buddhist teaching.

The Prajnaparamita Sutras attempt to go beyond this. Not only the categorial differentiations of natural phenomena are surpassed, and not only the subtle remaining remnants of a self or ego are gone beyond, but specifically the epistemological assumptions of the meditative means by which enlightenment is achieved—which are in some way assertable *on the way to* final wisdom but not *from* the position of final wisdom—these too are "gone beyond." The traditional assumptions and the means of enlightenment depend on theories of the impermanence of things, of the near omnipresence of suffering, of categories of desire that produce the phenomenal world, and of the complicated abidharma and its own system of categories and entities. This sophisticated philosophical psychology oriented toward a kind of philosophical-spiritual therapy is exactly what the Prajnaparamita goes beyond.

In Aeschylus's mythic account of the controversial seeing-from-both-sides origin of rhetoric, in Aristotle's description of rhetoric as a "seeing" of the means of persuasion that can cause a judgment on reality, and in Vico's argument that inventing and seeing the arguments is prior to criticizing them, we find something like a wisdom that has a knowledge of knowledge by way of a kind of seeing. In the Prajnaparamita literature, we also have a conception of wisdom that depends on a step back and a seeing of how conceptions of reality are produced—one that also includes a seeing of how complicated forms of desire produce the suffering that pervades that reality. However, the step back here is a contemplative one. It depends on a change in the organization of one's psyche—a re-formation. There are obvious and important differences here between the Western rhetorical tradition and the Mahayana/Prajnaparamita tradition. However, I want to focus instead on some of the less obvious similarities by concentrating on the contemplative features of rhetorical reflection. First, though, a look at the main features of wisdom in the Prajnaparamita literature in relation to the western tradition, and a very quick sketch in each instance of a possible dialogue with the rhetorical tradition.

The first feature of Prajnaparamita wisdom is that the primary conflicts the sutras address are not conflicts among competing claims about what is real or just or about the best course of action, but conflicts intrinsic to the human condition: we produce our own suffering, often by the very means by which we intend to escape suffering. Wisdom is liberation from the suffering that we ourselves inadvertently produce. The relation here with the rhetorical tradition is enormously complex. There is no question that the rhetorical tradition—and especially a deep rhetoric—is concerned with rhetoric as a way to address the suffering produced by conflict. However, it usually conceptualizes conflict as conflict among human groups (or mythically between human beings and gods). Nonetheless, the rhetorical tradition also shows a consistent interest in the internalization of rhetorical practices in the individual. As we saw in chapter 1, Isocrates notes this in his famous hymn to logos, where wisdom is internalized eloquence, where we think for ourselves with the same kinds of reasoning we use to deliberate with others. About 2,250 years after Isocrates, Chaim Perelman and Olbrechts-Tyteca devote a section of *The New Rhetoric* to "Self-Deliberating," and they note that deliberating with oneself, a kind of reflection, is often connected with a privileged kind of reasoning—less particular, more universal. So the rhetorical tradition has emphasized, perhaps, the civic and political uses of logos, but it has also recognized the inward and reflective use of rhetoric as well.[11]

A second feature of this Buddhist wisdom is its tendency toward so-called personification. The Heart Sutra begins with an invocation: "All homage to the perfection of wisdom, the lovely, the holy," and Edward Conze makes it clear that this is a woman (81). In fact, personification *and* deification are consistent themes in Buddhist efforts to communicate wisdom. The historical Buddha and all the Buddhas that follow represent wisdom in a human form, but there is also a counter-tendency to deify the Buddha—for example, in divine iconography in Buddhist art and in literature that calls him a teacher of the gods. The Diamond Sutra emphasizes the bodhisattva as a middle figure, the one who glimpses the unconditioned but turns back to alleviate the suffering of others. In the Heart Sutra, Avalokita, moving in the deep course of the wisdom that has gone beyond, *looks down* from *on high*. The need to personify and the tension set up between the human and something beyond the usual category of human pervade this tradition. As we will see, something similar to this oscillation takes place in other traditions and even in rhetoric itself.

Third, one moves toward wisdom through a process of disciplined study that includes meditative practice. This involves reflection, gaining knowledge of how experience is produced, and achieving a larger, outside (or deep inside) perspective that liberates and allows a new kind of agency. I will discuss this process of formation/education and its similarities with rhetorical training in the discussion below.

Fourth, wisdom produces an appreciation of apparent contradictions, which are experienced by the enlightened not as conflicts to be resolved but as useful for leading one toward the unconditioned. As one approaches the unconditioned, one stops being so captivated by the differentiating that causes contradictions to appear. As both Edward Conze and Donald Mitchell say of the Diamond Sutra, its teaching is that: (1) One should become a bodhisattva, and (2) there is no such thing as a bodhisattva.[12] Of course, there is a tradition of dialectical reasoning in the West that focuses on overcoming contradictions by in some way asserting both sides of the contradiction—in Hegel, for example, by "sublating." Marx develops his idea of dialectical materialism as a historical working through of contradictions. Derrida's notion of différence and "practicing the interval" is another way to avoid the mind-trap of binaries and the rigid, mutually exclusive contradictory propositions they help to form.

A different way, though, is found in Perelman and Olbrechts-Tyteca's *The New Rhetoric*. There, "dissociations" used in contradictions are produced and used to conduct conflict peacefully toward mutually acceptable logoi. To be perfectly clear here, the "contradictions" of rhetorical argumentation are not *logical* contradictions. They are instead "incompatibilities" because they present *choices* that are incompatible. There is a sense, then, in which "contradictions" have a mitigated reality in argumentation. Dissociations are produced by radical rhetorical invention to deal with incompatibilities, and argumentation offers many ways to avoid or undo or resolve incompatibilities. These rhetorical "contradictions" are fluid, and they are either useful or not; they are supposed to lead somewhere. Rhetoric's concern with becoming aware of how dissociations are produced aligns in part with the concerns of the sutras, but makes a different use of this awareness.[13]

Fifth, Buddhist meditation culminates in an experience of something like nirvana, the prajna-paramita, beyond all distinctions and differentiations. I will explore this, too, in the next section.

Contemplative Reflection

In the Buddhist wisdom tradition, wisdom is a lack of attachment or limitation to the specifics of a situation and an ability to have experience independently of that attachment and limitation. How does this kind of wisdom bear on the seeing involved in rhetoric's attempt to step back and envision the larger topological picture? From a rhetorical point of view, we usually think of communication's being made possible by certain limitations—for example, by a common language, a sense of what is significant, of what is worth arguing about, by common values, by common understandings of facts, and by common theories about how these things work together. Exactly what set of these things is active depends on the particular situation. However, because all communication depends on these temporarily available agreements which help to reveal things that are relevant for a particular purpose on a particular occasion in communication with particular others, any specific communicative situation is also "in the dark" about the things that would be revealed for other purposes, on other occasions, in communication with other people.

Imagine a situation that has been a reality for many American employers, especially in the public sector, for about the last twenty-five years. Imagine a city committee that is trying to develop a policy for granting benefits to same-sex domestic partners of employees in addition to opposite-sex spouses. A conflict arises because one member of the committee believes that "simply living together" does not represent the same kind of commitment that "covenantal" marriage does, and so concludes that city funds should not be used to extend benefits to people who have casual relationships with city employees. Another member believes that this misrepresents the reality, and she uses her own situation as an example: "My partner and I have lived together for ten years now. We have together cared for two children during those years. We have paid the mortgage together, shared living expenses, and lived as though married for those years. Before this relationship, I was married for ten months to someone else. Are you saying that my current partnership represents no commitment while my previous marriage did?" Part of this picture is that each of these people has a different view of the reality and range of how households and relationships function. However, both are also working with the language of "marriage" and "commitment" and "partnership" which itself may call up certain features of certain relationships and situations but may not capture accurately either the features of those situations that are most relevant or the range of different kinds of relationship that need to be examined to have a fruitful discussion.

This is why some people say that in all events of understanding there is both the revealed and the concealed, what exists (or comes to presence) and what does not. This lack of a complete perspective is sometimes, as in Buddhism, blamed for suffering, and often judged as what one must "go beyond" in order to mitigate suffering. In a rhetorical situation, one thinks of what the members of one's audience have experienced or are capable of experiencing, at the time, with their senses, in their thoughts, how they have been conditioned to experience and judge things in a certain way, and what they are conscious of most at the time and place of the communication. One knows that one is about to communicate not the essence of things but things as they are accessible and comprehensible and significant in some particular circumstance. One knows this against a background understanding that this is not the only way things can be understood, and so one's attachment to the particular way they are understood in this situation is not absolute, not an insistence or obsession or anxious attachment to this particular circumstance. The parallels with Buddhist wisdom are clear; rhetorical invention requires detachment. Rhetorical awareness means in part being aware of the range of possible understandings at play, and thus aware, too, to some extent, of how these possibilities shade off into unlikelihood at this time and place, or even into incomprehensibility.

In the example above, it may well not be too difficult for most parties to take gay and lesbian partnerships as seriously as heterosexual marriages, and this would expand the resources for reasoning about the conflict. However, if one continued on to consider the claims of seasonal or cyclical or group liaisons, or of people who did not live together at all but claimed a spiritual partnership, or began to consider why the desire and ability to couple or partner should have such an impact on the distribution of health benefits, one would begin to lose focus on the specific situation that was calling for a choice. So despite its essential tendency to take a larger perspective, rhetorical awareness is always sharply alert to the particular occasion, the knowledge that is at work here and now, because this is what choice and action and effective communication require. Too much attachment and one has lost perspective both on the larger reality and on the possibilities of change in the particular situation itself. Too little stake in the situation and one has lost the perspective that allows for timely and meaningful action, reasonable choice among alternatives, and successful communication.

Rhetorical meditation is in part an act of imagination that "sees" the limitations and opportunities of a particular occasion, the deep attachments and far-reaching possibilities, in the facts and values and theories and procedures and symbols and stories and arguments that make up the available resources for rhetorical action. Rhetorical wisdom then somehow knows how to keep to the border between the reality the interlocutors explicitly acknowledge at this moment and the reality that rhetorical meditations disclose. Locating this frontier is, so to speak, finding a mean, and having the self-control or sanity to stay near it. This is an old conception of wisdom, and rhetoric pretty clearly focuses mostly on keeping to this mean, while the Prajnaparamita literature concentrates mostly on going beyond it.

However, even from a rhetorical point of view, one might go beyond this meditative frontier for several reasons. First, one could take the larger perspective to see what arguments and persuasive actions are available, or possibly available, for the particular situation. One leaves the specific language and consciously acknowledged situation of the interlocutors or audience and explores possibilities they may not have considered in an effort to improve one's communication with them, perhaps to change their perspective or remind them of things they have forgotten, or provide them with a story that will focus their attention in the appropriate place. In this case, one crosses the meditative border in order to find resources to bring back and apply to the specific situation. (Note, though, that the border is crossed in two directions. One also replenishes the "larger perspective" with the historical newness constantly being created in the sphere of action.)

There are still other reasons to cross this boundary. One might cross this boundary in order to remember one's own larger perspective, which may not be relevant or even representable in a situation where the best resolution of a conflict does not align with it. In such a case, one crosses over in order not to lose touch with oneself, but to preserve an understanding of the relation between oneself and what is happening. The dialectic between self and situation here cannot be productive if the self is completely lost in the particular situation. One might also cross this border simply to preserve the contact with larger perspectives, to maintain a psychologically healthy independence from the deep emotional and cognitive attachments and anxieties of the parties to a conflict. At this point, rhetorical motives and Buddhist motives begin to merge. One might also cross this meditative border as a matter of discipline, in order to develop a habit of taking different perspectives, and so develop the intellectual virtues of open-mindedness, perseverance in learning, and the ability to argue from different sides, which, in turn, can lead to moral imagination and sympathy. Finally, one might cross this meditative border because it can generate, at times, a kind of delight in the sheer multiplicity and fullness of the possibilities of understanding things when one is not too deeply attached to any particular set of those possibilities. Again, this "seeing" can be a high pleasure in itself, and it is one of the ways wisdom sometimes gets conceptualized or analogized.

And yet just when "seeing" from this larger perspective seems attractive, rhetoric calls us back to its more concrete offices: one who is detached from ordinary desire and whose mind is mostly on the incomprehensible or on the very big or long term picture may have a difficult time speaking to a situation in which, say, peasants who are deeply attached to a particular piece of land, particular animals and plants and landscape, are having to defend themselves against attempts to remove them to another location. One must have a strong feeling and even sympathy for their attachments, a sympathy grounded in a detailed knowledge of the way the land may be integral to the culture and moral life of the peasants, in order to speak to the conflict they are facing. One must have a kind of compassion. One must also have detailed knowledge of, and even sympathy for, the ones who are attempting the removal, their motives, their own way of life, the legal and financial and political power they have, and so on. One must know in addition the psychologies and social psychologies involved, the fears and hopes, the senses of what can be sacrificed or compromised and what cannot, a knowledge of what will count as a reason for and a reason against for each party. This requires an immersion in the details of the particular occasion, an inside knowledge of and sympathy with groups of people in conflict. Hans-Georg Gadamer says that when we achieve this kind of understanding, there is a sense in which we are actually convinced of the position we are trying to understand. We could call this the road in, toward the specific and limited here and now, the road on which we come to imagine, and even to some degree become capable of experiencing, what someone else's rhetorical situation really is. However, there remains at the same time the road outward, going beyond. One who simply sees from the inside will be in no better position than the parties to an intractable conflict, or an audience that stands in need of reasonable choices or motivation or comfort.

We are of course deeply within rhetoric's realm, speaking of "roads" and "borders" of this kind, as if people's realities were geographical things, like countries, or like adjacent bodies in space. And we are bordering on a question that will generate one of rhetoric's most excellent tactics. The question is: is there another reality, a true reality that is not conditioned by time and place and the categories and ideas and images and stories and desires and values that make up the situation of any actual communicative event? Is there a vantage from which a perspective on perspectives themselves can be reached? Is there an intuition that has "gone beyond" all of this? The rhetorical move that is made in and out of this question is to divide reality into two: the lesser world of mere "appearance," the world of ordinary consciousness and communication, and the world of genuine "reality," a world that is true and complete in itself, apart from communication and the usual kind of awareness. Making this kind of distinction, say Perelman and Olbrechts-Tyteca, is philosophy's basic rhetorical move.[14]

This division into appearance/reality, practical knowledge/theoretical knowledge, consciousness/what is not limited to consciousness, or perspective/perspective on perspectives is also a judgment of value or even an ethical judgment about what is worth learning and pursuing in life. Reality has more importance than appearance; the unlimited is truer and ultimately more valuable than the limited. In fact, the "reality" term (whatever it may be) is used to judge the "appearance" term, to determine what in appearances is closer or more conducive to reality and what is not. Rhetoric itself (as well as any other kind of knowledge or wisdom) depends on some distinction of this kind, so let's explore a little how this move is at work in the way I have described deep rhetoric so far, in order to show how this distinction is both a division of appearance/reality and an ethical division.

We have already distinguished between two realities, the reality known to the rhetorician as such and the reality known to ordinary people in a communicative situation. For ordinary people not taking a deep rhetorical perspective, in any given situation there simply *are* certain facts and values and theories to which they hold and which are not arguable. What they have seen with their eyes and heard with their ears stands fast for them. The categories in which they organize things are solid. The stories and images that move them and the convictions that motivate them will not change in the course of the communication in question. Yet for the rhetorician (or anyone taking the deep rhetorical point of view), all these things are a temporary confluence of exigencies and chances. The people involved probably have a number of conflicting and even contradictory beliefs and attitudes and values. They are in some process of change; they may be susceptible to arguments and persuasions that they have not yet considered. The reality they acknowledge is the one that constitutes this particular rhetorical situation and not all rhetorical situations. In fact, it is their acknowledgment of each other's experience and language and thus of a shared reality that makes knowledge what it is. What counts as truth is thus communicative and kairotic; it takes place and changes in time.

Therefore, this important division is evidently a bit of a fiction. In actual situations, the deep rhetorical view and the ordinary view are both at work, mixed up in various ways in different people in relation to specific beliefs, values, and so forth. This is how rhetorical dissociation works. It takes something that looks like a unity and divides it into its more and less authoritative and valuable parts. Here we call them the "rhetorical" (reality) view and the "ordinary" (appearance) view. However, the point of such a separation is not merely to separate but to reorder and reevaluate the "appearances," ultimately in order to resolve incompatibilities and make reasoned choices. One could say: in order to discover logoi to which people can adhere and which will carry them in the right way and in the right direction. Ultimately, this fundamental distinction is an ethical one in the sense that it is not a metaphysical or epistemological descriptor but rather one that, in a situation, helps us to make the right choices that will aid in right action and the right kind of life.

In our example, this might allow us to think of three deep rhetorical divisions: (1) the true, (2) the kairotic, (3) the illusory. The true is the world experienced from the deep rhetorical point of view, a view of the many ways that kairotic realities form themselves. This is one stage of a kind of Buddhist meditation, but it is not the fully "gone beyond" wisdom of the Prajnaparamita literature. The kairotic is the view from within some acknowledged reality but with an awareness of its transient and provisional character and of its real possibilities. This might be said to be the rhetor's point of view. The illusory is the view from within a kairotic reality but with no experience of or perspective on its being anything else but the way things really are. In fact, and here is where this distinction again becomes an ethical one, what is characterized as a life of illusion is also often characterized as a burden, a mistake, sin, a prison or slavery, a way of life that produces suffering, and a condition one maintains by one's own thought and action.

For all of their important differences, there is in the end common ground between the Prajnaparamita literature and a deep rhetoric. For each, the fundamental categories we use to comprehend the world, ourselves, and each other eventually fail. The categories are produced by human desire and interest operating in specific ways at specific times. They are useful or not in particular times and places for the desires and interests they serve. So, from the perspective of the Prajnaparamita literature, they are useful "on the way" to wisdom, but they are no longer useful once wisdom is attained, which requires a "going beyond." In fact, as wisdom is approached, they become an impediment. A deep rhetoric, too, witnesses the way basic categories are generated by human activity and thought in particular situations. For a deep rhetoric, too, these categories are understood not so much to reflect the ultimately true nature of the world as to be useful for resolving incompatibilities and for making useful choices. They contribute to logoi that can be examined and evaluated, logoi to which one can adhere in order to act in a way and toward an end that shows itself as good. However, they are good for this transcendence, this movement. Once again, as Emerson writes: "All symbols are fluxional; all language is vehicular and transitive, and is good, as ferries and horses are, for conveyance, not as farms and houses are, for homestead" (1987, 238). Rhetoric's "wisdom" lies in skillful, right action in the world of logos and reason and choice. Whether it can conduct one to an arrival at a "gone beyond" is a question that takes one beyond the range of rhetoric, which lies in logos and in its power to "lead the soul."

Hebrew Wisdom

A competing idea of wisdom comes from the ancient Hebrew tradition of wisdom, which developed out of a folk tradition of practical wisdom, out of a search for order in nature, out of reflection on the national and historical experiences of the Jewish people, and out of attempts to address questions of theodicy. One theological strand centers on the attempt to discover once again how the God of Genesis who created the world as an act of wisdom might continue to reach out benevolently to human beings. Again, I cannot pretend to give anything like a comprehensive or scholarly account of this tradition in this context. It is possible, however, to trace briefly the general outlines of some specific movements of thought. What is distinctive in the strand of thought I will treat here is, in the words of Nozomi Miura (2004, 138), that "the most prominent feature . . . is the personification of wisdom" in a human figure of wisdom, a woman. Some writers look back to Canaanite or Egyptian goddesses to explain this figure. Christian theologians—Jürgen Moltmann (1981), for example—often look forward to its development into the second person of the Trinity, especially in the logos of the prologue to John's gospel.

Miura types Hebraic wisdom conceptions into three forms. First is "hidden wisdom," inaccessible to human beings. The example here is Job 28:12, where we find the following passage: "Where shall wisdom [*hokmah*] be found? And where is the place of understanding [*binah*]? Mortals do not know the way to it, and it is not found in the land of the living." Second is "accessible wisdom," and here personified wisdom seems to plays its most important role, for example in Ben Sirach 24 and Proverbs 8, where wisdom, a woman, cries out at the crossroads and beside the gates at the entrance to the town: "Does not wisdom [*hokmah*] cry out and understanding [*tevunah*] put forth her voice?" (Prov. 8:1). The dominant form of accessible wisdom in this tradition is probably law or Torah itself (and this is everywhere the assumption in the midrash on Proverbs),[15] but the figure of wisdom and the law are alike in this respect of making wisdom accessible, of *communicating* it. Third is "apocalyptic wisdom," in which wisdom is hidden from the many but revealed to the few visionaries or members of an avant-garde, and here some primary texts are Baruch 3, Enoch , and the Similitudes. I want to focus on the female wisdom figure of Proverbs and Sirach because it is here that the personification strategy is essential to the result, and it is here that we will encounter moves that are formally similar to some moves made in the twentieth century in an emerging philosophical rhetoric.

The challenge a translator or interpreter faces with these passages is to understand the pairing of *hokmah*/wisdom with *tevunah*/understanding (or *binah*/understanding). The paired terms are conceptually distinct and yet somehow unified in considerations of wisdom and in the appearance of the wisdom figure. The Hebrew words have their own complicated and controversial histories and traditions of commentary.[16] However, it may be helpful here to follow the Septuagint Proverbs' reading to grasp at least a central problem. In the Septuagint Proverbs, the translation of Wisdom's chapter 8 speech is rather remarkable. *hokmah* is rendered by *sophia* and *tevunah* by *phronēsis*. The issue becomes something like the relation of theoretical wisdom to practical wisdom. Theoretical wisdom/*sophia* is usually taken to be necessary for more practical wisdom/*phronēsis*. Yet without practical wisdom/*phronēsis*, theoretical wisdom/*sophia* does not touch ground, so to speak. So *sophia* and *phronēsis* are distinct conceptually and yet unified in the *person* of wisdom. This also makes clear an important fact about the wisdom figure—her wisdom is for human beings; it is human wisdom. She may have been present at creation, and she may also be the wisdom of nature, but if you call on her, you may get some practical help in living a human life. She appears in human space and time, she has a human voice, and she reveals wisdom to human beings. Further, one can and should rely on her without reservation. This distinguishes Hebraic wisdom from Gnostic wisdom, in which Wisdom's descent is a fall. The arguments about the interpretation of wisdom have to do both with how divine she is and how much of a hypostasis she is, and these controversies arise at all because she is very evidently figured as a woman, a person.

It is difficult here not to be reminded of Lady Rhetorica, difficult not to be reminded of Vico's Ciceronian dictum that eloquence is nothing but wisdom speaking. And, in line with the *Eumenides*, the need for a transference of wisdom from the divine to the human is surely part of the story of the personification of wisdom as a way to make wisdom accessible to humans, a way to make wisdom speak. However, it is more than this, and it becomes clear if we keep the contrast between hidden wisdom and accessible wisdom in mind. G-d's wisdom is incomprehensible. Like the Buddhist nirvana, it is beyond category. To make this wisdom "human" requires not only a go-between—a Bodhisattva or a Moses or a Lady Wisdom—but also a transference of authority from the divine to the human and so a humanization of wisdom or, one could also say, an apotheosis of human communication. There is still another dimension to this. The humanization of wisdom is also a transformation of wisdom from divine intuitive knowledge of all nature to a discursive practical wisdom of human affairs. The gnosis of an absolute nirvana or an apocalyptic insight into divine intention stand in contrast to the discursive and practical and humanly specific wisdom of personified wisdom.

So the abstract conceptual contours are these. First, the wisdom of a wholly other G-d is incomprehensible, beyond category, inaccessible and useless for human beings. All human wisdom is thus negative, an acknowledgment that human wisdom is not wisdom at all. Even though such negative wisdom is useful for defeating theodicies and idolatries, it is also practically intolerable. Some kind of human wisdom is necessary for living life, and so a second idea of wisdom arises, linked not to a wholly other G-d but to a benevolent one who makes wisdom accessible. Making accessible means humanizing, in the law, or in the figure of Wisdom. However, any actually human, historically existing wisdom is less than divine wisdom and so vulnerable to criticism. This leads to third conceptions of wisdom that attempt to comprehend both of the first two—first, to what Burton Lee Mack (1973) calls *Die entschwundene Weisheit*, because although Wisdom comes to dwell among human beings, she is rejected by them, and so departs; and second to what Nozomi Miura calls apocalyptic wisdom, because although personified wisdom is rejected, a direct visionary experience of wisdom comes to be claimed by some. These visionaries claim to be able to criticize existing claims about wisdom on that basis, and also to be able to make wise judgments themselves.

In some respects, this repeats a formal pattern familiar from the discussion of the Prajnaparamita literature. On the one hand, we have the hidden, beyond-category-and-desire incomprehensibility of nirvana, and on the other we have the accessible Bodhisattvas who "descend," so to speak, to bring enlightenment and liberation to others. These are united in the Diamond Sutra, which can be summarized, once again, in the paradox: "The Bodhisattva with Wisdom strives to lead all beings to nirvana . . . and . . . there is no Bodhisattva, no Wisdom, no beings, no nirvana" (1976, 55). The Book of Job presents us with incomprehensible, hidden wisdom. At the ending of chapter 28, the only wisdom (ḥokmah) finally available to human beings is not wisdom in any conventional sense at all but rather the "fear of God," who alone is wise. Yet Proverbs 8 offers a Wisdom who stands at the high points in the city as a woman, and calls out, and offers to lead those who pass through the gates. There are significant differences in these wisdom literatures and in their conceptions of wisdom, but there are nevertheless also interesting formal similarities. We will have a chance to develop more of these later, in the sections on Kenneth Burke and Chaim Perelman.

It would perhaps be remiss simply to settle with Miura's typology and not raise the question of the place of *Ecclesiastes* in this framework. Although that profound book presents many challenges, it could prove helpful in this context to risk a few generalizations and see whether they shed any light.

The complications are, however, not trivial. In one respect, *Ecclesiastes* presents us with a clear example of accessible wisdom. This teacher is said in the opening narration to be the son or descendant of David, and he has historically been associated with Solomon. Within the book, we learn from the teacher that he has devoted himself to seeking wisdom: "And I gave my heart to seek and search out by wisdom concerning all things that are done under heaven. . . . I gave my heart to know wisdom" (1:13, 17). At the end of the book, the narrator comes to the explicit conclusion that the teacher is wise and has given wise words, and much of the book is taken up with what are supposed to be wise sayings. Thus, this does seem to be a case of personified wisdom, accessible both in the person of the teacher and in the proverbs that are a kind of folk law.

The difficulty with this reading is that, although the teacher pursues wisdom and praises it in several of the book's cycles, the teacher also confesses that he has failed in his pursuit: "I said, I will be wise; but it was far from me. That which is far off, and exceeding deep, who can find it out?" (7:23–24, see also 8:16–17). And so wisdom seems also to be inaccessible. The teacher further admits that, where he seems to have uncovered wisdom, it has failed to have any beneficial effect in life. In some of the book's most memorable lines: "I returned, and saw under the sun, that the race is not to the swift, nor the battle to the strong, neither yet bread to the wise, nor yet riches to men of understanding, nor yet favour to men of skill; but time and chance happeneth to them all" (9:11). Wisdom and the wise are not exempt from the great cycles of chapter 3 or from the travail or vexation or vanity that attend human life everywhere in the book. In fact, sometimes wisdom just produces more misery: "And I gave my heart to know wisdom, and to know madness and folly: I perceived that this also is vexation of spirit. For in much wisdom is much grief: and he that increaseth knowledge increaseth sorrow" (1:17–18).

These facts create the cycle or oscillation between wisdom and its other: an immersion in the pleasures and occupations of life, those matters which, from the standpoint of the seeker of wisdom, sometimes seem vain and vexatious and toilsome. Among them are: mirth, pleasure, wine, laughter, wealth, property, marriage, and getting dressed up. In part of the cycle, these seem to be the wise practice of ordinary life to which wisdom leads. Perhaps if the practice of ordinary life is tempered with the folk wisdom expressed in the teacher's proverbs, then it will be enough. And yet looming death, the persistent and widespread injustices of life, the fact that everyone undergoes the suffering associated with the travail and the vanity of it all—these all lead one to the dark mood of the first part of chapter 7, where the day of one's death is said to be better than the day of one's birth and where we learn that "the heart of the wise is in the house of mourning" (7:4).

So wisdom seems accessible, inaccessible, and then it also seems to disappear altogether, as if what we thought was wisdom turns out not to be wisdom at all, as if there is nothing called wisdom. *Ecclesiastes* seems to cycle through all three kinds of wisdom, taking "disappeared" wisdom as its third kind. Perhaps, then, this cycling is a fourth kind of wisdom. Perhaps the three kinds of wisdom are not something we ever sort out intellectually. Perhaps the fourth kind of wisdom is to live through all three kinds of wisdom and their interdependent inevitability. To everything there is a season. Perhaps, but then there is the final judgment of the narrator, who seems to have the responsibility of bringing this philosophical excursion to its religious finale: "Let us hear the conclusion of the whole matter: Fear God, and keep his commandments: for this is the whole duty of man" (12:13). Thus, some ultimate kind of wisdom is accessible after all. It would be interesting to be able to know the teacher's response.

Socratic Wisdom

Socratic wisdom is just as hard to delimit and grasp as these other conceptions of wisdom because Socratic wisdom is from the ground up paradoxical. Socratic wisdom has several characteristics. First is the paradoxical characteristic of ignorance. The oracle at Delphi has pronounced that there is none wiser than Socrates.[17] However, Socrates is profoundly aware of his own ignorance; he knows that he does not possess wisdom. So he sets out to question those who have a reputation for wisdom, and he discovers that, under questioning, those with the greatest reputations were not wise at all but in fact were the most deficient. He continued this questioning of many kinds of people, and discovered that his so-called wisdom lay only in his knowledge of his own ignorance. While others believed they were wise but were not, he alone knew that he did not possess wisdom. This negative wisdom is the human wisdom of Socrates.

However, "lacking" is not altogether negative for Socrates, for lack creates a striving toward what one lacks. This is the second feature of Socratic wisdom. Ignorance, an awareness of what one lacks, gives rise to eros, the desire for what is missing. The comportment toward unpossessed wisdom is to desire it, to love it, to seek it. The desire is not to possess it; possessing wisdom would quench the erotic longing for it. In Plato's *Lysis*, this erotic desire for the beautiful and the good is analogous to having a friendship with them. Similarly, in Socratic wisdom, the issue is a seeking for wisdom that takes the form of a desire to have a friendship with wisdom. Both friendship and philosophy require a lack, a desire for something more than one possesses and even more than can possibly be possessed. This means that the relation to wisdom is a practical one and not a matter of knowledge. It is a kind of life defined by the comportment toward wisdom rather than the application of a possessed knowledge to practical affairs. So, first, Socratic wisdom is ignorance. Second, Socratic wisdom is erotic, a striving longing and desire.

Third, Socrates' wisdom is also a kind of loyalty—more specifically, a kind of friendship with law. When one is aware that one is essentially a lack of wisdom, and confirms that it is the same with others, and that thus there is no true wisdom in human beings, and yet wisdom is what is required to lead a life and to make choices, then one must look elsewhere for guidance. One must somehow cultivate one's friendship with wisdom into something concrete. Unable to rely solely on oneself, or on the conflicting knowledges in one's world, one must somehow form a loyalty to something outside oneself, something with more concrete reality than longed-for wisdom.

Plato explores this need and the temptation to deny it in the dialogue, *Crito*. Socrates has cultivated a loyalty to philosophy, a keeping faith with longing and striving themselves—the longing and striving for something worthy of one's loyalty, for wisdom. He is characterized essentially by what Josiah Royce would call a "loyalty to loyalty" or what Augustine might call a "love of love" or what Heidegger calls a "seeking of seeking." This loyalty to philosophy has caused him to fall out of favor with the city, and he faces a death sentence. His friend Crito visits him in prison and urges him to escape. In his response to Crito, Socrates imagines that he is having a dialogue with the laws themselves and that the discussion has come down to a single question: ought one to keep one's agreements or not? The laws point out that Socrates has made an agreement with them, a fundamental agreement to live in conformity with them. They point out that they have given him his very life and that they have nurtured him and formed him—that he is himself, as a citizen of the polis, a creation of the laws. Most pointedly, they ask: what will become of our conversations about justice and virtue if you violate your agreements with us? (53c-54a). They taunt him with the question of whether he would find any other cities that would allow him freedom for philosophy, and whether he would trade philosophy for security.

The words used for all the variations of "agree" and "conform with" in these passages come from the verb *homologeō*. The word usually means simply "to agree" or "to consent to" or more literally "to speak the same." However, it also has a history of use in legal settings where it has the meanings of "to admit to something" or "to consent" to someone's testimony or statement. It has a similar use in Plato, where Socrates is constantly seeking "agreement" or "admissions" from his interlocutors as he takes them through an elenchus. However, there is an intensifying of the meaning in Plato because this "agreement" must be sincere; there is, as Gregory Vlastos puts it, a "say what you believe" expectation that Socrates makes explicit with his interlocutors. One must not just "say the same" but one must in some way *be* the same as one's speech. One must in *The New Rhetoric*'s terms "adhere" to the logoi, one must stick to them, keep faith with them, be loyal to them, make a commitment that is informed by them. As Socrates sometimes says, he is not interested in arguing simply "for the sake of." Rather what is being tested are the interlocutors themselves. For example, in the *Protagoras*, at 331c, Protagoras responds to Socrates' questioning this way: "What does it matter? . . . If you like, we can take it that justice is holy and holiness just." Socrates reports his reply: "Oh no I can't. . . . It isn't this 'if you like' or 'if you think so' I want to examine, but me and you." It is Protagoras and Socrates who are being tested, and it is Protagoras who is beginning to register what kind of "examination" this is.

The argument of the *Crito* suggests that it is this kind of radical "agreement," this kind of common loyalty to *logoi* that makes possible the conversation between law and philosophy about justice, and thus holds open the difference between law and justice. It is also just this "homologousness" that makes possible Socratic resistance to the actually existing temper of the Athenians. For it is his loyalty to, his being homologous with, certain speeches about justice and excellence that lead him to give his great speech of resistance in the *Apology*. Socrates has "consented" to being a citizen of the polis. He has entered into a mutual testing with the laws, who have reminded him of his previous "agreements" with them. His loyalty to philosophy, to the possibility of the difference between law and justice, the possibility of a challenging philosophical conversation between them, requires him to maintain a loyalty to the laws themselves. The bitter irony of course, heavily emphasized by Plato, is that the Athenian with the greatest loyalty to the city is judged by the actual Athenians to be its enemy.

Another way of understanding wisdom, then, is in terms of some kind of loyalty. It is Socrates' loyalty to certain passionate conversations about justice and good and excellence that gives concrete shape to his "philosophy" as a way of life and guides his choices. A loyalty to certain *logoi* gives order and a modest integrity to one's life, some of the things one might associate with wisdom. However, one is led to this loyalty to something beyond oneself by the fact of one's own insufficiency, one's self-acknowledged lack of wisdom, and one's erotic longing to befriend it. The Socratic crisis is: a life without loyalties would be no real life at all; a life without integrity would not be one's own life. The logoi with which we cast our lots give our lives form and direction and whatever weak Socratic integrity we may achieve. It is in terms of these logoi that we practice our friendship with wisdom.

A final characteristic of Socratic wisdom is Socratic character. It is formed by Socrates' awareness of his ignorance; his consequent desire to get into an appropriate relation to what he, on his own, must continue to lack; his commitment to philosophical discourse; and his loyalty to the form of life that is hospitable to philosophy. In Plato's Socratic dialogues,

Socrates is himself a personification not of possessive wisdom but of the closest thing to wisdom available to human beings: the love and striving for wisdom. However, there is a sense in which we find in Socrates not only a "personification" of wisdom but also a kind of incarnation or humanizing of wisdom. The gods alone are wise, but this means that they know only a possessive wisdom. Only a human being can live a life shaped by Socratic wisdom because that wisdom is ignorance, a not-possessing; it is eros, a lack, and so a striving and a desire; and it is loyalty, a lack of self-sufficiency, and a dependence on something outside of oneself. Socratic wisdom is not divine; it can show up only in human beings, with their lack and limitations.

———

There are some obvious similarities and differences in these traditions, and we will explore them further in the context of the late-twentieth-century conceptions of rhetorical wisdom by Kenneth Burke and Chaim Perelman. However, I would like to characterize one of them just briefly as a way of making a transition to the discussion of Burke. In each tradition, there are competing notions of wisdom. One kind of wisdom is the absolute or contemplative wisdom that belongs to gods or God alone, and the other is a human wisdom, more practical, but in an important sense not really wisdom at all. This is clearest in the cases of Socratic and Hebraic wisdom, but it can be seen in a slightly different form in the Diamond Sutra as well, in which there both is a wisdom that one can strive for, with the help of those who are wise, and there is not—because wisdom itself, and the idea that there are wise people, are just more categories motivated by desire and by the endless acquisitive energies of the mind. So one could with justice say that there is only comic wisdom, that the concept of wisdom fails because of essential human limitations, and that wisdom, in its diminutive, comic form, lies in this awareness of limitation and fallibility. As we will see, Burke, too, seems to working out this same recognition.

Burkean Wisdom

In "Four Master Tropes," the last appendix to *A Grammar of Motives* and a concluding précis of the work as a whole, Kenneth Burke broaches something like the issue of wisdom, of getting a knowledge of knowledge or getting a perspective of perspectives. The context is Burke's discussion of what he calls irony-dialectic equations. "Where ideas are in action," he says, "we have drama; where the agents are in ideation, we have dialectic" (1969a, 512). Ideas go into action in concrete forms as human agents, or as characters in a drama, and so dramatic conflict is a conflict of different ideas, different perspectives on reality, perspectives lived out by human beings, or characters in a drama. Ideas themselves can in turn be thought of as abstract or "logical" versions of the perspectives of human agents, and then these develop not in action but in dialectic, as a conflict of ideas, conflicting perspectives on reality. Burke's concern with the master tropes—here, specifically, with irony and its literal equivalent, dialectic—is with "their role in the discovery and the description of 'the truth'" (503).

One important thing to hold in mind here is that by irony Burke does not mean "saying one thing and meaning the opposite." His concern with irony is complicated, but there are two primary senses to the term here. First, he is concerned with dramatic irony—with the irony that occurs when the audience knows more than, and so has a truer understanding than, the characters in a drama. In such cases, the audience is not limited to the partial perspectives of a character, but instead has a superior perspective on the perspectives, and so is wiser than the character. A second, related meaning of irony is a little different. If one is to get perspective on any particular character or idea, then one must do so by taking each one "ironically" and not only on its own terms. To comprehend any particular character, one must comprehend it from the perspectives of all the other characters. To comprehend any single idea, one must do so in light of its interaction with all the other ideas. The challenge is to see the whole from all the perspectives, to achieve a knowledge of the different knowledges, to learn the truth about the different truths, to achieve wisdom.

The problem Burke faces is that there are always before us multiple perspectives in conflict with one another, whether formed by ideas or represented by characters. How does one come to the proper perspective on these perspectives? How does one achieve a unified, comprehensive understanding of these different standpoints on knowledge in a way that will allow one *to make choices between them* when choices become necessary? The problem is not easily addressed, or even formulated, says Burke, because three powerful intellectual temptations block the way.

The first temptation is relativism, generated by taking ideas out of their dialectical context and privileging or absolutizing one set of terms, one central idea or character, thus isolating that set and depriving it of

its "irony," its habitat in a larger context of interacting ideas and characters. However, as Burke says, the more one absolutizes an idea, the more
unqualified one's own attachment to it, the greater the relativism and
subjectivity. When the action of drama or the arguments in a dialogue
are understood from the perspective of one character or one interlocutor,
one has relativism and no irony. Relativism is, as Burke puts it, "seeing
everything in but one set of terms," and so, paradoxically, the greater the
non-ironic absolutism, the greater the relativism and partiality. The way
to begin to move beyond this is, for Burke, to lead the ideas into interaction, to use all the terms. This means releasing one's attachment and
seeing from more than one perspective.

A second temptation is literalism. Dramas and dialectics have representative characters and ideas that tend to stand for and shed light on
the whole development or the overall goal. However, if one takes this
representativeness too literally, then one ignores the essential relations of
interdependence between the representative character or idea and all the
others. If one literalizes the synecdochic representation, one misses completely *what it represents*. However, if one does not take the representativeness seriously enough, one fails to discover grounds for making choices
among competing perspectives. These "temptations" are not external to
the development itself.

A third temptation, and the most treacherous one, is an assumption of
superiority in which one stands securely outside the dialectic/drama with
the true perspective on the perspectives. This "outside" might always
be judged to be just another kind of relativism, one more instance of a
perspective being privileged and given the authority to be the perspective of all perspectives. However, the even subtler danger lies elsewhere
because, for Burke, wisdom is not simply a seeing, not simply a matter
of knowledge, but of an attitude and comportment *toward* knowledge. It
requires humility, a power similar to *sōphrosune* or self-restraint, and in
fact it is an intellectual virtue in the sense that it aims to allow things to
show up as what they are. It is a counterforce to relativism and literalism
and to the superiority that attends the achievement of the most common
forms of dramatic irony. As we will see in a moment, this superiority is a
deepening of the problem and not a solution. It will not purify conflict
of violence; it will do quite the opposite.

Interestingly, it turns out that all three of these obstacles require something analogous to the ethically formative reflection of Buddhist practice:
releasing one's attachment to one set of terms, cultivating self-restraint,
and experiencing some kind of interdependence of perspectives. Or we

could say that something like Socratic "ignorance" is called for, if we take "ignorance" as a nonattachment to a specific kind of knowledge and an a-gnostic attitude toward some knowledge of knowledge.

If one escapes these temptations, and achieves the proper humility, then other sorts of comportment toward knowledge become possible. Against the fall or corruption of being isolated in a particular perspective, Burke imagines counter-possibilities that might express the view of the whole. He imagines the whole as a noun and the many contributing perspectives as adjectives. His phrases "perspective of perspectives" and the "resultant certainty" of such a perspective are attached to this idea. He imagines, dramatistically, the same ideal as one in which we allow each character to comment on all the others so that no perspectives are lost or denied. He recommends this, too, as a way of writing history—that is, without its being a story of simple supersession and progress. This kind of wisdom is "ironic" in that all the terms interact; no perspective speaks alone, for itself. The development of each occurs in a mutual development.

Burke also imagines this as a turn to law and its procedures, at one point calling the development of the whole an "orderly parliamentary development" of the characters or ideas. Contrasting this alternative with the attitude of relativism, Burke writes:

But insofar as terms are . . . encouraged to participate in an orderly parliamentary development, the dialectic of this participation produces . . . a "resultant certainty" of a different quality, necessarily ironic, since it requires that all the sub-certainties be considered as neither true nor false, but contributory voices . . . necessary modifiers. . . . (1969a, 513)

As Burke says, "Irony, as approached through either drama or dialectic, moves us into the area of 'law' and 'justice'" (516). The movement to law as a concrete instance of wisdom is of course familiar both from the Hebraic wisdom tradition and from the history of rhetoric itself, though here Burke's emphasis is on a process—and so it is more like the act of legislating or interpreting law than it is like a code. The "justice" involved here also returns us to considerations of violence and peace.

In the sense just described, the orderly parliamentary development, and so wisdom, is also aesthetic and creative. There is the requirement of *integritas*—the participation of all the terms, all the sub-certainties, in the conceptualization of the whole; there is the requirement of *proportionality* that is met in the giving of each voice its due in the orderly parliamentary development; and this produces *claritas*, the revealing of something in the resultant certainty. Burkean wisdom meets Aquinas's three requirements for beauty. But then wisdom is already lovely and holy in the Heart Sutra and in Proverbs 8.[18] So we have here a number of formal convergences.

Burkean wisdom concerns not so much knowing how to choose among available alternatives, but rather experiencing a specific need for *new* alternatives, *new* characters, and *new* perspectives. This creativity thus provides another link to the Hebraic tradition's *ḥokmah*, as well as to the rhetorical tradition's *inventio*. However Burkean wisdom is not simply the power of creation but also the ability to discern just what needs to be created. Burke actually *uses* the word "wisdom" only once in this essay. It is quite an important use because it exposes the temptation of superiority that lies in any possible advent of wisdom and the conversion one must undergo in order to escape it. Just after Burke notes that the only superiority the observer of drama and dialectic might possess is to "feel the need of more characters than the particular foolish characters under consideration" (514), he points out, in a recognition moment, that the superiority is cancelled by the realization that these "foolish" characters are *necessary*—that the new one is needed *only in relation to them*, is a function of them. One might, as Burke says, feel the need of more characters, more ideas (and so, we suppose, invent and imagine them), but one also needs the characters at hand, in all their partiality and incompleteness and limited perspectives. They are part of the development that calls for more characters, and the new characters will, as needed, stand in need of them.

And then comes the reversal that is the price of wisdom: the foolish characters one witnesses are not external to oneself. One is not above them or superior to them. They are contained within oneself; they make up parts of one's own psyche and one's own practices, even in one's creation of new ideas, new characters. And then, if Burke has not knocked us out already, the punchline lands: "Folly and villainy are integral motives, necessary to wisdom or virtue" (515). Wisdom is not moral perfection. Without facing up to their own villainy, the wise would not realize that they contain the enemy within, nor that they are, in Burke's religious word, "consubstantial" with the enemy. Without this recognition, they would remain lost in their superiority, and so they would fail to arrive at the only human wisdom possible, not a superior wisdom but a humble one.

Though reversal is clearly the theme, there is something troubling about this appendix to Burke's *Grammar of Motives* because the book begins with *ad bellum purificandum* and yet the final appendix ends with a reference to the *lex talionis* and the necessity of *peripeteia* in drama and dialectic:

Irony, as approached through either drama or dialectic, moves us into the area of "law" and "justice" (the "necessity" or "inevitability" of the *lex talionis*). . . . There is a level of generalization at which predictions about "inevitable" developments in history are quite justified. We may state with confidence, for instance, that what arose in time must fall in time (hence that any given structure in society must "inevitably" perish. . . . The developments that led to the rise will, by the further course of their development, "inevitably" lead to the fall. . . . (1969a, 516–17)

So are the inevitable dialectical punishments and reversals the final word? If so, what is purified?

Some subtleties of Burkean wisdom lie here. First, in the notion of a representative character or idea in each situation. Art and politics and practical choices *force* this on us. Some ideas or characters must be representative of others. However, this can be asserted without literalism or superiority and with an eye out for the reversals one is thereby putting into play. What is purified or refined is the quality of our allegiance to the representative idea and to its dialectical interplay with competing ideas. When one knows that all of the ideas and characters have their truth, and that changes and reversals are necessary, then one's attachment to the representativeness of an idea or character is never absolute. Choices force adherence, but the adherence, good for a time, is always provisional. When conditions have changed so dramatically that the original good that was achieved by an allegiance is now not only no longer achieved, but actually defeated by the allegiance, then allegiances change, too. Any conception of a good to be achieved will have to be attenuated as well; the dynamic whole it attempts to bear in mind is always changing.

A second subtlety lies in the felt need for more characters that we have already discussed. This "more" represents a limited but no less persistent "gone beyond." In Burke's "Prologue in Heaven," God's wisdom is expressed in "The Lord's" consistent response to "Satan." "It's more complicated than that," the Lord keeps saying. Preventing the last word refines tragedy of its fatality, keeps open the possibility of the return of a dead character, allows for yet more recognition and change. This is comic purification. And Burke is an actual believer in this regard: "With a few more terms in his vocabulary of motives, . . . the rabid advocate of racial intolerance could become a mild one; and the mild one would not feel the need to be . . . intolerant at all. And so . . . war can be refined to the point where it would be much more peaceful than the conditions we . . . now call peace" (305). This convergence of wisdom and peace is not knowledge, but a skillful and humble practice of conflict, purified war, conducted as art and parliamentary process.

Burke's essay ends with a connection between this awareness of a need for new characters, the awareness that belongs to wisdom, and an attempt to decide what the future will hold. The truth of irony and dialectic is inevitable change and a consequent exposing of the insufficiency of any particular perspective. In art, this involves the creation of new forms of anticipation and fulfillment/nonfulfillment. In politics and history, change requires new laws and institutions and practices and modes of sociality, and there, too, change and creation will take the formal appearance of recognition and reversal. Deciding exactly what new characters and ideas are being called for at some particular time might seem to require taking the perspective of perspectives and trespassing onto the ground of a "superior" wisdom. However, rhetorical wisdom is, contra all gnosticisms, anticipatory. It looks toward an emerging future and toward forming that future in a way that will allow it to emerge and evolve more peacefully than the conditions we now call peace. All such anticipations of a future good are tenuous, "beyond being," but they are a necessary part of any coming to a choice, any taking over of responsibility for transcendence toward a good that will allow for reasoned choice. One of wisdom's challenges is to have the conviction of one's choices but tempered with the comic/humble attenuation of allegiance that follows from an awareness of one's own inevitable villainy.

Thus rhetorical wisdom demands a virtually impossible ethical posture, or at least a fundamentally unstable one. Because if you judge that you have achieved the humility and virtue and ethical power and creativity to consider all the perspectives and create the new needed ones, and you evaluate controversies on this basis, then you obviously don't have the requisite humility and so are not qualified to judge. This is surely one reason why Socrates professes ignorance and why his inner voice prevents him from getting involved in politics. This impossibility is represented, too, in the humility and powerlessness of Jesus, who, as that word/logos/wisdom, renounced power and met a Socratic end. Hebraic wisdom, too, is neglected, crying out in the streets, disinherited. Plato, too, insists that the only qualified rulers will be the ones who do not want to rule, who do not want to judge, who prefer questioning to deciding and self-control to political power.

Burke's paradox is an old and persistent one. All of these wisdom characters seem to have their roles postponed to some future, anticipated by the wise but never scheduled. We ordinary humans are condemned to choose on the basis of a wisdom we can neither achieve nor escape—and in the face of the violent actions of those who have none of the subtle scruples that afflict the wise. Burke's comic wisdom seems to leave us with the challenge of having attenuated attachments to specific characters and ideas and a more powerful conviction regarding our choices of just which new characters and ideas are needed at some specific time. In addition, it demands of us an even stronger commitment not simply to characters and ideas but to a process that leads the inevitable reversals through a transition of power that is conducted with peace and justice, and so mitigates suffering. It is difficult not to recall here (from the first chapter) Mieczysław Maneli's preference for a "weak" social philosophy over a strong one, and his characterization of the ideal new rhetorical political agents: "The new rhetoric may be the only philosophy that praises those who ruminate, hesitate, are reluctant, doubtful, but ultimately able to act prudently" (1994, 13). These new political activists "are more critical than ever before and at the same time more tolerant in their beliefs and cooperation" (139). One might say, with qualifications, that they are more concerned with how history is made than they are with making history; however, the first qualification would be that history cannot be distinguished from how it is made.

To conclude with a little comparativist knowledge: first, although wisdom is focused on tractable social conflict in the rhetorical tradition, in the Prajnaparamita Sutras it is focused on intractable conflict *intrinsic* to the human condition. However, in these sutras and in Burke, reflective practices generate ethical formation that addresses both kinds of conflict. Second, in both the sutras and in Burke, wisdom tends to tolerate contradiction. What is said of the Bodhisattva in the Diamond Sutra could certainly be said of Burke's representative character: there both is and is not an idea or character that sums up the development of the whole. And consider too Burke's law of reversal: "What goes forth as 'A' will return as 'non-A'" (1969a, 517). Yet, in the sutras, an awareness of contradictions and how they are produced leads to an awareness that goes beyond the dualities on which contradictions depend. For Burke, the conflicting ideas are instead put into play with each other in such a way that their conflict is purified of "war" and the outcome is a new kind of peace.

Third, all the considerations of wisdom exhibit not simply personification effects but patterned oscillation between the divine and the human, personification and apotheosis, explicit in Buddhist and Hebraic wisdom but just as evident in Burke's constant use of religious terminology—and not just in "consubstantiation" as a key concept. For in the *Grammar of Motives, the* Creation is *the* representative act, and creation here is the essential feature of the wisdom that leads to new characters and new ideas. Explaining the ways in which Creation and creation are formally similar and yet radically distinct here would require extensive commentary, but

I hope that pointing this out nevertheless provides a little perspective by incongruity.

Fourth, wisdom in each tradition, and in Burke as well, is essentially linked to virtue and is a convergence term for the virtues. Wisdom is identified with intelligence, beauty, humility, self-restraint, law, equity, justice, peace, and creativity. Fifth, and finally, wisdom seems implicitly at least to be the goal and purpose of scholarship and knowledge. Wisdom is the knowledge of knowledge and essentially a recognition of the powers and limitations of knowledge. It is a creative comportment toward whatever knowledge has already been gained. However, by transcending the limits of knowledge, it also seems to lose some of the power of knowledge, just at the point at which it seems to need it the most.

However, the aim here is not simply to identify the similarities and differences among these attitudes toward wisdom, but to shed some light on Burke's conception of wisdom by putting it into a different context, with different characters and ideas, and to begin to test its fitness to be inter-illuminating with them, and to be a plausible representative of rhetorical wisdom in that milieu.

New Rhetorical Wisdom

One way the problem of wisdom appears in Perelman and Olbrechts-Tyteca's *The New Rhetoric* is this: a speaker faces what is called a "composite audience," that is, an audience composed of many different particular audiences, each of which holds to beliefs and values that are different from those of the others. Arguments that are convincing for one of these audiences will not be convincing for some of the others and in fact might work negatively. What can a speaker do? This practical problem is an expression of the question of wisdom—the question of how to make judgments in the face of multiple perspectives, competing knowledges, and incompatible desires—and it is addressed in the construction of a "universal audience." A universal audience has the capability to make such judgments.

Universal audiences are constructed by following rules or procedures that express a conception of how a more universal reasonableness is achieved. Some of the rules mentioned in *The New Rhetoric* are: (1) set aside all the obviously particular and local and limiting features of an audience and so pay attention only to the more universal ones. (2) Exclude from the audience people who are obviously incompetent or prejudiced. (3) Add audiences together. Begin with the particular audience under consideration but add other individuals or groups to it to make it more universal. Add people from other places or even from other times—past or future. (4) Let other audiences criticize the universal audience one has constructed this way—especially allow the particular audience under consideration to criticize it.

The New Rhetoric offers many such rules, and the first thing a careful reader notices about these rules is that they do not form a system, and in fact may not even be consistent with one another. Yet Perelman and Olbrechts-Tyteca offer no framework for resolving the inconsistencies. There is no theory of the different situations to which the different rules might apply, and there is no hierarchy of rules. One must set aside traditional rationalist or gnostic conceptions of universality to grasp how subtle and radical the move to this rhetorical universality really is. Rhetorical universality has little to do with the a priori or the necessary or the absolute or the certain. The rules themselves do not create a universal audience ex nihilo but are applied to some particular audience that is under consideration. They are a modification of a concrete particular. The rhetorical universal is not an absolute universal but a pragmatic universal, the universal of a particular—a universal that holds effectively for the degree of universality required in an argumentative situation. In the situation of some "composite audiences," the degree of universalizing required to construct a satisfactory audience might be relatively modest. In international law or in moral theory or in philosophy, the demands of universality might be far-reaching. However, as *The New Rhetoric* says, in each case, we construct a universal audience using our own limited knowledge as a starting point: "Each individual, each culture, has thus its own conception of the universal audience" (*NR* 333). And: "The universal audience is no less than others a concrete audience, which changes with time" (491).

Further, the rules are not intended as practical instructions for achieving a concept of what is actually universal, as if the universal audience existed somewhere and had only to be discovered. They are intended to describe how people have successfully reasoned in the context of demands for universality. If there is a fact that causes wonder in *The New Rhetoric*, wonder that is the beginning of knowledge, it is that people actually have reached reasonable agreements through argumentation about such matters as ethics and human rights and international law and many other matters. They actually have employed conceptions of universality that have worked to hold violence at bay. They have also failed disastrously, and as Perelman consistently reminds us, this has led to violence, often on vast scales. *The New Rhetoric* is an attempt to explain what makes nonviolent human community possible when we have differences that cannot be resolved by appeals to absolute or objective truths.

Three features of the conception of wisdom embodied in a universal audience are especially important here. First, the wisdom of a universal audience is practical wisdom, a practical power to make reasonable choices and decide issues. Further, though, the wisdom of a universal audience is in part a function of the wisdom involved in constructing a universal audience. Constructing a universal audience itself requires reasoning and argument, and, like all argumentation, this is a matter of making choices. A universal audience is not an object of knowledge or calculation. One is not compelled or forced, logically or otherwise, in constructing a universal audience. One does work within the limits of a situation—the limits of the audience and the exigencies at play and one's own limits, as well—but within those limits, one must make a choice about how one universalizes, a choice connected with some good to be achieved. Yet the choice is never arbitrary. One can always give reasons for the choice, arguing that one has followed the appropriate rules and procedures for constructing a universal audience. This forward-looking choice, made within the limits of the situation, and supported with arguments, expresses some of the practical wisdom that becomes incarnate in the universal audience itself. However, the challenge of explaining how this wisdom succeeds takes on much greater complexity when we consider the other features of wisdom.

Second, wisdom is human—it is a feature of real or imagined people, and the ultimate appeal to wisdom is an appeal to these people. The universal audience is an audience of imagined human beings, not a system of principles or rules or a body of knowledge. As *The New Rhetoric* says, this audience is historical and concrete. It is an imagined audience, but it is an imagined human audience, one with a particular form of receptivity. These humans are not in some sense ultimate perfected humans. The *New Rhetoric* insists that "each speaker's universal audience can from an external point of view be regarded as a particular audience" (30). The degree of universality one achieves in creating a capable enough audience for the rhetorical conflicts one faces in relation to a particular situation can always be challenged by taking up a standpoint outside of that situation. Since all universal audiences are constructed from particular audiences, every universal audience is from some perspective also a particular audience. Consequently, there can be no ultimate universal audience. The human beings that make up that audience are likewise limited. They are, like all human beings, to some degree historically and culturally specific. They are, however, paragons in relation to the conflict under consideration—models of the reasonableness to which the parties in conflict aspire. The members of the universal audience are the citizens of a society to which we would like to belong.

To imagine this audience, to conceive this wisdom, we must ourselves not only have a knowledge of it, but in some important respects we must also have achieved a kind of membership in it because we identify with its judgments, and we recognize them, at least with due reflection and perhaps with occasional surprise, as the judgments we would approve of ourselves. Perelman explains the humanity of wisdom by describing the person who has the capability to construct a universal audience. In his Genoa lectures on justice (1967), Perelman focuses on this incarnation of wisdom in the figure of the philosopher. The philosopher is not representative in the procedural sense that an elected or appointed legislator achieves representativeness. Neither is the philosopher representative in a way that could be empirically verified. In fact, the philosopher is not representative of any identifiable group at all. To capture the philosopher's role in wisdom and universality, Perelman quotes Husserl, who says that "philosophers are the civil servants of humanity."[19]

Perelman directly confronts the basic objection to incarnate wisdom, that the universality required of philosophy and the individuality of the philosopher cannot be reconciled. He calls the assumed dichotomy of individual and universal "chimerical." Any time an individual formulates a principle of action, he says, the purely arbitrary and subjective are overruled, and the possibility emerges of the principle's being accepted by other people (1967, 77). And no universal practical principle is ever a priori beyond objection—that is not the nature of any real universality that has ever been achieved. Instead, says Perelman, one finds a "progressive universalization" of principles that are locally generated and a gradual emergence of effective conceptions of universality.[20] So Perelman's philosopher is content neither with formal universality nor with local ethics and local law. Instead, the philosopher *formulates* and *proposes* potentially universal principles, an ideal of universality, and offers arguments in support of them.

How do we judge these proposals? They cannot be judged according to existing practices and principles because they are supposed to go beyond them, and as Perelman says, "furnish criteria for evaluating and judging experience and, if necessary, disqualifying certain aspects of it" (1967, 79). They cannot be judged purely logically because they are reached through defeasible natural language argumentation about substantive matters and do not pretend to certainty or formal universality. The philosopher has considered all the relevant opposing points of view, developed arguments out of precedents, and yet ultimately a choice must be made. None of the arguments are absolutely compelling. There is no philosophy of this kind without agency, and yet the philosopher does not have and does not appeal to any special faculty or knowledge in this regard. Instead, the appeal is to a universal audience, the final judge. When we ourselves judge this appeal, we are not judging a claim against a reality. We are judging, in part, an aspiration, a hope for universality, an act of philosophical freedom.

At this level of philosophical action, says Perelman, the philosopher is not simply reporting on a reality or on a belief about reality but is *making a commitment* to a hoped-for reality. "The philosopher who judges commits himself," he says, and then he adds: "in judging a philosophy we are also judging the man who is identified with it" (1967, 85). We are judging the aspirations of a person. It is to be expected that the proposals of any person will fail to some degree and especially over time. If we are successful in inheriting these preceding conceptions of universality in a process of "progressive universalization," we will continue these philosophical aspirations of specific individuals for, as Perelman explains it, "more rationality and justice, and less violence" (86).

Perelman's point is not that we must ultimately judge philosophical arguments on the basis of the philosopher's personal life or politics or any other biographical fact. He knows that human beings do not always follow through on their commitments. He knows, as the rest of us do, that a specific person can be practically wise about overcoming conflicts in some particular domain but ignorant and foolish about choices in some other domain. It is not very difficult to find examples of this, especially among philosophers. However, these kinds of considerations will be to some degree involved in the judgment. Philosophical/practical wisdom is located in individual human beings. It is connected with the individual limitations and possibilities and in general the form of life out of which it is formulated and proposed. This is why it can be substantive and not merely formal. If the substance of that form of life is too distant from the substantial conflicts of one's own society, then it is impossible to identify with that philosopher's aspirations. Whatever universality could be achieved would not be a relevant universality.

The philosopher is proposing a future, a form of life that will follow from adopting the new principle. She is proposing that we follow her into that form of life. She offers arguments for directing ourselves into that future, but none of them are compelling. We will make our choice based on those arguments, but it will still require an act of freedom to make our commitment. Some people are philosophical themselves, have the requisite knowledge and ability, can repeat for themselves the reasoning of the philosopher, and make a choice independently. However, Perelman seems to believe that for most people the philosopher serves as a model, a leader. He seems to believe that our judgment about the philosopher's commitment to a hoped-for future is connected with our judgment about the philosopher herself. We could say that the strength of the philosopher's logos is interdependent with the strength of the philosopher's ethos. Neither can meet the challenge of wisdom alone.

In any case, there are finally no criteria that can decide the questions that give rise to the demand for wisdom. Only a person can make the choice and the commitment involved. Wisdom takes a human form.

Third, wisdom is creative. A universal audience is the result of an act of imagination and not the product of a calculation or a generalization from empirical facts. There is an illuminating moment of this kind of creativity in Perelman's Genoa lectures on justice. He is facing the problem of a legally ordered political society and asking, first, whether the essential conflicts within that society are ultimately settled by law or whether there can be a continuing argument with the law—and, second, whether there is an alternative to violence when conflicting legal communities come into conflict. Perelman insists that positive law cannot be the final authority. He rejects the positivist answer because, he says, it is essentially violent. The political process operates within a framework of the specific facts and values accepted by a particular political community, or by its most powerful factions, and, within that process, those cannot be effectively questioned. To take them as the last word is, for Perelman, to abolish the argument between justice and the laws, to give up the project of universality—and to give this up is, for Perelman, tantamount to succumbing to violence. And yet there is no rational procedure, no process of formalization, that can yield universality. The work is an act of imagination and of *proposing* conceptions of universality. This wisdom is creative. However, it is not gnostic or mystical, and it is not absolute or unconditioned. Instead, it can be expressed and supported in language, and it is defeasible and corrigible. As Perelman says: "It will be for others who come after . . . to continue the efforts" (1967, 86).

We have already broached this in the discussion of wisdom as a form of incarnate human agency that proposes something new. However, this creative aspect of wisdom, familiar from ancient Hebraic wisdom, raises concerns about whether the question of wisdom has been fully addressed. There is no question that Perelman believes that wisdom is creative—and in a radical way. For his claim is that reality is not a simple empirical or even a metaphysical notion but is a normative idea with a rhetorical origin. The creation of an experience of reality as such, to which wisdom is connected, is a rhetorical and ethical event. Let's follow Perelman carefully here:

> Assertions that represent the systematic formulation of an ideal cannot be judged the way we judge factual judgments. Their role is not to conform to experience, but to furnish criteria for evaluating and judging experience, and, if necessary, for disqualifying certain aspects of it. This is exactly what a philosopher does who opposes reality to appearance through the establishment of a hierarchy of values among the diverse manifestations of reality. (1967, 79)

This is the new rhetoric going deep. Here Perelman employs the new rhetorical phenomenon of dissociation to clarify the creative role of rhetoric in generating conceptions of reality as such. Put briefly, according to *The New Rhetoric*, a concept of reality emerges like this.[21] We begin with experience in which appearances and reality have not yet been distinguished. However, experience includes incompatible appearances. Water appears in the distance, but as one approaches the water disappears. The stick is straight in air but bent in the water. It becomes very helpful on a practical level to distinguish between reliable appearances and unreliable appearances. This is dissociation, in which one undifferentiated phenomenon breaks into two distinct kinds. The philosopher formulates a systematic dissociation, in which reliable appearances coincide with reality and unreliable appearances with illusion. The dissociation generates reality, on the one hand, and appearance on the other. This concept of reality is, as Perelman says, normative. There are criteria associated with it, although these criteria are not agreed on among philosophers and they change in the history of philosophy. Without dissociation, there is no concept of reality and thus no experience of reality as such.

But note that an experience of reality in this sense is not only generated rhetorically, it is also dependent on the practical interests we have. It is useful for us—perhaps vital for us—to distinguish between appearance and reality in a highly developed and systematic way. Notice, too, that since this is, first of all, a practical project with practical aims, it is also guided by a purpose to be achieved. It is not purely theoretical. We dissociate in order to be successful in our actions, to predict and control outcomes. Prediction and control are criteria for testing claims about reality that are still very difficult to discharge even as conceptions of reality appear to become more theoretical and less practically oriented.

Perelman does not hesitate to draw deep rhetorical conclusions here:

Philosophers who have refused to recognize this primacy of practical reason have often exposed themselves to the criticism of the positivist by presenting ontologies and theories of being as if they were on the same level as scientific theories of reality. But reality as conceived by philosophers is always normative, for it aims at the devaluation of those manifestations of reality that are qualified as appearance or illusion. This is true as well of the positivists, for their conception of reality validates that of the natural sciences and dismisses all other approaches to reality as mythical or illusory. (1967, 79–80)

We have already established that for Perelman knowledge has to be completed by wisdom that is practical and specifically human. Now we see that something like this practical wisdom has a primacy over knowledge. Practical reason has primacy over scientific theories of reality and over philosophical ontologies that aim to be strictly theoretical. Philosophy and science as theoretical enterprises are *derived from* practical wisdom.

It is hard here not to be reminded of the title of Husserl's 1911 *Philosophy as Strict Science* and of Heidegger's move toward a more practically oriented conception of phenomenology in the analysis not of Dasein's consciousness but of its (more practical) existence and also of Levinas's full turn toward the primacy of ethics over ontology. Perelman is certainly writing out of the same milieu, but he has concentrated his attention on the way ontologies arise not simply from ethics in general but from reasoning that is from the ground up practical and so ethically specific from the start. For Perelman, rhetoric is the source of the intelligibility in terms of which philosophy and science build their conceptions of reality. Rhetorical wisdom is creative.

So Perelman's rhetorical wisdom is practical, it is human and finite, and it is creative. However, this creativity reaches into domains that make it very hard to track and that touch the limits of reason. We can follow rhetorical wisdom into these domains through the door of one of *The New Rhetoric*'s least mentioned but most important ideas—the idea of the undefined universal audience.

First, though, let us review. The question of wisdom arises because knowledge is insufficient. In *The New Rhetoric*, one faces a composite audience, a part of which accepts one set of facts, theories, and values, and a part of which accepts a different and apparently incompatible set. In order to invent arguments that will address this audience as a whole, one imagines yet another audience constructed from them, a more universal and paragon audience. Yet how does one know that the techniques by which one constructs this audience are the appropriate and legitimate techniques? This is especially a problem in philosophical argumentation, but it can be a continuing controversy in many practical conflicts, too. We know that there is no ultimate answer because any universal audience can, from an external perspective, appear as a particular audience. There is no ultimate audience and there is no ultimate solution—no direct intuition of truth and no certain, absolutely compelling arguments. So what is the decisive source of wisdom here? *The New Rhetoric* offers the following answer:

> It is the undefined universal audience that is invoked to pass judgment on what is the concept of the universal audience appropriate to . . . a concrete audience, to examine . . . the manner in which it was composed, which are the individuals who comprise it, according to the adopted criterion, and whether this criterion is legitimate. (*NR* 35)

So it is yet another audience, another instantiation of wisdom in human form, that judges our constructions of universal audiences. And yet this new, undefined universal audience is not directly or consciously constructed by us. It is not capable of being grasped or made because it remains undefined, in some important respect unknown.

However, it is not completely unknown. In setting out from a particular audience toward a universal audience, one establishes a direction. When one hears a new argument for a new practical principle proposed by a philosopher, and one recognizes it as a strong one, one does not always know that a new conception of universality has been expressed, or a new universal audience addressed, but one nevertheless recognizes the strength of the argument. One continues moving in a direction, toward something, some form of life in which the universality being progressively developed is realized concretely. One has an implicit sense of the rightness of the argument because one recognizes this direction. We are sometimes convinced by arguments without knowing explicitly what the criteria for judgment should be because this implicit skill at judgment is pointed in a practical direction in a particular case. And so we come again to one of the constants in discussions of wisdom. When knowledge for some reason comes to its limit, a practical virtue or disposition or skill completes the task of judgment.

Yet even this is more than *The New Rhetoric* gives us concerning this undefined audience. I have tried to interpret its brief remarks by speaking of virtues and dispositions, and although this is not entirely wrong, it could be misleading. Perelman and Olbrechts-Tyteca would certainly deny that this appeal to an undefined audience is an appeal to a faculty of any kind. What is leading us is an implicit awareness that is active in practical dispositions and virtues but is not for that reason necessarily authoritative. Our practical judgments of this sort can always be challenged. What is most important here is that the implicitly understood undefined universal audience is still an audience, a form of receptivity, fully human and fallible. As rhetorical receptivity, it is not simply a passive judge but also a form of rational agency, acting on us—drawing us forward, as if from outside of us. It is one more human embodiment of creative wisdom that projects a form of life.

A number of themes familiar throughout this chapter arise again here in Perelman's encounter with the question of wisdom. Beyond the three perspectives on wisdom provided by the notion of a universal audience, there is also the relation of wisdom and law. Hebraic wisdom becomes concrete and available in the Law. For Burke, parliamentary process is an image of the process of wisdom. For Socrates, too, some kind of loyalty to and identification with the laws is a feature of wisdom. It is difficult not to think here also of Giambattista Vico, who is well known for identifying wisdom with eloquence, which in turn is defined as the rhetorical capability of a culture to hold itself together in laws and civil institutions through what Vico called civil prudence. Mieczysław Maneli's positivism, discussed in chapter 1, is another example of a strong identification of wisdom with law. However, Perelman, a legal scholar and theorist, believes that, for positivism, law relies ultimately on force, and this cannot be for him a final justification of law. It may be a *cause* of law, but it cannot justify it.

Instead, Perelman aligns himself with the traditional conception of wisdom as incarnate—not wholly other and divine, and not simply expressed in positive law, but the wisdom of the human beings we would like to be, or at least of those we would approve of as judges. Law itself holds the authority of precedent, but it is never finished, and it is not self-justifying. Justice and justification depend on argumentation before a human audience. And yet, as we have seen, argumentation can accomplish this justification because it does so according to a just process and before an audience that is partly defined by its concern for justice. This audience is wisdom incarnate, though it is changeable and fallible wisdom.

Another pervasive theme is the idea of the rhetorical formation of character that develops a practical wisdom. This was treated most extensively in connection with Buddhism and rhetoric above; however, the notion that rhetoric carries an educational ideal has been evident from its origin through its entire history. In this book, it has perhaps been most notable in the discussions of rhetorical capabilities. It is important to stress this notion of rhetorical formation because the acknowledgment that argumentation requires, beyond all reasoning, a commitment to a specific future may appear to be a claim that we make reasonable choices *ultimately* on the basis of fundamental commitments. But this would be to throw things out of balance.

For Perelman, wisdom is not reducible simply to commitments. We make decisions out of everything we have become—our dispositions and habits of perception and capacity to reflect and be self-critical—all the deep skills we use to think and feel, skills we use to achieve whatever consciousness we have, and skills that make possible whatever transcendence we can manage, because wisdom includes a receptiveness to what is beyond us, beyond what we rationally control. Wisdom requires the temperance explored and exemplified, mostly in its absence, in Plato's *Gorgias*. It requires humility—the openness to discovering one's limitations and errors and a willingness to learn and change. It requires a kind of whole-hearted and passionate caring that can sustain one through the intellectual and psychological and social and sometimes political difficulties involved when no agreed-upon knowledge can help to mitigate a serious conflict. Quite simply, it requires all the capabilities necessary for a contact of minds and for the conduct of argumentation in conditions of justice. It also requires, *along with* these capabilities, casting our lot with some good and some form of life, identifying ourselves with something specific, at least provisionally.

Finally, for all of their significant differences, there is also a kind of agreement between Perelman and Burke here, and the agreement is about the necessity of reconciling apparent incompatibilities as part of the pursuit of wisdom. A choice is required, but the attachment is provisional, attenuated, purified of grasping and fanaticism and dogmatism. One continues in a seeking, following a kind of *via negativa*. And one's true attachment is to be faithful to the seeking, to the acknowledgment that what is sought cannot be finally possessed. Instead, one hopes, if anything, to continue to be drawn by it, not to lose one's way in the shiny attractions of the prevalence of beings—or characters or ideas or faculties or principles.

And although we identify with the philosopher as a seeker and not primarily a writer or speechmaker, there is yet no contempt for logos here, no escape from logoi. On the contrary, we are creatures of choice who must take responsibility for one another, for ourselves, and for our world through logoi. We live in logoi, and our choices are made in logoi. They are all, like our lives themselves, temporary, provisional, subject to review. We identify with the philosopher in her practical reconciliation of *both* the persevering seeking and the formulation of a logos by which to steer.

The capabilities required here are complex and present paradoxical challenges. Commitment and detachment. Choice and persevering seeking. To make choices is to participate, and to attenuate attachment is still to participate; both are required. So are these: to be grateful, to receive what is given, but still to long for a not-yet, and to give this dissatisfaction the shape, the logos, of a choice. The point is not to draw back from the incompatibilities but to endure them, and so to resolve them not simply in thought but in practice, in life, in time. This is the task of the only wisdom to which human beings can aspire. In a consideration of the challenge of imagining an audience that is sufficiently universal, and after an explicit recognition that whatever audience we imagine will be in some respects insufficient, that wisdom is not attainable, Perelman and Olbrechts-Tyteca come to a radical assertion of the ethical substrate of rhetorical wisdom:

Our effort and our good will in this regard are the only elements of rationality that we can grasp. (2010, 334)

Athena's Practical Wisdom

We return now to Athena. We left her after she had instituted a jury for resolving the dispute between Orestes and the Furies—an institution that would endure through time. She had also established rules for juridical rhetoric and procedure. Yet the jury had split six to six. Athena resolves the impasse she faces by deciding for Orestes—apparently in her divinely unconscious gender-based way, and yet perhaps not. Orestes declares his allegiance to Athens. The Furies declare their anger, threaten destruction, and portray the trial once again as a struggle between the older and the younger divinities.

The next part of the drama, following the failure of rhetorical logos to find wisdom in the juridical context, delivers the final manifestation of Athenian wisdom, not in the arguments of the speakers in a juridical setting but in the persuasive speech of Athena, as she walks the Furies into a conversion, into an acceptance of the outcome, and into a new self-understanding. In these passages, Athena's speech is not "logical" but "glossal." She appeals explicitly to the goddess Peithō (Persuasion) as she makes her case. And it is not especially easy. In the drama, she has six speeches of five lines or more before her judgment; she has eleven after the judgment, most of them persuasive speeches aimed at the Furies. It is easier to found a court system and judicial rhetoric than it is to appease angry gods. After Athena's judgment, the first four speeches of the Furies are all angry laments and threats.

In her first counter-speech to them, Athena explains that the ballot was fair and that the gods had ordered Orestes to take his action. She also promises the Furies a new role, under ground, beside a hearth, respected and honored by citizens, and she urges them to give up their anger and threats. In her second counter-speech, she takes the role of the awe-inspiring herself, and reminds them that she has Zeus on her side and knows where his thunderbolts are hidden. She assures them that the old order is not completely abolished and that they will, if they give up their anger, live with her and win the first fruits in offerings for children and marriage rites. That is, they will play central divine roles in the female concerns of hearth and marriage and children. Then you will say, she predicts to them, that my argument (*logon*) was good. Note that it is only *later* that they will say this. The grounds for judging are not yet available. They are being urged to help realize an order in which the grounds will become available.

In Athena's third counter-speech, she acknowledges that the Furies are older than she is, and she even says that they are more practically skillful. But she also claims that Zeus has given her practical wisdom. She makes a kind of causal argument herself: if they go away, they will regret it, because Athens will flourish and realize a peaceful future from which they would benefit, and she urges them again not to do harm to this future. In her fourth and culminating speech, she says that she will never cease telling these stories of the good things that will come to them so that they will never be able to say that elder gods were driven away by young Athena and by the citizens of Athens. At this point she says, "If you are filled with holy reverence for the goddess Persuasion, and with the soothing enchantments of my voice, then I hope that you are staying here with us" (885–87).

At this point, in response to persuasion and enchantment, the Furies become reasonable and begin to negotiate for place, power, and honor, and they give four speeches of blessing on Athens, the final one putting an end to blood revenge. In the end, even the Furies seem to be won over to a kind of wisdom, although it is still a question for Athena: "Are they taking thought to discover the road where speech goes straight?"

(988–89). Are they becoming practically wise? she asks. In any case, they go underground to bless Athens, and living, mortal women sing their praise in a processional as the play ends.

Just before the fourth, culminating blessing, the one that ends blood revenge, Athena sings her praise of Persuasion: "I love the eyes of Persuasion, who kept watch over my mouth and tongue when I spoke to these wild, refusing ones. But mighty Zeus watches over human assemblies, and good prevails in the contest" (970–75).

Athena/wisdom seems to have three forms of divine power in the drama: (1) She can create the possibility of rhetoric as forensic rhetoric and of rhetoric as a kind of wisdom itself by instituting a court and jury. (2) If this court and jury fail, as they do, then she can make a divine, sovereign judgment—on grounds that are not the ones that mortals would on their own acknowledge as relevant. (3) After that divinely sovereign decision, she can redress the damage done to the aggrieved who have lost the case, and she can do this not with a rhetoric appropriate to a court or an assembly but with a magical rhetoric of calming and soothing and with negotiation and divine payments.

This latter point is essential. It is one thing to pronounce a sovereign judgment when a jury splits. It is another matter entirely to persuade the losing (divine) party not to take revenge for its loss but instead to accept its new role and to perform its duties conscientiously—in fact, to feel honored in their performance. The Furies are obviously losing their place and power in public, political life. What will they receive in compensation? This is, on the one hand, a practical political matter. The Furies can make a mess of the city and force Athena to take violent action against them. Athena acts to prevent this outcome. However, this is also a matter of a justice beyond justice. If all practical wisdom and all justice is fallible, and if choices often require, at least to some degree, "winners" and "losers," as in a trial, then a more complete justice will have to work, by some other means, to redress the hurt or damage done to the losing party. This is partly a matter of preventing revenge or noncooperation, but it is also an acknowledgment of the imperfection of the wisdom expressed in a system of justice and an acknowledgment, too, of the imperfection of the justice of rhetorical argumentation.

And so Athena makes use of a different kind of rhetoric, a rhetoric of persuasion, not human but "divine" and so imbued with the power to placate the divinities who feel diminished by the outcome of the trial. Athena allies herself with Peithō, and resorts to divine persuasion, which includes threats and promises as well as negotiation and payments of honor and ritual and a ceremonial place in the life of the city. In the end, Athena's most powerful persuasion seems to rest in the picture she paints of a future Athens, one in which the Furies have a place of honor, secured in sacred rituals regarding marriage, home, and family. The Furies are finally persuaded by these images of secure divine roles and of a reverent city. Peithō, a "divine" power, is necessary for redressing the injustice that attends justice. This holy persuasion addresses what simple argumentation and reasoned judgment cannot—the diminishment of the losing party—and is a way of continuing the aspiration for justice with the proper humility.

The drama leaves us with many questions, as great dramas do. However, it also leaves us with a fairly clear judgment on rhetorical wisdom. Human reason that proceeds by way of argumentation cannot succeed autonomously. Athena's hope in rhetoric as justice founders when the divine impasse is simply encountered once more as a human, rhetorical impasse. So there is sovereign intervention. However, Athena cannot herself deliberate in a way that is based on reasons available to human beings, and she cannot achieve a perspective that puts the other perspectives into perspective—though she can effect a mythical/historical shift of political authority. This is why mortals must succeed, why they must develop the rhetorical capabilities that make effective reasoning about conflicts possible, as well as the rhetorical capabilities to speak to those who suffer losses.

After Athena

A final theme to be noted here, and we have come across it many times, is that wisdom refuses to be theorized, refuses to make itself comprehensible. Wisdom is an unstable concept, as difficult to control as the thing itself. Every conception of a sufficient wisdom turns out to be insufficient. In the Diamond Sutra, the truth of wisdom is that there both is and is not something called "wisdom." In the Hebraic tradition, wisdom is wholly other, and so inconceivable; incarnate in a wisdom figure or in law, and so fallible and susceptible to conflicts of interpretation and to rejection; and finally either "disappeared" or known directly only by a privileged faction. For Burke, wisdom is not a perfection at all. Rather, it is a defeat of the notion that one could ever achieve a superior perspective on human conflict, and it is a recognition of one's own partiality and "villainy." It is thus the practice of a special kind of humility. This feeling of an instability in the idea of wisdom, of its being in some sense incomprehensible and unachievable, takes us back again to Socratic ignorance and to the *Phaedrus*.

In a wonderful conclusion to his final speech of the dialogue at 278b-d, Socrates tells Phaedrus to go and tell Lysias that they "came down to the fountain and sacred place of the nymphs," where they were given words to repeat to anyone who writes at all—whether speeches, or poetry, or laws. The judgment is this: writing and speeches are not "serious." They are ruled by an element of play. They are not the proper object of one's deepest earnestness and investment. However if one can, by means of an experience of truth, support in a discussion what one has put into writing, thereby demonstrating an awareness of the insufficiency of writing, then one should not be called simply a speechwriter or poet or lawgiver. One should not take one's name from one's writings, but from, and we have come across this already in chapter 7, "the serious pursuit which underlies them."

Phaedrus: What titles do you grant them then?
Socrates: I think, Phaedrus, that the epithet "wise" is too great and befits God alone; but the name "philosopher," that is, "lover of wisdom," or something of the sort would be more fitting and modest for such a man.

The others, the ones whose goals are more evidently achievable kinds of knowledge-wisdom, the ones who take writing "seriously," but not necessarily the pursuit underlying it, can be called poets, speechwriters, writers of laws, and so on.

And so we come again to the notion that it is the pursuit itself, so frequently eclipsed by what is apparently pursued, that is in some sense the elusive goal. Deep rhetoric seems to converge with this thread in philosophy that conceives the *searching* for wisdom as the "good" toward which we aim. If wisdom is unattainable, the proper comportment toward it may not be. The hope or aspiration itself becomes the goal. As we have seen, for Perelman (1967, 82), the universal audience toward which we look is an audience with aspirations; we aspire to aspire the way it does. We seek that seeking. This seeking of seeking is a participation in the "authentic" transcendence of the philosopher explored in chapter 6, the transcendence that perseveres in seeking. Once again, this transcendence is supported by "dialogue," by moving through logoi, whether in actual dialogue or inner speech or whatever shape logoi are taking; seeking has the form of logos and is a way of participating in logos.

I said a moment ago that the seeking itself becomes the goal; however, as Heidegger pointed out, "goal" may no longer be the appropriate way to name this. Goals tend to be things that can be comprehended and incorporated into a strategy. They are part of a regime of beings we aim to master through knowledge, through control of actions and prediction of their consequences. They are almost by definition achievable. The reversal at play with wisdom and philosophy undoes this conception of a goal. Perhaps this is best figured a little more concretely—say, in Augustine's experiences of trying to seek G-d. The *Confessions* are built on the paradoxes of "seeking" G-d, and the eventual recognition and reversal moments occur when Augustine becomes aware, again and again, that G-d is not an object susceptible to being contained by the mind but instead is "teaching and guiding" in the very process of the seeking, closer, as Augustine says, than he is to himself. The aim becomes to stay in the seeking that is formed by the teaching and guiding. G-d is seeking Augustine in the very seeking with which Augustine seeks G-d, but Augustine is, as he catalogues brilliantly in the *Confessions*, bewitched by the sparkling prevailing of beings.

The religious example suggests still one more perspective here, this time on a different notion of transcendence. In this book, I have emphasized the humanism of rhetoric. However, I have been careful not to develop what Charles Taylor (2007) calls an "exclusive humanism" that takes a dogmatic stand on religious questions—specifically, that human flourishing is the ultimate purpose of human life *and* that such flourishing is essentially unconnected with and perhaps even defeated by a notion of something that transcends human life, such as G-d or a moral order in nature. A deep rhetoric could be developed along the lines of an exclusive humanism, even a thoroughly atheistic humanism, but it could also be developed along the lines of religious thinking that extends its concerns to "communication" with something that is transcendent in the religious sense. The transcendence with which I have been concerned here is the transcendence that human beings are, that is, their being essentially toward something—toward others, toward the world, toward their own next selves. To understand human beings, one cannot simply study them as objects. One must look at the ways in which their being takes place "outside" of them, in a meaningful social world, in their directing themselves "outward" and finding their being in terms of the meaningfulness of the world.

And yet this Heideggerian notion of "world" can also be restricting because transcendence in this sense seems to be limited to the beings of a specific historical culture and to the background but still historical and finite event of "being" that allows beings to come to presence the way they do. This background event may not be conceptualizable as just another being, and so it may transcend beings in some way, but it is limited to their history and to human history. The Heideggerian seeking of seeking is essentially a search for a way of comporting oneself toward being. However, this kind of reversal, as we have seen with the example of Augustine, has religious potential as well. If it is possible to overcome the ontic gravity of transcendence, and direct oneself toward transcendence itself, then questions can arise about whether it is possible to "encounter" what is not a being—whether this is "being" or the Levinasian other, or whether one moves into explicitly religious considerations. At that point, deep rhetoric would take a different turn and develop itself in relation to this further kind of transcendence and its communicative dimensions. In some limited respects, we have already engaged in preliminary considerations of the Heideggerian and Levinasian moves, although not of any explicitly religious moves, except to show their formal similarities to certain concerns of a deep rhetoric.

One concern I have regards the question of this relation between deep rhetoric and specifically religious or avowedly nonreligious attitudes. In this book, I have been concerned with a tradition of philosophical rhetoric in which rhetoric tends to replace religion or divinely sanctioned political power, and since this happens in degrees, I am interested in the line between this "secularization" and whatever remains of these divine sanctions. This rhetorical secularization is certainly in accord with a great many religious attitudes, including all those which see democracy and religion as compatible or recognize, to some degree, the value of a separation of political authority and religious authority.

However, from another perspective, it is also sometimes interesting to raise the question of apotheosis—of whether this is not a secularization but an "incarnation" or a process of theosis. In that case, one might attempt to think a convergence between (1) the *Phaedrus*'s raising the question about whether there is a specific *dynamis* of logos and answering it by saying yes, it is *psychagōgia* (leading the soul) and (2) the passage in the prologue to John where the logos has a different *dynamis*, which is to be *pros ton theon* (moving toward God), present from creation (a wisdom reference) and incarnate. This would make the process of secularization and rhetoric itself a process of theosis or incarnation, an essentially "religious" process.

This is, however, a very formal and philosophical approach to religion. A more serious concern here would be rhetoric's capability for shedding light on the communicative dimensions of religious experience itself. When Catherine Pickstock (1998) claims that liturgy is not an application of theology but that rather theology is a reflection on liturgy, she is calling attention to the fact that religion's truth is not philosophical truth but truth of a different order—a more original source of meaning that gives rise to philosophical-theological reflection. Could a deeper rhetoric plumb the path from the sources of meaning to the religious language in which we reflect on these sources? A genuine dialogue among world religions would have to be more than just a dialogical reflection on our reflections.[22]

There are of course a myriad of religious and nonreligious attitudes and theological and philosophical positions that could come into play here (from familiar ones to rather strange and weird ones). My own intent for this book has been to elaborate a preliminary account of a deep rhetoric that would help to frame these further developments for as many people, with as many different attitudes and positions, as possible. Actually creating a rhetorical framework for something like Gadamer's projected conversation among the world's religions would be a different task, an important one, and one to which I hope a deep rhetoric would contribute.

_____

Although I have tried to argue throughout this book that the philosophical dimensions of rhetoric are broader and deeper than is usually recognized, and that consequently rhetorical theory and informed rhetorical practice have much more intellectual and social importance than are usually granted them, I would like to end this chapter by noting some limits of a deep rhetoric. Philosophy has sometimes seen itself as a self-grounding project, an autonomous one, a project of questioning everything in its attempt to find what cannot be doubted. In some ways, a deep rhetoric aligns itself with this philosophical impulse, primarily in its attempt to look behind theories of rhetoric that make too many ontic assumptions and to explore the communicative and ethical realities occluded by such assumptions.

However, as we have seen, rhetoric and its wisdom are not self-grounding or autonomous or epistemologically pure or theoretically complete. The elaboration of a deep rhetoric is itself a rhetorical event. It relies on a world it inherits and in terms of which it understands itself. It places itself (well or not so well) in both a tradition and a contemporary institutional practice of scholarship and intellectual work, a tradition and practice that themselves have their small places in a much larger world. Deep rhetoric is to some degree a function of this past and present. Its concerns with logos and communication and "leading the soul" are thus empowered and inflected by other authorities, and the project is interdependent with them. All such work takes place in a context—religious, economic, political, civil, ethical, moral—that contributes to the work's meaning and makes it possible to be the work it is at all. This is not to mention the cultural and economic powers that increasingly govern and give form to our world through new media and the global flow of capital and so increasingly shape our practices and our goals. However, intellectual and scholarly work is never simply the function of a past and of a contemporary organization of power.

The project of a deep rhetoric reaches into a past, the rhetorical tradition, especially its late-twentieth-century phase. It interprets that past, selects from it, conceptualizes it, presents it, and brings it into dialogue with new interlocutors, new questions and concerns, as well as with other traditions—in light of a future toward which it looks. It does not simply carry out its work in the terms of the extant theories, past or present; neither does it offer a new rhetorical theory, at least not more than a few sketches of one. Rather, a deep rhetoric offers a philosophical matrix for developing rhetorical theories, new or renewed theories that will promote a more philosophically aware and less prejudicial understanding of how religions and corporations and political entities and educational systems and media and moralities and families and other powers come to presence and shape choices. It will be of special help in grasping the meaning and guiding the conduct of their conflict with one another.

Rhetoric, especially as argumentation, involves both an understanding and a practice of capabilities that will allow us to lead these social powers through their conflicts in just and peaceable ways. And, as persuasion, it will perhaps help us call these powers into closer continuing cooperation in changing conditions. And so deep rhetoric, despite its being philosophical, is also dependent on a conception of something "good," a future toward which it is worthwhile to lead each other, one in which we conduct our conflicts more justly and peacefully. That future requires much from us.

On the one hand, it requires continuing engagement with the philosophical dimensions of rhetoric, the dimensions that lie beyond rhetoric as a theory or a discipline. We have been exploring those dimensions in this book. On the other hand, it requires a renewed commitment to the study and teaching of rhetoric as a discipline—a discipline that has profound links with the history of democracy; an implicit and powerful commitment to the dignity of human beings; and a potential for mitigating violence, conducting conflict justly, and so achieving a dynamic peace that seems, at least to me, to belong to any robust conception of human well-being.

Notes

1.   The nineteenth- and twentieth-century institutional history
     of rhetoric has received a great deal of attention, though the
     narratives do not always align perfectly. For a short and to
     the point account, see Walker (2005). Glenn and Carcasson
     also have a helpful account that is pedagogically oriented. It
     appears in the *Sage Handbook of Rhetorical Studies* (Lunsford
     et al. 2009, 285–92), whose many essays have a frequent
     focus on the status of rhetoric as a discipline. A classic work
     here is Kitzhaber ([1954] 1990), which covers the years
     1850–1900. See also his (unfortunately) still pertinent report
     on the teaching of writing in the mid-twentieth century
     (1963). For a helpful, practically oriented piece that gives
     a short history of rhetoric's past as a way of envisioning its
     immediate institutional future, see Zarefsky (2004). A helpful
     bibliography of histories of the contemporary disciplines
     related to rhetoric may be found in Goggin (1999). For an
     account that includes an argument for a reunified rhetoric,
     see Mailloux (2006). Mailloux's continuing work in rhetori-
     cal pragmatism and rhetorical hermeneutics (1989, 1995,
     1998, 2004) is in its own way also an attempt to develop a
     more philosophical conception of rhetoric. Note how his
     recent work on *phronesis* (2004) intensifies that dimension of
     his project.
2.   The late-twentieth-century institutional resurgence of rheto-
     ric has taken place in philosophy as well, although under the
     rubrics of "informal logic" and "critical thinking.
3.   Conflicting conceptions of rhetoric have certainly had an
     impact on rhetoric's institutional history, too, a fact that

can be acknowledged without asserting an idealist version of institutional change or any simple causal model of the relation between ideas and institutions.

4. Paulo Freire gives a famous account of a "banking approach" to education in *Pedagogy of the Oppressed* (1970).

5. This can perhaps be clarified by comparing it to the practice of trying not to judge other people in positive or negative ways. This is an impossibility if taken as a literal or absolute goal. One would not be able to make choices about many important matters without making such judgments. And yet the practice is also useful, and allows one to stay open to learning new things about people and to interpreting their actions in new ways that might become unavailable if a judgment settles in and begins to work as a kind of theory.

6. Personal communication. May 16, 2008. Eugene, Oregon.

CHAPTER ONE

1. This Hebraic wisdom figure is discussed in chapter 5 below. In Proverbs 8, she cries out from the high places, and at the gates, of the city.

2. John's logos is the subject of the prologue to (the first chapter of) John's Gospel in the New Testament.

3. Gadamer writes a great deal about rhetoric and its history in many different places. For an excellent overview, along with an argument that Gadamer's philosophical account can have a salutary influence on debates that concern the discipline of rhetoric, see John Arthos, "Gadamer's Rhetorical Imaginary" (2008). See also Steven Mailloux's powerful arguments for including Gadamer as an important part of the rhetorical tradition in *Disciplinary Identities* (2006).

 Gadamer's idea that rhetoric is the "universal form of human communication" is one that will be explored and developed throughout the book, especially in the many discussions of logos. One can begin to raise the right questions and get a first hold on the idea by considering all human communication as a way people reach beyond themselves to someone else. Every instance of this is also an influencing of that other person. Deep rhetoric is concerned with the many dimensions of this communicative influence—from the ethical to the ontological to the political and beyond.

4. Although I will be engaging with ancient sources throughout this book, I will be doing my best to stay away from philological controversies—a futile endeavor, perhaps. As far as possible, I will keep the discussion of classical sources in English. Where it seems necessary to use the Greek terms, I will offer transliterations. Where I approach potentially controversial matters, and where I delve into Plato's text in chapter 3, I will add whatever linguistic precision seems necessary. Since I will be using some old Greek terms in new senses and in new contexts in English sentences, I will differentiate

between the Greek word and my transplanting of it by keeping the Greek word in italics and removing the italics for my new uses of the word. (The difference is not always precise.) New uses of words, "logos," for example, and "logoi" (its plural), will have to be given definition at several places as the argument develops. This is really no different from what will have to be done with the Greek word, which appears in Plato and in the Christian New Testament, but with quite different meanings in each case.

5. Thus, I am dissenting, too, with some trepidation, from Jeffrey Walker's studied account of the emergence of "rhetoric" in his *Rhetoric and Poetics in Antiquity* (2000). Walker takes Socrates to be exploiting similarities, and deliberately conflating the art of rhetoric with a general art of logos—and so misleading Phaedrus into agreeing that rhetoric is a dimension of a general art of logos and has an essential connection to philosophy.

6. Actually, Aristotle's conceptualization of rhetoric is many-layered. Although he writes about rhetoric as a *techne*, an art, he defines it at 1355b as a *dynamis*, a power or a capability.

7. Hegel makes this case in his *Lectures on the Philosophy of History*, an early-nineteenth-century Eurocentric account of the progress of freedom that is, for its time, very well informed and striking in its efforts to see the whole of history and to see history whole. Although its many limitations have become clear, it is still not only an intriguing work of philosophical history but a challenging attempt to conceptualize freedom in ways that are at once both philosophical and historical.

8. Gadamer makes this general argument in a number of places. See especially the first and last essays collected in *Reason in the Age of Science* (1981): "On the Philosophic Element in the Sciences and the Scientific Character of Philosophy" and "Philosophy or Theory of Science?"

9. Rhetoric produces universals both at the level of language and at the level of receptivity itself, in the form of universal audiences. I have attempted to track and explain these processes in "Universalities" (2010).

10. This idea occurs throughout Plato's works, but perhaps most significantly in the *Symposium* and in its characterization of *eros*. I have written on this in connection with the notion of friendship as it is at stake in the *Phaedrus* in "Giving Friendship: The Perichoresis of an All-embracing Service," in *Emerson and Thoreau: Figures of Friendship* (2010a). I will return to this idea in the final chapter, on rhetoric and wisdom, where it will figure prominently.

11. I will use "G-d" when we are not supposed to be thinking of an entity that can be known in the ways that entities are known, and "God" when the reference is to an entity that can be known as the greatest entity. This usage is intended to be helpful, or at least thought-provoking, even if it cannot be precise. There are many possible senses of "known" and "entity" in the contexts we will explore.

12. "For all symbols are fluxional; all language is vehicular and transitive, and is good, as ferries and horses are, for conveyance, not as farms and houses

are, for homestead." From "The Poet" in *The Essays of Ralph Waldo Emerson*
(1987, 238).

13. See especially Gaonkar, "The Idea of Rhetoric in the Rhetoric of Science,"
    in Gross and Keith (1997). That volume includes several critical responses
    to Gaonkar's work.

14. It will become even clearer in what follows that a deep rhetoric is informed
    by the Levinasian account of the ways in which ethics precedes ontology,
    especially the account found in *Otherwise than Being* (1981). As will also
    become clear, I have not gone as far as Levinas in the matter of granting
    a kind of infinite deference to the other but have instead followed Chaim
    Perelman in tracking down a deep rhetorical understanding of justice. For
    a provocative attempt to go further with Levinas as a way of rethinking
    rhetoric, see Diane Davis's very interesting *Inessential Solidarity: Rhetoric and
    Foreigner Relations* (2010), which came into my hands only as I was revising
    the manuscript for this book.

15. Maneli works out the relation between the philosophy of law and the new
    rhetoric in chapter 8 of *Perelman's New Rhetoric as Philosophy and Methodol-
    ogy for the Next Century* (1994). The chapter is titled "The New Rhetoric and
    Jurisprudence."

16. Inertia as a rhetorical principle is introduced and discussed in section 27
    of *The New Rhetoric*. It is connected with the rule of justice in section 52.
    I have developed an interpretation of the principle of rhetorical inertia in
    "Nature and Reason: Inertia and Argumentation" (2000).

17. The source here is Amartya Sen's *The Idea of Justice* (2009, 231). In what
    follows, I have relied primarily on Sen's elaboration of the capabilities ap-
    proach in that book. Martha Nussbaum's list of capabilities, found below,
    occurs in different versions as she developed it over the years. The one I
    consulted here may be found in her *Sex and Social Justice* (1999).

CHAPTER TWO

1. Hans Barth himself saw very clearly the possibility that this view would
   become the dominant one, but dissented nevertheless: "The reduction of
   intellectual content to social power is self-defeating. The ideas of truth and
   justice are not invalidated merely because under different conditions men
   hold different things to be true and just. Though all intellectual systems,
   including law and social theory, lay claim to these ideas, they may in practice well fall short of them. Yet this does not mean that the ideas themselves are reducible to other forms or modes of being, such as economic
   activity, folk spirit, culture soul, race, or social power" (1976, 194). And
   in a manifesto of unabashed humanism, he concludes: "On the contrary,
   the ideas are inherent in human nature. The disastrous effect of ideological thinking in its radical form is not only to cast doubt on the quality and
   structure of the mind that constitute man's distinguishing characteristic,

but also to undermine the foundation of social life. Human association is dependent on agreement, and the essence of agreement, be it concerned with common behaviour, rational action, or scientific investigation, is the idea of truth" (194). Barth wrote from Zürich and published these words in 1945.

Barth's work is in large part a confrontation with Karl Mannheim's *Ideology and Utopia* ([1929, 1936], 1985), which proposes an expansive notion of "ideology" as the subject matter of the sociology of knowledge. While Barth sees a skeptical relativism as the central threat to social life, Mannheim sees dogmatism as that threat. Mannheim quotes a character from Ranke's *Das Politische Gespräch*: "Truth always lies outside the realm where error is to be found. Even from all the forms of error taken together, it would be impossible to extract truth. Truth will have to be sought and found for its own sake, in its own realm. All the heresies in the world will not teach you what Christianity is—it can be learned only from the Gospel." Mannheim makes his own position clear. He addresses the theological hubris of the statement by saying that such naïve views assume an "intellectual Eden that knows nothing of the upheaval of knowledge after the Fall." He continues: "Only too often is it found that the synthesis, which is presented with the assurance that it embraces the whole, turns out in the end to be the expression of the narrowest provincialism." What Mannheim seeks, a total view, "is not an immediate and eternally valid vision of reality attributable only to a divine eye. It is not a self-contained and stable view. On the contrary, a total view implies both the assimilation and transcendence of the limitations of particular points of view. It represents the continuous process of the expansion of knowledge, and has as its goal not achievement of a super-temporally valid conclusion but the broadest possible extension of our horizon of vision" (1985, 106).

I cite these passages at length first because Perelman and Olbrechts-Tyteca, in their working out of a philosophical conception of rhetoric, identified skepticism and dogmatism as sources of irrationalism and violence; they were the alternatives over against which the new rhetoric defined itself. Deep rhetoric is in part a needed philosophical response to this classic controversy in the sociology of knowledge. Second, Mannheim is reaching for some way to acknowledge perspectivism without either collapsing into crude relativism or establishing some metaperspectival resolution to the conflict of perspectives. This is exactly the task Kenneth Burke set for himself and set about to address in a rhetorical framework in his essay "Four Master Tropes," an appendix to *The Grammar of Motives*, which will receive close attention in chapter 8.

2. Crowley's *Ancient Rhetorics for Contemporary Students* appeared in a first edition (1994) and a second (2004) and subsequent editions, the latter co-authored with Debra Hawhee. The accounts of ideology are a little different in each. I am following the more condensed first edition here.

3. See Thomas Conley's *Toward a Rhetoric of Insult* (2010), which elucidates in detail the "ideological" background without which insults would be impossible. The recognition that natural language is in some sense a distortion, or is "ideological," is an ancient one, and the reform of society and the development of clearer communication and sounder reasoning has been associated in the West with the reform of language since at least the older sophists' concern with orthography. Francis Bacon, too, in his famous account of the idols of the mind, included the idols of the marketplace, and his discussion there was primarily concerned with the way language diverts us from the truth.

4. Epidictic's role in argumentation is discussed in *The New Rhetoric* in section 11. I have tried to develop the new rhetorical interpretation of epidictic further in chapter 4 of *The Rhetoric of Reason* (104–8).

5. *The New Rhetoric*'s discussion of how reference groups support presumptions is found in section 17 of the book (70–74).

6. According to von Frank, Emerson first delivered the lecture form of this essay on March 4, 1867 at the Unity Church in Chicago. Apparently, he repeated the lecture five times in 1867, and delivered it twice again in 1868. He did not lecture on eloquence again—at least not under the title—until he gave his final lecture titled "Eloquence" on March 18, 1875, at the Academy of Music in Philadelphia. Emerson was two months short of his 72nd birthday. According to von Frank's note, "RWE is not clearly audible to the three thousand persons in attendance."

7. Gadamer treats the being of the work of art in part 1, section 2 of *Truth and Method*, "The Ontology of the Work of Art and its Hermeneutic Significance." He treats temporality specifically on pp. 119–25.

8. For a fine history of Antigone reception, see George Steiner's *Antigones*.

9. Interestingly enough, Toulmin claims in an interview (1993) that he saw the essential relation to jurisprudence only while concluding his work on *The Uses of Argument*.

10. How this is possible, and what it means for the project of a deep rhetoric, will be explored in chapter 7, "Reason and Justice."

11. Gadamer's arguments and insights on the priority of the question were what allowed me to develop the account of argumentation in my earlier work, *The Rhetoric of Reason*. Whether they were an immediate influence or not, something very like them seems to be active, too, in Michel Meyer's conceptualization of problematology in his *Of Problematology* (1995) and in his systematic rhetorical theory developed in *Principia Rhetorica* (2008).

CHAPTER THREE

1. This subject has of course received extensive controversy over a long period of time. In Plato's *Sophist*, Theaetetus and the Stranger discover that the elusive sophist has several different forms; see esp. 231 d-e. Recently, Takis

Poulakos has tried to condense the grounds of Plato's objections into five specific commonalities that sophists share (1995, 87–88), although he actually identifies many more. Susan Jarratt begins her rereading of the sophists with a review of the Platonically oriented history of negative judgments on the sophists (1991, xv-xiv, 1–4). Marina McCoy's introduction to her book-length treatment of the subject outlines seven distinct arguments concerning the way Plato distinguishes between philosophy and rhetoric in his treatment of the sophists (2008, 1–22). And in a much too neglected treatment of the subject, Laszlo Versényi (1963) offers a very balanced view that emphasizes the continuities between Socrates and the sophists at the same time that it distinguishes between the legitimate objections of Plato, on the one hand, and the exaggerations of Platonism and Platonic critiques of the sophists, on the other.

2. James Fredal has answered this question at length in "Why Shouldn't the Sophists Charge Fees?" (2008, 148–170). Fredal holds that Socrates' refusal to accept fees is a disguise for the fact that he is establishing a relationship of power that requires of the recipient certain subordinate reciprocations for the gift being bestowed. However, to avoid misunderstanding Socrates' practice, one must seriously consider Plato's thinking about philosophical friendship. I have sketched out the basics of that notion of friendship in "Giving Friendship: The *Perichoresis* of an All-embracing Service" (2010).

3. *Psychagōgia* has many meanings, from calling up the souls of the dead to the leading of the soul's own erotic reachings. Harvey Yunis offers a helpful discussion in which he links the word to its erotic uses and then develops its meaning more completely in its Platonic context (Yunis 2007, 82ff.).

4. I examine the way this "incompleteness argument" functions in the *Phaedrus* in *The Rhetoric of Reason* (1996, 224–30). Although I emphasize here the "incoherence" of the sophistic project because of its atelic character, there is also a sense in which that project is all too coherent because of its relentless deployment of a pure instrumentalism.

5. It is of course difficult and contentious to identify this mid-twentieth-century acceleration point. Eugene Dupreel's 1948 *Les Sophistes* is very sympathetic and comprehensive in its treatment of Gorgias. Dupreel himself is responding in part to Heinrich Gomperz's 1912 *Sophistik und Rhetorik*, which begins with a philosophical treatment of Gorgias. However, Untersteiner (1954) has had more influence on English language writers on rhetoric, partly because of Kathleen Freeman's translation of *I sophisti* into English, but partly, too, because of the sheer excitement of Untersteiner's prose and approach, as well as his deep sympathy for his subject. Werner Jaeger published the second and third volumes of his *Paideia* in the 1940s, but Jaeger gives attention to the sophists primarily as educators rather than as philosophers or theorists of rhetoric.

6. See Brian Vickers (1988) for a perhaps extreme expression of the traditional

reading. For a textbook version of the traditional view, see James L. Golden et al. (2003, 51–53).

7. James H. Nichols (1998) finds a different kind of continuity between philosophy and rhetoric, and a different importance for rhetoric, in the introduction to his translation of *Gorgias*. He takes rhetoric to be the crucial link between philosophy and politics. Harvey Yunis (2007) takes this kind of notion to characterize Plato's conception of political rhetoric but not Plato's conception of the philosophical rhetoric that is connected with education.

8. For a similar project with a similar goal but a different approach to the *Gorgias*, see Arthos (2008).

9. It is interesting that Socrates represents both Protagoras and himself as boxers, using martial strategies in a section of the *Protagoras* (339d-e).

10. See Gregory Vlastos (1983) for a good description of how this criterion works in connection with Socratic elenchus.

11. The more common word used for the rhetorical notion of the "fitting" or "appropriate" is *to prepon*.

12. See Albert Hofstadter's Introduction to his translations of Heidegger collected in Heidegger, *Poetry, Language, Thought* (1971). See also Hofstadter's "Being: The Act of Belonging" (1970).

CHAPTER FOUR

1. See Hannah Arendt, *On Violence* (1970); *Eichmann in Jerusalem* (1994); and *Thinking* (1978). On Arendt, agonism, and rhetoric, see also Patricia Roberts-Miller (2002) and my response to her (2002).

2. Jean Nienkamp has devoted an entire book to this idea and its relation to rhetoric: *Internal Rhetorics: Toward a History and Theory of Self-Persuasion* (2001). Lev Vygotsky (1962) is a classical source of this view in psychology, and Mary Watkins (1986) has drawn interesting and challenging developmental and therapeutic conclusions from it.

3. Derrida (1992) gives several of his own reasons for rereading Benjamin: (1) the essay reflects the crisis in liberal European democracy and the crisis in *droit* that is a part of it. (2) The essay is exemplary in lending itself to a deconstructive reading. (3) The essay participates in its own deconstruction.

4. Derrida (1992) undoes the force/violence distinction, as he does many of Benjamin's other distinctions.

5. It is difficult to know exactly what Benjamin is thinking here. However, the following facts come to mind. The "Critique" was published in 1921. The Weimar Republic was founded in late 1918, after years of war, with 1.8 million Germans dead, 4 million wounded, and the Republic severely impoverished. The violence of the early Weimar years followed, but it was violence to which the state reacted in specific ways: "Between 1918 and 1922, assassinations traced to left-wing elements numbered twenty-two;

of these, seventeen were rigorously punished, ten with the death penalty. Right-wing extremists, on the other hand, found the courts sympathetic: of the 354 murders committed by them, only one was rigorously punished, and not even that by the death penalty" (Gay 1968, 20). This is just one of the features of the violent milieu in which Benjamin wrote.

6. A more subtle rhetorical account may be found in *The New Rhetoric*. Both the means/end and the subject/object pair are examples of what Perelman and Olbrechts-Tyteca call dissociations, treated in part 3, chapter 4 of the book (411–59). As philosophical pairs, they behave with a specifically rhetorical logic. Means/end relationships are treated more specifically on 261–78.

7. "Practicing the interval" is a phrase from Derrida's early essay "Differance" in *Speech and Phenomena* (1973). Although I am often sympathetic to what this phrase seems to want to say, I believe that the rhetorical approach to philosophical pairs outlined in Perelman and Olbrechts-Tyteca's *The New Rhetoric* is more productive than the kind of deconstruction sketched in "Differance." See my "Rhetoric in the Wilderness: The Deep Rhetoric of the Late 20th Century" (2004).

8. Again, I want to let the religious dialectic unfold, but I must point out that the distinction between particularism and generalization that Benjamin makes here has been treated much more subtly by other theorists. John Rawls, for example, relates the two in his idea of a "reflective equilibrium" between particular judgments and more general principles of justice; we modify each in light of the other to achieve the best equilibrium we can. Five years after Benjamin's death, Chaim Perelman published *De la justice*, a work written under virtual house arrest in Brussels, in which he begins his own reflections on the impossibility of generalizing an acceptable concept of justice, and his difficulties will lead him directly to the ideas he elaborates in *The New Rhetoric*, a story I will tell in a later chapter.

9. And although we are supposed to be escaping the mythic, it is surprising again how Hindu Benjamin's world is beginning to appear: history is trapped in the violent cycles of Samsara. Governing forces are the Creative (Brahma) and the Preserving (Vishnu), but renewal demands destruction (Shiva.)

10. Here I have combined and modified the Jephcott and the Quaintance/Derrida translations to try to get Benjamin's distinctions into more readable English.

11. See Mieczysław Maneli (1994, 13).

12. For a more contemporary example of this self-*reductio* of critical theory, see the admittedly polemical speech of Slavoj Žižek (2009), in which his explanation of the abstract political goal of making "poverty" "impossible" leads to a judgment that "the worst slaveholders were kind to their slaves" because their kindness contributed to slavery's continuation. From a deep rhetorical perspective, Žižek's theorizing ends up concerned with

poverty as an abstract function of a social formation as a whole (much like Benjamin's "mythical violence"), but it is not at all concerned with the suffering of actual impoverished people, who do not speak in the theorizing.

13. This sentence is formed out of a recollection of something Stanley Cavell wrote, although I am unable to find the source.

CHAPTER FIVE

1. This is Saussure's famous founding distinction for linguistics, explained in the introduction to the *Course in General Linguistics*. *Langue* refers to language in the sense of the linguistic structure of a system of signs that make up a social institution. *Parole* is the actual use of language by individuals. The introduction to the *Course* makes interesting reading precisely for the way Saussure wrestles with this distinction, drawing it very sharply in chapter 3, where *langue* is "essential" and *parole* is "accidental," and then troubling the distinction when he describes their interdependencies in chapter 4, as if the distinction had not yet been drawn successfully. In any case, *langue* is clearly the hero of the science of linguistics.

2. Heidegger explores rhetoric most explicitly and directly in his 1924 Summer Semester lectures published in English as *Basic Concepts of Aristotelian Philosophy* (2009a). There he situates basic concepts of Aristotle's *Rhetoric* in the context of other Aristotelian writings, especially *Metaphysics*, *Politics*, *Nicomachean Ethics*, and *De Anima*. The work contains especially interesting accounts of pathos and of fear. The account of pathos seems to be a step in the development of what will emerge in *Being and Time* as an account of *Befindlichkeit* as an "existentiale." The account of fear seems to be a preliminary sketch of section 30 of *Being and Time*. Heidegger has picked up concepts from this encounter with rhetoric and incorporated them into his analysis of Dasein, but—as I will argue—without encountering rhetoric as a philosophical challenge in itself, despite his famous dictum: "Contrary to the traditional orientation, according to which rhetoric is conceived as the kind of thing we 'learn in school,' this work [the *Rhetoric*] of Aristotle must be taken as the first systematic hermeneutic of everydayness of Being with one another" (1962, 178). Heidegger also discusses rhetoric in his lectures on Plato's *Sophist* (1997). Susan Zickmund (2007) has developed the implications of those lectures for clarifying Heidegger's early conception of rhetoric.

Heidegger's importance for rhetoric has been explored by a number of other writers. Daniel Gross and Angmar Kemman's collection, *Heidegger and Rhetoric* (2005), examines the 1924 Summer Semester course on Aristotle's *Rhetoric*. I will discuss Gross's account further below. Gross and Kemman also include a bibliography that provides references to the texts in which Heidegger attempts to define rhetoric. Allen Scult's *Being Jewish/Reading*

Heidegger (2004) delivers not only an engaging conversation between Heidegger and the Jewish tradition but hosts this conversation in the context of a concern for conceptualizing rhetoric in new ways. In *The Call of Conscience: Heidegger and Levinas, Rhetoric and the Euthanasia Debate* (2001), Michael J. Hyde effects a convergence of philosophy and rhetoric around the euthanasia controversy with strong attention to Heidegger and his connections with rhetoric. In a number of works, Ernesto Grassi (see 1980a, 1980b, 1987) also pursued ways to conceptualize rhetoric in relation to Heidegger's thought and to unify philosophy and rhetoric. Many other writers have pursued this in some way or other.

3. Levinas takes the event of the saying and the said through a number of permutations in *Otherwise than Being, or, Beyond Essence* (1998), which often reads like a critical commentary on Heidegger. For Levinas, although the said may be mostly subordinate to the regime of beings, the saying-before-the-said always involves an ethical relation to an other, a neighbor.

4. Heidegger believed that this shift was not his own but was a feature of the matter of thinking itself. See Richardson (1974, xviii).

5. It is interesting how empirical cognitive science has recently caught up with this idea of deep dispositions and habits that are also a kind of knowledge and especially a practical knowledge. Although the idea is as old as Plato's *anamnesis* that recovers this implicit knowledge, and Aristotle's very important habits and dispositions that define the practically wise person, the notion was given powerful reformulations by Heidegger in his notion that knowing is grounded in our pretheoretical coping (Hubert Dreyfus's word) that exhibits an implicit and practical knowledge of the world. Gadamer parlayed this idea into his philosophical hermeneutics, in which he shows that the implicit and practical judgments we make before we begin some explicit examination are necessary features of the way we understand and reason.

6. That this, too, is Heidegger's view is clear in his comments on Aristotle's concept of logos, made in 1929–30: "What Aristotle sees quite obscurely under the title *sumbolon*, sees only approximately, and without any explication, in looking at it quite ingeniously, is nothing other than what we today call *transcendence*. There is language [*Es gibt Sprache*] only in the case of a being that by its essence *transcends*. This is the sense of Aristotle's thesis that a logos is *kata sunthēkēn*" (1995, 308). As we shall see, Heidegger also seemed to persevere in playing with a distinction between language and being, drawing the line in various ways at various times in his career; however, there is no denying that he holds open the door to the larger sense of logos, according to which logos is what it is as the medium of human transcendence.

7. This understanding of language and interpretation and historicity is central to Gadamer's account of human being as interpretive and "phronetic."

The critical discussion of "application" may be found in *Truth and Method* (1998, 307–12).

8. This dictum comes from what Kisiel and Sheehan call "the most famous of the versions of the introduction to a book on Aristotle that Heidegger was planning to write under the title 'Phänomenologische Interpretationen zu Aristoteles' ever since he taught his course of WS 1921–22 under that title" (Heidegger 2007, 168).

9. Daniel Gross (Gross and Kemman 2005) is very helpful in this regard, and especially helpful on the way pathos is conceptualized in the lectures (27–39). *Logos* without *pathos* is impossible because it is *pathos* that leads us both into language and into moments that require decisions. Our world is in no sense a world of pure data that are received with no feeling. This is why Heidegger is led, in these 1924 lectures, to speak of *pathos* as the "ground" (*Boden*) of *logos*. In 1927, in *Being and Time*, the *pathē* as such are absorbed into *Befindlichkeit*, which is then said to be "equiprimordial" with discourse. In the larger sense in which I have been using the word "logos," pathos is already an important factor in logos, since logos is, in Plato's language, the leading of the soul, the leading of one thing to another. This leading is similar to the "movement" of *pathos* that Heidegger notes—and which Gross explains very clearly in light of the Aristotelian context.

10. On the *alltägliche* and time in the 1924 lectures, see Nancy S. Struever's deeply perceptive account (2005).

11. Heidegger lectured on Heraclitus's teaching on logos in 1944, and that lecture is collected in the *Gesamtausgabe*, vol. 55, *Heraklit*. An English translation of a section on "Logos and Language" is available in *The Heidegger Reader* (Heidegger 2009b). David Farrell Krell and Frank A. Capuzzi include a translation of a related 1951 lecture, "Logos," in their collection, *Early Greek Thinking* (Heidegger 1975).

12. Heidegger's deficient conception of rhetoric has also been noted by Otto Pöggeler, "Heidegger's Restricted Conception of Rhetoric" (2005).

13. This story is related in Riccardo Dottori's wonderful, informative collection of interviews with Gadamer held in 1999–2000 and published in *A Century of Philosophy* (Gadamer 2006).

14. It is puzzling why Heidegger should forget the question here. After all, the entire possibility of fundamental ontology and the reason for the *Dasein-analysis* lies in the fact that Dasein raises the question of being and so shows that being is already in some indistinct way understood. There is a sense in which Gadamer has simply carried through on and developed one of Heidegger's own most essential insights.

15. I have developed this account in detail in *The Rhetoric of Reason* (1996, 51–101).

16. Taylor Carman's discussion of *Rede* in *Heidegger's Analytic* (2003, 204–63) both tracks Heidegger's inconsistencies and offers an interpretation that

attempts to give as much overall coherence to the idea as possible by describing *Rede* as the articulation of intelligibility *in our practical engagements*, and so as a phase of logos in between the fully implicit meaningfulness of world and the outspokenness of meaning in language.

17. Here I have merged Malik's and McNeill's translations, and made some further modifications of my own.

18. See Steven Shankman's inspired interpretation of Levinas on this point in his reading of Rembrandt's *The Sacrifice of Isaac* in the introduction to *Other Others* (2010). Shankman's book as a whole transforms Levinas's account of the otherwise than being into a promising framework for transcultural literary criticism.

CHAPTER SIX

1. I am relying here on George J. Gutsche's translation and comments in his essay "Moral Fiction" (1999).

2. Heidegger left *Contributions to Philosophy* in manuscript form, and it was not published until 1989, after his death. The work was published in an English translation in 1999. Both the publication and the translation have been controversial in Heidegger studies.

3. The translation here, as well as the ones that follow, are from Gonzalez (2008). I include Gonzalez's citations of the volumes and page numbers from Heidegger's *Gesamtausgabe* (GA).

4. This word "sigetical" is from the Greek word *sigan*, which means keeping silent.

5. See especially Heidegger, *Elucidations of Hölderlin's Poetry* (2000). In the discussion that follows, I will be using Jerome Veith's translation of "Wie wenn am Feiertage . . . ," "As When on a Holiday . . . ," from *The Heidegger Reader* (2009b).

6. One of Heidegger's clearest and simplest accounts of the poetic in this sense can be found in "Hölderlin and the Essence of Poetry" in *The Heidegger Reader* (2009b). However, see also "Building Dwelling Thinking" and ". . . Poetically Man Dwells . . ." in *Poetry, Language, Thought* (1971).

7. In his collection, *Friedrich Hölderlin: Poems and Fragments, a Bilingual Edition*, Michael Hamburger includes a variant text, as well as an English translation that conflicts with Heidegger's in interesting ways. In addition, the text adds the following startling lines to the end of the poem:

Doch weh mir! wenn von

Weh mir!

 Und sag ich gleich,

Ich sei genaht, die Himmlische zu schauen,
Sie selbst, sie werfen mich tief unter die Lebenden

Den Falschen Priester, ins Dunkel, das ich
Das warnende Lied den Gelehrigen singe.
Dort. (376)

In Hamburger's translation:

But, oh, my shame! When of

My shame!

  And let me say at once

That I approached to see the heavenly,
And they themselves cast me down, deep down
Below the living, into the dark cast down
The false priest that I am, to sing,
For those who have ears to hear, the warning song.
There

8. This theme is explored in compelling ways by Rüdiger Safranski in *Martin Heidegger: Between Good and Evil* (1998). See especially chapters 3 and 7.

9. See Hadot (1995, 82–83), but consider the complexity of the notion and even the appearance of the authenticity/inauthenticity pair in part 2 ("Spiritual Exercises") of *Philosophy as a Way of Life*. See *What is Ancient Philosophy?* (2002) for Hadot's full account. Hadot's overall judgment on Heidegger is especially interesting: "The movement of thought inaugurated by Heidegger and carried on by existentialism seeks—in theory and in principle—to engage man's freedom and action in the philosophical process, although, in the last analysis, it too is primarily a philosophical discourse" (1995, 272). Hadot is right to say "primarily" here, but primarily is not exclusively.

10. The translations of Jaspers are from Gonzalez (2008). I have included Gonzalez's citations of page numbers from Jaspers' works, which I have included in the list of works cited.

CHAPTER SEVEN

1. I have found Taro Shinoda's work helpful in pondering the way transcendence generates and transforms these body/world, internal/external boundaries. The idea is implicit in much of his work, but the first segment of the video *Reverberations* is especially provocative. Our internal can be the inside of our bodies, beneath our skin, but it can also be the inside of our habitat, a room or a house. Inside/outside is transformed when we are in a car, when our body and its movements stretch our boundary out to the vehicle's surface. One can go on from there, to larger buildings and even to cities and beyond, which in their forms resemble natural phenomena and establish internal/external boundaries that resemble and function as membranes and body/world boundaries. The idea of cities and especially

Tokyo as an artificial organism is widespread in Japanese thought and art, and it has both a threatening and a hopeful side. See also *Model of Oblivion*, a sculpture that attempts to capture the identity between the circulatory action in the body and the circulatory action of the cosmos. These works were viewed at the Mori Art Museum, Tokyo, Japan, October 27, 2010.

2. Walter Benjamin's "Über den Begriff der Geschichte" has been translated by Harry Zohn as "Theses on the Philosophy of History" and is included in *Illuminations* (1969). It has also been translated by Dennis Redmond as "On the Concept of History" (2001). Since Redmond's translation is posted at a website, I will refer to passages from this translation only by the section numbers.

3. For an interesting account of how fear works in contemporary ways to shape political reasoning, see Chaput, Braun, and Brown (2010).

4. I have explored this implicit connection between claiming and questioning in chapter 3 of *The Rhetoric of Reason* (1996).

5. Jeanne Fahnestock, whose magisterial *Rhetorical Figures in Science* (2002) shows with great clarity how figures have structured thought in science, explains just as clearly *The New Rhetoric*'s account of how style functions in argumentation in general in her 2008 keynote address, "The Art of Style in *The New Rhetoric*" (http://media.uoregon.edu/channel/2008/08/18/ the-promise-reason-jeanne-fahnestock-and-francis-j-mootz-iii/, accessed February 1, 2011). For the published version, see Fahnestock (2011).

6. Again, Michel Meyer has carefully elaborated the role that questions play in the life of propositions, and I have developed the larger context for assertions and their meaning in a process of argumentation that includes questioning, claiming, and giving reasons in *The Rhetoric of Reason* (1996).

7. I say "usually" here because once again we are capable of carrying out this dialogue with ourselves, capable of entertaining incompatible assertions by becoming a kind of other to ourselves.

CHAPTER EIGHT

1. Hegel is perhaps the most famous of modern historiographers who write about this transition, and his account of it as part of a logical transition to philosophy is contested in some contemporary writings on the sophists. Xavier Zubiri ([1944] 1981) offers a twentieth-century version of the Hegelian narrative—with strong Heideggerian inflections—in his tracking of wisdom from (1) possession of the truth about nature, to (2) wisdom as a vision of being, to (3) wisdom as a rational knowledge of things, to (4) wisdom *as* rhetoric and culture in the sophists. More recently, Christopher Lyle Johnstone (2006) has focused on the sophistic conception of wisdom once again, trying to flesh out the sophistic arête of wisdom in greater detail.

2. Garver (1994) develops the idea of Aristotelian rhetoric as a specifically political art that cannot be completely distinguished from practical wisdom,

and then exposes the absence of such a political context for rhetoric in contemporary life and so a severance of rhetoric from practical wisdom that can be repaired in each situation only by a new kind of *phronēsis*. Quite a challenge he leaves us! In many respects, Garver's writings on Aristotle and especially his work on practical reasoning (2004) come very close to many of the concerns of what I am calling a deep rhetoric, though they come from quite a different direction.

3. Cicero's conclusion is that wisdom (*sapientia*) without eloquence is simply of little use to states, but that eloquence without wisdom is positively harmful. In *De oratore*, prudentia—foresight, judgment, or "practical wisdom"—rises in relation to *sophia* as a competitor for the wisdom role in relation to eloquence. For an account of Cicero's use of "prudentia," and a lively exploration of its continuing significance, see Robert Hariman (2003). See, too, David DePew's similarly lively review (2004).

4. Of course, nothing in Augustine is simple. *On Christian Doctrine* is theological theory. If one instead reads Augustine through the lens of *Confessions* as a writer of philosophical literature, then matters look quite different. *Confessions* moves autobiographically, second personally, through a pretheoretical deep rhetorical region that charts the failure of theorizing. I will add here that there is a provocative discussion of wisdom in *Confessions* (2006, 12.3.20–21) in which Augustine describes both "uncreated wisdom" and "created" wisdom. It is an interesting passage in which Augustine's prayer to G-d turns suddenly toward this created wisdom (which is not God): "May my wanderings yearn out toward you, as I ask him who made you to let me, whom he made, become his in your habitation." Augustine's rhetoric forms here, and everywhere in *Confessions*, the vital meaning of the text, yet it is not made a theme that might compete with either kind of wisdom. I might venture, however, that rhetoric implicitly undergoes a possible apotheosis in book 10, where the inventory Augustine takes of himself in his search for God, pursued with intense Augustinian interrogative rhetoric, where speech to God is prayer (*oratio*) that is at the same time an attempt "to speak out what the heart holds true" (which requires an impossible honesty with oneself)—that taking of inventory becomes the very site of the "teaching and guiding" (251) that turn out to be G-d's own pursuit of Augustine. This is potentially undermined only by Augustine's persistent suspicion that he may, at still undiscovered depths, be writing the *Confessions* only for "vainglory," that is, to win praise.

5. John Arthos (2007) also develops the Renaissance idea in a contemporary context by explaining Hans-Georg Gadamer's recapitulation of practical wisdom in his philosophical-hermeneutical account of understanding, and so addresses one of the greatest obstacles to the broader emergence of a deep rhetoric—the neglect of Gadamer's reinterpretation of the rhetorical tradition in hermeneutical-ontological terms. And speaking of "the rhetorical tradition" makes perfect sense here since the philosophical tradition in which

Gadamer worked had defined itself over against what it had understood as the rhetorical tradition. This is also as good a place as any to point out that Gadamer would fail to see the point in skepticism about whether there *is* a rhetorical tradition. For Gadamer, the rhetorical tradition *is* in its reception, or more completely in the acts of its authors, the texts and artifacts they leave, and in their reception—as Gadamer says, in the "play" among them.

6. The case for this reading of Vico has been made at length and in detail by Michael Mooney (1985) in his illuminating *Vico in the Tradition of Rhetoric.*

7. The line numbers of passages from the *Oresteia* are from the Lattimore translation (1960). Lattimore took them from Smyth's Loeb edition of the drama, which was based on the Greek line numbers, from which they diverge in a few places.

8. That is, if *sōphronein*, ordinarily "sound-mindedness," can be construed as a kind of practical wisdom.

9. Most helpful to me have been Edward Conze's translations of and commentary on the Diamond and Heart Sutras in his *Buddhist Wisdom Books* ([1958] 2001). He combines the perspectives of the scholar and the practitioner as well as anyone. Heinrich Dumoulin's histories of Buddhism and his comparative work have also been very helpful. Dumoulin (1994) has a powerful and sound sense of just what questions need to be addressed. For a brilliant exposition of the relation between the theory of categories in the history of western philosophy and their role in Buddhist thought, see Tze-wan Kwan (1995).

10. This trend is widespread in contemporary Buddhist Studies, but a surprisingly helpful introduction to it can be found in Kevin Trainor's *Buddhism: The Illustrated Guide* (2001), with its emphasis on sangha (community), on artifacts and relics, on religious practices and festivals, and on art and architecture—though not to the neglect of Buddhist writings.

11. Once again, Jean Nienkamp has written extensively about this in her *Internal Rhetorics* (2001).

12. This paradox makes up the entire subject of Donald Mitchell's "The Paradox of Buddhist Wisdom" (1976).

13. Once again, *The New Rhetoric* develops its account of dissociation at 411–59. I have tried to explain how dissociation works in a practical controversy in "Rhetoric in the Wilderness: The Deep Rhetoric of the Late 20th Century" (2004).

14. See section 90 of *The New Rhetoric*, "The Appearance-Reality Pair."

15. See Visotzsky's very useful translation (1992).

16. *Tevunah* can also be used for personification, to refer to a teacher, for example. The *ḥokmah/binah* pair are famously important in Kabbalah.

17. Plato has Socrates give this famous account at 20d through 23c of the *Apology.*

18. In his account of Buddhist wisdom, Donald Mitchell makes this relation between wisdom and beauty explicit: "Perfect Wisdom (prajnaparamita) is

idealized and personified as the 'Mother' of the Tathagata in that it is Wisdom which begets enlightenment (bodhi). Like the Greek Sophia, Wisdom is viewed as the great Mother Goddess. She is the genetrix of enlightenment and truth. And through the aid of the Bodhisattvas, she nourishes goodness and beauty in the world" (1976, 65).

19. Perelman (1967, 72). The original remark may be found in E. Husserl (1954, 15).
20. I have explored this notion of universality and developed some of its political implications in an article titled "Universalities" [2010b]).
21. This account of dissociation is based on section 90 of *The New Rhetoric*.
22. John Arthos explores what seems to be a related question in *The Inner Word in Gadamer's Hermeneutics* (2009), where there is word (*verbum*) that is not quite language in any ordinary sense; however, I discovered Arthos's book only as I was concluding this project, and I have not had a chance to give it the study it deserves.

Works Cited

Abram, David. 1996. *The Spell of the Sensuous: Perception and Language in a More-than-Human World*. New York: Pantheon Books.

Adams, John Quincy. 1810. *Lectures on Rhetoric and Oratory*. Cambridge, Mass.: Hilliard and Metcalf.

Aeschylus. 1960. *Eumenides*. Translated by Richard Lattimore. In *Greek Tragedies*, vol. 3, edited by David Grene and Richard Lattimore, 1–41. Chicago: University of Chicago Press.

Althusser, Louis. 1971. "Ideology and Ideological State Apparatuses." In *Lenin and Philosophy and Other Essays*, 127–86. New York: Monthly Review Press.

Arendt, Hannah. 1970. *On Violence*. New York: Harcourt Brace Jovanovich.

———. 1978. *Thinking*. New York: Harcourt Brace Jovanovich.

———. 1994. *Eichmann in Jerusalem: A Report on the Banality of Evil*. New York: Penguin Books.

Aristotle. 2006. *On Rhetoric*. Translated by G. Kennedy. New York: Oxford University Press.

Arthos, John. 2004. "Almost Speaking a New Rhetoric: The Strangeness of the Text of *La Nouvelle Rhétorique*." *Southern Journal of Communication* 70 (1): 393–407.

———. 2007. "A Hermeneutic Interpretation of Civic Humanism and Liberal Education." *Philosophy and Rhetoric* 40 (2): 189–200.

———. 2008. "Gadamer's Rhetorical Imaginary." *Rhetoric Society Quarterly* 38 (2): 171–97.

———. 2009. *The Inner Word in Gadamer's Hermeneutics*. Notre Dame: University of Notre Dame Press.

Augustine. 1958. *On Christian Doctrine*. Translated by D. W. Robertson. New York: Liberal Arts Press.

———. 1991. *The Trinity*. Translated by Edmund Hill. Brooklyn: New City Press.

———. 2006. *Confessions*. Translated by Garry Wills. New York: Penguin Books.

Bacon, Francis. 1968. *The New Organon*. In *The Works of Francis Bacon*, edited by James Spedding, Robert L. Ellis, and Douglas D. Heath. New York: Garrett Press.

Barth, Hans. 1976. *Truth and Ideology*. Berkeley and Los Angeles: University of California Press.

Basso, Keith H. 1996. *Wisdom Sits in Places: Landscape and Language among the Western Apache*. Albuquerque: University of New Mexico Press.

Benjamin, Walter. 1969. "Theses on the Philosophy of History." In *Illuminations*, edited and with an introduction by Hannah Arendt, translated by Harry Zohn. New York: Shocken Books.

———. [1921] 1986. "Critique of Violence." In *Reflections: Essays, Aphorisms, Autobiographical Writings*, edited and with an introduction by Peter Demetz, translated by Edmund Jephcott, 277–300. New York: Shocken Books.

———. 2001. "On the Concept of History." Translated by Dennis Redmond. http://members.efn.org/~dredmond/ThesesonHistory.html (accessed July 9, 2012).

Bizzell, Patricia, and Bruce Herzberg. 2000. *The Rhetorical Tradition: Readings from Classical Times to the Present*. Boston: Bedford/St. Martins.

Berger, Peter L., and Thomas Luckmann. 1966. *The Social Construction of Reality: A Treatise in the Sociology of Knowledge*. Garden City: Doubleday.

Bolduc, Michelle, and David Frank. 2010. "Chaim Perelman and Lucie Olbrechts-Tyteca's 'On Temporality as a Characteristic of Argumentation'." *Philosophy and Rhetoric* 43 (4): 308–36.

Burke, Kenneth. 1968. *Counter-Statement*. Berkeley and Los Angeles: University of California Press.

———. 1969. *A Grammar of Motives*. Berkeley and Los Angeles: University of California Press.

Carman, Taylor. 2003. *Heidegger's Analytic: Interpretation, Discourse, and Authenticity in Being and Time*. Cambridge: Cambridge University Press.

Cavell, Stanley. 1976. "Must We Mean What We Say?" in *Must We Mean What We Say?* 1–43. Cambridge: Cambridge University Press.

———. 1990. *Conditions Handsome and Unhandsome*. Chicago: University of Chicago Press.

Chaignet, Antelme Édouard. 1888. *La Rhétorique et son histoire*. Paris: F. Wieveg.

Chaput, Catherine, M. J. Braun, and Danika M. Brown. 2010. *Entertaining Fear: Rhetoric and the Political Economy of Social Control*. New York: Peter Lang.

Cherwitz, Richard A. 1990. *Rhetoric and Philosophy*. Hillsdale, N.J.: L. Erlbaum Associates.

Cicero, Marcus Tullius. 1960. *De inventione. De optimo genere oratorum. Topica*. With an English translation by H. M. Hubbell. Cambridge, Mass.: Harvard University Press.

———. 2001. *On the Ideal Orator. (De Oratore)*. Translated by James M. May and Jakob Wisse. New York: Oxford University Press.

Conley, Thomas M. 1990. *Rhetoric in the European Tradition*. New York: Longman.

———. 2010. *Toward a Rhetoric of Insult*. Chicago: University of Chicago Press.

Consigny, S. 2001. *Gorgias: Sophist and Artist*. Columbia: University of South Carolina Press.

Conze, Edward. [1958] 2001. *Buddhist Wisdom: The Diamond Sutra and the Heart Sutra*. Translated and commentary. New York: Vintage Books.

Crosswhite, James. 1995. "Is There an Audience for this Argument? Fallacies, Theories and Relativisms." *Philosophy and Rhetoric* 28 (2): 134–45.

———, 1996. *The Rhetoric of Reason*. Madison: The University of Wisconsin Press.

———. 2000. "Nature and Reason: Inertia and Argumentation." In *Argumentation at the Century's Turn: Proceedings of the 1999 Ontario Society for the Study Argumentation meeting*, edited by Christopher W. Tindale, Hans V. Hansen, and Elmar Sveda. CD-Rom. Peterborough, Ontario: OSSA.

———. 2002. "Conflict in Concert: Fighting Hannah Arendt's Good Fight." *JAC: Rhetoric, Writing, Culture, Politics* 22 (4): 948–60.

———. 2004. "Rhetoric in the Wilderness: The Deep Rhetoric of the Late 20th Century." In *A Companion to Rhetoric and Rhetorical Criticism*, edited by Walter Jost and Wendy Olmsted, 372–88. Malden, Mass.: Blackwell Publishing.

———. 2010a. "Giving Friendship: The *Perichoresis* of an All-embracing Service." In *Emerson and Thoreau: Figures of Friendship*, 151–71. Bloomington: Indiana University Press.

———. 2010b. "Universalities." *Philosophy and Rhetoric* 43 (4): 430–48.

Crowell, Steven. 2007. "Conscience and Reason: Heidegger and the Grounds of Intentionality." In *Transcendental Heidegger*, edited by Steven Galt Crowell and J. E. Malpas, 43–62. Stanford: Stanford University Press.

Crowley, Sharon. 1994. *Ancient Rhetorics for Contemporary Students*. New York: Macmillan.

Dahlstrom, Daniel. 1994. "Heidegger's Method: Philosophical Concepts as Formal Indications." *Review of Metaphysics* 47 (June): 775–97.

Davis, Diane. 2010. *Inessential Solidarity: Rhetoric and Foreigner Relations*. Pittsburgh: University of Pittsburgh Press.

DePew, David. 2004. Review of *Prudence: Classical Virtue, Postmodern Practice* by Robert Harriman. *Philosophy and Rhetoric* 37 (2): 167–75.

Derrida, Jacques. 1973. *Speech and Phenomena, and Other Essays on Husserl's Theory of Signs*. Translated by David B. Allison. Evanston: Northwestern University Press.

———. 1992. "Force of Law: The 'Mystical Foundation of Authority.'" In *Deconstruction and the Possibility of Justice*, edited by Drucilla Cornell, Michael Rosenfeld, and David Gray Carlson, translated by Mary Quaintance, 3–67. New York: Routledge.

Dumoulin, Heinrich. 1994. *Zen Buddhism: A History*, vol. 1: *India and China: With a New Supplement on the Northern School of Chinese Zen*. Translated by James W. Heisig and Paul Knitter. New York: Macmillan.

Dupreel, E. 1948. *Les Sophistes*. Neuchâtel: Editions du Griffon.

Eemeren, Frans H. van, Rob Grootendorst, and T. Kruiger. 1987. *Handbook of Argumentation Theory*. Dordrecht-Providence: Foris.

Eemeren, Frans H. van, and Rob Grootendorst. 1995. "Perelman and the Fallacies." *Philosophy and Rhetoric* 28 (2): 122-33.

Emerson, Ralph Waldo. 1904. "Eloquence." In *The Complete Works of R. W. Emerson*, vol. 8: *Letters and Social Aims*, edited by Edward Waldo Emerson, 109–33. Boston: Houghton Mifflin.

———. 1911. "The Fugitive Slave Law." Delivered March 7, 1854. In *The Complete Works of R. W. Emerson*, vol. 11: *Miscellanies*, edited by Edward Waldo Emerson, 215-44. Boston: Houghton Mifflin.

———. 1987. *The Essays of Ralph Waldo Emerson*. Edited by Alfred Riggs Ferguson and Jean Ferguson Carr. Cambridge, Mass.: Harvard University Press.

Fahnestock, Jeanne. 2002. *Rhetorical Figures in Science*. New York: Oxford University Press.

———. 2011. "No Neutral Choices: The Art of Style in The New Rhetoric." In *The Promise of Reason: Semi-Centennial Studies in "The New Rhetoric,"* edited by John Gage, 29–47. Carbondale: Southern Illinois University Press.

Fish, Stanley. 1989. "Rhetoric." In *Doing What Comes Naturally: Change, Rhetoric, and the Practice of Theory in Literary and Legal Studies*, 471–502. Durham, N.C.: Duke University Press.

Fox, Michael V. 2000. *The Anchor Bible: Proverbs 1–9*. Translation and Commentary. New York: Doubleday.

Fredal, James. 2008. "Why Shouldn't the Sophists Charge Fees?" *Rhetoric Society Quarterly* 38 (2): 148–70.

Freire, Paulo. 1970. *Pedagogy of the Oppressed*. Translated by Myra Bergman Ramos. New York: Seabury Press.

Gadamer, Hans-Georg. 1982. *Reason in the Age of Science*. Translated by Frederick G. Lawrence. Cambridge, Mass.: MIT Press.

———. 1986. *The Relevance of the Beautiful and Other Essays*. Translated by Robert Bernasconi. Cambridge: Cambridge University Press.

———. 1990. "Reply to My Critics." In *The Hermeneutic Tradition: From Ast to Ricoeur*, edited by Gayle L. Ormiston and Alan D. Schrift, 273–97. Albany: State University of New York Press.

———. 2003. *Truth and Method*. Translated by Joel C. Weinsheimer and Donald G. Marshall. New York: Continuum.

———. 2006. A Century of Philosophy: A Conversation with Riccardo Dottori. New York: Continuum.

Gaonkar, Dilip. 1997. "The Idea of Rhetoric in the Rhetoric of Science." In Gross and Keith 1997, 25–85.

Garver, Eugene. 1994. *Aristotle's Rhetoric: An Art of Character*. Chicago: University of Chicago Press.

———. 2004. *For the Sake of Argument: Practical Reasoning, Character, and the Ethics of Belief*. Chicago: University of Chicago Press.

Gay, Peter. 1968. *Weimar Culture: The Outsider as Insider*. New York: Harper & Row.

Goggin, Maureen Daly. 1999. "The Tangled Roots of Literature, Speech Communication, Linguistics, Rhetoric/Composition, and Creative Writing: A Selected Bibliography on the History of English Studies." *Rhetoric Society Quarterly* 29 (4): 63–87.

Golden, J., G. Bergquist, W. Coleman, and J. Spoule. 2003. *The Rhetoric of Western Thought*. Dubuque: Kendall Hunt.

Gomperz, H. 1912. *Sophistik und Rhetorik*. Leipzig: Teubner.

Gonzalez, Francisco. 2008. "And the Rest is *Sigetik*: Silencing Logic and Dialectic in Heidegger's *Beiträge zur Philosophie*." *Research in Phenomenology* 38 (3): 358–91.

Gorgias. 1972. *Encomium of Helen*. Translated by G. Kennedy. In *The Older Sophists*, edited by R. Sprague, 50–54. Columbia: University of South Carolina Press.

Grassi, Ernesto. 1980a. *Rhetoric as Philosophy: The Humanist Tradition*. Translated by John Michael Krois and Azizeh Azodi. University Park: Pennsylvania State University Press.

———. 1980b. "Italian Humanism and Heidegger's Thesis of the End of Philosophy." Translated by John Michael Krois. *Philosophy and Rhetoric* 13 (2): 79–98.

———. 1987. "The Ordinary Quality of the Poetic and Rhetorical Word: Heidegger, Ungaretti, and Neruda." Translated by Lavinia Lorch. *Philosophy and Rhetoric* 20 (4): 248–60.

———. 1988. *Renaissance Humanism: Studies in Philosophy and Poetics*. Translated by Walter F. Veit. Binghamton: Medieval and Renaissance Texts and Studies.

Gross, Alan G. 1990. *The Rhetoric of Science*. Cambridge, Mass.: Harvard University Press.

Gross, Alan G., and William M. Keith. 1997. *Rhetorical Hermeneutics: Invention and Interpretation in the Age of Science*. Albany: State University of New York Press.

Gross, Daniel M., and Ansgar Kemmann. 2005. *Heidegger and Rhetoric*. Albany: State University of New York Press.

Gutsche, George J. 1999. "Moral Fiction: Tolstoy's 'Death of Ivan Il'ich'." In *Tolstoy's Death of Ivan Il'ich: A Critical Companion*, edited by Gary R. Jahn, 55–101. Evanston: Northwestern University Press.

Habermas, Jürgen. 1979. "Consciousness-raising or Redemptive Criticism: The Contemporaneity of Walter Benjamin." Translated by Philip Brewster and Carl Howard Buchner. *New German Critique* 17 (Spring): 30–59.

———. 1990a. "A Review of Gadamer's *Truth and Method*." In *The Hermeneutic Tradition: From Ast to Ricoeur*, edited by Gayle L. Ormiston and Alan D. Schrift, 213–44. Albany: State University of New York Press.

———. 1990b. "The Hermeneutic Claim to Universality." In *The Hermeneutic Tradition: From Ast to Ricoeur*, edited by Gayle L. Ormiston and Alan D. Schrift, 245–72. Albany: State University of New York Press.

Hadot, Pierre. 1995. *Philosophy as a Way of Life: Spiritual Exercises from Socrates to*

Foucault. Edited with an introduction by Arnold I. Davidson; translated by Michael Chase. Malden, Mass.: Blackwell Publishing.

———. 2002. *What Is Ancient Philosophy?* Translated by Michael Chase. Cambridge, Mass.: Harvard University Press.

Hanssen, Beatrice. 2000. *Critique of Violence: Between Poststructuralism and Critical Theory*. London: Routledge.

Hariman, Robert, ed. 2003. *Prudence: Classical Virtue, Postmodern Practice*. University Park: Pennsylvania State University Press.

Hauser, Gerald, ed. 2007. *Philosophy and Rhetoric in Dialogue: Redrawing their Intellectual Landscape*. University Park: Pennsylvania State University Press.

Hegel, Georg Wilhelm Friedrich. 1967. *Hegel's Philosophy of Right*. Translated with notes by T. M. Knox. New York: Oxford University Press.

———. 1975. *Lectures on the Philosophy of World History: Introduction, Reason in History*. Translated by Hugh Barr Nisbet. Cambridge: Cambridge University Press.

———. 1995. *Lectures on the History of Philosophy*. Translated by E. S. Haldane. Lincoln: University of Nebraska Press.

Heidegger, Martin. 1962. *Being and Time*. Translated by John Macquarrie and Edward Robinson. New York: Harper.

———. 1969. *The Essence of Reasons*. Translated by Terrence Malick. Evanston: Northwestern University Press.

———. 1971. *Poetry, Language, Thought*. Translated by Albert Hofstadter. New York: Harper and Row.

———. 1975. *Early Greek Thinking*. Translated by David Farrell Krell and Frank A. Capuzzi. New York: Harper and Row.

———. 1982. *The Basic Problems of Phenomenology*. Translated by Albert Hofstadter. Bloomington: Indiana University Press.

———. 1985. *Phänomenologische Interpretationen zu Aristoteles: Einführung in die phänomenologische Forschung*. Edited by Walter Bröcker and Käte Bröcker-Oltmanns. Frankfurt am Main: Klostermann.

———. 1995. *The Fundamental Concepts of Metaphysics: World, Finitude, Solitude*. Translated by William McNeill and Nicholas Walker. Bloomington: Indiana University Press.

———. 1997. *Plato's Sophist*. Translated by Richard Rojcewicz and André Schuwer. Bloomington: Indiana University Press.

———. 1998. "On the Essence of Ground." Translated William McNeill. In *Pathmarks*, ed. William McNeill, 97–135. New York: Cambridge University Press.

———. 1999. *Contributions to Philosophy: From Enowning*. Translated by Parvis Emad and Kenneth Maly. Bloomington: Indiana University Press.

———. 2000. *Elucidations of Hölderlin's Poetry*. Translated by Keith Hoeller. Amherst, N.Y.: Humanity Books.

———. 2001. *Sein und Wahrheit*. Freiburger Vorlesungen Sommersemester 1933 und Wintersemester 1933/34. Edited by Hartmit Tietjen. Frankfurt am Main: Klostermann.

———. 2007. *Becoming Heidegger: On the Trail of his Early Occasional Writings, 1910–1927*. Edited by Theodore J. Kisiel, and Thomas Sheehan. Evanston: Northwestern University Press.

———. 2009a. *Basic Concepts of Aristotelian Philosophy*. Translated by Robert D. Metcalf and Mark B. Tanzer. Bloomington: Indiana University Press.

———. 2009b. *The Heidegger Reader*. Edited by Günter Figal and Jerome Veith. Bloomington: Indiana University Press.

Hofstadter, A. 1970. "Being: The Act of Belonging." In *Agony and Epitaph*, 199–257. New York: George Braziller.

Hölderlin, Friedrich. 1967. *Friedrich Hölderlin: Poems and Fragments, a Bilingual Edition*. Translated by Michael Hamburger. Ann Arbor: University of Michigan Press.

Horkheimer, Max, and Theodor W. Adorno. 1976. *Dialectic of Enlightenment*. Translated by John Cumming. New York: Continuum.

Husserl, Edmund. 1954. *Gesammelte Werke*, vol. 6. The Hague: Nyhoff.

Hyde, Michael J. 2001. *The Call of Conscience: Heidegger and Levinas, Rhetoric and the Euthanasia Debate*. Columbia: University of South Carolina Press.

Isocrates. 1956. "Antidosis." In *Isocrates: On the Peace. Areopagiticus. Against the Sophists. Antidosis. Panathenaicus*. Translated by George Norlin. Cambridge, Mass.: Harvard University Press.

Jaeger, Werner. 1943. *Paideia: The Ideals of Greek Culture*, vol. 2: *In Search of the Divine Center*. Translated from the German Manuscript by Gilbert Highet. New York: Oxford University Press.

———. 1944. *Paidea: The Ideals of Greek Culture*, vol. 3: *The Conflict of Cultural Ideals in the Age of Plato*. Translated from the German Manuscript by Gilbert Highet. New York: Oxford University Press.

Jarratt, Susan. 1991. *Rereading the Sophists: Classical Rhetoric Revisited*. Carbondale: Southern Illinois University Press.

Jaspers, Karl. 1989. *Notizen zu Martin Heidegger*. Munich: Piper.

———. 1994. *Philosophie*. Munich: Piper.

Jauss, Hans Robert. 1989. *Question and Answer: Forms of Dialogic Understanding*. Translated by Michael Hays. Minneapolis: University of Minnesota Press.

Johnstone, Christopher Lyle. 2006. "Sophistical Wisdom: Politike, Arete and Logosophia." *Philosophy and Rhetoric* 39 (4): 265–89.

Johnstone, Henry. 1970. *The Problem of the Self*. University Park: Pennsylvania State University Press.

———. 1978. *Validity and Rhetoric in Philosophical Argument: An Outlook in Transition*. University Park: Dialogue Press of Man and World.

———. 1990. "Rhetoric as a Wedge: A Reformulation." *Rhetoric Society Quarterly* 20 (4): 333–38.

Jost, Walter, and Wendy Olmsted. 2006. *A Companion to Rhetoric and Rhetorical Criticism*. Malden, Mass.: Blackwell Publishing.

Kant, Immanuel. 1998a. *Critique of Pure Reason*. Translated by Paul Guyer and Allen W. Wood. Cambridge: Cambridge University Press.

———. 1998b. *Groundwork of the Metaphysics of Morals*. Translated by Mary J. Gregor. Cambridge: Cambridge University Press.

———. 2000. *Critique of the Power of Judgment*. Translated by Paul Guyer. Cambridge: Cambridge University Press.

Kennedy, George. 1980. *Classical Rhetoric and its Christian and Secular Tradition from Ancient to Modern Times*. Chapel Hill: University of North Carolina Press.

Kerferd, G. 1981. *The Sophistic Movement*. Cambridge: Cambridge University Press.

Kitzhaber, Albert R. 1963. *Themes, Theories, and Therapy: The Teaching of Writing in College*. New York: McGraw-Hill.

———. [1954] 1990. *Rhetoric in American Colleges, 1850–1900*. Introduction by John Gage. Dallas: Southern Methodist University Press.

Kwan, Tze-wan. 1995. "The Doctrine of Categories and the Topology of Concern: Prologomena to a Topology of Culture." *Analecta Husserliana* 46, edited by Anna-Teresa Tymieniecka, 243–302. Dordrecht: Kluwer Academic Publishers.

Laclau, Ernesto, and Chantal Mouffe. 1985. *Hegemony and Socialist Strategy: Towards a Radical Democratic Politics*. London: Verso.

Lanham, Richard. 2006. *The Economics of Attention*. Chicago: University of Chicago Press.

Lear, Jonathan. 2006. *Radical Hope: Ethics in the Face of Cultural Devastation*. Cambridge, Mass.: Harvard University Press.

Levinas, Emmanuel. 1990a. *Difficult Freedom: Essays on Judaism*. Translated by Sean Hand. Baltimore: Johns Hopkins University Press.

———. 1990b. "Prefatory Note to 'Reflections on Hitlerism'." Translated by Sean Hand. *Critical Inquiry* 17:62–71. (Originally published in 1934 in *Esprit*.)

———. 1998. *Otherwise than Being, or, Beyond Essence*. Translated by Alphonso Lingis. Pittsburgh: Duquesne University Press.

Lunsford, Andrea A., Kirt H. Wilson, and Rosa A. Eberly. 2009. *The SAGE Handbook of Rhetorical Studies*. Los Angeles: SAGE.

Mack, Burton Lee. 1973. *Logos und Sophia: Untersuchungen zur Weisheitstheologie im hellenistischen Judentum*. Göttingen: Vandenhoeck & Ruprecht.

MacRae, George W. 1970. "The Jewish Background of the Gnostic Sophia Myth." *Novum Testamentum* 12 (2): 86–101.

Mailloux. Steven. 1989. *Rhetorical Power*. Ithaca: Cornell University Press.

———. 1995. "Introduction: Sophistry and Rhetorical Pragmatism." In *Rhetoric, Sophistry, Pragmatism*, edited by Steven Mailloux, 1–31. Cambridge: Cambridge University Press.

———. 1998. *Reception Histories: Rhetoric, Pragmatism, and American Cultural Politics*. Ithaca: Cornell University Press.

———. 2004. "Rhetorical Hermeneutics Still Again: or, On the Track of Phronesis." In *A Companion to Rhetoric and Rhetorical Criticism*, edited by Walter Jost and Wendy Olmsted, 457–72. Malden, Mass.: Blackwell Publishing.

———. 2006. *Disciplinary Identities: Rhetorical Paths of English, Speech, and Composition.* New York: Modern Language Association of America.

Maneli, Mieczysław. 1994. *Perelman's New Rhetoric as Philosophy and Methodology for the Next Century.* Dordrecht: Kluwer Academic Publishers.

Mannheim, Karl. 1985. *Ideology and Utopia: An Introduction to the Sociology of Knowledge.* Translated by Louis Wirth and Edward Shils. San Diego: Harcourt Brace Jovanovich.

Marion, Jean-Luc. 1991. *God without Being: Hors-texte.* Translated by Thomas A. Carlson. Chicago: University of Chicago Press.

Marx, Karl. 1904. *A Contribution to the Critique of Political Economy.* Chicago: Charles H. Kerr.

McComiskey, B. 2002. *Gorgias and the New Sophistic Rhetoric.* Carbondale: Southern Illinois University Press.

McCoy, M. 2008. *Plato on the Rhetoric of Philosophers and Sophists.* Cambridge: Cambridge University Press.

McKeon, Richard. 1987. *Rhetoric: Essays in Invention and Discovery.* Woodbridge, Conn.: Ox Bow Press.

Meyer, Michel. 1994. *Rhetoric, Language, and Reason.* University Park: Pennsylvania State University Press.

———. 1995. *Of Problematology: Philosophy, Science, and Language.* Translated by David Jamison and Alan Hart. Chicago: University of Chicago Press.

———. 2008. *Principia Rhetorica: Théorie générale de l'argumentation.* Ouvertures. Paris: Fayard.

Mitchell, Donald. 1976. "The Paradox of Buddhist Wisdom." *Philosophy East and West* 26 (1): 55–67.

Miura, Nozomi. 2004. "A Typology of Personified Wisdom Hymns." *Biblical Theology Bulletin* 34 (4): 138–49.

Moltmann, Jürgen. 1981. *The Trinity and the Kingdom: The Doctrine of God.* Translated by Margaret Kohl. San Francisco: Harper & Row.

Mooney, Michael. 1985. *Vico in the Tradition of Rhetoric.* Princeton: Princeton University Press.

Murray, Les A. 2000. "An Absolutely Ordinary Rainbow." In *Learning Human: Selected Poems,* 6–7. New York: Farrar, Straus and Giroux. Originally published in 1969 in *The Weatherboard Cathedral.* Sydney: Angus and Robertson.

———. 1999. *Fredy Neptune: A Novel in Verse.* New York: Farrar, Straus and Giroux.

Nelson, John S., Allan Megill, and Deirdre N. McCloskey. 1987. *The Rhetoric of the Human Sciences: Language and Argument in Scholarship and Public Affairs.* Madison: University of Wisconsin Press.

Neusner, Jacob. 1992. *The Incarnation of God: The Character of Divinity in Formative Judaism.* Atlanta: Scholars Press.

Nienkamp, Jean. 2001. *Internal Rhetorics: Toward a History and Theory of Self-persuasion.* Carbondale: Southern Illinois University Press.

Nussbaum, Martha C. 1999. *Sex and Social Justice.* Oxford: Oxford University Press.

Perelman, Chaim. 1945. *De la justice*. Brussels: Office de publicité. Translated into English as "Concerning Justice" in Perelman 1963, 1–60.

———. 1963. *The Idea of Justice and the Problem of Argument*. Translated by John Petrie. New York: Humanities Press.

———. 1967. *Justice*. Translation of 1964 Genoa lectures by Chaim Perelman and Susan Rubin. New York: Random House.

———. 1980. "The Use and Abuse of Confused Notions." In *Justice, Law and Argument*, edited by Harold Berman, 95–106. Dordrecht: D. Reidel, 1980. First presented at the Iowa Colloquium on Rhetoric and Public Philosophy in January 1978.

———. 1984. "The New Rhetoric and the Rhetoricians." *Quarterly Journal of Speech* 70 (2): 188–96.

Perelman, Chaïm, and Lucie Olbrechts-Tyteca. 1958. *Traité de l'argumentation: la nouvelle rhétorique*. Paris: Presses Universitaires de France.

———. 1969. *The New Rhetoric: A Treatise on Argumentation*. Translated by J. Wilkinson and P. Weaver. Notre Dame, Ind.: University of Notre Dame Press.

———. 2010. "On Temporality as a Characteristic of Argumentation." In Bolduc and Frank 2010, 315–36.

Pickstock, Catherine. 1998. *After Writing: On the Liturgical Consummation of Philosophy*. Oxford: Blackwell Publishers.

Plato. 1956. *Phaedrus*. Translated by Benjamin Jowett. Indianapolis: Bobbs-Merrill.

———. 1961a. *Letter VII*. Translated by L. A. Post. In *The Collected Dialogues of Plato, Including the Letters*, edited by Edith Hamilton and Huntington Cairns, 1574–98. Princeton: Princeton University Press.

———. 1961b. *Euthyphro, Apology, Crito, Phaedo, Phaedrus*. Translated by H. Fowler. Cambridge, Mass.: Harvard University Press.

———. 1977. *Protagoras*. Translated by W. Lamb. Cambridge, Mass.: Harvard University Press.

———. 1980. *Gorgias*. Translated by Terence Irwin. Oxford: Clarendon Press.

——— 1984. *Plato's Protagoras: A Socratic Commentary*. Translated with a commentary by B. A. F. Hubbard and E. S. Karnofsky. Chicago: University of Chicago Press.

———. 1991. *The Republic of Plato*. Translated by Allan David Bloom. New York: Basic Books.

———. 1998. *Gorgias*. Translated by James H. Nichols. Ithaca: Cornell University Press.

———. 1996. *Plato's Sophist: The Professor of Wisdom*. Translated with an introduction by Eva Brann, Peter Kalkavage, and Eric Salem. Newburyport: Focus Philosophical Library.

Pöggeler, Otto. 2005. "Heidegger's Restricted Conception of Rhetoric." In Gross and Kemmann 2005, 161–76.

Polt, Richard. 2001. "The Event of Enthinking the Event." In *Companion to Heidegger's "Contributions to Philosophy,"* edited by Charles E. Scott, Susan M.

Schoenbaum, Daniela Vallega-Neu, and Allejandro Vallega, 81–104. Bloomington: Indiana University Press.

Poulakos, T. 1995. *Sophistical Rhetoric in Classical Greece*. Columbia: University of South Carolina Press.

Rawls, John. 1971. *A Theory of Justice*. Cambridge, Mass.: Belknap Press of Harvard University Press.

Richardson, William J. 1974. *Heidegger: Through Phenomenology to Thought*. The Hague: M. Nijhoff.

Ricoeur, Paul. 1989. "Rhetoric—Poetics—Hermeneutics." In *From Metaphysics to Rhetoric*, edited by Michel Meyer, 137–50. Dordrecht: Kluwer Academic Publications.

Roberts-Miller, Patricia. 2002. "Fighting without Hatred: Hannah Arendt's Agonistic Rhetoric." *JAC: Rhetoric, Writing, Culture, Politics* 22 (3): 585–601.

Rousseau, Jean-Jacques. 2002. *The Social Contract; and, the First and Second Discourses*. Edited and translated by Susan Dunn, with essays by Gita May et al. New Haven: Yale University Press.

Safranski, Rüdiger. 1998. *Martin Heidegger: Between Good and Evil*. Cambridge, Mass.: Harvard University Press.

Saussure, Ferdinand de. 1986. *Course in General Linguistics*. Edited by Charles Bally and Albert Sechehaye in collaboration with Albert Reidlinger; translated by Wade Baskin. LaSalle, Ill: Open Court.

Schiappa, Edward. 1999. *The Beginnings of Rhetorical Theory in Classical Greece*. New Haven: Yale University Press.

———. 2001. "Second Thoughts on the Critiques of Big Rhetoric." *Philosophy and Rhetoric* 34 (3): 260–74.

Scult, Allen. 1976. "Perelman's Universal Audience: One Perspective." *Communication Studies* 27 (3): 176–80.

———. 2004. *Being Jewish/Reading Heidegger: An Ontological Encounter*. New York: Fordham University Press.

Sen, Amartya. *The Idea of Justice*. Cambridge, Mass.: Harvard University Press, 2009.

Shankman, Steven. 2010. *Other Others: Levinas, Literature, Transcultural Studies*. Albany: State University of New York Press.

Smith, P. Christopher. 1995. "The Uses and Abuses of Aristotle's Rhetoric in Heidegger's Fundamental Ontology: The Lecture Course, Summer, 1924." In *From Phenomenology to Thought, Errancy, and Desire: Essays in Honor of William J. Richardson, S.J.*, edited by William J. Richardson and Babette E. Babich, 315–34. Dordrecht and Boston: Kluwer Academic.

Snyder, Gary. 1990. *The Practice of the Wild: Essays*. San Francisco: North Point Press.

Sokal, Alan. 1996. "Transgressing the Boundaries: Toward a Transformative Hermeneutics of Quantum Gravity." *Social Text* 46/47 (Spring/Summer): 217–52.

Sprague, R., ed. 1972. *The Older Sophists*. Columbia: University of South Carolina Press.

Stauffer, D. 2006. *The Unity of Plato's "Gorgias": Rhetoric, Justice, and the Philosophic Life*. Cambridge: Cambridge University Press.

Steiner, George. 1996. *Antigones: How the Antigone Legend Has Endured in Western Literature, Art, and Thought*. New Haven: Yale University Press.

Struever, Nancy S. 2005. "Alltäglichkeit, Timefulness, in the Heideggerian Program." In Gross and Kemmann 2005, 105–30.

———. 2009. *Rhetoric, Modality, Modernity*. Chicago: University of Chicago Press.

Taylor, Charles. 2007. *A Secular Age*. Cambridge, Mass: Belknap Press of Harvard University Press.

Thoreau, Henry David. 1971. *Walden*. Princeton: Princeton University Press.

Tolstoy, Leo. 1960. *The Death of Ivan Ilych, and Other Stories*. Translated by Alymer Maude. New York: New American Library.

Toulmin, Stephen. 1958. *The Uses of Argument*. Cambridge: Cambridge University Press.

———. 1972. *Human Understanding*. Princeton: Princeton University Press.

———. 1993. "Literary Theory, Philosophy of Science, and Persuasive Discourse: Thoughts from a Neo-Premodernist." Interview with Gary Olson. *JAC* 13 (2): 283–309.

Trainor, Kevin. 2001. *Buddhism: The Illustrated Guide*. Oxford: Oxford University Press.

Untersteiner, M. [1948] 1954. *The Sophists*. Translated by K. Freeman. New York: Philosophical Library.

Verene, Donald Phillip. 2007. "Philosophical Rhetoric." *Philosophy and Rhetoric* 40 (1): 27–35.

Versényi, Laszlo. 1963. *Socratic Humanism*. New Haven: Yale University Press.

Vickers, B. 1988. *In Defence of Rhetoric*. Oxford: Oxford University Press.

Vico, Giambattista. [1709] 1990. *On the Study Methods of our Time*. Translated with an introduction and notes by Elio Gianturco. Ithaca: Cornell University Press.

Visotzsky, Burton L., trans. and intro. 1992. *The Midrash on Proverbs*. New Haven: Yale University Press.

Vitanza, V. 1996. *Negation, Subjectivity, and the History of Rhetoric*. Albany: State University of New York Press.

Vlastos, G. 1983. "The Socratic Elenchus." In *Oxford Studies in Ancient Philosophy*, edited by Julia Annas, 1:35–38. Oxford: Clarendon.

Vries, Hent de. 2002. *Religion and Violence: Philosophical Perspectives from Kant to Derrida*. Baltimore: Johns Hopkins University Press.

Vygotsky, Lev. 1962. *Thought and Language*. Translated by Eugenia Hanfmann and Gertrude Vakar. Cambridge, Mass: MIT Press.

Walker, Jeffrey. 2000. *Rhetoric and Poetics in Antiquity*. Oxford: Oxford University Press.

———. 2005. "A Short Institutional History of Rhetoric in North America after the 18th Century." https://webspace.utexas.edu/jw2893/www/Inst-Hist-Rhet-North-America.htm (accessed January 31, 2011). Published, in German, in *Historisches Wörterbuch der Rhetorik*, 7:1734–40. Tübingen: Niemeyer, 2005.

Wardy, R. 1996. *The Birth of Rhetoric: Gorgias, Plato, and Their Successors*. London and New York: Routledge.

Watkins, Mary. 1986. *Invisible Guests: The Development of Imaginal Dialogues*. Hillsdale, N.J.: The Analytic Press.

Walton, Douglas N. 1998. *The New Dialectic: Conversational Contexts of Argument*. Toronto: University of Toronto Press.

Yunis, H. 2007. "Plato's Rhetoric." In *A Companion to Greek Rhetoric*, ed. Ian Worthington, 75–89. Oxford: Blackwell.

Zarefsky, David. 2004. "Institutional and Social Goals for Rhetoric." *Rhetoric Society Quarterly* 34 (3): 27–37.

Zickmund, Susan. 2007. "Deliberation, Phronesis, and Authenticity: Heidegger's Early Conception of Rhetoric." *Philosophy and Rhetoric* 40 (4): 406–15.

Žižek, Slavoj. 2009. "First as Tragedy, Then as Farce." Speech delivered to the Royal Society for the Encouragement of Arts, Manufactures and Commerce. November 24. http://www.thersa.org/events/vision/vision-videos/slavoj-zizek-first-as-tragedy,-then-as-farce (accessed August 10, 2010).

Zubiri, Xavier. 1981. *Nature, History, God*. Translated by Thomas B. Fowler Jr. Washington, D.C.: University Press of America. Originally published in 1944 as *Naturaleza, Historia, Dios*. Madrid: Editora Nacional.

Index